eMbedded Visual Basic: Windows CE and Pocket PC Mobile Applications

Chris Tacke and Timothy Bassett

SAMS

201 West 103rd St., Indianapolis, Indiana, 46290 USA

eMbedded Visual Basic: Windows CE and Pocket PC Mobile Applications

International Standard Book Number: 0-672-32277-3

Library of Congress Catalog Card Number: 2001093574

Printed in the United States of America

First Printing: November 2001

04 03 02 01 4 3 2 1

Associate Publisher
Linda Engelman

Acquisitions Editor
Karen Wachs

Development Editors
Susan Shaw Dunn
Laurie McGuire

Managing Editor
Charlotte Clapp

Project Editors
Sheila Schroeder
Christina Smith

Copy Editor
Linda Seifert

Indexer
Rebecca Salerno

Proofreader
Rowena Rappaport

Technical Editors
Marc Zimmermann
Joe Mize

Team Coordinator
Lynne Williams

Media Developer
Dan Scherf

Interior Designer
Gary Adair

Cover Designer
Alan Clements

Page Layout
Susan Geiselman

Contents at a Glance

Contents

About the Authors

Christopher Tacke, MCSD, is an associate at Rubicon Technologies, Inc., in Reston, Virginia, as well as cofounder and president of Innovative Decision Support Systems, Inc. He has a bachelor's in geology from the University of Montana and a master's in project management from the Keller Graduate School of Management in Illinois. He has written software with uses ranging from text games on his Vic-20 to seismic data analysis to assembly-line automation, but now focuses largely on mobile computing programming, including Windows CE, Palm, and RIM. Chris lives with his wife, Erin, and their black Lab, Zoe, in Maryland.

Tim Bassett, MCSE, MCSD, MCT, MCP+Site Building, has more than eight years of experience as a lead programmer on many emerging technologies. He received a bachelor's in business administration, focused in management information systems, from Ohio University in Athens, Ohio. As Mobile Application Group Manager at Rubicon Technologies, Inc., Tim was responsible for a large prercentage of Rubicon's research and development, as well as the training of Rubicon's associates. Currently Tim does independent consulting for mobile applications running on both Windows CE and Palm OS. He lives with his wife, Cori, in Washington D.C.

You can contact Chris via e-mail at `ctacke@innovativedss.com`. Tim Bassett can be contacted via `pocketpcbook@yahoo.com`. Be aware, though, that we get a whole lot of e-mail in a day and although we try to read and answer them all, responses may not always be quick. If you're looking for technical help on a problem, we highly recommend searching the archive of and posting to developer community Web sites, newsgroups, and listservers.

About the Technical Editors

Marc Zimmermann is a professional software developer and has written software for industrial automation systems, data acquisition, and data analysis, using various PC operating systems and programming languages. He volunteers his spare time helping users of Microsoft products in Internet newsgroups and has consequently been recognized by Microsoft as an MVP (Most Valuable Professional) since 1995. He is also well known in the Pocket PC community for writing reviews, tips, and how-tos for Microsoft's PocketPC.com Web site. Marc lives in Germany and can be reached via e-mail at `marc@zimac.de` or via his Web page at `www.zimac.de`. He works for GeNeSys, an independent software vendor for client projects and products. The corporate Web site can be found at `www.genesys-e.de` (currently in German only).

Joe Mize, MCP, has been programming for seven years in Visual C++ and Visual Basic. The last two years have centered on development for hand-held devices. He has a master's in mathematics from the University of Central Florida.

Acknowledgements

Writing a book is an arduous task, and although we the authors get the vast amount of credit for the final product, many people—in and out of the publication process—lead to a successful book.

I want to thank, first and foremost, my wife, Erin, for her amazing patience with me sitting at the dinner table typing away into the night. I'm sure there are a hundred other things I could, and maybe should, be doing.

I also want to thank Karen Wachs, Susan Dunn, and the rest of the staff at Sams for helping us put together what I feel is the best book on the subject.

I also want to thank Marc Zimmermann and Joe Mize who did the technical editing for the book. They definitely helped keep me on the right track and caught the errors that late-night coding produces.

Lastly, I want to thank everyone else who has helped me with, shown me the way on, or given me the opportunity to play with development. From newsgroups and listservers to good employers, it takes a great environment to make a great programmer.

—Chris Tacke

Although authoring is something I've always dreamed of, I want to thank Chris for giving us the opportunity to write this book.

I also want to show appreciation to Cori, my wife, who helped endure this effort while we were getting married and she too was producing the largest effort of her professional career.

There have been people along my way (both personal and professional) I want to thank; I would never be here if it weren't for them. My parents are the first of these people that encouraged me early, for it was they who bought my first computer. Next, I want to thank my cousin, Mike Bubb, who's also a computer geek, for giving me many different perspectives, both technical and nontechnical, throughout my life.

Without Rubicon Technologies, I would never have had the same opportunity to learn so much about Windows CE; for that I thank them. Of course I would like to thank the folks at Sams Publishing. And—this could go on forever—but lastly, all the industry partners who have further increased my Windows CE knowledge, such as Pocket PC Group at Microsoft (Joel and Vidur), Odyssey Software, and Extended Systems.

—Tim Bassett

Tell Us What You Think!

As the reader of this book, *you* are our most important critic and commentator. We value your opinion and want to know what we're doing right, what we could do better, what areas you'd like to see us publish in, and any other words of wisdom you're willing to pass our way.

As an Associate Publisher for Sams Publishing, I welcome your comments. You can fax, e-mail, or write me directly to let me know what you did or didn't like about this book—as well as what we can do to make our books stronger.

Please note that I cannot help you with technical problems related to the topic of this book, and that due to the high volume of mail I receive, I might not be able to reply to every message.

When you write, please be sure to include this book's title and author as well as your name and phone or fax number. I will carefully review your comments and share them with the author and editors who worked on the book.

Fax: 317-581-4770

E-mail: `feedback@samspublishing.com`

Mail: Linda Engelman, Associate Publisher
Sams Publishing
201 West 103rd Street
Indianapolis, IN 46290 USA

Introduction

Today, PDAs (personal digital assistants) are selling in large quantities. Pagers now have 386-processors, megabytes of memory, and power to run applications. Mobile phones have full GUI interfaces and can do far more than simply place a call. Technology, as always, is pushing for smaller and faster, and we're now in the age of mobile computing.

One major operating system for mobile computing is Microsoft's Windows CE, used on the popular PocketPC devices. Windows CE offers the look and feel of the desktop Windows environment and uses a robust set of programming interfaces from the desktop as well.

With the large numbers of these devices sold each month and the astounding number of Visual Basic developers out there, I was quite surprised when I began mobile application development with the limited amount of resources available on VB development for Windows CE.

I spent far too much time fighting and debugging applications, only to find that what I was trying to do was to be done in a completely different way or just wasn't supported at all. This book is a collection of knowledge that both Tim and I have gained from writing actual, real-world applications for Windows CE devices.

We've tried to avoid the mundane and simple stuff and focus on things that we feel have a distinct value in the programming community. Hopefully you will find the sample applications useful beyond what they teach you about the development environment.

Who This Book Is For

We make a few assumptions from the outset in this book. Obviously, we expect that you'll know your way around some newer version of the Windows operation system, but we also expect you'll know a fair amount about Visual Basic as well.

The chapters are written assuming that you can create VB projects, lay out forms, and handle most of VB's general syntax. That's not to say that you must be an expert in Visual Basic to use this book—things will just make a lot more sense if you have a knowledge of the basics. In fact, after you get your feet wet with Visual Basic, there's no reason you can't continue to learn in the Windows CE world rather than the desktop world.

NOTE

If you're looking for technical help on a problem, we highly recommend searching the archive of and posting to developer community Web sites, newsgroups, and list-servers.

How This Book Is Organized

Because we assume that you're new to eMbedded Visual Basic, Chapter 1 covers the basics of installing eMbedded Visual Tools and the Pocket PC Platform SDK. Chapter 1 also covers some of the basic differences of debugging an application in eVB versus debugging with Visual Basic 6.

Chapter 2 outlines the differences between eMbedded Visual Basic and Visual Basic 6, highlighting those items unsupported in eVB and providing workarounds for those that apply.

With the exceptions of Chapters 1, 2, and 9, each chapter covers a specific library or set of associated libraries usable in eMbedded Visual Basic. Each chapter walks you through using as much of the covered libraries as practical by writing a sample application.

We didn't feel that you should be forced to move through the book chapter by chapter to get use out of later chapters, so the sample applications in later chapters don't depend on code from earlier chapters. Be aware, though, that tips and workarounds are explained the first time they are used, so if something doesn't make full sense, you may want to peruse the earlier chapters.

Chapter 9 covers the Windows CE API. Rather than use a sample application, the chapter focuses on several examples on how to use the APIs to achieve things not natively supported in eVB.

The following is a brief listing of the chapters in this book and what they cover:

- Chapter 1, "An Introduction to Windows CE," give you a quick overview of Windows CE and its platforms and covers the installation of eMbedded Visual Basic.
- Chapter 2, "Introducing eMbedded Visual Basic," outlines the differences between Visual Basic 6 and eVB.
- Chapter 3, "Manipulating Files," covers file manipulation using the Windows CE TreeView, FileSystem, and File controls.
- Chapter 4, "Working with Menu Controls for Pocket PC," discusses how to create and use menus with the MenuBar control.
- Chapter 5, "Using the Windows CE WinSock for IR Communication," demonstrates socket communications using TCP/IP or IrDA with the WinSock control.
- Chapter 6, "The Pocket Outlook Object Model: Accessing Contacts and Calendar Items," demonstrates manipulating Contacts and Appointments using the Pocket Outlook Object Model (POOM).
- Chapter 7, "Storing and Retrieving Data with ActiveX Data Objects CE," covers data manipulation using ADOCE.

- Chapter 8, "Using SQL Server in a Mobile Environment," discusses using Microsoft SQL Server CE for storing and transferring data.
- Chapter 9, "Harnessing the Windows CE API," highlights how you can use the Windows API with Windows CE.

Finally, Appendix A gives full outlines of object models used throughout the book, listing and briefly describing all supported methods, properties, and events.

Conventions Used in This Book

Interspersed in each chapter are graphic elements that help you identify special information:

TIP

Tips offer advice or suggest easier or alternative methods of doing something.

NOTE

Notes indicate additional information that may help you avoid problems or that you should consider when using the described features.

CAUTION

Cautions alert you to possible problems or hazards and advise you on how to avoid or fix them.

You also will find certain typographical conventions used throughout this book:

- Names of all dialogs and dialog options use initial capital letters.
- Messages that appear onscreen, as well as all program code, appear in a special monospaced font, as in the following example: `Variable undefined`. Text that you are to type appears in **`monospaced boldface;`** syntax variables that you need to replace with an appropriate value appear in *`monospace italic`*.
- When a choice is given for code parameters, a pipe symbol (|) is used.

An Introduction to Windows CE

CHAPTER

1

IN THIS CHAPTER

Microsoft's Windows operating systems provide a rich graphical environment in which software can run. All the versions have a similar look and feel, and a large number of users are comfortable using them.

Now that mobile computing is becoming more and more common, from PDAs to smart phones, it only makes sense that Microsoft has developed and deployed a smaller version of Windows, Windows CE, for these devices. Windows CE takes advantage of user- familiarity with desktop versions of Windows as well as Windows significant market penetration and, judging by recent reports and trends in the industry, is gaining acceptance.

With a large—and growing—user base, it naturally follows that there is a fairly large demand for developers for the platform, and historically developers have come in two general flavors: Visual C++ developers and Visual Basic developers. This book is designed for you, the Visual Basic developer.

This chapter takes a brief look at Windows CE's different platforms, the installation of eMbedded Visual Basic, creating a basic eVB project, and a few tools that you have at your disposal.

> **NOTE**
>
> Microsoft doesn't use the Windows CE name in marketing any more, but instead uses Windows Powered.

The goals of this chapter are to

- Discuss the features of Pocket PCs, Handheld PCs, and Palm-size PCs and highlight their differences.
- Install eMbedded Visual Basic from the eMbedded Visual Tools installation CDs.
- Install the Pocket PC Software Development Kit (SDK) and emulator.
- Create a Pocket PC project.
- Explore the Zoom and Control Manager remote tools.

After you complete this chapter, you'll be set to begin developing Pocket PC applications with eMbedded Visual Basic.

CE Platforms

To complicate things a bit more than with the desktop versions of Windows, Windows CE has the notion of platforms, which can be markedly different even within the same version of

Windows CE. Early commercially available Windows CE devices, such as the Casio E-10, ran Windows CE 1.0 and then 2.0 on the Palm-size PC platform. Then came Windows CE 2.11 and the Handheld PC and Handheld PC Pro platform, and most recently Windows CE 3.0 and the Pocket PC and HPC 2000 platforms.

Palm-Size PC

The earliest platform supported by eMbedded Visual Basic, and probably the earliest platform you can find anymore, is the Palm-size PC.

The Palm-size PC tried to keep the look and feel of the desktop Windows operating systems, but in a smaller package. There is still a taskbar at the bottom of the screen and a Start button at the lower left corner (see Figure 1.1), and the typical action to perform is a double screen tap, just like a double-click on the desktop.

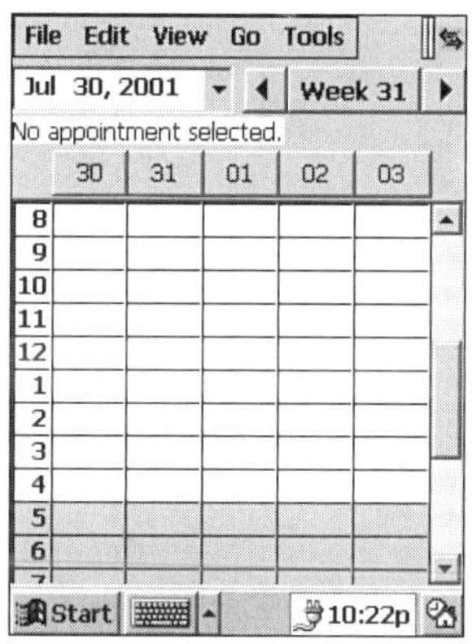

FIGURE 1.1
The typical layout of a Palm-size PC screen.

Handheld PC (HPC)

The Handheld PC (HPC) platform comes in various flavors. Some devices run Windows CE 2.11 (HPC and HPC Pro) and some run Windows CE 3.0 (HPC 2000). Also, different devices have different screen sizes, ranging from smaller clamshell devices with about 50% more real estate than the Palm-size PCs, up to laptop and notepad sized screens.

Before Windows CE 2.11, all devices were referred to as a Handheld PC. When Windows CE 2.11 was released, two versions became available: Professional came with Pocket Access embedded in the device ROM, whereas the standard HPC did not.

The HPC platform almost always has a physical keyboard, and usually has at least one full-size PCMCIA slot, which has made them a popular choice for industrial and heavy use applications. This has led to the development and manufacture of rugged, water-resistant devices with built-in wireless connections.

Other than the physical dimensions, the screen of an HPC looks remarkably like the desktop PC, with a taskbar, start button, and program icons (see Figure 1.2).

FIGURE 1.2
The Handheld PC desktop, regardless of actual screen size, is remarkably similar to the desktop for PC-based Windows operating systems.

Pocket PC

Probably the most prevalent platform for Windows CE for the everyday user is the Pocket PC. The Pocket PC runs Windows CE 3.0 and has a single screen size of 240×320 pixels.

The Pocket PC platform is the most significant modification to the Windows look-and-feel so far. The familiar Start button at the lower left of the screen is gone, replaced by the Windows logo at the upper left (see Figure 1.3). Navigation and other behaviors have also been changed to make it faster and less complex, requiring fewer stylus taps to get to desired features and applications.

For example, you no longer double-tap items for action, but instead only single-tap. Applications have no concept of minimizing or maximizing, they just fill the entire screen, and few Pocket PC applications actually shut down. Instead, when you are finished using an application, you just proceed to the next. Eventually, if memory resources become low, the operating system will either reallocate program memory or even shut down running applications that are idle.

You can check to see what is running and shut down applications manually by selecting Settings on the menu and then selecting Memory from the System tab (see Figures 1.4 through 1.6).

FIGURE 1.3
The Pocket PC Today Screen.

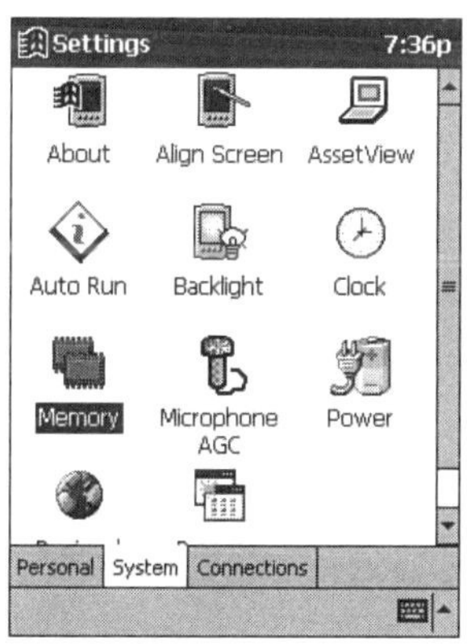

FIGURE 1.4
The current memory status can be accessed through Settings on the System tab.

Despite all these changes, under the hood the Pocket PC still is based on the Palm-size PC platform, and in fact most Palm-size PC applications will run on the Pocket PC, provided, of course, that the application was compiled for the device's processor type.

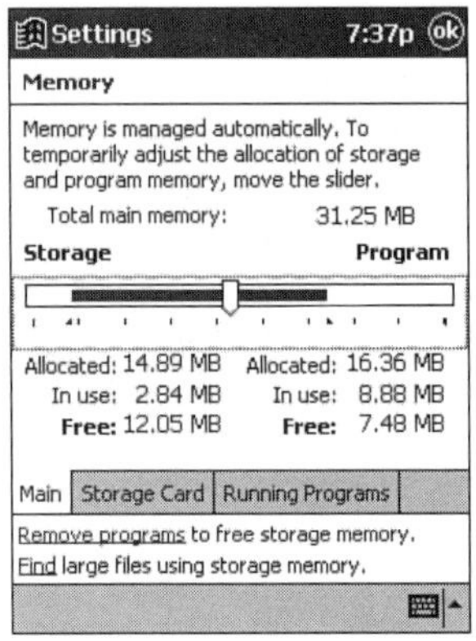

FIGURE 1.5

The main Memory Settings window. Here you can view available and in-use memory resources as well as manually allocate them.

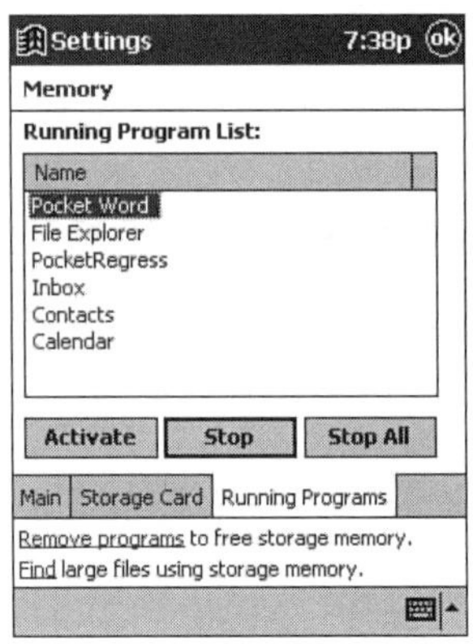

FIGURE 1.6

The Running Programs Settings window. Here you can view all running programs as well as stop any or all programs currently in memory.

Processors

An interesting, as well as significant, difference between Windows CE and the desktop versions of Windows is that the OS must support multiple processor architectures. This difference is in the process of being changed with a standardization of processor architecture, but applications intended for use on the current set of devices already in users' hands must deal with different processors.

We often take for granted when developing desktop applications that all our target machines are based on the Intel *x*86 processor. This isn't the case with Windows CE devices. A number of potential processors are available to device manufacturers—SH3, SH4, MIPS, ARM and more—and the code that runs on them varies, meaning that for a single code base, there are often multiple compiled versions—one for each processor family.

Fortunately for you, eVB doesn't care what processor your program runs on, but the support files and controls that you may have to distribute will very likely have different versions.

Each version you need will be nicely ordered in directories when you install eMbedded Visual Tools, so finding it won't be a major challenge. Just keep in mind that there are differences, which often makes distribution and maintenance of Windows CE applications, no matter what language they've been developed in, a larger challenge.

eMbedded Visual Basic

eMbedded Visual Tools comes with two development environments: eMbedded Visual Basic (eVB) and eMbedded Visual C++ (eVC). eVB is, especially at first glance, a lot like its big brother Visual Basic 6, but they aren't interchangeable. If you want to do development for PocketPC devices, you need to install eVB.

Installing eVB

The installation set comes as two free (except for shipping) CDs from Microsoft. At the time I'm writing this, the installation is also available for download, but the availability and location has changed quite a bit over the last year, so providing a Web location would likely be invalid by print time. A search for "eMbedded Visual Tools" at `www.microsoft.com` or `www.PocketPC.com` should get you there pretty easily.

Installing from the CD is a straightforward operation. If the setup doesn't autostart, you can run setup.exe from the CD's root directory. You should be prompted with the first eMbedded Visual Tools 3.0 installation dialog (see Figure 1.7).

The second dialog is the usual Microsoft EULA (end user license agreement) that you have to accept to continue.

The third dialog requires a license key (although because the tools are free, I'm not sure why) and your name. Your company name is optional. The downloadable version of eMbedded Visual Tools comes with a text file that contains the license key.

The fourth dialog is important. It allows you to choose eMbedded Visual Tools as well as the software development kits (SDKs) you want to install (see Figure 1.8). Each SDK comes with an emulator to let you run and test your applications to some degree without a device.

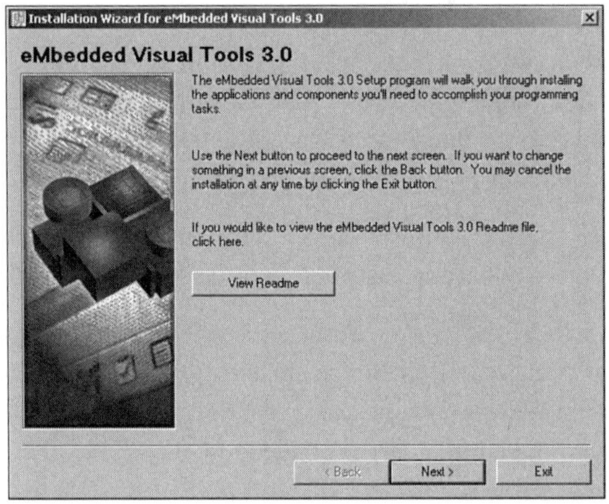

FIGURE 1.7

The first dialog in the eMbedded Visual Tools installation process.

NOTE

While you can install eMbedded Visual Tools on a Windows 9x machine, the emulators require Windows NT 4.0/2000/ME/XP to run.

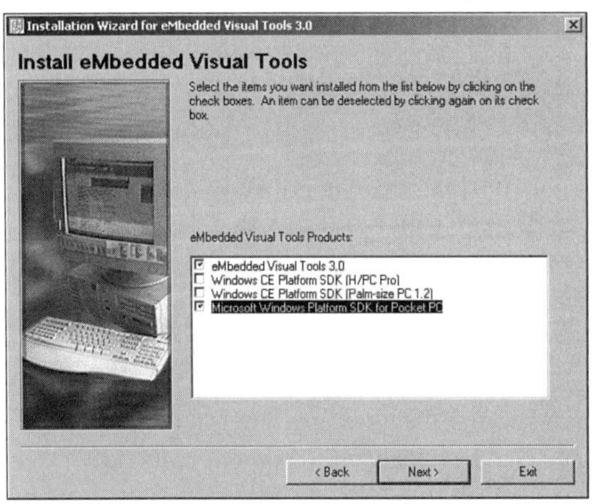

FIGURE 1.8

Selecting eMbedded Visual Tools and the Pocket PC SDK for installation.

Next, you'll be asked to provide an installation path for the Windows CE Tools. Interestingly, this is *not* where the eMbedded Visual Tools will be installed (you don't have a choice there); instead, it's where the SDKs, the controls, and the libraries are located. Most everything you'll need to reference in a project or distribute with an application will be somewhere in this folder. It's a directory that you'll get to know well if you do much Windows CE development, so after installation browse through it to familiarize yourself with its layout and the files included.

Next, you'll be presented your Product ID or License Number. It says to write it down, but you can get it at any time through the Help menu in eVB.

Next is another important dialog (see Figure 1.9). You get to choose what development environments you want to install. Of course, you'll want to install eVB, and the Common Components are actually necessary to run as well. eVC is large, and you don't have to install it, but keep in mind that if you start doing a lot of API programming (see Chapter 9), you may want to look through some of the header files for external libraries. Installing eVC will give you a lot of those headers. Of course, it also gives you the capability and joy of developing in C++ as well.

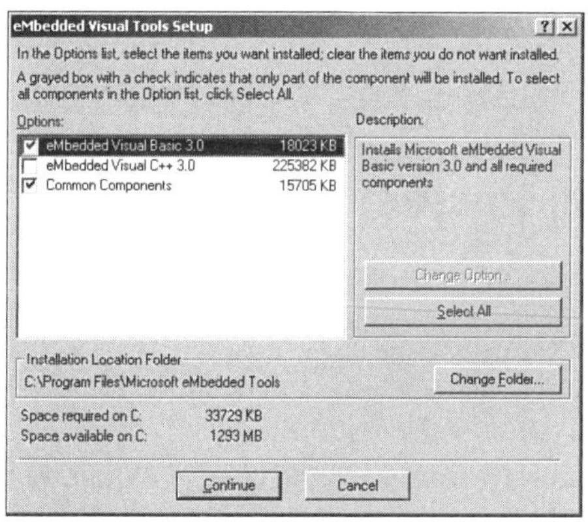

FIGURE 1.9
Selecting the eMbedded Visual Tools Components to install. eVB and the Common Components are required.

Next, you'll go through a couple of dialogs as the installation copies over files and completes. Next it prompts you for CD 2. This is where all the SDKs reside, so if you decide to add on later, you only need to install from disk 2.

If you selected only the Pocket PC SDK, you'll get the first installation screen that says, `To continue, click Next`. This takes you, again, to a EULA.

Accepting the EULA takes you to the next dialog, which is very important. This dialog allows you to enter your user name and organization, but more importantly it allows you to install the

SDK for just yourself or for everyone on your machine (see Figure 1.10). Because the Windows NT family of operating systems is security conscious, it's important that you choose well here. If you are installing while logged in as the user account you always use, and therefore your default account has administration privileges, choosing Only For Me is fine. If you use a different user account, be sure you choose Anyone Who Uses This Computer.

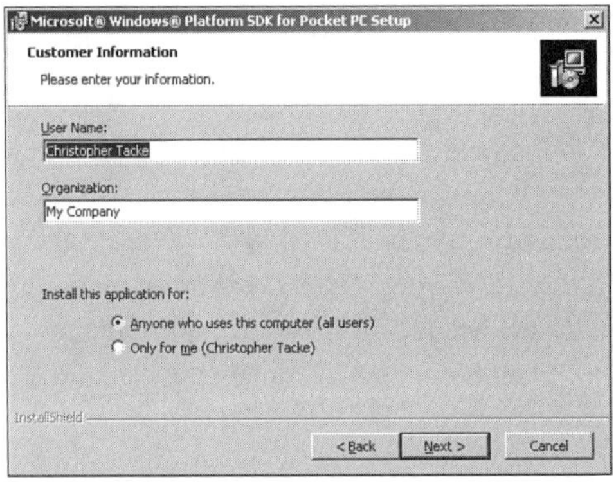

FIGURE 1.10
Choosing the account on which to install the SDK. Choosing Anyone Who Uses This Computer is the safest.

Creating a New Project

After you install eMbedded Visual Tools and the Pocket PC SDK, you're ready to start writing applications.

You first need to create a new project, which is done in the same basic way as with Visual Basic 6. You'll be prompted with the New Project dialog (see Figure 1.11) from which you'll have at least two types of projects from which to choose: Windows CE for the Pocket PC Project and Windows CE Formless project. If you've installed more SDKs, you'll have more options.

The only difference between the Formless and the Pocket PC templates is that the Formless creates a project with a single module with the program entry point of `Sub Main`, whereas the Pocket PC project creates a project with a single form with the entry point at `Form_Load`. Either one can be converted to the other easily by adding either a form or module and changing the entry point.

Let's create a simple `Hello World` application so we can get a feel for some of the differences between eVB's IDE and Visual Basic's IDE.

Select the Pocket PC project template and click Open. You should see a familiar IDE screen. The only notable difference at this point from VB6 is that the form is all white (Pocket PC backgrounds are white instead of the Windows gray). You also have your familiar set of stock controls in the toolbox at the left.

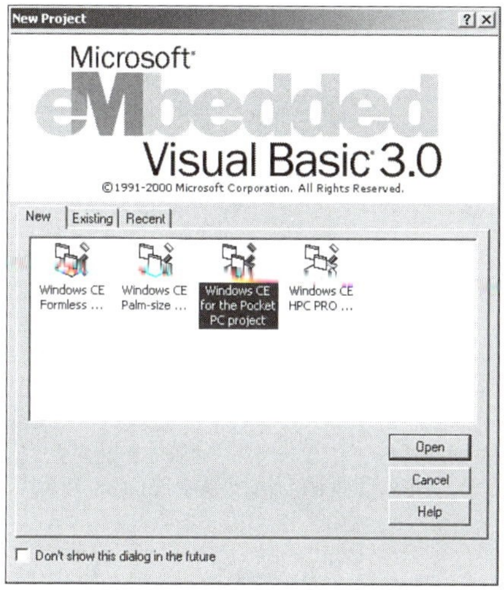

FIGURE 1.11

The New Project dialog with the Pocket PC template selected. Notice that I've also installed the HPC Pro and Palm-size PC SDKs.

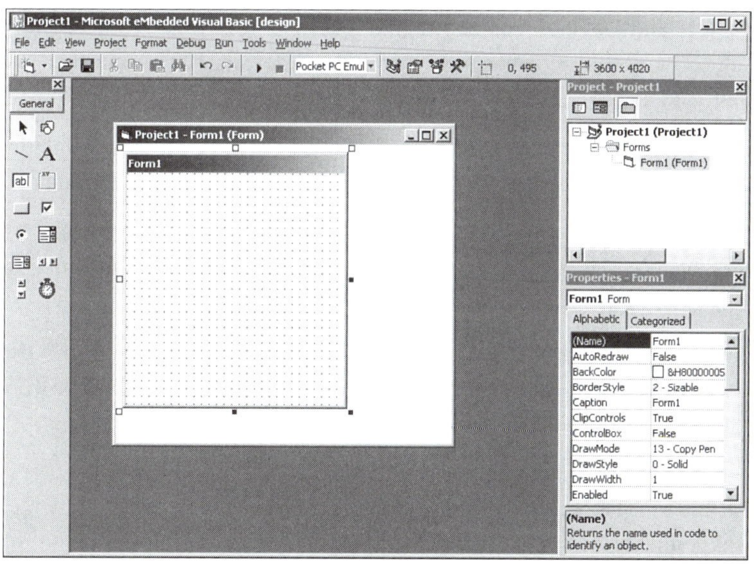

FIGURE 1.12

The eVB IDE looks and feels just like Visual Basic 6. Notice, though, that the form is white instead of gray.

Next, go ahead and drop a single command button on the form, leaving its name `Command1`, and go to its `Click` event handler.

You'll probably notice that the code page already has a single method in it that looks like this:

```
Private Sub Form_OKClick()
    App.End
End Sub
```

The Pocket PC form has, by default, a small OK button in the upper-right corner where the desktop Windows Close button usually resides. This method gives the same functionality to the OK button by closing the application. You may rightfully wonder why it doesn't just have the `End` command; eVB doesn't support a global `End` command, instead it has an `End` method as part of the `App` object.

Now add the `Command1_Click` event handler, something like this:

```
Private Sub Command1_Click()
    MsgBox "Hello World!", vbExclamation, "My First App"
End Sub
```

Running and Debugging

Now that you have your first application, let's look at the debugging tools available, or, as you'll soon see, unavailable.

First notice that in the toolbar you'll have a ComboBox with two items: Pocket PC Emulation and Pocket PC (Default Device). You choose the former if you want to debug with the emulator and the latter if you want to debug with a connected device. For a connected device, you must be currently connected with ActiveSync.

Let's look at the emulator, so be sure that the ComboBox says Pocket PC Emulation. Put a break point on the `MsgBox` code line in your `Command1_Click` event handler and click the Run button.

The first thing that should happen is that eVB attempts to connect to your device, which is the emulator in this case. If the emulator isn't running, eVB will launch it.

After a short while, the emulator should appear with your form at the front. If it doesn't appear, try minimizing eVB to see if it came up behind it. Figure 1.13 shows eVB running with the emulator.

Click `Command1` to get it to break on your breakpoint. Notice the debug toolbar. It's missing the familiar Pause button. The only way to stop execution of an eVB application while running is through a breakpoint.

Go ahead and click `Run` and revel in the splendor of your first application (see Figure 1.14).

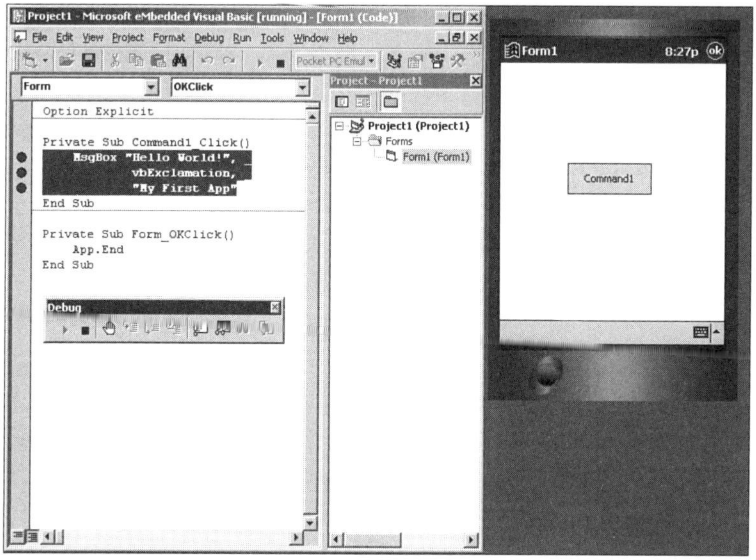

FIGURE 1.13
The full debugging environment for eVB. I've squished it all onto one screen to make it easier to see.

FIGURE 1.14
The first application, running bug-free.

Another thing to be aware of that we can't really explore in this sample is that breakpoints don't always work, or they don't work reliably, regardless of whether you're using the emulator or a physical device for debugging.

If you find that execution is running past your breakpoint without stopping, there are two things to try:

- Try setting the breakpoint at the `Form` level. This means placing the breakpoint in `Form` event handling code before it goes into another sub or function. These breakpoints work more reliably.
- Try placing three or four breakpoints on consecutive lines. This often causes an uncooperative debug session to behave better, although it still may break on a completely different line of code than the breakpoint.

Another major missing piece in eVB that VB6 has is the Locals window. You can't view all your current variables, nor can you traverse the call stack in eVB. You simple get the immediate window.

Debugging is probably one of the largest frustrations I have with eVB. We'll cover more of the limitations later in the book and you'll undoubtedly discover how well the IDE behaves on your machine and how to get around some of the quirks. Above all, remember that the MsgBox is a valuable debugging tool that reliably stops execution.

Remote Tools

Installing eMbedded Visual Basic also installs some nice tools that aren't really explained in any documentation, and often developers don't go exploring through them. It took me nearly a year to realize that some of the tools that are installed are great for tasks that I had been doing the hard way.

We'll cover three tools in this book: Windows CE Zoom, the Control Manager, and the Windows CE Registry Editor. The first two are covered in this chapter; the Registry Editor is covered in Chapter 9, where you'll make good use of it.

All Windows CE Remote Tools are available from the eVB IDE. Simply choose Remote Tools from the Tools menu for a list (see Figure 1.15).

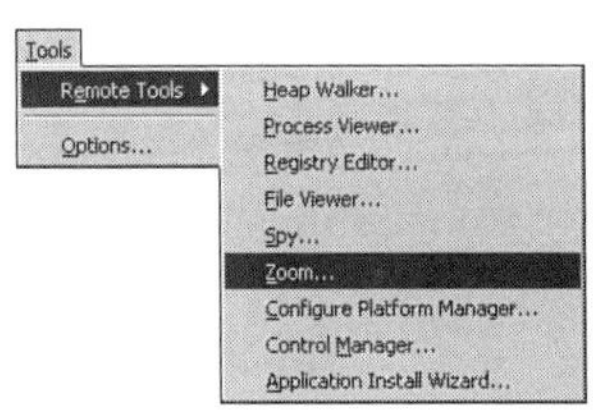

FIGURE 1.15
All Remote Tools are available from the Remote Tools menu of the eVB IDE.

Zoom

Zoom is a simple yet ingenious tool that enables you to take a screen capture of the device connected via ActiveSync. While this seems like a basic thing, I spent six months doing desktop screen captures and cropping them to the emulator before I discovered Zoom, and I hope to steer you away from needless frustration and busy work.

When you launch Zoom, if you have a device connected, it will automatically copy its client file and grab the current screen image for you (see Figure 1.16).

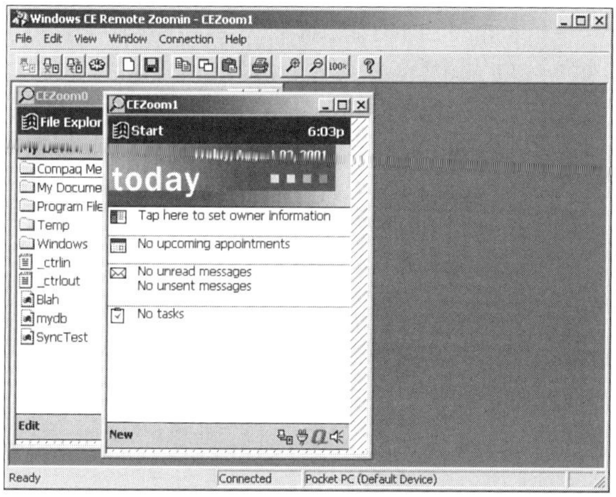

FIGURE 1.16
Zoom creates a bitmap the size of your device's screen.

You can refresh the current image with F5 (or choosing Refresh from the Connection menu) or grab the current device screen as a new image with Ctrl+N. Zoom creates a 256-color bitmap with the same dimensions as your connected device's screen and fills it with the device's screen contents, pixel for pixel. This allows you to trap everything, including pop-up menus. If you do much documentation, article writing, or GUI specification writing, Zoom will save you a lot of time and frustration.

NOTE

Zoom only works with a physical device. With the emulator, you still have to do a screen print and crop the resulting image.

Microsoft has also released the Remote Display Control PowerToy that has Zoom's functionality along with some additional features. It, along with other neat PowerToys, can be downloaded for free at `www.Microsoft.com/mobile/pocketpc/downloads/powertoys.asp`.

Control Manager

Control Manager is another great tool that took me months to discover. Rather than manually copy and register controls, or create a `.CAB` file specifically for a set of controls (which I did before discovering Control Manager), Control Manager allows you to selectively register and unregister ActiveX controls on the device from your desktop.

When Control Manager is launched, it has a TreeView of all your device options on the left side of the window and an empty ListView on the right (see Figure 1.17).

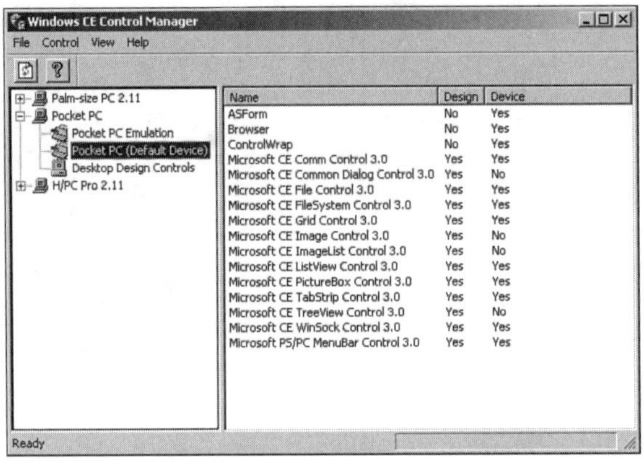

FIGURE 1.17

Use the Control Manager to see what's now installed on the device as well as to add or remove controls from the device.

You can expand the TreeView to access either the emulator, any physical device, or the desktop design controls. Selecting a device, emulator included, will provide you a list of all your available controls and whether each one is currently installed on the selected device.

Summary

We've briefly covered all the devices you're likely to see in use today, and installed eVB and the Pocket PC SDK. We also looked at some of the differences between the eVB IDE and Visual Basic 6's IDE, and even looked at a couple of handy Windows CE tools.

We've only begun to scratch the surface of the Pocket PC development world, but you're almost ready to dive in. While I'm sure you're itching to start coding, I strongly suggest that before you do you take the time to read through Chapter 2, "Introducing eMbedded Visual Basic," which explains in more detail the differences between eVB and Visual Basic 6. Knowing the differences will save you some time (and headaches) when coding and debugging.

Introducing eMbedded Visual Basic

CHAPTER

2

IN THIS CHAPTER

This chapter explores everything I've found that eVB doesn't expose or support but Visual Basic 6.0 does support. The list is fairly long, but don't let it trouble you; throughout the rest of the book, we'll explore ways to get past most of these limitations.

I've heard it said—and believe that probably a large contingent of programmers would agree—that eVB is fine for application prototyping but is unsuitable for enterprise-level or production-quality application development. This seems to come largely from the Windows CE C++ developer community, and the notion just isn't true. There's no reason you can't use eVB to develop a commercial mobile piece for even the largest enterprise applications. You must be careful to avoid some of the pitfalls, which you'll be exposed to throughout this book, but I've developed commercial applications with a high degree of success in deployment and a low cost of support.

eVB allows enterprises to tap into a large pool of Visual Basic developers and often into in-house domain knowledge. It provides for rapid GUI-based application development that, time-wise, just can't be matched with C++. Of course, there are always applications for which C++ is better suited, but when you're deciding what development environment to use, don't discount eVB simply because it's eVB or because you may have heard that it's inferior. My hope is that by laying out all the unsupported items, you can make an informed decision about eVB's viability in your development.

Since the early days of Windows CE, development languages have largely been limited to C++ and assembly. Although this allowed for great access to low-level functions, it meant that rapid application development was difficult at best and the pool of available developers was limited.

After CE 2.0 was released, the Windows CE Toolkit for Visual Basic, commonly called VBCE, was released. VBCE was an add-in that used the standard Visual Basic 6 IDE and allowed any VB developer to write applications for CE devices.

When a developer new to the CE world first sees eVB, the typical thought is, "Great! I know Visual Basic so I can easily use my knowledge to create CE applications as well." Although a lot of the basic knowledge is transferable, it's imperative that you understand that eVB isn't VB. It has many limitations and nuances and often requires a completely different development approach.

Even with all these nuances, eVB can provide you with the ability to provide high-quality mobile applications suitable for use in most production environments. Knowing what you can and can't do, though, is the key to building a successful application.

Compiled Versus Interpreted Code

One of eMbedded Visual Basic's major differences to its desktop brother is that it doesn't provide a compiled binary executable. Instead, it produces an interpreted p-code file that must be run through an interpreter. This difference has several consequences:

- eVB applications have slower performance. When an eVB application is run, the p-code must be interpreted at runtime, which requires processor cycles. This means that eVB isn't a great choice for lots of high-level mathematics, intensive graphics, and other processor-hungry applications.
- eVB applications must be deployed with an *interpreter*, an application to run the p-code. eVB compiles applications to a file with a .vb extension. Because these must be run through the pvbload.exe interpreter, pvbload.exe must exist on the target device.
- Pvbload.exe isn't the only thing you'll need to deploy. Pvbload.exe has its own dependencies and requirements. The base requirements for any eVB application are
    - Your .vb file
    - pvbload.exe
    - pvbform2.dll
    - pvbhost2.dll
    - vbscript.dll

  Also, if you add any controls or references to your project, you will have to deploy the necessary files for them. I'll cover those specifically when we use them in later chapters.
- Because the application uses an interpreter, and .vb files are simply associated with the interpreter (clicking a .vb file automatically calls pvbload.exe), all eVB applications have the same icon, which is the pvbload.exe icon. Getting around this requires that you write a C++ launcher application with your desired icon, and that application must pvbload.exe with your .vb file as a command-line parameter.

On the positive side, because eVB applications are interpreted, you don't have to be concerned with the target device's processor type. With C++, when an application is compiled, the resulting binary is processor specific, and therefore multiple versions must be made for multiple processor types. This increases maintenance and deployment costs. With eVB, your final .vb file can be run on any processor without recompile.

All Things Are `Variant`

Another major difference between eVB and VB6 is that eVB is far closer to VBScript and, as such, doesn't support strong-typed variables. All variables in eVB are `Variants`, even if you declare them otherwise. Using the `As` *`variable_type`* syntax simply gives you IntelliSense for objects, making development a bit easier.

However, again, this has consequences to be aware of. First, a variable won't get initialized. Consider the following:

```
Dim iMyInteger As Integer
```

In VB6, after this declaration, `iMyInteger` is equal to zero; in eVB, it's just an empty variant. This can sometimes cause logic errors that are difficult to debug, so you should get in the habit of initializing all eVB variables.

Assuming that we have a new project with a single form, `Form1`, consider this code snippet:

```
Dim frmMyForm As Form
Dim iMyInteger As Integer

frmMyForm = True
frmMyForm = frmMyForm + 1
Set iMyInteger = Form1
frmMyForm = iMyInteger.Caption
iMyInteger = iMyInteger.Left + 1
```

In VB6, this won't even compile, but in eVB it will actually run, with `frmMyForm` ending up as `Form1` and `iMyInteger` ending up with the value 1 (or something similar). Again, this can cause some difficult-to-debug logic errors if you mix variable types, and is a strong argument for always using `Option Explicit` and Hungarian notation.

Unsupported VB6 Features

The list of features not supported by eVB is fairly extensive, but don't let that discourage you. Many of the programming techniques you know from VB6 will transfer, and I'll give you workaround tips for most of the bigger issues.

`GoTo` and Error Handling

Error handling in Visual Basic has always been a sore point with many developers, and eVB further limits what you can do. The only `On Error` option in eVB is `On Error Resume Next`. You can't have an error handler at the bottom of a procedure and simply use a `GoTo` to jump to it; in fact, you can't use `GoTo` at all in eVB.

Instead, you must use line-by-line error handling. You have to be aware of what types of errors a code line might throw when you write it, because you'll likely have to check for and handle each one.

To minimize the amount of error-handling code you need, try to validate most data that you pass into functions to ensure that data that may cause an error never gets there.

Another good catchall for development and testing is to write a generic error trap at the end of your functions, something like this:

```
Public Function MyFunction() As Boolean
    On Error Resume Next
```

```
    ' Implementation code

    If Err.Number <> 0 Then
        MsgBox Err.Description, vbCritical, "MyFunction Error"
    End If
End Function
```

This displays a message box if any error occurs in the function and helps you to pinpoint both the location and the type of error for which you may need to add a handler.

Other unsupported error-handling features are `Erl` and `Resume`.

New, CreateObject, and Events

The `New` operator isn't supported in eVB. All object creation must be done with `CreateObject` or `CreateObjectWithEvents` and, as the latter suggests, `With Events` isn't supported for variable declarations.

Creating Objects with Events

To create an object and still be able to handle that object's event, you must use the `CreateObjectWithEvents` method, which takes two parameters: the object's `ProgID` and the `Event` prefix you want to use.

For example, if you want to create a WinSock control and be able to handle its events, you would use something like the following:

```
Set objSocket = CreateObjectWithEvents("Winsock.Winsock", "MySocket_")
```

This tells eVB to create the object and that all the object's events will start with `MySocket_`. For example, the `Connect` event for our created socket would be `MySocket_Connect()`.

Let's look at an example that you can actually run in eVB. You can create a WinSock control and immediately try to connect with it. Because you haven't told it where to connect to, the call will fail and fire the WinSock's `Error` event, which you trap in `MySocket_Error`:

```
Sub Main()
    On Error Resume Next
    Dim objSocket As WinSock.WinSock
    Dim vData As String

    Set objSocket = CreateObjectWithEvents("Winsock.Winsock", "MySocket_")

    objSocket.Connect
End Sub

Public Sub MySocket_Error(Number As Integer, Description As String)
    MsgBox Description
End Sub
```

Chapter 5, "Using the Windows CE WinSock for IR Communication," covers the details of socket programming; this snippet just serves as an example of using `CreateObjectWithEvents`.

`CreateObject`'s Memory Leak

To add to the challenge of creating objects, the Microsoft implementation of `CreateObject` in eVB has a memory leak. The leak boils down to this: when you call `CreateObject` to create any object with an enumeration (which almost all objects have), eVB allocates space for that enumeration. When the variable goes out of scope or is set equal to `Nothing`, the memory isn't released.

This means that every call to `CreateObject` will consume enough space for the enumeration(s) and not release that space until your application ends. The more enumerations the object has and the more times you create it, the worse the problem becomes.

No fix has been made publicly available by Microsoft, although Knowledge Base article Q286504, "eVB CreateObject Function Causes Memory Leak," acknowledges that it does exist. This means that you must program defensively against this leak.

The best method that I've come up with is to be sure that you create an object only once for your application and to reuse that object rather than create a new one every time.

Chapter 3, "Manipulating Files," gives more information and a full working example of a workaround for the `CreateObject` leak.

No Class Support

eVB projects support only two types of files: forms and standard modules. You can't create a Class Module, nor can you create your own classes with eVB.

This means that many programming techniques and styles must be "unlearned."

No `Validate` Events

eVB controls, such as the TextBox, don't have `Validate` events, so any validation must be achieved in another way. One option is with the `LostFocus` event. Here is one way to validate a TextBox to ensure that it has numeric data:

```
Private Sub Text1_LostFocus()
    If Len(Text1.Text) = 0 Then Exit Sub

    If Not IsNumeric(Text1.Text) Then
        MsgBox "Invalid Data"
    End If
End Sub
```

Menus Are Different

eVB has no Menu Editor like VB6's, but the Pocket PC doesn't support menuing the way a desktop PC does. Instead, eVB provides a MenuBar control, which is covered in Chapter 4, "Working with Menu Controls for Pocket PC," for the application menus. Pop-up menus aren't supported by eVB at all, but Chapter 9, "Harnessing the Windows CE API," shows an implementation that mimics their behavior.

Optional Isn't an Option

eVB doesn't support creating functions with optional parameters (although you can call C++ functions with optional parameters). This can make extending functions without breaking the interface difficult at best.

One option that you can use is to pass an array as the last parameter to a function, and simply add to the array for additional parameters. For example, consider the following function that takes a Grid control, an ADOCE recordset, and a variant array, and then formats and fills the control:

```
Public Function DisplayRecords(objGrid As GRIDLibCtl.GridCtrl, _
                adoRecordSet As Variant, _
                OptParams() As Variant)
    '----------------------------------------------------
    '----- MetaData is a 1 dimensional array
    '----- Element 0: Maximum column width
    '----- Element 1: Number of rows to preserve on redraw
    '----- Element 2: Row Height
    '----- Element 3: Minimum column width
    '----------------------------------------------------

    Dim intRowHeight As Integer
    Dim intMaxWidth As Integer
    Dim intMinWidth As Integer
    Dim intPreserveRows As Integer

    If OptParams(0) <> 0 Then
        intMaxWidth = OptParams(0)
    End If

    Select Case UBound(OptParams)
        Case 1
            intPreserveRows = OptParams(1)
        Case 2
            intPreserveRows = OptParams(1)
            If OptParams(2) <> 0 Then
                intRowHeight = OptParams(2)
            End If
```

```
        Case 3
            intPreserveRows = OptParams(1)
            If OptParams(2) <> 0 Then
                intRowHeight = OptParams(2)
            End If
            If OptParams(3) <> 0 Then intMinWidth = OptParams(3)
    End Select

    ' Implementation Code

End Function
```

I've left out the implementation code because I want to focus on the variant array of "optional" parameters. I've defined them as `MaxColWidth`, `PreserveRows`, `RowHeight`, and `MaxColWidth`. By using a `Select Case` on the upper bound of the array, the caller can opt not to use all the parameters. For example, to call it with only `MaxColWidth` and `PreserveRows`, you could use this:

```
Public Sub Main
    Dim vParams(3) As Variant

    vParams(0) = 1200
    vParams(1) = 1

    DisplayRecords grdMyGrid, objRs, vParams
End Sub
```

The limitations are that you can't omit a variable *in the middle* of the list, and you must provide at least `MaxColWidth`. Both of these could be fixed with some ingenuity if you need to get past these limitations, but I'll leave that as an exercise.

ActiveX Controls, DLLs, and EXEs

Another substantial limitation of eVB is that it doesn't support the ability to create ActiveX controls (often called *user controls*), ActiveX DLLs, or ActiveX executables. To make any of these, you have to use eVC.

Control Arrays

Control arrays aren't supported in eVB, so writing common code for multiple controls is more challenging. Usually moving the implementation to a single function and having all controls call that function is the easiest way to handle this problem:

```
Private Sub Text1_Change()
    HandleTextChange Text1
End Sub
```

```
Private Sub Text2_Change()
    HandleTextChange Text2
End Sub

Private Sub Text3_Change()
    HandleTextChange Text3
End Sub

Private Sub HandleTextChange(txtControl As TextBox)
    MsgBox txtControl.Name & " changed"
End Sub
```


User-Defined Data Types

eVB doesn't support user-defined types, also called UDTs or *structures*. This makes calling API calls that require UDTs difficult. Chapter 9 provides a workaround and samples for getting past this limitation.

`With` Blocks

Using a `With` block for shortcut coding isn't supported in eVB. The following code

```
With frmMain
    .Caption = "My Form"
    .Left = (Screen.Width - .Width) / 2
    .Top = (Screen.Height - .Height) / 2
End With
```

must be rewritten like this:

```
frmMain.Caption = "My Form"
frmMain.Left = (Screen.Width - frmMain.Width) / 2
frmMain.Top = (Screen.Height - frmMain.Height) / 2
```

Modal Forms

You can't show a form modally in eVB. This means that if you have an application with multiple forms, be aware that the user may change to another form at any point, sometimes by accidentally clicking outside the current window if it isn't full screen.

To help avoid this, use only full-screen forms and set the `Visible` property of background forms to `False`. Another option is to use only a single form for the entire application and use frames for each *screen* the user will view.

Using the Windows CE Emulators

Each Windows CE SDK comes with its own emulator, and the emulator can be a useful tool. It allows you to do some development without a physical device. Loading an application on the emulator is often faster than loading the application on a device through ActiveSync, and the emulator is convenient.

But beware—the emulator isn't infallible. In fact, the emulator is about only 80 percent accurate in emulating device behavior. Obviously you can't do infrared, socket, or serial communications with the emulator because you can't physically connect to it, but the bigger problems arise when it simply behaves differently than an actual device.

Behavior differences crop up especially during database work. For example, doing a large number of record inserts to a table on the emulator almost always causes an error, but the same code on an actual device works fine.

To avoid the headache of trying to find errors that are emulator-caused, use the emulator to do initial screen layouts and GUI work, such as screen-to-screen navigation; but when you start doing the bulk of the work and application logic, develop directly on a physical device.

Other Differences

Many additional differences between eVB and VB6 are either self-explanatory or don't warrant an entire paragraph to describe. The following is a list of those differences:

- Some project files have changed extensions. Forms in eVB end in .ebf; project files end in .ebp.
- eVB controls support only 256-color graphics. Trying to load a PictureBox with a 32,000 color image causes an ambiguous error that's difficult to debug, so be sure that all picture files have a color depth of 256 colors or less.
- You can't write custom add-ins for eVB, nor are any supplied from Microsoft.
- Because eVB is interpreted, `AddressOf` isn't supported. Similarly, you can't use `VarPtr` or `StrPtr` to retrieve the address of a variable.
- SQL in ADOCE doesn't support the `UPDATE` command. You must either use `DELETE` and `INSERT` or create an ADOCE recordset and use its `Update` method.
- The SQL `INSERT` command can take only a `VALUES` list. It can't contain subqueries.
- You can't `JOIN` more than four tables.
- You can't have ambiguous column names in a join (i.e. the same column name in two tables).

- The only `JOIN` supported is the `INNER JOIN`.
- Only `JOIN`s on equal fields are permitted.
- The `Format()` function isn't supported. Several new formatting procedures have been added: `FormatDateTime`, `FormatPercent`, `FormatNumber`, and `FormatCurrency`. Any other type of formatting requires you to roll your own procedure.
- The `Load` and `Unload` commands (that is, `Load Form1`) are unsupported. Be sure to clean up control modifications on loaded forms such as where you've added to collections (TreeView nodes, ListView items, and so on) if the form is to be conceptually loaded again.
- The conditional compiling directives (`#If...Then...#Else`, `#Const`) are unsupported.
- The `Shell()` command is unsupported. Use the `CreateProcess` API instead (see Chapter 9).
- Static variables are unsupported.
- The `Left()` string function is unavailable in a form's code page because eVB interprets it to be the form's `Left` property. `Left()` works fine in a module.
- `DoEvents` isn't supported. A workaround is provided in Chapter 9.
- The `SaveSetting` and `GetSetting` Registry functions aren't supported. See Chapter 9 for implementations for Windows CE.
- Custom properties (that is, `Property Set` and `Property Get`) aren't supported. Instead, twin methods must be used. See Chapter 3 for an example.
- The eVB ListBox doesn't support the CheckBox style.
- eVB doesn't support the `Date`, `Time`, or `Timer` statements. See Chapter 9's examples for `GetLocalTime` and `GetTickCount`.
- `Option Base` and `Option Type` aren't supported.
- Arrays can't have a lower bound other than zero.
- Collections aren't supported.
- The `!` operator (as in `objRs!Field1`) is unsupported.
- `GoSub` is unsupported.
- Line numbering isn't allowed.
- `End` is unsupported. Instead, use `App.End`.
- The following conversion functions are invalid: `Str`, `Val`, `Cvar`, and `CVDate`.
- eVB has no `Debug` object, so `Debug.Print` and `Debug.Assert` are invalid.
- The `TypeOf` function is unsupported.
- Select statements using `Is` or `To` are invalid (for example, `Case obj Is Nothing`, `Case 1 To 5`).

- `Beep()` is unsupported. See Chapter 9 for the `PlaySound` API.
- All string commands containing the `$` character (`Left$`, `Right$`) are unsupported.
- `LSet` and `RSet` are unsupported.
- The `Like` operator isn't supported.

CAUTION

Just because something comes up in IntelliSense does not mean eVB supports it! The eVB IDE was very likely derived from the VB6 IDE, and therefore some VB6 functions will show up in IntelliSense. When in doubt, check the eMbedded Visual Tools help files. As a general rule, if it isn't in the help files as an eVB function, it isn't supported.

Summary

We've covered many of the differences between eVB and Visual Basic 6 in this chapter, but don't be surprised if you run into something I haven't listed. Different programming styles tend to uncover different things. Again, when in doubt, check Help for eMbedded Visual Tools. If it doesn't appear in Help, it probably is unsupported.

Knowing eVB's limitations will help you design you applications and prevent debugging unsupported code. Armed with the knowledge of what you can't do, you're ready to start looking at what you can do.

Manipulating Files

CHAPTER

3

IN THIS CHAPTER

Most Visual Basic programmers today access files through the familiar Win32 File System Object (commonly called the fso). The fso provides an easy-to-use and quick-to-develop-with object model that works for most text file applications.

When it comes to binary or random access, the fso falters, and VB developers then turn to what's often called *free filing*—probably named as such due to using the `FreeFile()` method to get an available file number. Free filing is an older, procedural-based method of access files that's valid for any file access, but isn't quite as easy to use as the object-oriented fso.

Although the eVB's FileSystem and File controls don't have the extensive object model that the fso has, they provide just about everything developers could want or need for accessing any type of file-binary or text, sequential or random.

In fact, I find that using these controls has distinct advantages over file programming in Win32 because they wrap the functionality of both free filing and the fso in a nice, compact set of methods and properties. Whether accessing small text configuration files or large binary data files, the FileSystem and File controls are all you'll need.

This chapter explores some of the functionality behind the two controls in the `MSCEFileCtl` library: FileSystem and File. The controls' uses are limited only by the applications in which they are used and by your coding imagination; an exhaustive treatment of all the entire library's uses could be a book in itself. We'll cover some of their more common uses, give you ideas on where else you might use them, and add in the use of the TreeView control as well.

In this chapter you will

- Learn about the object models for the FileSystem and File controls
- Discover the differences between the `FileControl` functions and Visual Basic's well-known File System Object (fso)
- Learn about the object model for the native CE TreeView control
- Read and traverse a directory tree
- Use the Open, Read, Write, and Close text files
- See how to retrieve file attributes, such as size and modify date
- Examine how to minimize the impact of the `CreateObject` memory leak
- Work around the lack of support for properties

As we'll do with all chapters, we will also uncover some of eVB's more subtle nuances that can cause problems and headaches, as well as give coding tips applicable to any eVB application.

The FileSystem and File Controls

The Microsoft FileSystem and File controls are distributed with the platform SDK for each CE platform. They are both included in the MSCEFile.dll library. Controls are added to projects in eVB in the same manner as in other versions of Visual Basic (by choosing Components from the Tools menu). You can add the File and FileSystem controls specifically to your project via the Microsoft CE FileSystem Control 3.0 component library (see Figure 3.1).

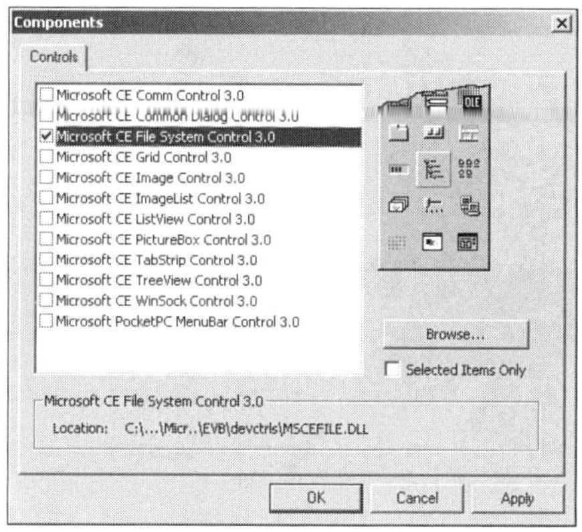

FIGURE 3.1
Adding the FileSystem control library to your project.

Adding the reference places both controls into the eVB toolbox. The File control's button shows a small file icon, whereas the FileSystem control shows a small two-drawer filing cabinet (see Figure 3.2).

The Controls' Object Models

This chapter will cover a large amount of the File and FileSystem controls' object models. Covering the entire object model for any library in a single project is difficult and often impractical. Many methods are used in just about every project, whereas others are used only for specific, narrowly focused uses.

The following is a list of the methods and properties used in this chapter:

File Control	*FileSystem Control*
`Close`	`Dir`
`Input`	`FileDateTime`
`LinePrint`	`FileLen`
`Open`	`GetAttr`
`EOF`	`Kill`

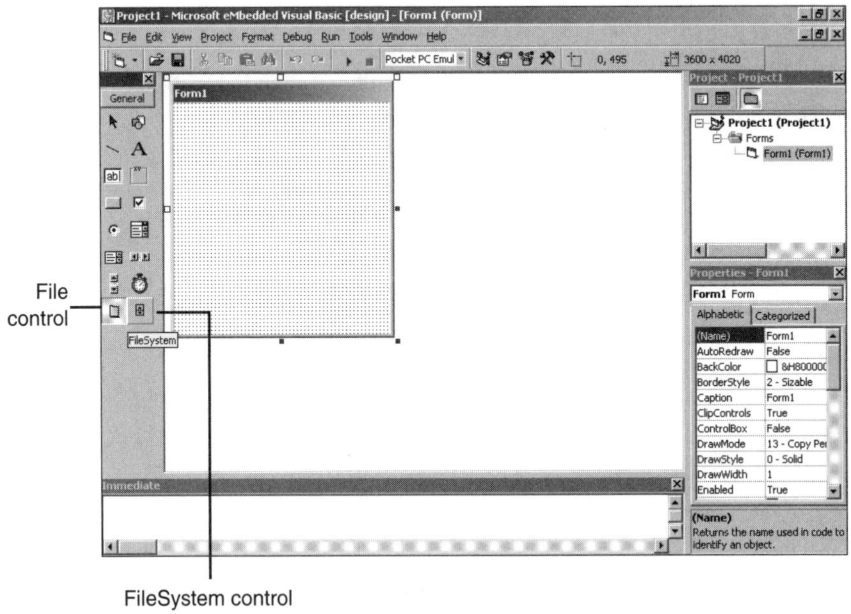

FIGURE 3.2

The eVB toolbox with the standard controls, the File control and the FileSystem control.

As a reference guide, Appendix A includes all the object models for the File and FileSystem controls.

The Windows CE TreeView Control

The application developed in this chapter provides a pretty good look at the Windows CE version of the familiar TreeView control. As you can expect, the object model is smaller and the features are fewer than what you get with the Win32 TreeView control, but it's sufficiently robust to provide all the common functionality TreeViews are used for without having to hunt for or write your own custom control.

The following is a list of the TreeView control's methods and properties used in this chapter:

```
Close
Input
LinePrint
Open
EOF
Dir
```

```
FileDateTime
FileLen
GetAttr
Kill
```

Again, I feel it's useful to have a full object model reference to be able to refer to in not only this project, but for any other project you work on as well. Appendix A lists the full object model for the Windows CE TreeView control.

The TreeView is in its own control library, MSCETreeView.dll, and, just like the FileSystem and File controls, can be added to a project's toolbox through the Project Components dialog. Simply select Microsoft Windows CE Treeview Control 3.0.

Creating the PocketExplorer Utility

The best way to familiarize yourself with the FileSystem and File controls is to dive in and begin using them for a meaningful purpose. To do that, we're going to write a small utility application called PocketExplorer that's somewhat of a mix between the standard Windows Explorer and Notepad.

PocketExplorer will allow you to navigate through all the folders on your PocketPC as well as view the files within the folders and their attributes. It will also allow you to open and edit any file, though only in text mode.

Setting Up the Project

PocketExplorer uses two forms—`frmMain` and `frmView`—and one module, `modMain`.

Listings 3.1 and 3.2 contain all the heading information for `frmMain` and `frmView`, respectively. For clarity, I have included listings only for properties that I modified from their defaults. Figure 3.3 shows what my project looks like.

LISTING 3.1 Heading Information from frmMain.ebf

```
Begin VB.Form frmMain
   Caption         =   "PocketExplorer"
   ClientHeight    =   4005
   ClientLeft      =   60
   ClientTop       =   840
   ClientWidth     =   3630
   ShowOK          =   -1  'True
   Begin FILECTLCtl.FileSystem fsMain
      Left            =   2220
```

LISTING 3.1 Continued

```
    Top              =   180
      _cx            =   2200
      _cy            =   1400
   End
   Begin MSCETREEVIEWLibCtl.TreeViewCtl tvwFolders
      Height         =   1755
      Left           =   30
      Top            =   0
      Width          =   3555
      LabelEdit      =   1
      LineStyle      =   1
      PathSeparator  =   "/"
      Style          =   6
   End
   Begin VBCE.Label lblFiles
      Height         =   255
      Left           =   2160
      Top            =   3720
      Width          =   495
      Caption        =   "Files:"
      Alignment      =   1
   End
   Begin VBCE.CommandButton cmdDelete
      Height         =   315
      Left           =   1380
      Top            =   3660
      Width          =   615
      Caption        =   "Del"
   End
   Begin VBCE.CommandButton cmdNew
      Height         =   315
      Left           =   720
      Top            =   3660
      Width          =   615
      Caption        =   "New"
   End
   Begin VBCE.ComboBox cboFilter
      Height         =   300
      Left           =   2700
      Top            =   3660
      Width          =   855
      Text           =   ""
   End
   Begin VBCE.CommandButton cmdEdit
```

LISTING 3.1 Continued

```
      Height          =   315
      Left            =   60
      Top             =   3660
      Width           =   615
      Caption         =   "Edit"
      Enabled         =   0   'False
   End
   Begin VBCE.ListBox lstFiles
      Height          =   1785
      Left            =   30
      Top             =   1800
      Width           =   3555
   End
End
```

NOTE

Listings 3.1 and 3.2 don't show the entire headings, but show all control settings that I've changed from their defaults.

LISTING 3.2 Heading Information from frmView.ebf

```
Begin VB.Form frmView
   Caption         =   "FileName"
   ClientHeight    =   4005
   ClientLeft      =   60
   ClientTop       =   345
   ClientWidth     =   3630
   ShowOK          =   -1  'True
   Begin VBCE.CommandButton cmdSave
      Height          =   375
      Left            =   2400
      Top             =   3600
      Width           =   1035
      Caption         =   "Save"
   End
   Begin VBCE.TextBox txtView
      Height          =   3495
      Left            =   30
      Top             =   30
      Width           =   3555
```

LISTING 3.2 Continued

```
      Text             =    ""
      MultiLine        =    -1  'True
      ScrollBars       =    3
   End
End
```

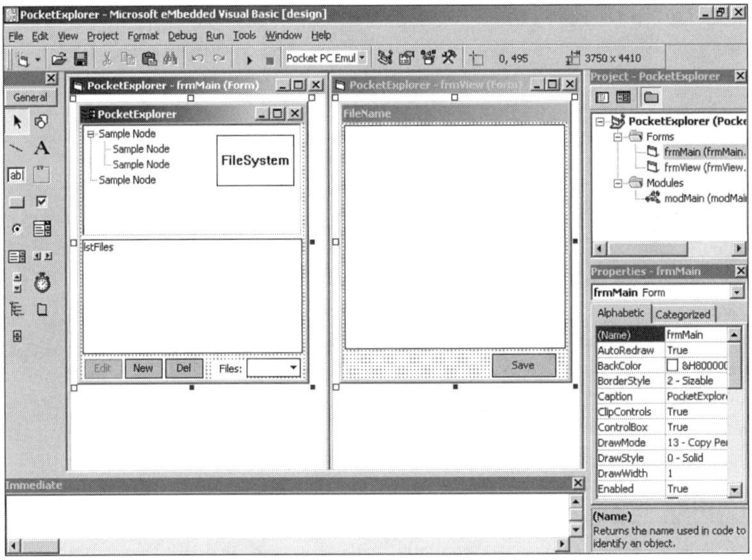

FIGURE 3.3
The final Form layouts for PocketExplorer.

Getting Directory Contents

One primary function of PocketExplorer is to display directory contents, so you need to write a *workhorse* function that can be called to do so. You want the function to read a directory, and then populate the TreeView with any subfolders in the directory as well as populate the textbox with all the directory files, provided they meet your filter conditions.

To make the code a little easier to reuse in other projects, it's a good idea to make it a function that's entirely independent of this project. That means you should have no direct references to any of the forms' controls, so what you need is a function that will take all this information as input parameters.

Call the `ReadDirectory` function and put it in the code module `modMain`.

```
Public Sub ReadDirectory(Path As String, _
                        fsFileSystem As FILECTLCtl.FileSystem, _
                        tvwTreeView As MSCETREEVIEWLibCtl.TreeViewCtl, _
                        nodParentNode As MSCETREEVIEWLibCtl.Node, _
                        lstListBox As ListBox, _
                        strFilter As String)
```

When giving the parameter types, it's important to provide the libraries they come from (that is, `FILECTLClt.FileSystem` instead of just `FileSystem`) because without them, you won't get IntelliSense for the object inside the function.

Next, you populate the controls passed in, and the simplest way to do that is one at a time. Listing 3.3 extracts all the subdirectories from the directory passed in as the `Path` parameter.

LISTING 3.3 Extracting All Subdirectories from a Directory

```
Dim strDir As String
Dim strFile As String

On Error Resume Next

' Ensure path is slash terminated
If Right(Path, 1) <> "\" Then Path = Path & "\"

' ----- First get all directories -----
' Priming Read
strDir = fsFileSystem.Dir(Path & "*", fsAttrDirectory)

' Iterate through directory
Do While strDir <> ""
    ' add directories to TreeView
    tvwTreeView.Nodes.Add nodParentNode.Key, tvwChild, strDir, strDir

    ' if the node already exists, ignore the error
    If Err.Number = 35602 Then
        ' ignore duplicate node adds - the add will fail anyway
    ElseIf Err.Number <> 0 Then
        MsgBox Err.Description, vbExclamation, "Error adding node!"
    End If

    strDir = fsFileSystem.Dir
Loop
```

The code in Listing 3.3 first allows for the incoming path to either be backslash-terminated or not by simply checking for it and adding it if necessary.

Next, it does a priming read with the FileSystem control's `Dir()` method. The first time you call `Dir()`, you must specify the path you want to read as well as any filtering options you want enforced. It returns a string of the first item that meets those conditions or an empty string if nothing meeting your conditions was found. In this priming read, you send in your path and `"*"` and specify `fsAttrDirectory`, which brings back all directories.

All subsequent calls to `Dir()` require no parameters and simply fetch the next item matching your criteria from the same directory until no more are found, at which point it returns an empty string. In Listing 3.3, this is handled with a simple `Do...While` loop.

If you call `ReadDirectory` with an already populated path, it will try to add duplicate nodes to the TreeView, which will cause an error (specifically, error 35602—`Key already exists in collection`).

You can handle this error by either keeping track of which directories you have already read or by checking to see if the node you are trying to add to already has children, but then you also have to determine if anything had been added, removed, or changed. You also can clear all the node's children and repopulate it, but this seems inefficient, because most often there won't be any differences. I've opted to look specifically for just error 35602 and ignore it. The error prevents duplicates and anything new will be added.

Next, you need to get all the files in the directory and populate the passed-in ListBox. Use the same logic of a priming read with the `Dir()` function followed by a `Do...While` Loop. This time in the priming read, you will send in a filter condition and specify `fsAttrNormal`, which will return files with normal attributes (see Listing 3.4).

LISTING 3.4 Extracting a Filtered File List from a Directory

```
' ----- Next get all files -----
' Clear ListBox
lstListBox.Clear

' Priming Read
strFile = fsFileSystem.Dir(Path & strFilter, fsAttrNormal)

' Iterate through directory
Do While strFile <> ""
    'Add Files to ListBox
    lstListBox.AddItem strFile
    strFile = fsFileSystem.Dir
Loop
```

Notice that because you clear the ListBox every time, you don't need to trap an error.

Before you can call `ReadDirectory`, though, you need to get all the information required by the function's parameter list. First up is the path.

The TreeView control works nicely for helping to store the current path with which the user is working. The control enables you to define a path delimiter, so by using a backslash delimiter and setting each node's text to that of a directory, you can almost get the exact string you need just by reading a node's `FullPath` property. The only problem is that it appends your root node's text to the beginning of the path.

To correct this, you simply need to remove the root node's text. I've done this by using the `Replace` function, and because you will need to get the path from multiple places in your code, I've wrapped this all in its own small function. Because the code is specific to your TreeView, I've placed the code on `frmMain`'s code page:

```
Private Function GetPath() As String
    GetPath = Replace(tvwFolders.SelectedItem.FullPath, "My Device", "")
End Function
```

The next four parameters to `ReadDirectory` are simple. Just pass in references to controls on `frmMain`.

The final parameter is the filter, which you can use to display all files by passing in `"*.*"` or to limit the files displayed by passing a filter. For example, passing in `"*.txt"` would show only files ending in .txt.

You can get this information from the `cboFilter` ComboBox on `frmMain`.

Because the code will call `ReadDirectory` from multiple places, I've also wrapped a call to it in another simple function and placed it on `frmMain`'s code page:

```
Private Sub RefreshForm()
    ' read the selected directory and populate the form
    ReadDirectory GetPath(), fsMain, tvwFolders, _
                tvwFolders.SelectedItem, lstFiles, cboFilter.Text
End Sub
```

Although this isn't absolutely necessary, it's easier for coding because now you can simply call `RefreshForm` any time you want to read the currently selected directory.

Displaying the Directory Tree

Now that you have created functions to get the contents of any directory, let's display the directory tree in the TreeView control.

Before adding anything to the TreeView control, you must first initialize it by creating and adding the root node. Every node in the TreeView will be a child of this node. A good example of this is the My Computer root node in the standard Windows Explorer TreeView on your desktop machine.

Following this model, call your root node My Device. To add the node to the TreeView, use the `Add` method, passing in both the `Key` and `Text` you want to display. Leave both the `Relative` and `Relationship` parameters blank because the root has no siblings or parent. The `Add` method also returns a reference to the created node, which you can then use to directly call its properties and methods. In the `Form_Load` event for `frmMain`, add the following code:

```
Dim nodRoot As MSCETREEVIEWLibCtl.Node

' Initialize the TreeView
tvwFolders.Nodes.Clear
Set nodRoot = tvwFolders.Nodes.Add(, , "Root", "My Device")
```

The reason you are holding a reference to the root node isn't immediately apparent, but you will want to call a couple of methods of the root on startup, so you might as well put the code in now to hold it.

`Form_Load` is a good time to do any other initialization of the application as well, so put a couple of filter options into the `cboFilter` ComboBox and set its default as well:

```
' Initialize the Filter combobox
cboFilter.AddItem "*.*"
cboFilter.AddItem "*.txt"

' This will fire the ComboBox Change event,
'  which will populate the first set of directories
cboFilter.Text = "*.*"

' Clean up
Set nodRoot = Nothing
```

This adds a filter for `".txt"` files and all files. Feel free to add whatever else you would like.

Setting the default filter to `"*.*"` causes the `Change` event for `cboFilter` to fire, just as the user changing it does. You need to add some code to be sure that these changes refilter the ListBox. Likewise, when the user taps the ComboBox to change it, you also want to handle that event. Add the code in Listing 3.5 to `frmMain`'s code page.

LISTING 3.5 Allowing Users to Filter the Files They Want to View

```
Private Sub cboFilter_Change()
    ' Refresh the form
    RefreshForm
```

LISTING 3.5 Continued

```
    ' Disable the Edit button
    cmdEdit.Enabled = False
End Sub

Private Sub cboFilter_Click()
    Dim strFilter As String

    ' The ComboBox Text get set AFTER the Click event,
    ' so we must get it manually
    strFilter = cboFilter.List(cboFilter.ListIndex)

    ' Read the selected directory and populate the form
    ReadDirectory GetPath(), fsMain, tvwFolders, _
        tvwFolders.SelecteItem, lstFiles, strFilter

    ' Disable the Edit button
    cmdEdit.Enabled = False
End Sub
```


NOTE

A ComboBox's events in eVB fire *in a different order* than they do in VB. This is extremely important, and knowing it will save you some headaches trying to debug apparent logic error in the future. The Text property gets set after the `Click` event fires, so checking the Text property in the `Click` event handler will actually return the text that the user changed it from, not the new selection. It does, however set the ListIndex property to the new value before the event, so to get the text of the user's selection, you must get the List value at the current ListIndex.

Notice that the code in Listing 3.5 disables the Edit button in both events because the file list is getting repopulated and there will no longer be a file selected. When the user selects a file, you need to re-enable it, so add code to the ListBox's `Click` event:

```
Private Sub lstFiles_Click()
    ' If a file is selected, enable the View button
    If lstFiles.ListIndex >= 0 Then
        cmdEdit.Enabled = True
    Else
        cmdEdit.Enabled = False
    End If
End Sub
```

Now the only thing left to do is to populate the node that the user selects by using the `RefreshForm` method. Handle it in the TreeView's `NodeClick` event like this:

```
Private Sub tvwFolders_NodeClick(ByVal Index As Long)
    ' Repopulate the form
    RefreshForm

    ' Disable the View button
    cmdEdit.Enabled = False
End Sub
```

Finally, a nice feature would be to display all the files and subdirectories in the root directory on startup. The easiest way to do this is to manually select the root node in `Form_Load`, which will fire the `NodeClick` event. Then it's just a matter of setting the node's `Expanded` property to `True`.

The modified `Form_Load` event now looks like the code in Listing 3.6.

LISTING 3.6 `Form_Load` Modified to Select and Expand the Root Node

```
Private Sub Form_Load()
    Dim nodRoot As MSCETREEVIEWLibCtl.Node

    ' Initialize the TreeView
    tvwFolders.Nodes.Clear
    Set nodRoot = tvwFolders.Nodes.Add(, , "Root", "My Device")

    ' Select the root node
    nodRoot.Selected = True

    ' Initialize the Filter combobox
    cboFilter.AddItem "*.*"
    cboFilter.AddItem "*.txt"

    ' This will fire the ComboBox Change event,
    '  which will populate the first set of directories
    cboFilter.Text = "*.*"

    'Expand the root node
    nodRoot.Expanded = True

    ' Clean up
    Set nodRoot = Nothing
End Sub
```

Running the application at this point gives you pretty good navigation functionality. Figure 3.4 shows PocketExplorer running.

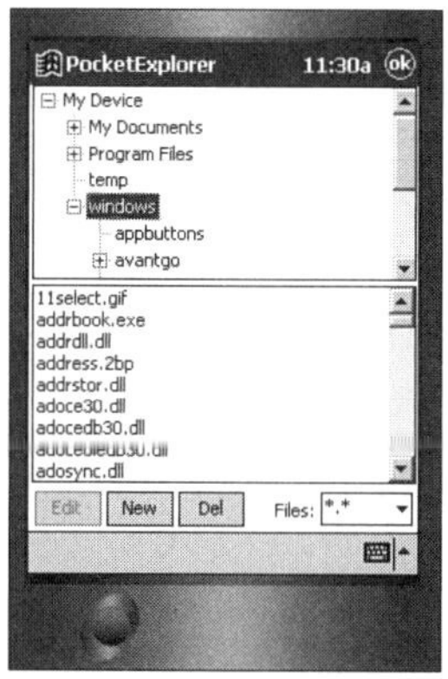

FIGURE 3.4
PocketExplorer's TreeView and File list in action.

Getting a File's Attributes

The next feature to add to PocketExplorer displays the attributes of a specific file when it is double-clicked in the file list. To add this functionality, use the FileSystem control's `Attr()`, `FileLength()`, and `FileDateTime()` methods.

First, write a function that returns a string representation of any file's attributes. Again, to make it more generic, and therefore more reusable, remove any references to the project's controls and instead pass them in. Listing 3.7 shows the full code for `GetFileAttributes()`.

LISTING 3.7 Getting a File's Attributes Given Its Path

```
Public Function GetFileAttributes(Path As String, _
                                  fsFileSystem As FILECTLCtl.FileSystem) _
                                  As String

    Dim FileAttr As FileAttrEnum
    Dim lFileLength As Long
    Dim dtFileDate As Date
    Dim strAttributes As String
    Dim strFileName As String

    On Error Resume Next
```

LISTING 3.7 Continued

```
    ' Get the attributes.  A file can have many
    FileAttr = fsFileSystem.GetAttr(Path)

    ' Check if it's a system file
    If FileAttr And fsAttrSystem Then
        strAttributes = strAttributes & "System File" & vbCrLf
    End If
    If FileAttr And fsAttrReadOnly Then
        strAttributes = strAttributes & "Read-Only" & vbCrLf
    End If
    If FileAttr And fsAttrArchive Then
        strAttributes = strAttributes & "Archive File" & vbCrLf
    End If

    ' Get file's date
    dtFileDate = fsFileSystem.FileDateTime(Path)
    strAttributes = strAttributes & dtFileDate & vbCrLf

    ' Get file's length
    lFileLength = fsFileSystem.FileLen(Path)

    ' format the size a little nicer
    ' Since Format() isn't supported, we'll use integer/float division
    '   as a workaround.
    If lFileLength < 1024 Then
        strAttributes = strAttributes & CStr(lFileLength) & " bytes"
    ElseIf lFileLength < 1048576 Then
        ' Go out 1 decimal place
        strAttributes = strAttributes & _
               CStr((lFileLength \ 102.4) / 10) & "k bytes"
    Else
        ' Go out 2 decimal places
        strAttributes = strAttributes & _
               CStr((lFileLength \ 10485.76) / 100) & "M bytes"
    End If

    ' Return the attributes
    GetFileAttributes = strAttributes
End Function
```

The function is pretty straightforward. First, it determines all the `Attr()` values for the file, such as `Hidden`, `Read-Only`, or `System`. It then calls `FileDateTime` to get the file's last modification date and `FileLen` to get the file's length in bytes.

Because eVB doesn't support the `Format()` function, and I thought it a bit ugly to show the exact number of bytes for large files, I've implemented a small workaround that formats numbers greater than 1,024 to either kilobytes or megabytes, depending on size.

Figure 3.5 shows the attributes in a MessageBox from the list's `DblClick` event handler (see Listing 3.8).

LISTING 3.8 Displaying a File's Properties on a Double Tap

```
Private Sub lstFiles_DblClick()
    Dim strPath As String
    Dim strAttributes As String
    Dim strFileName As String

    ' Make sure the user double-clicked a valid item
    If lstFiles.ListIndex < 0 Then Exit Sub

    ' Get the filename
    strFileName = lstFiles.List(lstFiles.ListIndex)

    ' Get the file's path
    strPath = GetPath() & "\" & strFileName

    ' Show the file's attributes
    strAttributes = GetFileAttributes(strPath, fsMain)

    ' Display the info to the user
    MsgBox strAttributes, vbInformation + vbOKOnly, strFileName
End Sub
```


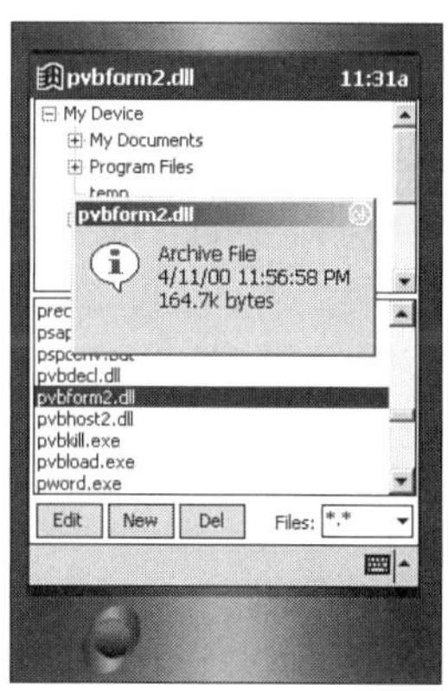

FIGURE 3.5
Displaying a file's attributes.

Opening, Editing, and Writing Text Files

The next features you will add to PocketExplorer are similar to those you get on a desktop PC through Notepad—the capability to create, open, and edit text files. The functions you need to implement these features are found in the File control.

Creating the `File` Object Without Leaking Memory

This is a good opportunity to demonstrate a few of eVB's features. Rather than drop a File control onto `frmMain`, you can use `CreateObject()`.

As I mentioned in Chapter 2, `CreateObject` also creates a memory leak. Every time you call it, you lose a chunk of memory, and if you call it often enough, you probably force users to reset their devices.

One way to avoid multiple calls to `CreateObject` is simply to call it the first time you need the object, and then keep the object around for the life of your application. Rather than create a new object every time you need one, just reuse the original. This increases the overall memory your application requires because you can never release the object, but minimizing the impact of `CreateObject`'s memory leak is more important.

NOTE

This is a trade-off you need to think about for any project that uses `CreateObject`. If the object is large and rarely used, you may want to destroy and re-create it only when used to conserve memory. Be aware, however, that each time you call `CreateObject`, you'll lose memory until your application is fully shut down.

Another frustrating aspect of using `CreateObject` in eVB is that the library and class names exposed to the Object Browser and IntelliSense aren't always the same as the names used in the object's type library. The File control falls into this category. If we look in the Object Browser or use IntelliSense, it seems that we would want to create a `FILECTLCtl.File` object, but using this as a parameter to `CreateObject` will result in error 429, `ActiveX Component can't create object`. This is because the library name isn't actually `FILECTLCtl`, but just `FILECTL`. (Notice the omission of the last three letters, `Ctl`.)

TIP

As a rule of thumb, if you get an error 429 when trying to create an object that ends in `Ctl`, `Lib`, or some combination of them, try creating the object without those letters:

```
CreateObject("FILECTL.File")
```

Another option for finding the name is to open the library's typelibrary or typelibrary cache. These are usually files with the same name as the DLL, but with a .tlb or .oca extension. In this case, it's MSCEFILE.oca and it can be found in the \Program Files\Microsoft eMbedded Tools\EVB\devctrls directory of your development PC. Opening the file with Notepad displays largely unprintable garbage, but all the library and class names should be readable. Be careful not to modify the file's contents.

CAUTION

.oca and .tlb files are binary files used by the system. Modifying them in any way can render their associated controls unusable.

With all that said, let's create a global `File` object variable and a function that both creates it and returns a reference to it. This way you can just call this function whenever you need your File control and let the function handle whether it actually needs to call `CreateObject()`. First, in the General Declarations section of `modMain`, add the variable declaration:

```
Private m_FileObject As FILECTLCtl.File
```

And then add the function shown in Listing 3.9.

LISTING 3.9 Minimizing the Impact of the `CreateObject` Memory Leak

```
Public Function GetFileObject() As FILECTLCtl.File
    On Error Resume Next

    ' If we haven't created the File object yet, do so
    If IsEmpty(m_FileObject) Then
        ' Create a File control
        Set m_FileObject = CreateObject("FILECTL.File")

        ' Ensure the object was created successfully
        If Err.Number <> 0 Then
            MsgBox "Failed to create File object." & vbCrLf & _
                "Ensure MSCEFile.dll has been installed and registered.", _
                vbCritical, "Error"
            Exit Function
        End If
    End If

    ' Return our global File object
    Set GetFileObject = m_FileObject
End Function
```

Deleting a File

Deleting a file is probably the simplest file function, so it is covered first. When the user selects a file in PocketExplorer and taps the Delete button, you call the `Kill` function of your `FileSystem` object. As a courtesy, it's always a good idea to give a warning message to ensure that the user really wants to delete the file. Listing 3.10 shows the event handler for the Delete button, and Figure 3.6 shows the Delete dialog.

LISTING 3.10 Event Handler for the Delete Button in frmMain.cbf

```
Private Sub cmdDelete_Click()
    Dim strPath As String
    Dim strFileName As String

    On Error Resume Next

    ' Make sure a file is selected
    If lstFiles.ListIndex < 0 Then Exit Sub

    ' Get the path to the file
    strFileName = lstFiles.List(lstFiles.ListIndex)
    strPath = GetPath() & "\" & strFileName

    ' Make sure the user wants to delete the file
    If MsgBox("Delete file?: " & vbCrLf & strFileName, _
            vbYesNo, "Delete File?") = vbNo Then Exit Sub

    ' Delete the file
    fsMain.Kill strPath

    ' Check for success
    If Err.Number <> 0 Then
        MsgBox "Unable to delete file.  It may be in use or protected", _
                vbExclamation, "Error"
    End If

    ' Repopulate the form
    RefreshForm
End Sub
```

Reading a File's Contents

Reading the contents of a sequential text file is a straightforward operation similar to using the fso in Win32. Essentially, you open the file, loop through the contents until you hit EOF, and then close the file. We'll use the `GetFileTextContents` function in Listing 3.11 to return the contents of any text file as a `String`.

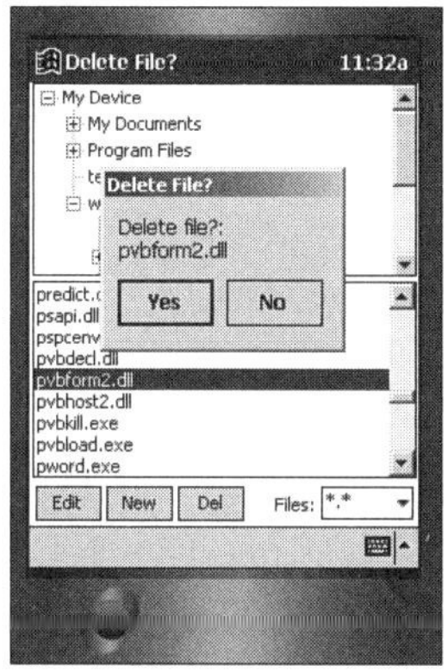

FIGURE 3.6
Asking before you delete a file is a general courtesy.

LISTING 3.11 Extracting the Contents of a Text File as a String

```
Public Function GetFileTextContents(Path As String) As String
    Dim filFile As FILECTLCtl.File
    Dim strInput As String

    On Error Resume Next

    ' Get our application File object
    Set filFile = GetFileObject()

    ' Open the File
    filFile.Open Path, fsModeInput, fsAccessRead

    ' Make sure the call to Open was successful
    If Err.Number <> 0 Then
        MsgBox "Open Method failed." & vbCrLf & _
            "The file could not be read.", _
            vbCritical, "Error"
    End If

    ' Loop through file, filling our input buffer
    Do While Not filFile.EOF
        strInput = strInput & filFile.Input(1)
    Loop

    ' Close the file
    filFile.Close
```

LISTING 3.11 Continued

```
    ' Release the File Object
    Set filFile = Nothing

    ' Return the text
    GetFileTextContents = strInput
End Function
```

When the user taps the Edit button, use the function to read the file's contents and fill the multiline TextBox on `frmView` (see Figure 3.7).

FIGURE 3.7
Editing a file with PocketExplorer.

Just like Notepad, you don't hold the file open while it's being viewed, so you need to store the filename somewhere so you know where to save any changes the user makes. A simple way would be to just set a global variable in either `frmView` or `modMain`, but let's take this opportunity to implement a workaround to the fact that eVB doesn't support user-defined properties.

Just like a property, you need to have a member variable in which to keep the value and implement both a `Set` and `Get` method to set or get that member variable's value. In `frmView`'s General Declarations section, add the following member variable:

```
Private m_strPath As String
```

And then add the following code:

```
' Since Properties aren't supported, we'll use a Set/Get
'   method pair as a workaround
```

```
Public Sub SetPath(NewPath As String)
    ' Store the full path to the current file
    m_strPath = NewPath
End Sub

Public Function GetPath() As String
    ' Retrieve the full path to the current file
    GetPath = m_strPath
End Function
```

You don't get a single name like you would for an actual property, but these two functions otherwise perform just like a property.

As another courtesy to users, keep track of whether they've saved their changes to the file so you can prompt them before they exit. To do this, keep a *dirty* flag in `frmView`, turning it off when they save and on when they make changes. When you first load the file, you need to clear the flag. Add the following to the General Declarations section of `frmView`:

```
Private m_bDirty As Boolean
```

And then add a function to clear the flag:

```
Public Sub ClearDirty()
    ' We must clear this flag every time we show the form
    m_bDirty = False
End Sub
```


While you're at it, you might as well add code that turns the flag back on. It's safe to assume that any stylus tap in the `txtView` TextBox will be a change to the file, so we'll turn the flag on in that event handler like so:

```
Private Sub txtView_KeyPress(ByVal KeyAscii As Integer)
    m_bDirty = True
End Sub
```

Now let's look at the implementation of the event handler for the Edit button (see Listing 3.12). Get the path to the selected file, set your new property to that value, get the file's contents, fill `frmView`'s TextBox, clear the dirty flag, and then lastly, hide `frmMain`.

LISTING 3.12 Opening and Displaying a Text File for User Modification

```
Private Sub cmdEdit_Click()
    Dim strPath As String
    Dim strContents As String
    Dim strFileName As String

    ' Build the path to the file
```

LISTING 3.12 Continued

```
    strPath = GetPath()
    strFileName = lstFiles.List(lstFiles.ListIndex)
    strPath = strPath & "\" & strFileName

    ' Set frmView's Path "property"
    frmView.SetPath strPath

    ' Get the file contents as text
    strContents = GetFileTextContents(strPath)

    ' Set frmView's caption
    frmView.Caption = strFileName

    ' Show frmView
    frmView.Show

    ' Populate the View textbox
    frmView.txtView.Text = strContents

    ' Set the form's dirty flag
    frmView.ClearDirty

    ' Hide frmMain
    frmMain.Hide
End Sub
```

Creating a New File

All that's left to do now is to add the capability to create a new file and save the changes the user makes to existing files. Both tasks can be handled with a single function.

Rather than determine what changes a user actually made to a file, it's much simpler to just overwrite the entire file. What you need then is a function that accepts the path to your file and your file's text as parameters (a new file will just have no text passed in). The function then needs to either create the file if it doesn't exist or overwrite it if it does, and write the passed-in text to it.

Again, you can write a generic function that can be reused in other projects (see Listing 3.13). A generic name such as `CreateFile` also facilitates reuse.

LISTING 3.13 Creating and Populating a Text File

```
Public Sub CreateFile(Path As String, Contents As String)
    ' This function performs double duty. We use it to create
    '   new files as well as overwrite old files

    Dim filFile As FILECTLCtl.File

    On Error Resume Next

    ' Get our application File object
    Set filFile = GetFileObject()

    ' Open the file, if it doesn't exist, it will be created
    ' fsModeOutput means overwrite
    filFile.Open Path, fsModeOutput, fsAccessWrite, fsLockWrite

    ' Make sure the call to Open was successful
    If Err.Number <> 0 Then
        MsgBox "Open Method failed." & vbCrLf & _
            "The file could not be created.", _
            vbCritical, "Error"
    End If

    ' Write our data to the file if it's not empty
    If Contents <> "" Then
        filFile.LinePrint Contents
    End If

    ' Close the file
    filFile.Close

    ' Release the File Object
    Set filFile = Nothing
End Sub
```


Now you need to add a call to `CreateFile` from `frmMain`'s New button. Prompt for a new filename by using the `InputBox` function. If the user doesn't enter a name or taps Cancel, `InputBox` returns an empty string.

Also add a default .txt extension to the filename if the user didn't provide one (see Listing 3.14).

LISTING 3.14 Getting a Filename from the User and Checking for an Extension

```
Private Sub cmdNew_Click()
    Dim strFileName As String
    Dim strPath As String

    ' Get a filename from the user - omit white spaces
    strFileName = Trim(InputBox("Filename to create:", "New File"))

    ' If the return was blank, exit
    If strFileName = "" Then Exit Sub

    ' Check for an extension by checking for a period
    If InStr(strFileName, ".") = 0 Then
        ' If an extension wasn't provided, default to .txt
        strFileName = strFileName & ".txt"
    End If

    ' Get the currentpath and append our filename
    strPath = GetPath() & "\" & strFileName

    ' Create the file
    CreateFile strPath, ""

    ' Repopulate the form
    RefreshForm
End Sub
```

Finally, you need to add a call from `frmView`'s Save button:

```
Private Sub cmdSave_Click()
    ' Save the file
    CreateFile GetPath(), txtView.Text

    ' Clear the dirty flag
    m_bDirty = False
End Sub
```

Adding the Final Touches

That pretty much completes PocketExplorer. You do need to add a few finishing touches to make it a bit more user friendly, though.

The PocketPC standard for exiting most forms is to tap the OK button in the upper-right corner of the form's title bar. The OK button has its own event handler to make this simple.

When users finish editing a file and tap OK, you should check to see whether they've saved all their changes and allow them to do so if they haven't. Do this with a simple `MsgBox` call (see Figure 3.8).

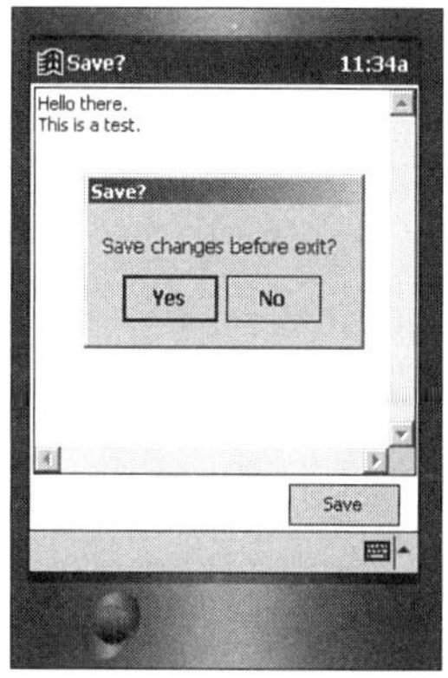

FIGURE 3.8
The Save Changes dialog.

Listing 3.15 shows `frmView`'s `OKClick` event handler.

LISTING 3.15 Asking to Save Changes Before Closing the Application

```
Private Sub Form_OKClick()
    ' check to see if there are unsaved changes
    If m_bDirty Then
        ' Prompt to save changes
        If MsgBox("Save changes before exit?", vbYesNo, "Save?") = vbYes Then
            ' Save changes
            CreateFile GetPath(), txtView.Text
        End If
    End If

    frmMain.Show
    frmView.Hide
End Sub
```

When the user exits the application by tapping OK on `frmMain`, you want to be sure to clean up after yourself, releasing any objects created. In the case of PocketExplorer, you should release the File control you created. Because the File control is held privately in `modMain`, you will need an access method to release it:

```
Public Sub ReleaseFileObject()
    Set m_FileObject = Nothing
End Sub
```

And finally, call your release method from `frmMain`'s `OKClick` event handler and end the application:

```
Private Sub Form_OKClick()
    ' Clean up our File object
    ReleaseFileObject

    ' End app
    App.End
End Sub
```

Summary

Writing PocketExplorer has given you a good look at the TreeView, FileSystem, and File controls and provided you with a tool not supplied with the PocketPC that you can actually use.

Of course, the File control has a lot of functionality that I didn't touch on for manipulating delimited text, binary, and random-access files, and I fully recommend exploring those functions. I commonly use the File and FileSystem controls for handling things such as configuration and .ini files for applications, but you could use them to save data or even save application state. The uses are limited only by your imagination and inclination.

You also saw examples of how to work around such problems as the `CreateObject` memory leak, the lack of `Format()` support, and the lack of user-defined properties. You even looked at making functions reusable by making them generic. These lessons can be applied to almost any eVB application, and you'll see similar code practices throughout the rest of the book.

If you want to do more exploration by extending the PocketExplorer application, the following modifications come to mind:

- Add images to the TreeView for folders.
- Save the state of the application so when users next launch PocketExplorer, it starts in the same folder from which they exited.
- Replace the Edit, Delete, and New buttons with a MenuBar (see Chapter 4).
- Add a Save As feature to `frmView` so users can rename the file when saving.
- Allow users to rename files or folders from `frmMain`.
- Add delimited file support (look at the `InputFields` and `WriteFields` methods).
- Add a popup menu for file operations.

Working with Menu Controls for Pocket PC

CHAPTER

4

IN THIS CHAPTER

The Pocket PC menu is implemented via an ActiveX control distributed with the Pocket PC SDK. Unlike Visual Basic, eMbedded Visual Basic has no native menu functionality. Another disadvantage is that there is no visual designer for this menu control. All design for the menu must be completed at runtime via programmatic control. One advantage to this is that it forces you as the programmer to have full control over the menu at all times. Toward the end of this chapter, we will investigate a dynamic menu system that's another design that lends itself to the limited menu support of eVB.

The menu control has a few events and a collection of objects. These collections are a multi-level hierarchical representation of the menu bars currently present on the menu.

The Pocket PC menu has a distinctly different appearance than Visual Basic menu controls. The two major differences are no cascading menus and buttons. Buttons are placed on the top-level menu bar itself. Cascading menus would be difficult to control and implement in such a small amount of real estate. Users would also be hard-pressed to get three perfectly placed stylus taps onto the menu. If a cascading menu is desired, use a menu with an ellipsis (…) and a small form to choose the next option. Buttons placed directly on the menu bar are a quick substitute toolbars. There really is no room for a docking toolbar (except in certain applications such as Pocket Excel and Pocket Word, but I still have difficulties working with the small amount of space left over after I turn on all the toolbars in these applications).

With all that in mind, in this chapter you will:

- Create a project reference to component for menu control
- Add a menu control to form
- Populate menu options
- Use graphics on menus
- Learn how to respond to menu events
- Investigate implementing a dynamic menu
- See how to implement a New menu button

Setting Project References For MenuBar Control

After your project is open, you need to set a reference to the ActiveX component that ships with eMbedded Visual Basic. To set the reference, choose Components from the Project menu.

This presents you with a dialog box allowing you to choose components to add to your project (see Figure 4.1). You need to choose Microsoft Pocket PC MenuBar Control 3.0. If you plan to use menu buttons with images, also set a reference to Microsoft CE ImageList Control 3.0.

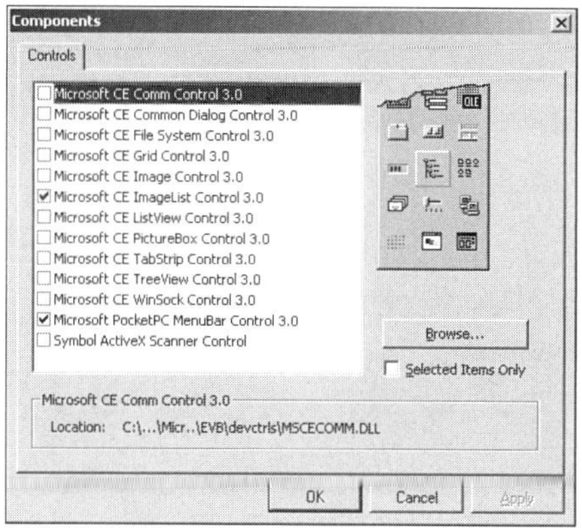

FIGURE 4.1

In the ActiveX Components dialog box, select the desired components for your project: Microsoft Pocket PC MenuBar Control 3.0 and Microsoft CE ImageList Control 3.0.

After setting reference to the components, your toolbar will contain two new controls. The ImageList and MenuBar controls are located at the bottom of Figure 4.2.

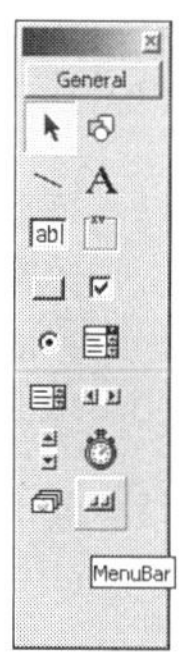

FIGURE 4.2

The eVB toolbox with the standard controls, the MenuBar control, and the ImageList control.

Next, add the menu control to your form. Values for `Top`, `Left`, `Height` and `Width` don't matter as the actual control will be invisible at runtime. Figure 4.3 shows a Menu control on an otherwise empty form.

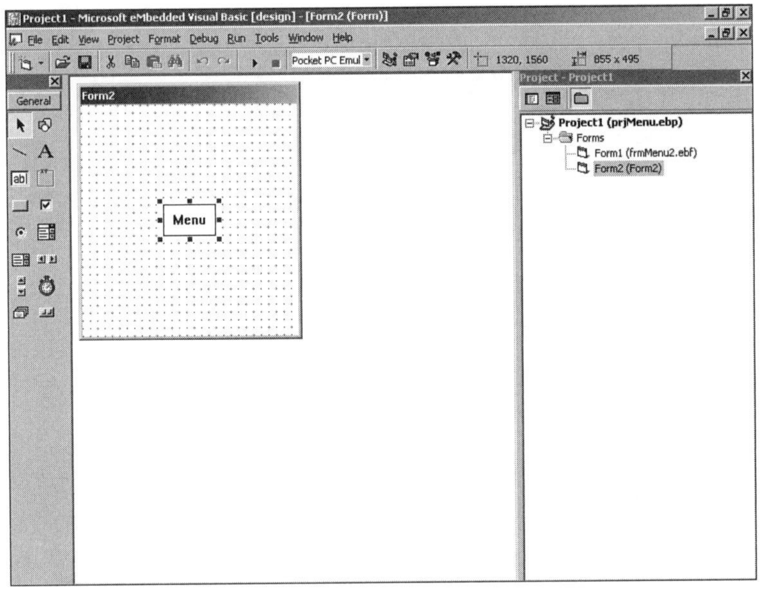

FIGURE 4.3
Once the MenuBar control is added to the form, it can be used to display menus, buttons, and button groups.

Creating Menu Bars

Let's start with a simple menu. In the sample application, there's a button with the caption Simple. In this button's `Click()` event, we'll clear the current menu bar, and add two menus and three menu items to each menu.

To add each menu to the command bar, use the `AddMenu` method of the `Controls` collection. Both the `Key` and `Prompt` parameters are provided to set these properties on the items. The `Key` property uniquely identifies the menus. Don't use the `Caption` property to identify the menus because the caption may change, causing bugs or extra maintenance coding. This becomes especially apparent when an application is internationalized.

In Listing 4.1, the `cmdSimple.Click` event creates two menus with three menu items on each. Figure 4.4. shows the menus created and the three menu items on the first menu.

LISTING 4.1 Creating a Simple Menu

```
Private Sub cmdSimple_Click()

    Dim objMenu As MenuBarLib.MenuBarMenu
    Dim objBar As MenuBarLib.MenuBarMenu
```

LISTING 4.1 Continued

```
    ' clear all buttons and menus from the menu bar control
    MenuBar1.Controls.Clear

    ' add 1st "root" prompt
    Set objMenu = MenuBar1.Controls.AddMenu("Prompt 1", KEY_SIMPLE_ROOT1)

    ' add 1st bar to the 1st root prompt
    ' set the key as part of the Add method
    Set objBar = objMenu.Items.Add(, KEY_SIMPLE_BAR1_PROMPT1, "Bar 1a")
    ' add a tag
    objBar.Tag = "Tag For Bar 1a"

    ' add 2nd bar to the 1st root prompt
    ' reuse objBar because we're done with 1st one
    Set objBar = objMenu.Items.Add(, KEY_SIMPLE_BAR1_PROMPT2, "Bar 1b")
    objBar.Tag = "Tag For Bar 1b"

    ' add 3rd bar to the 1st root prompt
    Set objBar = objMenu.Items.Add(, KEY_SIMPLE_BAR1_PROMPT3, "Bar 1c")
    objBar.Tag = "Tag For Bar 1c"

    ' add 2nd "root" prompt
    Set objMenu = MenuBar1.Controls.AddMenu("Prompt 2", KEY_SIMPLE_ROOT2)

    ' add 1st bar to the 2nd root prompt
    Set objBar = objMenu.Items.Add(, KEY_SIMPLE_BAR2_PROMPT1, "Bar 2a")
    objBar.Tag = "Tag For Bar 2a"

    ' add 2nd bar to the 2nd root prompt - again reuse
    Set objBar = objMenu.Items.Add(, KEY_SIMPLE_BAR2_PROMPT2, "Bar 2b")
    objBar.Tag = "Tag For Bar 2b"

    ' add 3rd bar to the 2nd root prompt - again reuse
    Set objBar = objMenu.Items.Add(, KEY_SIMPLE_BAR2_PROMPT3, "Bar 2c")
    objBar.Tag = "Tag For Bar 2c"

End Sub
```


Responding to Menu Taps

Now that the menu is displaying, the application needs to react to the user selecting one of its menu items. Use the MenuBar control's `MenuClick` event for this response. The menu item tapped is passed as the only parameter to the `MenuClick` event as an `Item`.

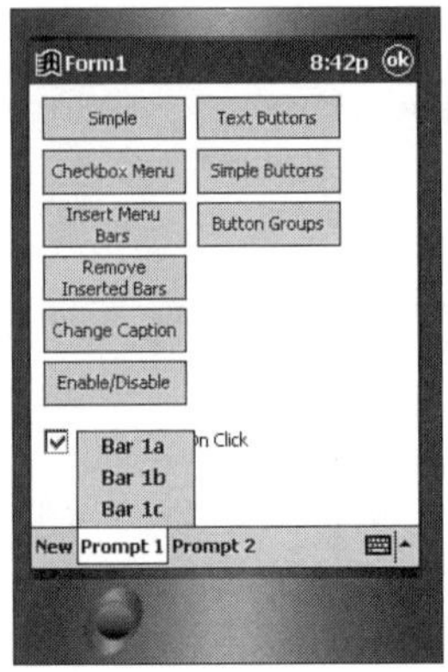

FIGURE 4.4

The first "root" menu is activated, displaying the three menu items attached. Notice the New button is displayed; the default value for the New button is `Enabled = True`.

In Listing 4.2, the sample application uses `MenuClick` to display the values of some of the properties of the tapped menu item, as shown in Figure 4.5. Then, depending on which menu is being displayed via your choices, the event will be passed to the proper subroutine.

FIGURE 4.5

When the menu item "Bar 1a" is tapped, the `MenuClick` *event responds and displays the current values of properties on the menu item.*

LISTING 4.2 Responding to a `Menu.Click` Event

```
Private Sub MenuBar1_MenuClick(ByVal Item As MenuBarLib.Item)

    Dim strMessage As String

    'check to see if MsgBox should be displayed
    If chkShowMsgBox.Value Then

        ' build message string
        strMessage = "You clicked:" & vbCrLf

        ' add the caption
```

LISTING 4.2 Continued

```
        strMessage = strMessage & "Caption:" & Item.Caption & vbCrLf

        ' add the key
        strMessage = strMessage & "Key:" & Item.Key & vbCrLf

        ' add the index
        strMessage = strMessage & "Index:" & Item.Index & vbCrLf

        ' add the checked state of item
        strMessage = strMessage & "Checked:" & Item.Checked & vbCrLf

        ' add the tag
        strMessage = strMessage & "Tag:" & Item.Tag & vbCrLf

        MsgBox strMessage
    End If

    ' since we're using several different "menus"
    ' let's use the first letter of the .Key property to
    ' let us know what menu we're using
    ' and send the event to different Subs for each menu

    Select Case Mid(Item.Key, 1, 1) 'can't use Left() function
        Case "S" ' simple
            Simple_MenuClick Item
        Case "C" ' checked
            Checked_MenuClick Item
        Case Else
            MsgBox "Unknown Menu"
    End Select
End Sub
```


In Listing 4.2, the menu item tapped is actually passed as an `MenuBarLib.Item` type. For this sample application, a message box is displayed, informing you of the values of the menu item tapped. Notice that after the message box is displayed, the Item is passed along to the appropriate subroutine (`Simple_MenuClick` or `Checked_MenuClick`). This is a good methodology to keep a menu virtually discreet within an eVB application.

Checkmark Menus

The Pocket PC MenuBar control can display checked menu items. The `Item` object has a `Checked` property. If this `Checked` property is set to `True`, the menu item will have a check mark placed to the left of the caption.

The sample application has a command button labeled Checkmark Menu. In this button's `Click` event, as shown in Listing 4.3, a menu is created with two groups of checkmarked menu items, as shown in Figure 4.6. A menu separator separates these two groups.

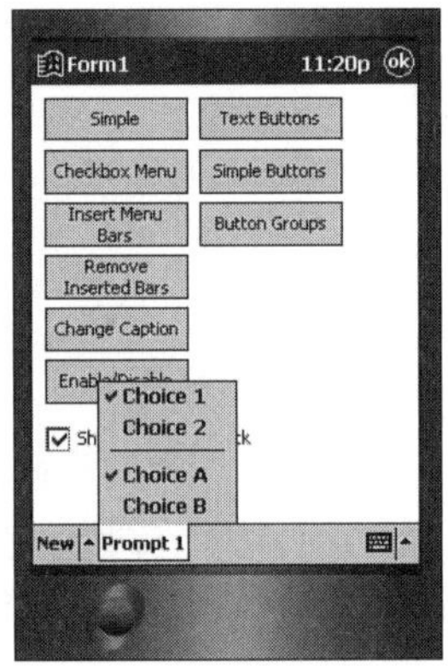

FIGURE 4.6
The checked menus are created and then marked with a check mark by setting `Checked` *to* `True`.

LISTING 4.3 Creating Checkmark Menu Items

```
Private Sub cmdMoreComplex_Click()

    Dim objMenu As MenuBarLib.MenuBarMenu

    ' this time we'll use "Item" so we can
    ' use extended properties
    Dim objBar As MenuBarLib.Item

    ' clear all buttons and menus from the menu bar control
    MenuBar1.Controls.Clear

    ' add 1st "root" prompt
    Set objMenu = MenuBar1.Controls.AddMenu("Prompt 1", KEY_COMPLEX_ROOT1)

    ' add 1st bar of 1st set of
    ' checked prompts to the 1st root prompt
    ' set .Prompt & .Key property in Add method
    Set objBar = objMenu.Items.Add(, KEY_COMPLEX_BAR1_PROMPT1, "Choice 1")
    objBar.Checked = True

    ' add 2nd bar of 1st set of
    ' checked prompts to the 1st root prompt
```

LISTING 4.3 Continued

```
    Set objBar = objMenu.Items.Add(, KEY_COMPLEX_BAR1_PROMPT2, "Choice 2")

    ' let's get a separator bar in there
    Set objBar = objMenu.Items.Add(, , , mbrMenuSeparator)

    ' add 1st bar of 2nd set of
    ' checked prompts to the 1st root prompt
    Set objBar = objMenu.Items.Add(, KEY_COMPLEX_BAR1_PROMPT3, "Choice A")
    objBar.Checked = True

    ' add 2nd bar of 2nd set of
    ' checked prompts to the 1st root prompt
    Set objBar = objMenu.Items.Add(, KEY_COMPLEX_BAR1_PROMPT4, "Choice B")

End Sub
```

In Listing 4.3, a reference to the first menu is retrieved. A menu item is added to this menu, and then its `Checked` property is set to `True`. Another item is added that is a complimentary menu item to the first one. A separator bar is added and another group of two menu items are added with the first one checked as well.

When one of the checkmark menu items is tapped, the application needs to handle unchecking the tapped menu item and checking the complimentary menu item. The `MenuClick` event handler farms the call to the `Checked_MenuClick` subroutine (See Listing 4.4) to accomplish this.

LISTING 4.4 Handling Taps to Checkmark Menu Items

```
Private Sub Checked_MenuClick(ByVal Item As MenuBarLib.Item)

    Dim objItem As MenuBarLib.Item

    ' check to see if already checked
    If Item.Checked Then
        ' ignore the click because it is already checked
        Exit Sub
    End If

    Select Case Item.Key
        Case KEY_COMPLEX_BAR1_PROMPT1
            ' if it's checked let's uncheck it
            ' if it's unchecked, let's check it
            Item.Checked = Not Item.Checked
```

LISTING 4.4 Continued

```
        ' retrieve the 2nd item in
        ' this set of checkmark prompts
        ' using the .Key value
        Set objItem = Item.Parent.Items(KEY_COMPLEX_BAR1_PROMPT2)

        ' set the checked property to
        ' the opposite of the other item
        objItem.Checked = Not Item.Checked

    Case KEY_COMPLEX_BAR1_PROMPT2
        ' if it's checked let's uncheck it
        ' if it's unchecked, let's check it
        Item.Checked = Not Item.Checked

        ' retrieve the 2nd item in
        ' this set of checkmark prompts
        ' using the .Key value
        Set objItem = Item.Parent.Items(KEY_COMPLEX_BAR1_PROMPT1)

        ' set the checked property to
        ' the opposite of the other item
        objItem.Checked = Not Item.Checked

    Case KEY_COMPLEX_BAR1_PROMPT3
        ' if it's checked let's uncheck it
        ' if it's unchecked, let's check it
        Item.Checked = Not Item.Checked

        ' retrieve the 2nd item in
        ' this set of checkmark prompts
        ' using the .Key value
        Set objItem = Item.Parent.Items(KEY_COMPLEX_BAR1_PROMPT4)

        ' set the checked property to
        ' the opposite of the other item
        objItem.Checked = Not Item.Checked

    Case KEY_COMPLEX_BAR1_PROMPT4
        ' if it's checked let's uncheck it
        ' if it's unchecked, let's check it
        Item.Checked = Not Item.Checked
```

LISTING 4.4 Continued

```
            ' retrieve the 2nd item in
            ' this set of checkmark prompts
            ' using the .Key value
            Set objItem = Item.Parent.Items(KEY_COMPLEX_BAR1_PROMPT3)

            ' set the checked property to
            ' the opposite of the other item
            objItem.Checked = Not Item.Checked

    End Select
End Sub
```

In Listing 4.4, `Checked_MenuClick` first checks whether a menu item tapped is already checked. If the menu item is already checked, the `routine` is `exited` because no action needs to be taken. Next, a `Select Case` decides which menu item was tapped and retrieves a reference to it. It then inverts its `Checked` property value (turns `False` to `True`; turns `True` to `False`). Then it retrieves a reference to its complimentary menu item and inverts its `Checked` property value as well.

Dynamic Menus

If it doesn't seem necessary or the best methodology to re-create the menu items wholly on-the-fly in your application, you can dynamically add and remove menu items.

A menu item can be inserted in place in a currently populated menu. If the `Index` parameter is used in the `AddMenu` method, the menu item will be inserted before the menu item with the index value. All menu items with an index value equal to or greater than the inserted index value will be renumbered one `Index` value greater. For example, if there are three menu items and a menu item is inserted with an `Index` value of 2, the menu item currently with an Index of 2 will become 3, and 3 will become 4. To insert a menu item in the middle, specify the index that it should be inserted before.

This sample application includes a button labeled Insert Menu Bars. In Listing 4.5, the `Click` event for this button adds two menu items to the first menu. The first menu item added is inserted before the top menu item. The item is inserted at the top by specifying an `Index` value of 1 in the `AddMenu` method. The second menu item added is inserted at the bottom below the lowest menu item. The second inserted menu item doesn't specify an index value, therefore it's added at the end (or bottom). Each prompt will still use a unique key. These key values (as with the other items) help to identify the items for manipulation, removal, and so on.

LISTING 4.5 Inserting a Menu Dynamically

```
Private Sub cmdInsert_Click()

    Dim objMenu As MenuBarLib.MenuBarMenu
    Dim objBar As MenuBarLib.MenuBarMenu

    ' check to make sure there are menus
    If MenuBar1.Controls.Count < 1 Then
        Exit Sub
    End If

    ' check to make sure simple menu is displayed
    If MenuBar1.Controls.Item(1).Key <> KEY_SIMPLE_ROOT1 Then
        Exit Sub
    End If

    ' grab the 1st prompt on the "root" menu bar
    Set objMenu = MenuBar1.Controls.Item(KEY_SIMPLE_ROOT1)

    ' add a bar to the 1st root prompt
    ' index = 1 places before the 1st prompt
    Set objBar = objMenu.Items.Add(1, KEY_SIMPLE_BAR_INSERTED1, _
        "Inserted Prompt 1")

    ' add a bar to the 1st root prompt
    ' leaving index empty places
    ' the prompt at the bottom
    Set objBar = objMenu.Items.Add(, KEY_SIMPLE_BAR_INSERTED2, _
        "Inserted Prompt 2")

End Sub
```

First, the code in Listing 4.5 checks to make sure that at least one menu is present on the control. Then, it ensures that the menu displayed is created by the simple menu button.

Next, a reference to the first menu is retrieved. This reference is then used to `Add()` the menu item to the top by using an `Index` value of 1. Then, another menu item is added to the bottom by not specifying an `Index` value. After these inserts occur, the menu should look like that in Figure 4.7.

Removing Menu Items

You also can remove a menu item. The `Remove` method of the `Items` collection accepts either an `Index` value or the `Key` value. If the application will be adding and removing menu items, it's best not to use the `Index` value because the items will have different `Index` values as they are added and removed. The application should use the `Key` property to ensure retrieval of the proper item.

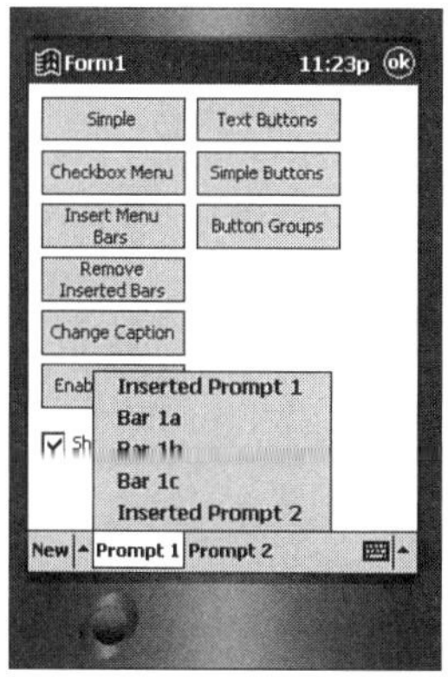

FIGURE 4.7

After building a simple menu by using the Simple button in the sample application, the Insert Menu Bars creates two menu items on-the-fly—one at the top and one at the bottom.

The sample application has a button on the form with the caption Remove Inserted Bars. Listing 4.6 shows the `cmdRemove.Click` event. This button removes the menu items inserted in the `cmdInsert.Click` event shown in Listing 4.5.

LISTING 4.6 Removing the Inserted Menu Items

```
Private Sub cmdRemove_Click()
    Dim objMenu As MenuBarLib.MenuBarMenu
    Dim objBar As MenuBarLib.MenuBarMenu

    ' check to make sure there are menus
    If MenuBar1.Controls.Count < 1 Then
        Exit Sub
    End If

    ' check to make sure simple menu is displayed
    If MenuBar1.Controls.Item(1).Key <> KEY_SIMPLE_ROOT1 Then
        Exit Sub
    End If

    ' grab the 1st prompt on the "root" menu bar
    Set objMenu = MenuBar1.Controls.Item(KEY_SIMPLE_ROOT1)

    ' remove the inserted bar at the top
    objMenu.Items.Remove (KEY_SIMPLE_BAR_INSERTED1)
```

LISTING 4.6 Continued

```
    ' remove the inserted bar at the bottom
    objMenu.Items.Remove (KEY_SIMPLE_BAR_INSERTED2)

End Sub
```

In Listing 4.6, again, a check is made to ensure that a menu exists and that it's the correct menu for this action.

Next, the application retrieves a reference to the first menu. It then removes the menu items that were dynamically inserted. Notice that it uses the `Key` values to address these items.

Changing Captions

Another aspect of dynamic menus is changing the captions. Even if the application doesn't use dynamic menus in the sense of manipulating the number or types of menu items, manipulating the captions can be an important strategy for localizing an international application. Note that the root menu prompts—the prompts are always visible on the bottom of the menu—can't be changed. This is a seriously deficient design (or defect) in the control.

The sample application has a button labeled Change Caption. This button's `Click` event, shown in Listing 4.7, first checks to make sure a menu is present on the menu control. Next, a check is made to ensure that the first item on the menu control is a menu (and not a menu button). Then, it displays an `InputBox` dialog box prompting for a new caption. It then changes the `Caption` of the currently top menu item on the first menu.

LISTING 4.7 Dynamically Changing Prompts on Menu Items

```
Private Sub cmdPrompt_Click()
    Dim objMenu As MenuBarLib.MenuBarMenu
    Dim objBar As MenuBarLib.MenuBarMenu
    Dim strCaption As String

    ' check to make sure there are menus
    If MenuBar1.Controls.Count < 1 Then
        Exit Sub
    End If

    ' make sure item is a menu bar
    If MenuBar1.Controls.Item(1).Type <> mbrMenuBar Then
        Exit Sub
    End If
```

LISTING 4.7 Continued

```
    ' grab the 1st "root" prompt
    Set objMenu = MenuBar1.Controls.Item(1)

    ' get the new caption
    strCaption = InputBox("Caption")

    Set objBar = objMenu.Items(1)

    objBar.Caption = strCaption
End Sub
```

Manipulating Enabled State

Windows design standards state menus should become disabled when their context isn't valid. To implement this on the Pocket PC MenuBar control, set the `Enabled` property to `False`.

The sample application has a button labeled Enable/Disable. As shown in Listing 4.8, the `Click` event of the button makes the two checks to see whether a menu exists and whether it's a menu item (not a button). This button changes the `Enabled` state of the first menu item of the first menu. If the menu item is currently enabled, it will disable it; if it's disabled, it will enable it.

LISTING 4.8 Enabling and Disabling Menu Items

```
Private Sub cmdEnable_Click()
    Dim objMenu As MenuBarLib.MenuBarMenu

    ' this time we'll use "Item" so we can
    ' use extended properties
    Dim objBar As MenuBarLib.Item

    ' check to make sure there are menus
    If MenuBar1.Controls.Count < 1 Then
        Exit Sub
    End If

    ' make sure item is a menu bar
    If MenuBar1.Controls.Item(1).Type <> mbrMenuBar Then
        Exit Sub
    End If

    ' add 1st "root" prompt
```

LISTING 4.8 Continued

```
    Set objMenu = MenuBar1.Controls.Item(1)

    Set objBar = objMenu.Items(1)
    objBar.Enabled = Not objBar.Enabled
End Sub
```

This code uses the same methodology to retrieve the first menu item of the first menu. It then changes its `Enabled` state to the opposite of current value. When the menu item has its `Enabled` property set to `False`, it should resemble Figure 4.8.

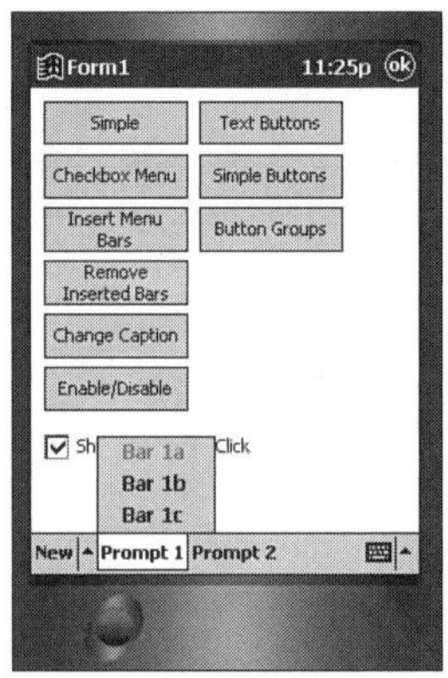

FIGURE 4.8
A simple menu with the first menu item disabled.

Implementing Menu Buttons

Menu buttons can only be placed directly on the menu control itself. You can see an example of menu buttons used in Pocket Internet Explorer. Menu buttons should be used for functionality that's not only common to all forms, but frequently used.

Populating the ImageList

Although you can use a menu button with only a caption, most buttons are best served with an image. To use an image on a menu button, the ImageList control must be present and populated.

First, make sure a reference to the ImageList control is set for the project. Add an instance of the ImageList to the form.

Moving Files to a Development Environment

Moving files to an actual device is fairly simple. To add files to the physical device, use ActiveSync. (See the ActiveSync documentation for this.)

Moving files to the emulator is a bit trickier, but much easier with Windows CE 3.0. In the Windows CE Tools folder (default installation is c:\Windows CE Tools\), follow the path to the Palm300 folder. This folder is essentially the root folder of the emulator's file system and can be found at c:\Windows CE Tools\wce300\MS Pocket PC\emulation\palm300. The sample application uses the bitmap files from the Windows folder; your application's design may require the files to be placed into another folder.

To load the images into the ImageList control, call the `Add` method. The `Add` method has only one parameter—the actual filename of the image to load. All images used in the sample application are loaded in `PopulateImageList`, as shown in Listing 4.9.

LISTING 4.9 Using Images

```
Private Sub PopulateImageList()

    ' maximum height to use
    ImageList1.ImageHeight = 16
    ' maximum width to use
    ImageList1.ImageWidth = 16

    ' add image
    ImageList1.Add "\windows\save.bmp"
    ' set the handle to the count
    lngImageHandleSave = ImageList1.Count

    ' add image
    ImageList1.Add "\windows\Open.bmp"
    ' set the handle to the count
    lngImageHandleOpen = ImageList1.Count

    ' add image
    ImageList1.Add "\windows\New.bmp"
    ' set the handle to the count
    lngImageHandleNew = ImageList1.Count

    ' add image
    ImageList1.Add "\windows\Left Justify.bmp"
    ' set the handle to the count
    lngImageHandleLeftJustify = ImageList1.Count
```

LISTING 4.9 Continued

```
    ' add image
    ImageList1.Add "\windows\Center Justify.bmp"
    ' set the handle to the count
    lngImageHandleCenterJustify = ImageList1.Count

    ' add image
    ImageList1.Add "\windows\Right Justify.bmp"
    ' set the handle to the count
    lngImageHandleRightJustify = ImageList1.Count

    ' add image
    ImageList1.Add "\windows\Full Justify.bmp"
    ' set the handle to the count
    lngImageHandleFullJustify = ImageList1.Count

    ' add image
    ImageList1.Add "\windows\Cascade.bmp"
    ' set the handle to the count
    lngImageHandleCascade = ImageList1.Count

    ' add image
    ImageList1.Add "\windows\Tile Horizontal.bmp"
    ' set the handle to the count
    lngImageHandleTileHorizontal = ImageList1.Count

    ' add image
    ImageList1.Add "\windows\Tile Vertical.bmp"
    ' set the handle to the count
    lngImageHandleTileVertical = ImageList1.Count

End Sub
```

In Listing 4.9, the ImageList is set up and populated. This subroutine is called from the `Form.Load()` event. The first task is to set the maximum height and width of the images using the `ImageHeight` and `ImageWidth` properties. Then, all images required for the sample application are added. Be sure to use the proper path and save your files so they are available in your device (or emulator).

After each image is loaded, a corresponding `Public` variable is set to the `Count` of the ImageList; this will be the `Index` of the loaded image. Because there is no collection of images on the ImageList and therefore no `Key` property, these public variables keep track of each image's assigned `Index`. These indexes are always assigned sequentially, so they can be hard-coded or `Const(s)` can be declared for their value, but that can lead to more error-prone code if images are inserted or deleted from the application.

As soon as the ImageList is initialized and the images are loaded, they can be used on buttons placed on the menu bar. On the sample application's form is a button labeled Simple Buttons. Listing 4.10 show this button's `Click` event. Tapping this button will `Clear()` the menu and add three buttons, giving each an image by assigning the value to the `Image` property. The `Image` property value corresponds to the index value of the image in the ImageList control. It uses the three distinct images loaded previously in the `PopulateImageList()` subroutine.

LISTING 4.10 Adding Buttons to the Menu Control

```
Private Sub cmdButtonsSimple_Click()

    Dim objButton As MenuBarLib.MenuBarButton

    ' clear all items off the menu
    MenuBar1.Controls.Clear

    ' set the ImageList on the MenuBar
    MenuBar1.ImageList = ImageList1.hImageList

    ' add the button to the menu bar
    Set objButton = MenuBar1.Controls.AddButton(KEY_SIMPLE_BUTTON_BUTTON1)

    ' set the button to the index value
    ' of the save button
    objButton.Image = lngImageHandleSave

    ' add another button to the menu bar
    ' reuse the objButton variable as
    ' we're done with it
    Set objButton = MenuBar1.Controls.AddButton(KEY_SIMPLE_BUTTON_BUTTON2)

    ' set the button to the index value
    ' of the open button
    objButton.Image = lngImageHandleOpen

    ' add another button to the menu bar
    ' reuse the objButton variable as
    ' we're done with it
    Set objButton = MenuBar1.Controls.AddButton(KEY_SIMPLE_BUTTON_BUTTON3)

    ' set the button to the index value
    ' of the open button
    objButton.Image = lngImageHandleNew

End Sub
```

In Listing 4.10, all items are cleared from the menu as in other examples. Then the MenuBar control must be informed which ImageList control will be used. This exchange takes place by setting the `MenuBar.ImageList` property to the `ImageList.hImageList` value. The `ImageList.hImageList` value is actually the handle to that window. This is its only intended use.

After this setup is complete, buttons are added to the MenuBar, as shown in Figure 4.9. These buttons are then given an image by setting the `Image` property on each button. This `Image` property is the index to the images handled by the ImageList control. Setting the `Index` property to 1 (`Image = 1`) sets the button's image to the first image contained by the ImageList control.

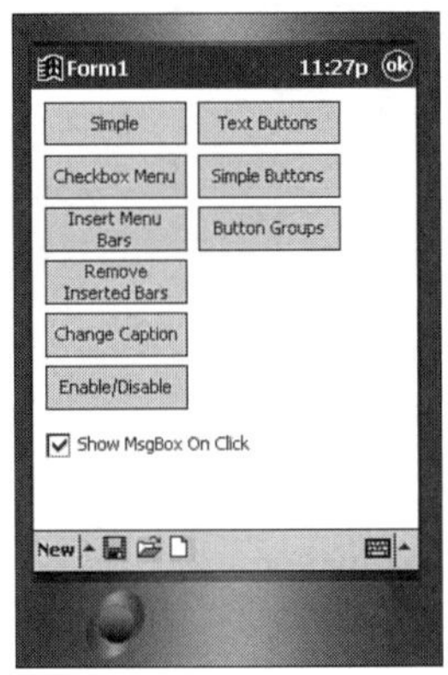

FIGURE 4.9
`Image` *displays the button groups created by* `cmdButtonsSimple_Click()`.

Responding to Button Taps

Another event of the MenuBar control is `ButtonClick`. This event is fired whenever a button is tapped. The only parameter for this event is a reference to the button actually tapped. This reference is of type `MenuBarButton`, different from the `MenuClick` (passed only as `Item`).

In the sample application, a similar approach to the `MenuClick` message box display is taken in the `ButtonClick` event, as shown in Listing 4.11. More properties are displayed, but the approach in `ButtonClick` is the same as `MenuClick`.

LISTING 4.11 Handling a Tap on a Menu Button

```
Private Sub MenuBar1_ButtonClick(ByVal Button As MenuBarLib.MenuBarButton)
    Dim strMessage As String
```

```
'check to see if MsgBox should be displayed
If chkShowMsgBox.Value Then
    ' build message string
    strMessage = "You clicked:" & vbCrLf

    ' add the Caption
    strMessage = strMessage & "Caption:" & Button.Caption & vbCrLf

    ' add the Enabled state - should always be true
    strMessage = strMessage & "Enabled:" & Button.Enabled & vbCrLf

    ' add the Image
    strMessage = strMessage & "Image:" & Button.Image & vbCrLf

    ' add the Index
    strMessage = strMessage & "Index:" & Button.Index & vbCrLf

    ' add the Key
    strMessage = strMessage & "Key:" & Button.Key & vbCrLf

    ' add the MixedState
    strMessage = strMessage & "MixedState:" & Button.MixedState & vbCrLf

    ' add the Style
    strMessage = strMessage & "Style:" & Button.Style & vbCrLf

    ' add the Tag
    strMessage = strMessage & "Tag:" & Button.Tag & vbCrLf

    ' add the ToolTip
    strMessage = strMessage & "ToolTip:" & Button.ToolTip & vbCrLf

    ' add the Type
    strMessage = strMessage & "Type:" & Button.Type & vbCrLf

    ' add the Value
    strMessage = strMessage & "Value:" & Button.Value & vbCrLf

    ' add Visible state - should always be true
    strMessage = strMessage & "Visible:" & Button.Visible & vbCrLf

    ' add the width
    strMessage = strMessage & "Width:" & Button.Width & vbCrLf
```

LISTING 4.11 Continued

```
        MsgBox strMessage
    End If

    ' decide which buttons are currently
    ' on the menu

    ' compare the left 2 char of the key
    ' they *should* always let us know
    ' which buttons are on the menu

    ' use Mid- left does not work
    Select Case Mid(Button.Key, 1, 2)
        ' use left 2 of the an example button
        ' since left two are the same
        Case Mid(KEY_SIMPLE_BUTTON_BUTTON1, 1, 2)
            ' here we would send the button to
            ' a specific sub
        Case Mid(KEY_BUTTONGROUP_GROUP1_BUTTON1, 1, 2)
            ' here we would send the button to
            ' a specific sub
        Case Mid(KEY_TEXT_BUTTON_BUTTON1, 1, 2)
            ' here we would send the button to
            ' a specific sub
        Case Else
            MsgBox "Unknown Button Type!"
    End Select
End Sub
```

In Listing 4.11, a reference to the tapped button is passed to the `ButtonClick` event. Unlike `MenuClick`, this parameter is more tightly typed as `MenuBarButton` (whereas `MenuClick` receives an Item, rather than `MenuBarMenu`). The implementation starts with a check to make sure that the message box should be displayed. This choice is more important with the button groups (below). A string of text of the properties and their current values is composed and displayed.

Then, a decision is made as to which menu is currently displayed by using the first two characters of the `Button.Key` value. Each Key value was defined and set when the buttons were added to the MenuBar control. Although no implementation takes place here, it would be possible to "farm-out" a button to a distinct subroutine for each menu type displayed.

It may be possible for your application to consolidate all response code for either `ButtonClick` or `MenuClick` into one subroutine. This would allow all implementation code for responding to events (ButtonClick or MenuClick) in one code segment. Because almost all functionality could be driven by the Key value itself, simply pass the reference for the button to this subroutine. Remember to use properties only available on the Item type and not button-specific properties (like Image)

Using Button Groups

Buttons groups are similar to radio buttons, but are placed on the MenuBar. Only one button in a button group may be selected at one time. An example of a button group is the different view states of a list view control (for example, File Explorer - Large Icons, Small Icons, List, Details). You can place more than one button group on the MenuBar by placing a separator between them.

In the sample application is a command button labeled Button Groups. This button's Click event, as shown in Listing 4.12, creates two separate groups of buttons on the menu bar. The first group is a set of three buttons for arranging windows (Cascade, Tile Horizontally, and Tile Vertical). The second group is from Microsoft Word (Left, Center, Right, and Full Justify).

LISTING 4.12 Creating Button Groups

```
Private Sub cmdButtonGroups_Click()

    Dim objButton As MenuBarLib.MenuBarButton

    ' clear all items off the menu
    MenuBar1.Controls.Clear

    ' set the ImageList on the MenuBar
    MenuBar1.ImageList = ImageList1.hImageList

    ' add the button to the menu bar
    Set objButton = MenuBar1.Controls.AddButton(KEY_BUTTONGROUP_GROUP1_BUTTON1)

    ' set the style of the button to button group (mbrButtonGroup)
    ' this will cause the button to work
    ' like a OptionButton
    objButton.Style = mbrButtonGroup

    ' set the button to the index value of the image
    objButton.Image = lngImageHandleCascade

    ' add another button to the menu bar
    ' reuse the objButton variable as
```

LISTING 4.12 Continued

```
    ' we're done with it
    Set objButton = MenuBar1.Controls.AddButton(KEY_SIMPLE_BUTTON_BUTTON2)

    ' set the style of the button to button group
    ' this will cause the button to work
    ' like a OptionButton
    objButton.Style = mbrButtonGroup

    ' set the button to the index value of the image
    objButton.Image = lngImageHandleTileHorizontal

    ' add another button to the menu bar
    ' reuse the objButton variable as
    ' we're done with it
    Set objButton = MenuBar1.Controls.AddButton(KEY_SIMPLE_BUTTON_BUTTON3)

    ' set the style of the button to button group
    ' this will cause the button to work
    ' like a OptionButton
    objButton.Style = mbrButtonGroup

    ' set the button to the index value of the image
    objButton.Image = lngImageHandleTileVertical

    Set objButton = MenuBar1.Controls.AddButton()

    ' set the style of the button to separator
    ' this will cause the button groups to be independent
    objButton.Style = mbrSeparator

    ' add another button to the menu bar
    ' reuse the objButton variable as
    ' we're done with it
    Set objButton = MenuBar1.Controls.AddButton(KEY_SIMPLE_BUTTON_BUTTON4)

    ' set the style of the button to button group
    ' this will cause the button to work
    ' like a OptionButton
    objButton.Style = mbrButtonGroup

    ' set the button to the index value of the image
    objButton.Image = lngImageHandleLeftJustify

    ' add another button to the menu bar
    ' reuse the objButton variable as
```

LISTING 4.12 Continued

```
    ' we're done with it
    Set objButton = MenuBar1.Controls.AddButton(KEY_BUTTONGROUP_GROUP2_BUTTON1)

    ' set the style of the button to button group
    ' this will cause the button to work
    ' like a OptionButton
    objButton.Style = mbrButtonGroup

    ' set the button to the index value of the image
    objButton.Image = lngImageHandleCenterJustify

    ' add another button to the menu bar
    ' reuse the objButton variable as
    ' we're done with it
    Set objButton = MenuBar1.Controls.AddButton(KEY_BUTTONGROUP_GROUP2_BUTTON2)

    ' set the style of the button to button group
    ' this will cause the button to work
    ' like a OptionButton
    objButton.Style = mbrButtonGroup

    ' set the button to the index value of the image
    objButton.Image = lngImageHandleRightJustify

    ' add another button to the menu bar
    ' reuse the objButton variable as
    ' we're done with it
    Set objButton = MenuBar1.Controls.AddButton(KEY_BUTTONGROUP_GROUP2_BUTTON3)

    ' set the style of the button to button group
    ' this will cause the button to work
    ' like a OptionButton
    objButton.Style = mbrButtonGroup

    ' set the button to the index value of the image
    objButton.Image = lngImageHandleFullJustify
End Sub
```


In Listing 4.12, the menu control is cleared. Then, the `ImageList` property is set from the `hImageList` property value as in the other button code. After each button is added, the `Style` property is set to `mbrButtonGroup`; this is what causes the button to act in a button group, such as an OptionButton. Each button's `Image` property is then set to the corresponding handle for the image.

Between the two button groups, a button is added and a `Style` property value of `mbrMenuSeparator` is assigned. This separator enables each set of buttons to act independently. The menu control should now show two button groups (see Figure 4.10).

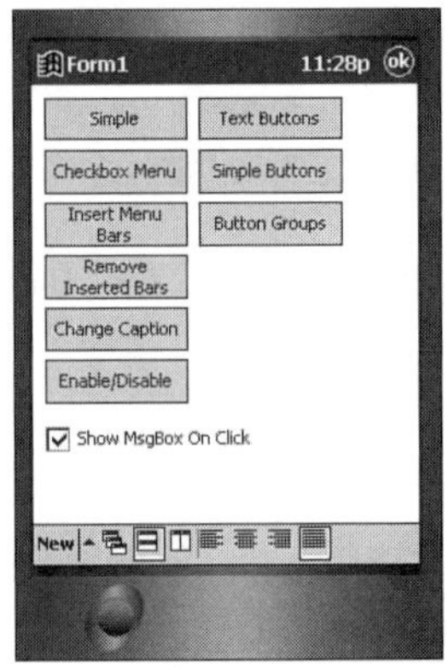

FIGURE 4.10
Image displays the button groups created by `cmdButtonGroups_Click()`.

Using Caption Buttons

Caption buttons seem to be one of those items that you may never think of using, but sometimes they do work well. A caption button is a button with no image placed directly on the menu bar. Nothing is special about programmatically creating a caption button except that its `Caption` property is set instead of its `Image` property. Its appearance is similar to a root menu prompt, but it has no menu bars and triggers a `Menu.Button_Click` event directly when tapped. Caption buttons do present the challenge of using a lot more real estate on the menu bar, but if your application can afford it, it may have its place.

In the sample application is a Text Buttons command button named `cmdTextButton`. This button's `Click` event (see Listing 4.13) clears the menu, adds three buttons to the menu and labels them with a caption (see Figure 4.11).

LISTING 4.13 Creating Text Buttons

```
Private Sub cmdTextButton_Click()

    Dim objButton As MenuBarLib.MenuBarButton

    ' clear all items off the menu
    MenuBar1.Controls.Clear
```

LISTING 4.13 Continued

```
    ' add the first button to the menu bar
    Set objButton = MenuBar1.Controls.AddButton(KEY_TEXT_BUTTON_BUTTON1)
    ' set its caption
    objButton.Caption = "Button 1"

    ' add the second button to the menu bar
    Set objButton = MenuBar1.Controls.AddButton(KEY_TEXT_BUTTON_BUTTON2)
    ' set its caption
    objButton.Caption = "Button 2"

    ' add the third button to the menu bar
    Set objButton = MenuBar1.Controls.AddButton(KEY_TEXT_BUTTON_BUTTON3)
    ' set its caption
    objButton.Caption = "Button 3"

End Sub
```

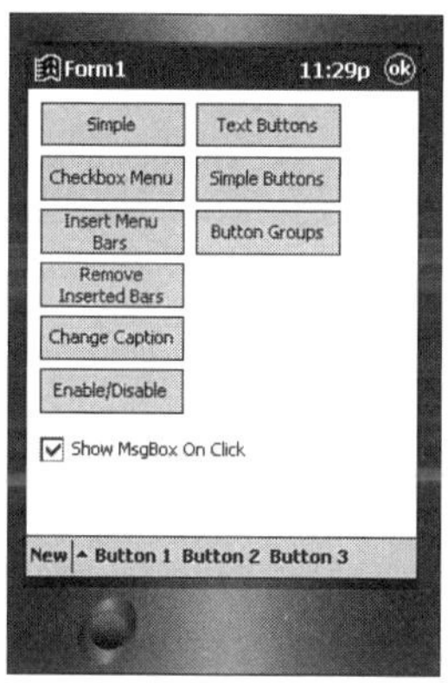

FIGURE 4.11
The three buttons created on the menu bar take up a lot of real estate with just simple captions; use caption buttons judiciously.

Adding the New Button

The New button is a common element to Pocket PC applications. It's found in applications such as Contacts, Calendar, Inbox, Tasks, Pocket Excel, and Pocket Word. The intention of this button is to trigger an event that allows the application to create a new instance of the document/record currently displayed. The button is made present or absent from the menu bar via the `MenuBar.NewButton` property. It's set to `True` by default and is read-only at runtime.

You can use a setting in the device's Control Panel to enable the new button menu. To enable this setting, from the Start menu choose Control Panel, Settings, and then Menus. On the New Menu tab, select Turn On New Button Menu. If this setting is checked, there will be a combobox-style arrow on the right of the application's New button. When this combobox arrow is tapped, the new button expands into a menu that offers each item registered on the device for New, as shown in Figure 4.12. Each item on the New menu is registered on the device to receive this event and provide a prompt. This registration takes place via a DLL and can't be directly accomplished in eVB.

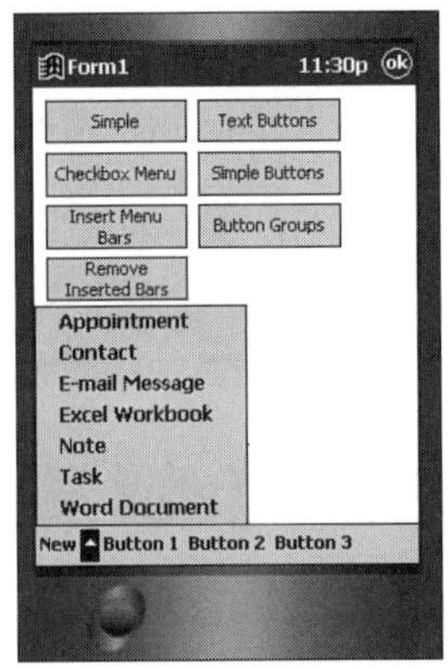

FIGURE 4.12

The New button, when tapped on the arrow, displays a menu item for each item registered on the device.

If the New button is included in an application, be aware that if the user selects a "new" document/record from a different application, your application will become inactive.

NOTE

Pocket PC keeps these tasks in memory. Pocket PC keeps only one instance of the application running, so when the application is requested, it's simply brought to the front. This is different behavior than Palm-Sized PC (Windows CE 2.x), especially for eVB. Using eVB for Palm-Sized PC, you had to manually intervene using API calls to prevent the device from opening multiple instances of the application.

The response to the New button when tapped is simple. The third and last event on the MenuBar control is `NewClick`. No parameters are passed as there can be only one New button on a MenuBar control.

Summary

Although creating menus programmatically is more challenging than using the menu build in Visual Basic, it's not that daunting a task. Experience has shown that re-creating the entire menu by refreshing it is a sound strategy. Using the knowledge gained in this chapter should put you on course to develop functional, robust menus for your applications.

One of the best practices for menus is to use the `Key` property. Without using `Key` to your advantage, the application can quickly become unwieldy and error-prone.

It's easy to notice that there is no way to use the MenuBar control to create shortcut menus. Although it's beyond the scope of this book, they can be created in different ways. One method is to use API calls. Context-sensitive menus can also be mimicked using a borderless form with Frame and Label controls. And, another mimic is to use an invisible list control that's manipulated, moved, and made visible.

Using the Windows CE WinSock for IR Communication

CHAPTER

5

IN THIS CHAPTER

Socket communications are generally the same regardless of the development environment. For Windows there is the Windows Sockets standard, and for Unix there is the Berkeley Sockets standard, but the differences—especially for our purposes—aren't important.

Socket communication in eMbedded Visual Basic is almost identical to Visual Basic 6, so the information covered here isn't as environment specific as the rest of the book.

"Why include it then?" you might ask. The answer is that transferring data to or from a Pocket PC requires some mode of connectivity, and socket communication is probably the simplest.

The WinSock control included with VB 6 has two protocols available, TCP/IP and UDP. eVB doesn't support UDP, but it does give us the addition of infrared, or IrDA, support. You'll see that using the IrDA port is almost transparent.

With a strong understanding of socket communication, you'll be well on your way to being able to build your first distributed or enterprise solution.

This chapter explores most of the power and functionality of socket programming exposed through the `MSCEWinsockCtl` library. The usefulness of a Pocket PC application grows exponentially when it can communicate with other Pocket PCs, desktop PCs, and even enterprise servers. In addition the simplicity and ease of using the WinSock control makes it a natural choice for communication.

In this chapter you will learn about

- The basics of socket communication
- Connecting to another Pocket PC or desktop PC through a socket
- Listening for connection requests from any socket server
- Establishing two-way communication between your Pocket PC and another
- Transferring text back and forth in a "chat" program
- Transferring text files to another socket client
- Creating and using a custom progress bar

You will also briefly review the use of the MenuBar.

As we'll do with all the chapters, we will also uncover some of eVB's more subtle nuances that can cause problems and headaches, as well as give coding tips applicable to any eVB application.

A Brief Socket Tutorial

Sockets are simply a software "layer" between your application and your transfer protocol, which is usually TCP/IP. TCP/IP in turn talks to your networking hardware, which in turn sends your data somewhere or receives it from somewhere.

The sockets, and the WinSock control, make talking to TCP/IP simple, because you don't need to be concerned with packets, headers, or the like. You just need to know who you are and to whom you want to talk.

Socket communication requires two pieces: a sender, or client, and a receiver or server. The server listens through a socket on a port for any connection requests. The client uses a socket to request a connection to the server through its IP and port. When the server receives the request, it accepts the request and a connection is established.

From this point on, you can transfer data in both directions. Typically, a sender will tell the receiver how much data it's going to send. The receiver acknowledges this and sends back an "OK" and then data is sent. The Windows CE WinSock control even keeps these formalities behind the scenes.

Generally speaking, to use socket communication, you must have a TCP/IP stack, which on a PC generally means you must have a network card installed and the TCP/IP protocol loaded. On the Pocket PC this isn't necessarily the case, which means that even without a network card, you can write and use the sample application in this chapter. If you do have a network card installed, though, you can make a socket connection to any exposed IP address on your network or the Internet, provided that you have access rights.

If you have a device connected to your PC with ActiveSync through a serial or USB connection, there is actually a TCP/IP connection between the two, and any IP address requested by the device will get routed automatically to the PC. The Windows CE WinSock control also wraps the IrDA port on the device, so you can use the IR port as though it were a TCP/IP connection. Both features can be very valuable, as you'll see as we progress though the chapter.

NOTE

Because the Pocket PC emulator doesn't have an IR port, can't connect to ActiveSync, nor can it have a network card, you can't make a socket connection with it. This means that to take full advantage of this chapter, you will need a physical Pocket PC device.

Understanding the WinSock Control

The Microsoft WinSock control is distributed with the platform SDK for each Windows CE platform. It's included in the MSCEWinsock.dll library. The control is added to projects in eVB is the same manner as in other versions of Visual Basic by choosing Components from the Tools menu. You can specifically add the WinSock control to your project by adding the Microsoft CE WinSock Control 3.0 component library, as shown in Figure 5.1.

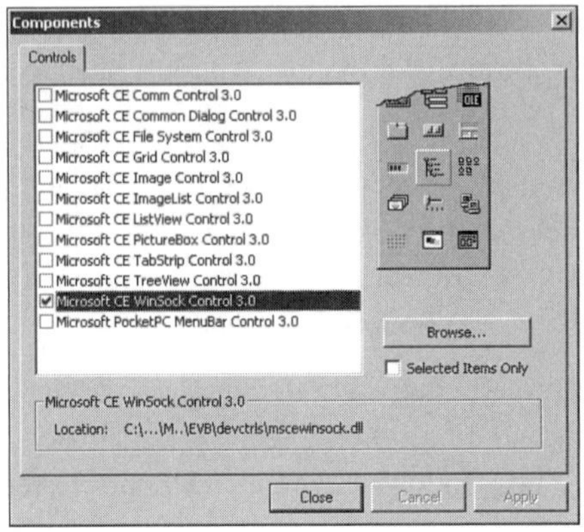

FIGURE 5.1
Adding the WinSock Control library to your project.

Adding the reference places the WinSock controls into the eVB Toolbox. Its icon looks like two PCs connected with a red line, which you can see in Figure 5.2.

FIGURE 5.2
The eVB toolbox with the standard controls and the WinSock control.

The Control's Object Model

The following is a list of the methods, properties, and events used in this chapter:

Methods	*Properties*	*Events*
`Accept`	`BytesReceived`	`Close`
`Close`	`LocalHostName`	`ConnectionRequest`
`Connect`	`LocalPort`	`Connect`
`GetData`	`Protocol`	`DataArrival`
`Listen`	`RemoteHost`	`Error`
`SendData`	`RemoteHostIP`	`SendComplete`
	`RemotePort`	`SendProgress`
	`SocketHandle`	
	`State`	
	`ServiceName`	

If you compare this list to the Object Model, you will see that we cover everything except `LocalIP`, `Name`, `Parent`, and `Tag`. Essentially, once you are finished with this chapter, there should be nothing within the control's capabilities that you can't do.

Writing the PocketChat Application

To explore socket communications, we're going to write PocketChat, an application that revolves around the WinSock control.

By the end of the chapter, PocketChat will provide you with a good understanding of not just socket communications, but also a plethora of ideas on what else you can use sockets for.

You'll have a small chat application that works over a TCP/IP connection or through the IrDA port and also allows us to send files to a remote user.

PocketChat is meant to be a springboard to bigger, better applications and utilities. The lessons learned here will be the foundation for almost any application you might develop that requires communication.

PocketChat is designed to talk specifically with another copy of PocketChat on another device. Because socket communications require a physical device, and because many developers don't have two devices, you need another client to talk to.

At the end of this chapter (see Listings 5.17 and 5.18), I've included the code listing and form header for a Visual Basic 6 project called PCChat, which you can use as a substitute for a second device. Simply run PCChat on your ActiveSync host PC, with ActiveSync running and connected to your device.

Running PCChat from the VB 6 IDE will actually give you the opportunity to see both sides of the socket communication at the same time by placing break points in both the VB and eVB projects.

PCChat uses a large amount of code copied directly or slightly modified from PocketChat. There are inline comments, so I haven't included any explanation text for the project.

Project Setup

PocketChat uses only one form, `frmMain`, and one module, `modMain`.

Listing 5.1 contains heading information for `frmMain`. For clarity, I have only included listings for properties that I modified from their defaults. You will also need to add the Picturebox, MenuBar, and WinSock controls to the project through the Project Components dialog.

LISTING 5.1 Heading Information from frmMain.ebf

```
Begin VB.Form frmMain
   Caption         =   "PocketChat"
   ClientHeight    =   4005
   ClientLeft      =   90
   ClientTop       =   840
   ClientWidth     =   3630
   ShowOK          =   -1  'True
   Begin PictureBoxCtl.PictureBox picProgress
      Height          =   195
      Left            =   60
      Top             =   3780
      Width           =   3495
   End
   Begin MenuBarLib.MenuBar mnuMain
      Left            =   1560
      Top             =   120
      NewButton       =   0    'False
   End
   Begin WinSockCtl.WinSock wskMain
      Left            =   2460
      Top             =   120
   End
   Begin VBCE.Label lblConnect
      Height          =   255
      Left            =   2370
      Top             =   1020
      Width           =   1215
      Caption         =   "Disconnected"
      ForeColor       =   16777215
      Alignment       =   2
   End

 Begin VBCE.Label lblStatus
```

LISTING 5.1 Continued

```
Height              =    255
      Left               =    30
    Top               =    1020
    Width             =    2175
    BackColor         =    -2147483643
    BackStyle         =    1
    Caption           =    "Waiting..."
    ForeColor         =    8388608
  End
  Begin VBCE.TextBox txtRecv
    Height            =    2415
    Left              =    30
    Top               =    1320
    Width             =    3555
    BackColor         =    14737632
    Text              =    ""
    Alignment         =    0
    Locked            =    -1   'True
    MultiLine         =    -1   'True
    ScrollBars        =    2
  End
  Begin VBCE.TextBox txtSend
    Height            =    915
    Left              =    30
    Top               =    60
    Width             =    3555
    BackColor         =    -2147483643
    Enabled           =    0    'False
    ForeColor         =    16711680
    Text              =    ""
    MultiLine         =    -1   'True
  End
End
```

Figure 5.3 shows what my project looks like in the IDE.

Project Flow

Before you begin, let's take a look at what you are trying to accomplish and the general strategies you can take to get there.

First, because you know that you'll be connecting to another PocketChat application, you know that one of the instances will have to request a connection and the other will have to receive and accept that request. It makes good sense, then, to start the application and begin listening for a request immediately, stopping only when you try to make a connection, when a connection request comes in, or when the application is shut down.

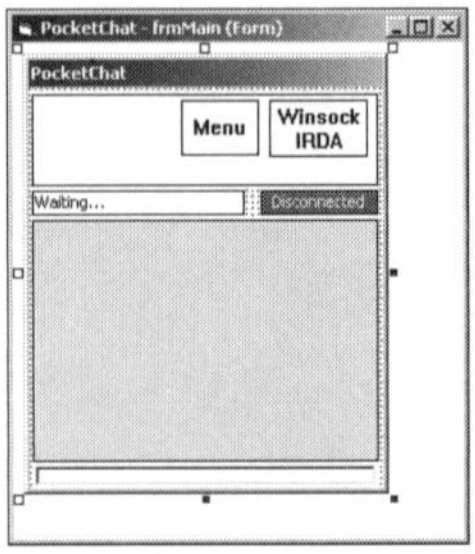

FIGURE 5.3
The final project layout, as seen in the eVB integrated development environment (IDE).

It's also going to be useful to display not only the chat text, but also a label or tag for who said it, and you'll be implementing your own properties (or, more correctly, your property workaround) for storing and retrieving this information.

The next step will be making a connection. For the request, you'll prompt users for an IP or host name to connect to, but hard code the port to 5000. You can set this to any valid port that you want, and if you're on a network behind a firewall, your network administrator might want you to use something else.

After you make the connection, you'll need to transfer the chat text to either the remote client or a file. To keep user interaction to a minimum (you don't really want users to have to tell the application after every line comes in what kind of data it is), the receiver will have to be able to distinguish chat text from file text itself. For this, use XML-like tags to bracket the data, and then parse it out on the receiving end. Of course, this makes the transmitted data a bit longer, but makes for a friendlier application.

That's the general plan. Of course, there's a bit more to it, but the specifics will be covered as we come to them, so let's begin.

Initializing the Application

Most projects use global settings and variables that need to be set up right away and persist throughout the application. PocketChat is no exception. Application startup is usually the best time to perform those tasks, and my preference is usually to do these tasks either in `Sub Main` or in a procedure called from it.

The problem with doing initialization in a Form_Load event is that the form itself isn't fully instantiated during the event and modifying the form in its own Load event handler doesn't always work.

As we've already discussed, you want to start up in a listening state. With the WinSock control, this is handled by calling the Listen method, but before you can begin listening in your application, you want to do a couple of other tasks. First, you need to tell the socket what protocol to listen with: TCP/IP or IrDA. You also need to load the main form so you can inform the user that you are listening.

Startup is also a good time to get the local user's name, because it probably won't be changing during a session, and you might as well begin by writing the methods to store this "property." While you're at it, create a similar pair of methods to store the name of the remote user you are connected to as well.

In modMain's General Declarations section, create two member variables to store the information:

```
Private m_LocalHostName As String
Private m_RemoteHostName As String
```

And then add the implementation procedures directly below the declarations:

```
' the LocalHostName "Property"
Public Function GetLocalHostName() As String
    GetLocalHostName = m_LocalHostName
End Function

Public Sub SetLocalHostName(NewName As String)
    m_LocalHostName = NewName
End Sub

' the RemoteHostName "Property"
Public Function GetRemoteHostName() As String
    GetRemoteHostName = m_RemoteHostName
End Function

Public Sub SetRemoteHostName(NewName As String)
    m_RemoteHostName = NewName
End Sub
```

We can also set our port as a global constant, allowing users to easily change it in one place. Add the following to the General Declarations section:

```
Public Const SOCKET_PORT = SOCKET_PORT
```

Lastly in the General Declarations section, define a variable as the incoming data buffer, the use of which is covered later. Add the following line to general declarations:

```
Public m_strRecv As String
```

Now look at the application's entry point. Listing 5.2 shows `Sub Main`.

LISTING 5.2 Initializing the WinSock Control

```
Public Sub Main()
    ' Set our protocol to TCP/IP
    frmMain.wskMain.Protocol = sckTCPProtocol

    ' Get our local host name and set the property
    SetLocalHostName frmMain.wskMain.LocalHostName

    ' Show frmMain
    frmMain.Show

    ' We'll assume we're a socket server to begin with
    ' So we put the socket into listen mode
    frmMain.wskMain.Listen

    ' Set up the MenuBar
    frmMain.MenuBarInit
End Sub
```

Notice that we're simply calling `SetLocalHostName` with the `LocalHostName` property of the WinSock control. This seems a bit pointless. Wouldn't it be easier to just use the WinSock control's native property? Well, yes, but only if you intend to use the name of the local device to identify the user. If you want to allow users to enter their names in the future, you'll have to go back and modify every place that you call `frmMain.wskMain.LocalHostName`. By adding and using your own property, it will make any future modifications much simpler.

Lastly call `MenuBarInit`, which you still need to write. Not surprisingly, you will use this method to initialize your application's MenuBar control.

Adding the Application's MenuBar

PocketChat's feature set is pretty small, so your MenuBar can be simple and still meet your needs. You'll need a button to connect and disconnect, a button to send a file, and two buttons for the current protocol, only one of which can be selected at a time. To make it a more aesthetically pleasing, Listing 5.3 shows a couple of added separators as well.

LISTING 5.3 Initializing the MenuBar in a Single Location

```
Public Sub MenuBarInit()
    Dim btnTemp As MenuBarLib.MenuBarButton
    Dim mnuTemp As MenuBarLib.MenuBarMenu

    ' ----- Set up menu buttons -----
    ' Add the send button to the menubar
    Set btnTemp = mnuMain.Controls.AddButton("Send")
    ' Set the button's properties
    btnTemp.Caption = "Send"
    btnTemp.Enabled = False
    btnTemp.Width = 800

    ' Add the connect button to the menubar
    Set btnTemp = mnuMain.Controls.AddButton("Connect")
    ' Set the button's properties
    btnTemp.Caption = "Conn..."
    btnTemp.Width = 750

    Set btnTemp = mnuMain.Controls.AddButton("Xfer")
    ' Set the button's properties
    btnTemp.Caption = "Xfer..."
    btnTemp.Enabled = False
    btnTemp.Width = 700

    ' Add the button to the menubar
    Set btnTemp = mnuMain.Controls.AddButton("Sep1")
    ' Set the button's properties
    btnTemp.Caption = ""
    btnTemp.Style = mbrSeparator

    ' Add the button to the menubar
    Set btnTemp = mnuMain.Controls.AddButton("TCP")
    ' Set the button's properties
    btnTemp.Caption = "TCP"
    btnTemp.Width = 450
    btnTemp.Style = mbrButtonGroup
    btnTemp.Value = mbrPressed

    ' Add the button to the menubar
    Set btnTemp = mnuMain.Controls.AddButton("IrDA")
    ' Set the button's properties
    btnTemp.Caption = "IR"
    btnTemp.Width = 350
    btnTemp.Style = mbrButtonGroup
```

LISTING 5.3 Continued

```
    ' Add the button to the menubar
    Set btnTemp = mnuMain.Controls.AddButton("Sep2")
    ' Set the button's properties
    btnTemp.Caption = ""
    btnTemp.Style = mbrSeparator

    ' Clean up
    Set btnTemp = Nothing
End Sub
```

We've already covered the MenuBar very thoroughly, and PocketChat's use of the control is pretty basic, so I won't spend a whole lot of time explaining how things work here. If you need some clarification or would like to make the MenuBar a little nicer, refer to Chapter 4, "Working with Menu Controls for Pocket PC."

Because all the MenuBar controls are buttons, you can handle all stylus taps in a single event handler, `mnuMain_ButtonClick()`. Use a `Select...Case` control handler block to determine the key of which button was clicked, and therefore take appropriate action. The skeleton for the event handler is shown in the following code and you can add implementation code to it as you go.

```
Private Sub mnuMain_ButtonClick(ByVal Button As MenuBarLib.MenuBarButton)
    ' Determine which button was clicked and take action
    Select Case Button.Key
        Case "Send"
        Case "Connect"
        Case "Xfer"
        Case "TCP"
        Case "IrDA"
    End Select
End Sub
```

Figure 5.4 shows what the final MenuBar looks like.

Changing the Connection Protocol

When PocketChat is in its listening state, the simplest action that users can take is to change the connection protocol by tapping either the TCP or IR buttons on the MenuBar.

To change the protocol, the socket must be closed, so when the user taps either button, close the socket, change the protocol, and start listening again. These tasks are simple enough that they can be handled right in the MenuBar's `Click` event handler.

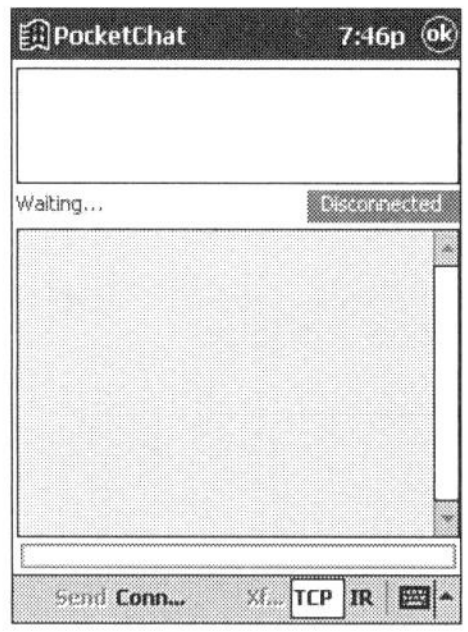

FIGURE 5.4
The application MenuBar when the application is in "listen" state.

The last two cases in `mnuMain_ButtonClick` now look like this:

```
Case "TCP"
    ' Close the socket
    wskMain.Close

    ' Change connection protocol to TCP/IP
    wskMain.ServiceName = ""
    wskMain.Protocol = sckTCPProtocol

    ' Set the socket to listen again
    wskMain.Listen
Case "IrDA"
    ' Close the socket
    wskMain.Close

    ' Change connection protocol to IrDA
    wskMain.Protocol = sckIRDAProtocol
    wskMain.ServiceName = "PocketChat"
    ' Set the socket to listen again
    wskMain.Listen
```

The `ServiceName` property is used only for IrDA mode. `ServiceName` acts somewhat like the IP address in TCP/IP mode, helping to keep communications straight in the presence of multiple IR signals.

Connecting to a Remote Device

The next task is to make a connection with another device, and this can be initiated in two ways:

- Users can initiate the connection by tapping the toolbar's Connect button.
- Remote users can make a connection request that is received by us.

In the first case, when the user requests a connection by tapping Connect, the first thing to do is to handle the MenuBar button tap. This will be another `Case` in the `mnuMain_ButtonClick` event handler:

```
Case "Connect"
    If wskMain.State = sckListening Then
        ' User click "Connect"
        If Not ConnectToPeer() Then Exit Sub

        ' Show the SIP
        SIPVisible = True

        'Set focus to txtSend
        txtSend.SetFocus
    End If
```

You know that you want to call `Connect` only if you aren't currently connected, so check the current state of the WinSock control. If you are not connected, first call `ConnectToPeer`, which I will discuss momentarily. Next, to make this application as user friendly as possible, assume that if users are connecting, the next thing they will probably want to do is send some chat text. To decrease the potential number of screen taps users will need to perform, ensure the built-in keyboard is shown by setting `SIPVisible` to `True` and setting the application focus to `txtSend` where they can begin typing their message.

Next, you need to know a few details. You need to know the host to which users want to connect (either the IP address or the host name), the port through which the connection should be made, and the protocol to use when connecting.

You have already handled the protocol with the protocol buttons, and you have set the port to our global constant (5000), so the only thing left to get is the remote host name or IP. The simplest way to get this is to prompt the user for the information with the `InputBox` function, which you can see in the `ConnectToPeer` function in Listing 5.4.

LISTING 5.4 Using the WinSock Control to Connect to a Peer

```
Private Function ConnectToPeer() As Boolean
    Dim Peer As String

    ' Set our return value
    ConnectToPeer = True

    ' Get name of peer to connect to - This can be an IP or a host name
    ' With a serial or USB connection, _any_ IP (not host name though)
```

LISTING 5.4 Continued

```
    '    will connect to the ActiveSync host
    Peer = InputBox("Enter host to connect to:", "Remote Host", "ctacke")

If Peer = "" Then
        ConnectToPeer = False
        Exit Function
    End If

    ' Set the remote host properties
    wskMain.RemoteHost = Peer

    ' Take the socket out of Listen state
    wskMain.Close

    ' Set the socket remote port
    wskMain.RemotePort = SOCKET_PORT
    ' Update the status label.
    ' Since the Connect call blocks, we must do it now and refresh
    lblStatus.Caption = "Connecting..."

    ' Refresh to get rid of the InputBox and draw the label
    frmMain.Refresh

    ' Make a connection
    wskMain.Connect
End Function
```

Let's look more closely at what's happening in `ConnectToPeer`. First, because it is a function, it will return a value, and it is set in the first line. I like to set the default, or most likely, return value at the outset, so that I don't have to remember to set it at exit.

In this case, the return value is a Boolean indicating whether we've made a successful call to connect. This doesn't necessarily mean the connection is successful, however. That information is handled with the WinSock control's events, which are covered shortly.

Next call the `InputBox` function:

```
Peer = InputBox("Enter host to connect to:", "Remote Host", "ctacke")
```

For a default, I'm using `"ctacke"` so I don't have to type in my own computer name every time I run the application, which is especially useful during debugging. You might want to change this to your computer name, IP, or leave it out completely. Figure 5.5 shows what the InputBox looks like.

Next, check to be sure the user has actually entered a name. If the user taps Cancel or taps OK with nothing in the TextBox, you get the same result: a return value of an empty string. If that's the case, set the return value to `False` and exit the function:

```
If Peer = "" Then
    ConnectToPeer = False
    Exit Function
End If
```

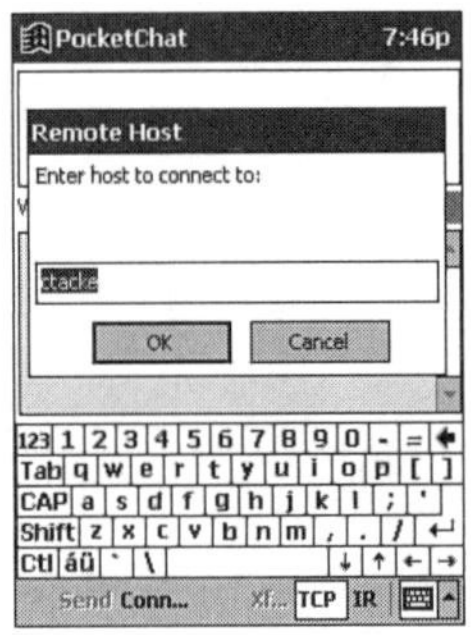

FIGURE 5.5
Prompting users for a remote host name or IP.

The rest of the function is really the "nuts and bolts" of initiating a connection. You must set the `RemoteHost` property of the WinSock control, because the control uses this when it tries to make the connection. Next take the control out of the "listen" state by calling `Close`. Calling `Connect` with a socket already in the listen state results in an error.

Next, set the `RemotePort` you want to connect to, update the status label, and call the `Refresh` method for the form. Refreshing here will not only ensure that the label gets drawn properly, but it will also get rid of the "ghost" that the InputBox will likely place over your form.

Finally, make a call to the `Connect` method. As you can see, `Connect` takes no parameters. Instead, it depends on the programmer to have previously set the `Port`, `RemoteHost`, and `Protocol` properties.

NOTE

If you are using a serial or USB connection, *any* IP or host name will connect to the ActiveSync host.

Accepting a Connection Request

If everything works as planned, we have a valid `RemoteHost`, `Port`, and `Protocol` and there is actually a socket server out there listening, the server's socket will fire a notification event: `ConnectionRequest`. At this point, all you need to do is call the WinSock control's `Accept` method to complete the connection process.

Because you're designing PocketChat to essentially connect with itself—albeit another copy running on another device—you need to add the code to handle this event in your project:

```
Private Sub wskMain_ConnectionRequest()
    ' Accept the request
    wskMain.Accept

    ' Set the GUI to show we're connected
    DisplayConnected
End Sub
```

I've also added a call to `DisplayConnected`, which you can see in Listing 5.5. `DisplayConnected` simply makes some changes to the GUI to let the user know that we've made the connection. It also changes the state of some of the MenuBar buttons.

LISTING 5.5 Letting Users Know They're Connected

```
Private Sub DisplayConnected()
    ' Adjust the connect label
    lblConnect.Caption = "Connected"
    lblConnect.BackColor = vbGreen
    lblConnect.ForeColor = vbBlack

    ' Change the "connect" button's caption
    mnuMain.Controls("Connect").Caption = "Bye"

    ' Set the status label to the remote host
    lblStatus.Caption = wskMain.RemoteHost

    ' Enable "Send" and "Xfer" buttons
    mnuMain.Controls("Send").Enabled = True
    mnuMain.Controls("Xfer").Enabled = True

    ' Enable txtSend
    txtSend.Enabled = True
```

LISTING 5.5 Continued

```
    ' Disable protocol buttons
    mnuMain.Controls("TCP").Enabled = False
    mnuMain.Controls("IrDA").Enabled = False

    ' Show we're connected
    txtRecv.Text = txtRecv.Text & "<Connected>" & vbCrLf
End Sub
```

Because we're connected, the user can now send information, so we enable both the Send and Xfer buttons. We change the Connect button's caption to Bye so we can reuse the button for disconnecting. This saves us some real estate onscreen by eliminating the need for separate buttons for connecting and disconnecting. As a nicety for users, we display the name of the RemoteHost in the `lblStatus` filed and lastly, because we can't change protocols while connected, we disable both Protocol buttons.

Receiving the Connection Notification

Back on the client, where you initially tapped the Connect button and entered the RemoteHost name, you still have some work to do. You've sent out a request for a connection by calling `Connect` and the server has accepted the connection by calling `Accept`. However you still need to let the user know that the connection was accepted.

When the remote socket host accepts the connection, you receive a notification event: `Connect`. This event fires to let the caller know when and if the connection has been accepted.

Because you have already written a function that changes the GUI to indicate a connected state (`DisplayConnected`), you might as well make use of it by calling it from your event handler like so:

```
Private Sub wskMain_Connect()
    ' Called when the remote machine accepts a connection
    ' Set the GUI to show we're connected
    DisplayConnected
End Sub
```

After you make the connection, both devices should resemble Figure 5.6.

Disconnecting

After you make a successful connection, it's important to allow a graceful disconnection without requiring the user to disconnect their LAN, USB, or serial cable in the case of a TCP/IP connection or move out of range in the case of an IR connection.

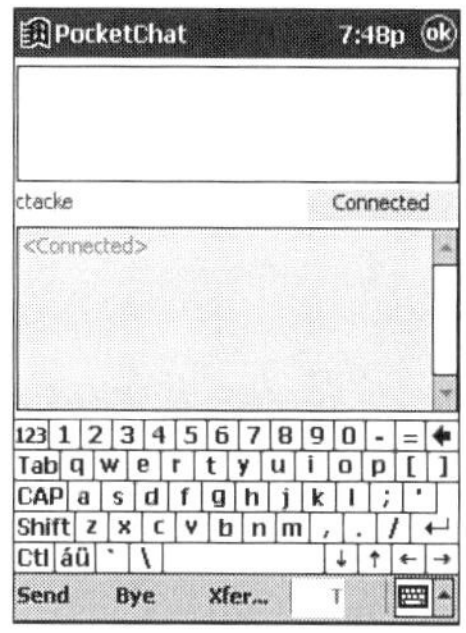

FIGURE 5.6
The device display when you are successfully connected to another device.

You've already changed the text of the Connect button to Bye, so let's look at the implementation. First, on the device where the user taps Bye, you handle this in the now-familiar `mnuMain_ButtonClick` event handler. You've already added code for the `Case "Connect"` for when you are connected; you now need to add an `Else` clause to the `If` statement, making the entire `Case` look like this:

```
Case "Connect"
    If wskMain.State = sckListening Then
        ' User click "Connect"
        If Not ConnectToPeer() Then Exit Sub

        ' Show the SIP
        SIPVisible = True

        'Set focus to txtSend
        txtSend.SetFocus
    Else
        ' User clicked "bye"
        ' Disconnect
        wskMain.Close

        ' Inform the user
        txtRecv.Text = txtRecv.Text & "<Disconnected>" & vbCrLf

        ' Set socket back to listen state
        SetListenState
    End If
```

As you can see, it's rather straightforward. You simply close the socket by calling the WinSock control's `Close` method. Again, to keep the user informed, we not only display `<Disconnected>` in `txtRecv`, we also make a call to `SetListenState`. `SetListenState` in

Listing 5.6 is essentially the inverse of the `DisplayConnected` subroutine as far as the GUI goes. The only other function it performs is to call the WinSock control's `Listen` function to set it back into listen state.

Figure 5.7 shows the GUI after the user disconnects.

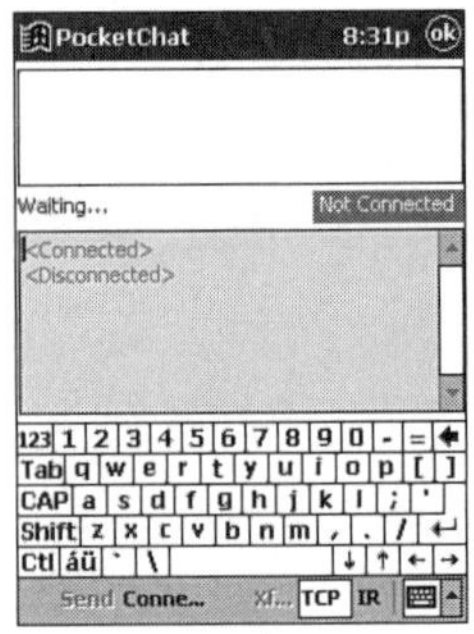

FIGURE 5.7
PocketChat after a disconnect.

LISTING 5.6 Encapsulating the "Listen" Code in a Single Method

```
Private Sub SetListenState()
    On Error Resume Next

    ' Set socket back to listen state
    wskMain.Listen

    ' Set the status label
    lblStatus.Caption = "Waiting..."

    ' Set connection label
    lblConnect.Caption = "Not Connected"
    lblConnect.BackColor = vbRed
    lblConnect.ForeColor = vbWhite

    ' Disable "Send" and "Xfer" buttons
    mnuMain.Controls("Send").Enabled = False
    mnuMain.Controls("Xfer").Enabled = False

    ' Disable txtSend
    txtSend.Enabled = False

    ' Set "Connect" button caption
    mnuMain.Controls("Connect").Caption = "Connect..."
```

LISTING 5.6 Continued

```
    ' Enable protocol buttons
    mnuMain.Controls("TCP").Enabled = True
    mnuMain.Controls("IrDA").Enabled = True

    ' This is a good general error handling method for debugging
    If Err.number <> 0 Then
        MsgBox "SetListenState:" & vbCrLf & Err.description, _
            vbCritical, "Error"
        Err.Clear
    End If
End Sub
```

This is a good opportunity to show another example of how you can approach error handling in eVB. eVB doesn't always act as you would expect when it encounters an error. Sometimes, even without calling `On Error Resume Next`, an error might not get thrown immediately, but might "linger" until the end of another procedure. Sometimes after it throws the error it won't show you the offending line of code or even the offending procedure.

One way around this is to add a general error handler like the one I've added to `SetListenState`. At the end of the procedure, check to see if the `Err` object's number is zero. If it isn't, display the procedure name and the error description, and then clear the error object.

Although this doesn't gracefully handle the error, it's a useful tool while debugging and developing to give you an idea of where a more robust error-handling routine should be used.

As with most of the WinSock methods, the other end of the connection fires a notification event when `Close` is called and you need to handle it. If we don't, our socket will remain in a undesired state and the remote user might not be aware that the connection was closed.

In the case of the `Close` event being called, the remote device's WinSock control will fire the `Close` event. This doesn't actually cause the remote socket to close; it just notifies it that its partner has closed, so we must do the cleanup ourselves. Again, it's important to let users know what's going on through the GUI.

```
Private Sub wskMain_Close()
    ' A request to close was sent, we still must call Close
    wskMain.Close

    ' Inform the user
    txtRecv.Text = txtRecv.Text & "<Disconnected>" & vbCrLf

    ' Go back to a Listen state
    SetListenState
End Sub
```

Sending Chat Text

Sending and receiving text through the WinSock control is a pretty simple, straightforward task. The challenge lies in being able to handle the text efficiently. PocketChat will allow users to send and receive not only chat text, but text files. It's important that the application be able to distinguish between the two so it knows what to do with the data. It would be very user-unfriendly if after every line of text was received you asked the user what to do with it. Users expect an application to be at least somewhat smart and these are the details that help make an application successful.

One of the easiest ways to make data distinguishable, especially text data, is to attach metadata to it. *Metadata* is simply "data about data," or a descriptor of the data within itself. XML is probably the best example of this, and because it works well and there's no point in reinventing the wheel, let's use XML-like tags to identify our data.

By tagging the data, we not only know what the data is, we also know where it begins and ends. This is vital with larger data sets because the WinSock control will start breaking the data into packets. Rather than send 10,000 bytes of text at one time, it will break the data into smaller chunks and send them one at a time for you to reassemble on the other side. Although this sounds somewhat complicated, the WinSock control actually handles most of it for you. We will examine this more in depth when we cover sending and receiving files.

In PocketChat, the user simply enters text into a textbox, txtSend, and taps the Send button and the remote user sees the text appear in `txtRecv`. Let's start at the beginning of the process.

Again, turn to the `mnuMain_ButtonClick` event handler. When the user taps Send, you simply step into `Case Send` and call out to a procedure in `modMain` called `SendText`:

```
Case "Send"
    ' Send chat text
    SendText txtSend.Text
```

`SendText` takes the text being sent as an input parameter (see Listing 5.7). It then prefixes the text with your hostname, wraps your tags—`<PocketChat Text>` and `</PocketChat Text>`—around it, and sends it through the WinSock control.

LISTING 5.7 Sending Text Through an Active Connection with a Call to `SendText`

```
Public Sub SendText(strSend As String)
    Dim ilength As Integer

    ' Append our local name
    strSend = GetLocalHostName & ": " & strSend

    ' Send the data with our custom tags
```

LISTING 5.7 Continued

```
    frmMain.wskMain.SendData "<PocketChat Text>" & strSend & "</PocketChat
Text>"

    ' Move it to the "recv" textbox
    frmMain.txtRecv.Text = frmMain.txtRecv.Text & strSend & vbCrLf

    ' Clear the "Send" textbox
    frmMain.txtSend.Text = ""

    ' Set focus back to the send textbox
    frmMain.txtSend.SetFocus
End Sub
```

Again, to make the application more user-friendly, it copies the text you sent, without tags, to `txtRecv`, clears `txtSend`, and sets the focus back to `txtSend` from the MenuBar. Figure 5.8 shows the screen when sending text.

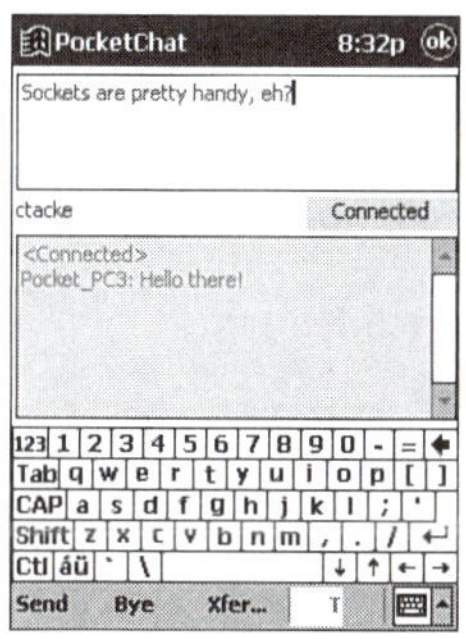

FIGURE 5.8
Sending text to a remote PocketChat user.

To make the application even more user-friendly, you can make it behave like most other IM applications and automatically send when the user taps the Return key.

```
Private Sub txtSend_KeyPress(ByVal KeyAscii As Integer)
    ' If the user presses the Return key, send the text
    If KeyAscii = 13 And wskMain.State = sckConnected Then
        ' Setting KeyAscii to 0 will NOT prevent the key.
        ' We must use a workaround

        ' Send the text
        SendText txtSend.Text
    End If
End Sub
```

Of course when you send the text, you don't want to send the final Return key as text; you just want to use it to call `SendText`. This is a great opportunity to look at another known bug in eVB.

Typically in Visual Basic 6, if you had a similar problem, you would just set the `KeyAscii` value back to 0 in the `KeyPress` event, and the Return keypress would be ignored. Not so in eVB. In fact, modifying `KeyAscii` in the `KeyPress` event in eVB has no effect at all.

What you do know is that when eVB enters this event handler, the TextBox's text hasn't yet appended the `KeyAscii` value, so in this case, `txtSend.Text` doesn't have the return (`KeyAscii = 13`) appended. This means that if you send `txtSend.Text` directly to `SendText` from here, the final Return key won't be transferred to the remote device.

The keystroke doesn't disappear though. If you just use this event handler, you will get a Return in `txtSend` after you send the text, essentially leaving the user on the second line of `txtSend`. If they don't delete it, it will get sent as the first character of their next line of chat text.

The easy way around the problem in this case is to check to see if `txtSend` contains only a Return, and the easiest time to check is when `txtSend`'s `Text` property changes. By checking in the `txtSend_Change` event handler, if you find that the text is just a return (`vbCrLf`), you can clear the text.

```
Private Sub txtSend_Change()
    ' Part of the Keypress(13) workaround
    If txtSend.Text = vbCrLf Then
        txtSend.Text = ""
    End If
End Sub
```

Receiving Chat Text

After the text has been sent, you get a notification event at the receiving end, `DataArrival`, and with it you get the number of bytes of data that have arrived. Because the data might come in packets, rather than the entire message at once, the number of bytes received might not be all the bytes being sent. If you are receiving packets, you will receive a `DataArrival` event for each packet, so you have to be cognizant of this when you code the event handler.

Data coming into the WinSock control is placed in a buffer. You can read the buffer at any time by calling the WinSock control's `GetData` method. `GetData` returns a string of the entire contents of the buffer, and it's important to know that `DataArrival` will only fire after the first time if you have retrieved the data from the WinSock's data buffer with `GetData`. This means that it's good practice to immediately call `GetData` in the `DataArrival` event, even if it is to put the data into another application buffer.

You will follow this model in PocketChat. As data comes in, you will append it to a member variable and then scan the variable for one of our terminating XML tags. Listing 5.8 shows what the event handler looks like.

LISTING 5.8 Firing the `DataArrival` Event When Data Is Received Through the WinSock Control

```
Private Sub wskMain_DataArrival(ByVal bytesTotal As Long)
    Dim InBuffer As String

    ' Get the data in the Winsock's buffer
    wskMain.GetData InBuffer

    ' Append the received data to our app buffer
    m_strRecv = m_strRecv & InBuffer

    Do While Len(m_strRecv) > 0
        ' If no end tag has been received, we'll keep appending
        If InStr(m_strRecv, "</PocketChat Text>") Then
            ' We've received a Chat message
            DisplayText m_strRecv

            ' Remove handled data from buffer
            m_strRecv = Mid(m_strRecv, InStr(m_strRecv, _
                    "</PocketChat Text>") + _
                    Len("</PocketChat Text>"))
        ElseIf InStr(m_strRecv, "</PocketChat File>") Then
            ' We've received a file
            WriteFile m_strRecv

            ' Remove handled data from buffer
            m_strRecv = Mid(m_strRecv, InStr(m_strRecv, _
                    "</PocketChat File>") + _
                    Len("</PocketChat File>"))

        End If
    Loop
End Sub
```

As the data comes in, we append it to our member variable buffer, `m_strRecv`. We then look for either `</PocketChat Text>` or `</PocketChat File>`. Either tag indicates that this is the end of the data being sent, and so you can handle the data appropriately by calling either `DisplayText` for chat text or `WriteFile` for file text. We also wrap the search for `</PocketChat Text>` or `</PocketChat File>` in a `Do...While` loop to handle the possibility of either multiple messages or data coming in after the closing tag.

`DisplayText`, which follows, simply strips the XML tags from the data because you don't want to display them, and appends it to `txtRecv`.

```
Private Sub DisplayText(TextToDisplay As String)
    ' First strip the tags
    TextToDisplay = Replace(TextToDisplay, "</PocketChat Text>", "")
    TextToDisplay = Replace(TextToDisplay, "<PocketChat Text>", "")

    'Display the text
    txtRecv.Text = txtRecv.Text & TextToDisplay & vbCrLf
End Sub
```

Figure 5.9 shows the GUI output for `DisplayText`. `WriteFile` is a bit more complex, and we will cover it in the next section.

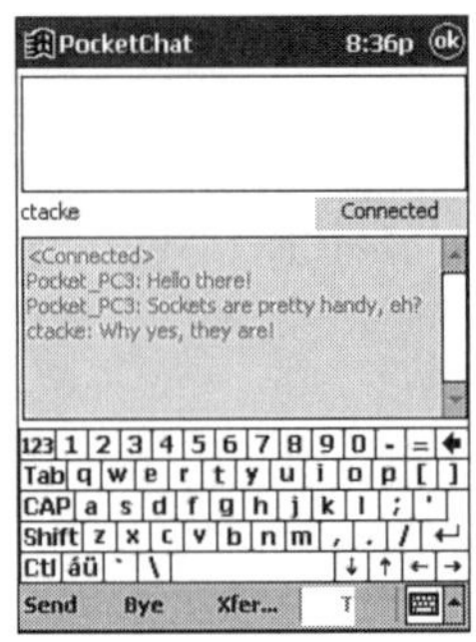

FIGURE 5.9
PocketChat, after sending and receiving text. Notice the usernames prefix each line to make the dialog more readable.

Sending a Text File

The final primary task that PocketChat performs is sending a text file through the WinSock control. This is initiated by the user by tapping the Xfer button on the MenuBar. This is also the final MenuBar function you need to write, so it's a good time to look at the full implementation for `mnuMain_ButtonClick` in one place (see Listing 5.9).

LISTING 5.9 Handling the `ButtonClick` Event for PocketChat's Application Menu

```
Private Sub mnuMain_ButtonClick(ByVal Button As MenuBarLib.MenuBarButton)
    ' Determine which button was clicked and take action
    Select Case Button.Key
        Case "Send"
            ' Send chat text
            SendText txtSend.Text
```

LISTING 5.9 Continued

```
    Case "Connect"
           If wskMain.State = sckListening Then
               ' User click "Connect"
               If Not ConnectToPeer() Then Exit Sub

               ' Show the SIP
               SIPVisible = True

               'Set focus to txtSend
               txtSend.SetFocus
           Else
               ' User clicked "bye"
               ' Disconnect
               wskMain.Close

               ' Inform the user
               txtRecv.Text = txtRecv.Text & "<Disconnected>" & vbCrLf

               ' Set socket back to listen state
               SetListenState
           End If
       Case "Xfer"
           ' Send a text file
           SendFile
       Case "TCP"
           ' Close the socket
           wskMain.Close

           ' Change connection protocol to TCP/IP
           wskMain.ServiceName = ""
           wskMain.Protocol = sckTCPProtocol

           ' Set the socket to listen again
           wskMain.Listen
       Case "IrDA"
           ' Close the socket
           wskMain.Close

           ' Change connection protocol to IrDA
           wskMain.Protocol = sckIRDAProtocol
           wskMain.ServiceName = "PocketChat"
           ' Set the socket to listen again
           wskMain.Listen
   End Select
End Sub
```

Notice that the newest addition—`Case "Xfer"`—is simply a call to the `SendFile` function. `SendFile` is similar to the `SendText` function in Listing 5.7 in that it creates a full "image" of what you need to send, including XML tags, and pushes it through the WinSock control.

Of course, it isn't quite as simple as sending chat text because you need to ask the user what file they want to send and you need to attach a bit more information, namely the filename, to the file text itself.

Let's take a look at the function in Listing 5.10.

LISTING 5.10 Getting a Text File's Contents and Sending It Through the WinSock Control

```
Public Sub SendFile()
    Dim strPath As String
    Dim strFileName As String
    Dim strContents As String
    Dim iStartPos As Integer

    strPath = InputBox("Enter name of file to send (include full path)", _
            "Send File")

    ' if the user hit Cancel of OK with a blank input, exit
    If strPath = "" Then Exit Sub

    ' Refresh frmMain to get rid of InputBox "ghost"
    frmMain.Refresh

    ' Get the file's contents
    If GetFileTextContents(strPath, strContents) = True Then
        ' Bracket file contents in tags
        ' Add filename tags
        iStartPos = InStrRev(strPath, "\")
        If iStartPos <= 0 Then iStartPos = 1
        strFileName = Mid(strPath, iStartPos)

        ' Inform the user we're beginning and hide the SIP
        frmMain.txtRecv = frmMain.txtRecv & "Sending file: " _
               & strFileName & vbCrLf
        frmMain.Refresh

        ' Start building data stream
        strContents = "<Filename>" & strFileName & "</Filename>" & strContents

        ' Add PocketChat tags
        strContents = "<PocketChat File>" & strContents & "</PocketChat File>"
```

LISTING 5.10 Continued

```
        ' Send the file
        frmMain.wskMain.SendData strContents

        ' Inform the user we've sent the file
        frmMain.txtRecv.Text = frmMain.txtRecv.Text & "Sent File: " _
            & strFileName & vbCrLf
    Else
        ' failed to get contents.  Likely file doesn't exist
        MsgBox "Cannot locate file to send", vbCritical, "Error sending"
    End If

End Sub
```

First, ask the user for the path and name of the file you want to send (see Figure 5.10). It would be friendlier to add a File Explorer type interface to allow them to navigate to the file. However, you've already covered how to write this type of interface in Chapter 3, "Manipulating Files," and it would add a lot of extraneous code to this project.

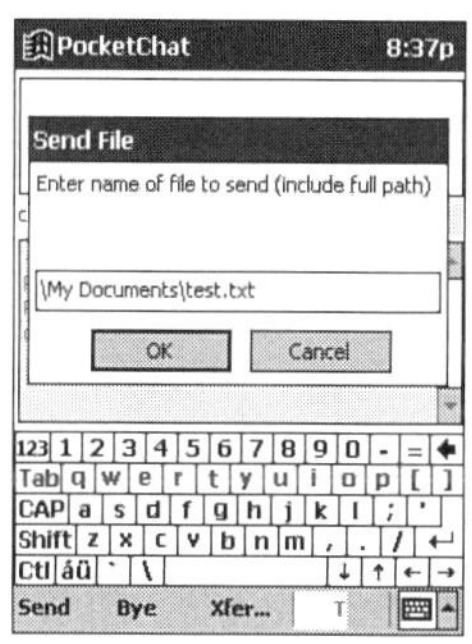

FIGURE 5.10
Sending a file to a remote PocketChat user.

After getting the filename, refresh `frmMain`. Any time you display either a MsgBox or InputBox, it's good practice to call `Refresh` on the underlying form. If you don't, and the application must do a little work before it automatically refreshes the form, you'll get a "ghost" that whites out part of your form. Although it won't affect the application itself, it's a bit unsightly and could cause the user to think your application has locked up.

Next get the file's contents by calling `GetFileContents` (see Listing 5.11).

LISTING 5.11 Extracting the Contents of a File Given the File's Full Path

```
Public Function GetFileTextContents(Path As String, _
                                    ByRef Contents As String) As Boolean
    Dim filFile As FILECTLCtl.File

    On Error Resume Next

    ' Set our return value
    GetFileTextContents = True

    ' Get our application File object
    Set filFile = GetFileObject()

    ' Open the File
    filFile.Open Path, fsModeInput, fsAccessRead

    ' Make sure the call to Open was successful
    If Err.number <> 0 Then
        GetFileTextContents = False
        Exit Function
    End If

    ' Loop through file, filling our input buffer
    Do While Not filFile.EOF
        Contents = Contents & filFile.Input(1)
    Loop

    ' Close the file
    filFile.Close

    ' Release the File Object
    Set filFile = Nothing
End Function
```

You might recognize this function, and rightfully so—it's almost identical to the `GetFileContents` function we used in Chapter 3. The only difference is that in Chapter 3, the function returned the contents of the file; here, you pass a variable `ByRef` (although `ByRef` is the default for function parameters, I've added it explicitly here for clarity) that the function populates with the file contents. Then it returns a Boolean to signify success or failure.

Otherwise, the function is the same as the one used previously. If you need further clarification, feel free to refer to Chapter 3. Note that the function still calls `GetFileObject`, which again is from Chapter 3 and this function is identical.

LISTING 5.12 Minimizing the `CreateObject` Memory Leak by Wrapping a Global `File` Object with an Accessor Function

```
Public Function GetFileObject() As FILECTLCtl.File
    On Error Resume Next

    ' If we haven't created the File object yet, do so
    If IsEmpty(m_FileObject) Then
        ' Create a File control
        Set m_FileObject = CreateObject("FILECTL.File")

        ' Ensure the object was created successfully
        If Err.number <> 0 Then
            MsgBox "Failed to create File object." & vbCrLf & _
                "Ensure MSCEFile.dll has been installed and registered.", _
                vbCritical, "Error"
            Exit Function
        End If
    End If
    ' Return our global File object
    Set GetFileObject = m_FileObject
End Function
```

Looking back at the `SendFile` function in Listing 5.10, the next thing you do is inform the user you are about to send the file. Because this could be a lengthy operation, it's nice to let the user know you've begun.

Next, add your XML tags and metadata. Prefix the file data with the filename in its own `<Filename>` tag set. You'll use this on the receiving end.

Lastly, inform the user that you are finished with a message box (see Figure 5.11). This helps prevent users from assuming the device has either locked up or failed to perform the transfer.

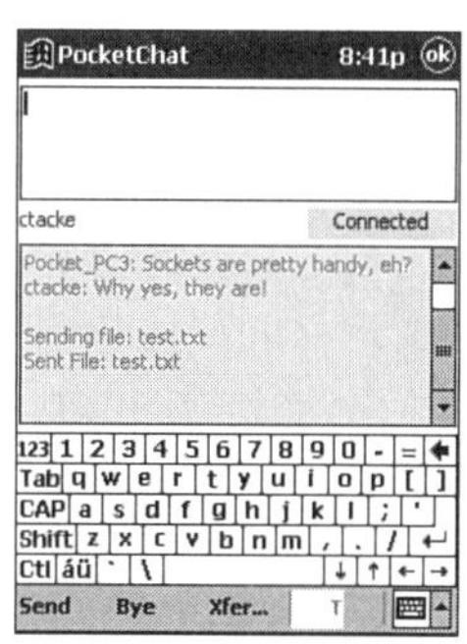

FIGURE 5.11
Informing users before you send a file and after you're done sending lets them know what the application is up to.

A ProgressBar Workaround

Because sending files can take some time, especially over IR, it would be nice to provide the user with a little more than just a `Sending file` notice, and the WinSock control can help us.

Whenever you send text—even short amounts that aren't broken into packets—the WinSock control fires two events: `SendProgress` and `SendComplete`. `SendProgress` provides the number of bytes sent so far and the number of bytes remaining to be sent. This can easily be turned into a percentage representing overall progress.

Displaying this progress to the user as a ProgressBar would be nice, but unfortunately there isn't one in the eVB toolkit. There is a native ProgressBar in the Pocket PC's API. Why Microsoft chose not to expose it through eVB, I'm not sure, but because they didn't, we need a workaround.

Fortunately, this is a simple one, easier than writing API calls to get the native ProgressBar to appear.

First, drop a PictureBox onto your form, giving it the height, width, and positioning of the desired ProgressBar. Now "draw" a colored box in the PictureBox, starting at the left side, a certain distance across the PictureBox using the `DrawLine` function. The entire procedure looks like Listing 5.13.

LISTING 5.13 Adding ProgressBar Functionality by Filling a PictureBox with a Color

```
Public Sub DrawProgress(picProgress As PictureBoxCtl.PictureBox, _
                        PercentDone As Integer, DrawColor As Long)
    Dim sngPercentWidth As Single
    Dim sngDrawWidth As Single

    ' Check for valid input
    If PercentDone < 0 Then PercentDone = 0
    If PercentDone > 100 Then PercentDone = 100

    ' Allow for decimal representation of percent
    If PercentDone < 1 Then PercentDone = PercentDone * 100

    ' Determine the width of one percent
    sngPercentWidth = picProgress.Width / 100

    ' Determine the width to draw
    sngDrawWidth = PercentDone * sngPercentWidth

    ' Fill the picturebox in White
    If PercentDone = 0 Then
```

LISTING 5.13 Continued

```
picProgress.DrawLine 0, 0, picProgress.Width, _
            picProgress.Height, RGB(255, 255, 255), True, True
    End If

    ' Draw the progress bar - essentially a filled rectangle
    picProgress.DrawLine 0, 0, sngDrawWidth, _
        picProgress.Height, DrawColor, True, True

    ' Without Refresh, the progress is not displayed until done
    picProgress.Parent.Refresh
End Sub
```

I've even added a few features to make it more robust by allowing you to tell the function with what color to draw the bar (using an RBG integer or eVB constant) as well as making it semi-intelligent by allowing either whole number percentages (0–100) or decimal percentages (0–1). The only drawback occurs when drawing a progress of 1. Does that mean 1% or 100%? I've opted to assume it means 1%.

Now that you have a ProgressBar, let's see it in action. You know that `SendProgress` gives you enough information to calculate a percentage, so call `DrawProgress` from there:

```
Private Sub wskMain_SendProgress(ByVal bytesSent As Long, _
                                 ByVal bytesRemaining As Long)
    Dim iProgress As Integer

    ' Determine progress
    iProgress = CInt((bytesSent / (bytesSent + bytesRemaining)) * 100)

    ' Update the progress bar
    DrawProgress picProgress, iProgress, vbBlue
End Sub
```

And once the data has been fully sent, `SendComplete` fires, so you can reset the ProgressBar by calling `DrawProgress` with a progress of 0:

```
Private Sub wskMain_SendComplete()
    ' Reset the progress bar
    DrawProgress picProgress, 0, vbBlue
End Sub
```

If you send small amounts of data, especially through a USB or LAN connection, the transfer could happen too fast for you to notice any ProgressBar at all. In fact, if the data doesn't get broken into packets, you'll likely see nothing. If you want a really quick test to see it working without having to find or create a large text file, just write a simple loop in `Sub Main`, something like this:

```
Dim pct As Integer

For pct = 100 to 10000
    DrawProgress pct/100
next pct
```

Receiving a Text File

Again, you have to handle to receiving end of your feature, this time the reception of a text file. Remember in our `DataArrival` event handler you checked for the existence of the `</PocketChat File>` tag? From there you call `Writefile`, which handles all the file data (see Listing 5.14).

LISTING 5.14 Extracting the File Text from the Incoming Data Buffer and Writing It to Your Local Machine

```
Public Sub WriteFile(FileString As String)
    Dim filFile As FILECTL.File
    Dim strFileName As String
    Dim iEndPos As Integer

    Set filFile = GetFileObject()

    ' First strip the tags
    FileString = Replace(FileString, "</PocketChat File>", "")
    FileString = Replace(FileString, "<PocketChat File>", "")

    ' Next get the filename
    FileString = Replace(FileString, "<Filename>", "")
    iEndPos = InStr(FileString, "</Filename>")
    strFileName = Left(FileString, iEndPos - 1)

    ' Strip the filename and tags from the file contents
    FileString = Mid(FileString, iEndPos + Len("</Filename>"))
    ' Open the file
    filFile.Open App.Path & "\" & strFileName, fsModeOutput

    ' Write the data
    filFile.LinePrint FileString

    ' Close the file
    filFile.Close
End Sub
```

Once again you call GetFileObject to retrieve a File object with which you'll write the file. Then you strip off the <PocketChat File> tag set.

Next you extract the filename from the beginning of the data and save the file to the application directory using the same filename.

Handling WinSock Errors

You have covered everything for normal socket operation. Unfortunately, there will always be instances where things won't be quite "normal." What if a user tries to connect to a host that doesn't exist, or his device isn't connected to a network? What if the remote user shuts down his PocketChat application without closing the socket? What if his device crashes?

A whole host of things can go wrong with socket communications, and fortunately handling them isn't difficult. When any error occurs, the WinSock control will fire its Error event.

There are a lot of potential errors (check out the object model in the appendix for a full listing), but with a bit of testing you can determine which ones will most likely occur in your application. From there you can determine which specific errors you want to handle and which ones you'll pass through a generic error handler.

In PocketChat we'll look for a timeout error, an address not available error, and the host not found error. All others will fall into Case Else. Interestingly, the WinSock control adds the error number to the error description, so I've provided some code in Case Else that will extract just the description (see Listing 5.15).

LISTING 5.15 Firing the Error Event

```
Private Sub wskMain_Error(ByVal number As Long, ByVal description As String)
    Dim strMsg As String
    Dim iPos As Integer
    Dim iProgress As Integer

    Select Case number
        Case sckTimedout
            MsgBox "Timed out.", _
                vbExclamation, "Error Connecting"
        Case sckAddressNotAvailable
            MsgBox "Could not contact remote IP or Host name.", _
                vbExclamation, "Error Connecting"
        Case sckHostNotFoundTryAgain
            ' Likely tried to connect to a device in TCP protocol
            MsgBox "Couldn't get a response from remote device.  " _
                & "Ensure remote device is set to IrDA", vbExclamation, _
                "Error Connecting"
```

LISTING 5.15 Continued

```
    Case Else
            ' Separate the error number from description
            iPos = InStr(description, vbLf)
            strMsg = Right(description, Len(description) - iPos)
            MsgBox strMsg, vbExclamation, "WinSock Error"
    End Select

    ' Make sure the socket is closed
    wskMain.Close

    ' We should wait for the socket to finish closing
    iProgress = 0

    Do While True
        ' Increment our progress bar
        iProgress = iProgress + 5
        If iProgress > 100 Then iProgress = 0

        DrawProgress picProgress, iProgress, vbBlue

        ' Check the winsock state
        If wskMain.State = sckClosed Then
            ' Reset the progress bar
            DrawProgress picProgress, 0, vbBlue

            ' Exit the loop
            Exit Do
        End If
    Loop

    ' Set socket back to listen state
    SetListenState
End Sub
```

If the control raises an error for any reason, such as a failed IR connection, you can display a MessageBox like the one shown in Figure 5.12.

Regardless of the error, the socket connection either is broken or is in an unstable state, so you should gracefully close out the local socket by calling the `Close` method. Depending on what happened, the WinSock control might take a little while to fully close the socket, and you should always wait for it to complete. Here you sit in a polling loop waiting for it to close, updating the ProgressBar as you wait.

FIGURE 5.12
When an error occurs, the `Error` *event fires. This provides you the opportunity to give the user helpful feedback.*

CAUTION

> Sitting in a continuous loop, or *polling*, is often undesirable. It can cause the active thread to consume large amounts of the processor time and essentially lock your device, especially if you expect the loop to take more than a very short period of time. If you must poll, it's a good idea to allow system events to occur by using the `DoEventsCE` workaround found in Chapter 9.

Adding Final Touches

As with most applications, there are niceties that you can add to make the user's experience a little better. In PocketChat we've already done some of this type of work, showing the SIP (Soft Input Panel, the onscreen keyboard) when the user connects, for example. When the SIP is shown, though, it overlaps `txtRecv`, and if the user has done much chatting, the area where data is getting appended will be beneath the SIP. Of course the user can always hide the SIP to see it, but it's far friendlier to simply prevent the SIP from overlapping the textbox.

This is achieved by changing the height of `txtRecv` whenever the SIP is shown or hidden, and nicely enough eVB exposes an event for the form called `SIPChange` that fires whenever the SIP state changes.

By adding the code in Listing 5.16, you can avoid the SIP ever overlapping `txtRecv`.

LISTING 5.16 Making Sure the SIP Doesn't Overlap Input or Display Fields

```
Private Sub Form_SIPChange(bSIPVisible As Boolean)
    If bSIPVisible Then
        ' If the SIP is visible, we need to shrink txtRecv
```

LISTING 5.16 Continued

```
        txtRecv.Height = 1450

        ' It also means they're probably about to type
        If txtSend.Enabled Then
            txtSend.SetFocus
        End If
    Else
        ' If the SIP is hidden, we need to expand txtRecv
        txtRecv.Height = 2415
    End If
End Sub
```

Notice that when the SIP becomes visible, we make the assumption that the user will likely want to begin typing, so set the application focus to `txtSend` for them.

You also need to do some clean up of the `File` object if it has been created. Just as you did in Chapter 3, you handle this by calling `ReleaseFileObject` from `frmMain`'s `OKClick` event just before ending the application:

```
Private Sub Form_OKClick()
    ' Clean up our File object
    ReleaseFileObject

    ' End app
    App.End
End Sub
```

`ReleaseFileObject` simply sets the `File` member variable to `Nothing`:

```
Public Sub ReleaseFileObject()
    Set m_FileObject = Nothing
End Sub
```

PCChat

PocketChat was designed to "talk" with another copy of PocketChat on another device. If you only have one Pocket PC device, you can use PCChat to simulate the other device.

The PCChat project consists only of a single form, `frmMain`. You will need to add two component references: the Microsoft WinSock Control and the Microsoft Windows CE File Control. Nicely enough, the Windows CE controls work just fine under the full Win32 environment.

The relevant form header code is in Listing 5.17. The full project code shown in Listing 5.18 should be placed in `frmMain`'s code page.

LISTING 5.17 Heading Information from frmMain.frm of PCChat

```
Begin VB.Form frmMain
   Caption         =   "PCChat"
   ClientHeight    =   4335
   ClientLeft      =   60
   ClientTop       =   345
   ClientWidth     =   6360
   Begin VB.CommandButton cmdXfer
      Caption         =   "Xfer"
      Height          =   435
      Left            =   2160
      Top             =   3720
      Width           =   1155
   End
   Begin FILECTLCtl.File filMain
      Left            =   120
      Top             =   3660
   End
   Begin VB.CommandButton cmdSend
      Caption         =   "Send"
      Height          =   435
      Left            =   840
      Top             =   3720
      Width           =   1155
   End
   Begin VB.TextBox txtRecv
      Height          =   2595
      Left            =   60
      Locked          =   -1  'True
      MultiLine       =   -1  'True
      Top             =   960
      Width           =   6075
   End
   Begin VB.TextBox txtSend
      Height          =   855
      Left            =   60
      MultiLine       =   -1  'True
      Top             =   60
      Width           =   6075
   End
   Begin MSWinsockLib.Winsock wskMain
      Left            =   5040
      Top             =   60
   End
End
```

LISTING 5.18 Complete Code for PCChat

```
Option Explicit

Private Sub cmdSend_Click()
    SendText
End Sub

Private Sub cmdXfer_Click()
    SendFile
End Sub

Private Sub Form_Load()
    ' Set the port we'll be using - you may have to modify this
    wskMain.LocalPort = SOCKET_PORT

    ' Set the port to listen mode
    wskMain.Listen
End Sub

Private Sub wskMain_Close()
    wskMain.Close

    ' Inform the user
    txtRecv.Text = txtRecv.Text & "<Disconnected>"

    wskMain.Listen
End Sub

Private Sub wskMain_ConnectionRequest(ByVal requestID As Long)
    wskMain.Close

    wskMain.Accept requestID
End Sub

Private Sub wskMain_DataArrival(ByVal bytesTotal As Long)
    Dim InBuffer As String
    Static strRecv As String

    wskMain.GetData InBuffer

    strRecv = strRecv & InBuffer

    ' If no end tag has been received, we'll keep appending
    If InStr(strRecv, "</PocketChat Text>") Then
        ' We've received a Chat message
```

LISTING 5.18 Continued

```
        DisplayText strRecv

        ' Clear the input buffer
        strRecv = ""
    ElseIf InStr(strRecv, "</PocketChat File>") Then
        ' We've received a file
        WriteFile strRecv

        ' Clear the input buffer
        strRecv = ""
    End If
End Sub

Private Sub WriteFile(FileString As String)
    Dim strFileName As String
    Dim iEndPos As Integer

    ' First strip the tags
    FileString = Replace(FileString, "</PocketChat File>", "")
    FileString = Replace(FileString, "<PocketChat File>", "")

    ' Next get the filename
    FileString = Replace(FileString, "<Filename>", "")
    iEndPos = InStr(FileString, "</Filename>")
    strFileName = Left(FileString, iEndPos - 1)

    ' Strip the filename and tags from the file contents
    FileString = Mid(FileString, iEndPos + 11)

    'now write the file - We can use the CE File object!!
    ' 73k v. the 145k scrrun.dll (fso)

    ' Open the file
    filMain.Open App.Path & "\" & strFileName, fsModeOutput

    ' Write the data
    filMain.LinePrint FileString

    ' Close the file
    filMain.Close
End Sub

Private Sub DisplayText(TextToDisplay As String)
    ' First strip the tags
```

LISTING 5.18 Continued

```
    TextToDisplay = Replace(TextToDisplay, "</PocketChat Text>", "")
    TextToDisplay = Replace(TextToDisplay, "<PocketChat Text>", "")

    'Display the text
    txtRecv.Text = txtRecv.Text & TextToDisplay & vbCrLf
End Sub

Private Sub SendText()
    Dim strSend As String

    ' Get the data to send
    strSend = Trim(txtSend.Text)

    ' Append our local name
    strSend = GetLocalHostName & ": " & strSend

    ' Send the data with our custom tags
    wskMain.SendData "<PocketChat Text>" & strSend & "</PocketChat Text>"

    ' Move it to the "recv" textbox
    txtRecv.Text = txtRecv.Text & strSend & vbCrLf

    ' Clear the "Send" textbox
    txtSend.Text = ""

    ' Set focus back to the send textbox
    txtSend.SetFocus
End Sub

Private Function GetLocalHostName() As String
    GetLocalHostName = "ctacke"
End Function

Public Sub SendFile()
    Dim strPath As String
    Dim strFileName As String
    Dim strContents As String
    Dim iStartPos As Integer

    strPath = InputBox("Enter name of file to send (include full path)", "Send
File")

    ' Get the file's contents
    If GetFileTextContents(strPath, strContents) = True Then
```

LISTING 5.18 Continued

```
        ' Bracket file contents in tags
        ' Add filename tags
        iStartPos = InStrRev(strPath, "\")
        If iStartPos <= 0 Then iStartPos = 1
        strFileName = Mid(strPath, iStartPos)
        strContents = "<Filename>" & strFileName & "</Filename>" & strContents

        ' Add PocketChat tags
        strContents = "<PocketChat File>" & strContents & "</PocketChat File>"

        ' Send the file
        frmMain.wskMain.SendData strContents

        ' Inform the user we've sent the file
        frmMain.txtRecv.Text = frmMain.txtRecv.Text & "Sent File: " _
            & strFileName & vbCrLf
    Else
        ' failed to get contents.  Likely file doesn't exist
        MsgBox "Cannot locate file to send", vbCritical, "Error sending"
    End If

End Sub

Public Function GetFileTextContents(Path As String, _
                                    Contents As String) As Boolean
    ' I've just modified the CE version of the method to use filFile

    On Error Resume Next

    ' Set our return value
    GetFileTextContents = True

    ' Open the File
    filMain.Open Path, fsModeInput, fsAccessRead

    ' Make sure the call to Open was successful
    If Err.Number <> 0 Then
        GetFileTextContents = False
        Exit Function
    End If

    ' Loop through file, filling our input buffer
    Do While Not filMain.EOF
        Contents = Contents & filMain.Input(1)
```

LISTING 5.18 Continued

```
    Loop

    ' Close the file
    filMain.Close
End Function
```

Summary

PocketChat (and PCChat, if you've decided to use it) has provided you with working code for just about the entire WinSock object model, plus given you a small working example of the MenuBar in a full project. In addition, it has given you a simple, reusable progress bar.

Admittedly, PocketChat, as it now stands, can't be used to solve a great many problems, but it does provide a very strong foundation on which to build. It isn't much of a stretch to get the application to connect with a more common instant messenger service. A little research on the Internet can provide the specifics of many of the IM services available.

Another more exciting and extensible direction in which to take the application is to extend what you've learned about file transfer to full data transfer. After reading about ADOCE in Chapter 7, "Storing and Receiving Data with ActiveX Data Objects CE," try passing an entire Recordset as XML to another client and re-creating the Recordset there. Or pass it to a desktop VB application. After you accomplish that, the uses are unlimited.

If you're after an even larger challenge, read the explanation in Chapter 9, "Harnessing the Windows CE API," of working around eVB's lack of structure or UDT support and apply that knowledge to transferring binary data instead of text through the control. Just because the documentation states that only text and integer arrays can be passed through the control doesn't mean that you can't get it to pass binary data. It just isn't as straightforward.

So, if you're looking for more things to do with sockets and PocketChat, consider the following as challenges and/or feature upgrades:

- Add a File Explorer type interface for selecting a file to send—you could roll your own or use the Common Dialog control.
- Have the application save state. That is, have it remember the last host it connected to so the user doesn't have to type it in. You could keep this information in a file, the registry or even a database.
- Allow the user to save the text of a session as a text file.
- Have the text box hold only a certain amount of text. Trim the oldest text off as new text comes in to prevent the textbox from using large amounts of memory.

- Allow connections to a common IM service.
- Allow connections to multiple clients at one time to provide a chat room, where all clients see all messages.
- Send an ADOCE Recordset's data as XML to a remote machine and re-create the Recordset there.
- Send binary (non-text) data through a socket connection.

The Pocket Outlook Object Model: Accessing Contacts and Calendar Items

CHAPTER

6

IN THIS CHAPTER

Microsoft provides the Pocket Outlook Object Model (POOM) to access, modify, and delete the native Pocket PC Personal Information Manager (PIM) data. Currently implemented in POOM are contacts, appointments, and tasks, but not e-mail. POOM can be very powerful, allowing eVB developers to extend the PIM applications or replace their GUI applications while leaving the data-store and current synchronization in place.

In this chapter, we'll investigate Contacts, Appointments, and Tasks. How to access, modify, copy, display, delete and beam via infrared these items are explained and demonstrated. The library is relatively simple, but does have some limitations in eMbedded Visual Basic (eVB).

In this chapter you will discover

- How to obtain and install the POOM SDK
- The POOM object model
- How to use the POOM Contact object (`ContactItem`)
- How to build PocketPIM, a sample application that uses POOM to extend functionality of the native PIM applications

Installing POOM

POOM is already installed on most Pocket PCs and Handheld PC 2000s. But, to enable IntelliSense in eVB, you need to install POOM to your development machine. To install POOM, you must obtain it from the Microsoft Web site (`www.microsoft.com/MOBILE/downloads/developer/poomsdk.asp`). If the SDK is no longer available at this address, search `msdn.microsoft.com` or `microsoft.com` for POOM.

NOTE

The POOM SDK page mentions that POOM isn't compatible with the emulator. Although this is true for other platforms, the Pocket PC emulator allows for POOM development.

After downloading POOM, you need to run the setup program, PIMSTORE.EXE. This guides you through an installation that is essentially just an archive expansion or unzipping. The package installs five files:

- eula.txt, the End User License Agreement.
- pimstore.h, a header file for eMbedded Visual C++.
- Pocket Outlook Object Model.doc, POOM's documentation. Mostly C++ centered, but yet very useful.

- Readme.txt, instructions for installation.
- Pimstore_******.dll, a collection of pimstore (POOM) DLL files. One for each processor type (for example, pimstore_sa1100.dll for the Intel StrongArm processor).

Installation onto Your Device

Most Pocket PC devices ship with the pimstore.dll on them, some don't, and some have outdated versions. After testing POOM on your device, if you find that POOM doesn't work correctly or doesn't work at all, you will need to place the proper pimstore.dll onto the device.

NOTE

A device with POOM installed will have a DLL named pimstore.dll in the \windows directory. If this file isn't present or you have problems using POOM, you will need to install POOM. Before installing it, be sure that this is the problem, as installing POOM from the SDK may break functionality.

First, you need to determine which processor type your device has. Refer to your user manual or the manufacturer's Web site for this information. After you determine the processor type, the DLLs that correlate are as follows:

DLL	*Processor*
pimstore_i486	Intel x86 processors
pimstore_sa1100	StrongArm SA1100
pimstore_r3000	MIPS 3000 family
pimstore_r4100	MIPS 4000 family
pimstore_sh3	Hitachi SH3
pimstore_sh4	Hitachi SH4

If you find that you need to place or replace the pimstore.dll on the device, you need to choose the correct file (as described in preceding the list). Then rename the file to pimstore.dll. By Using ActiveSync, copy the renamed file to the device's \Windows directory. After copying, you need to register the DLL by using REGSVRCE.EXE. REGSVRCE.EXE is the Windows CE version of RegSrv32.exe and can be used to register any ActiveX CE DLL server.

You can find REGSVRCE.EXE in a processor-specific subfolder in the \target folder of your development machine's Windows CE Tools directory. In the default installation, the StrongArm version of REGSVRCE.EXE is found at C:\Windows CE Tools\wce300\MS Pocket PC\target\arm\REGSVRCE.EXE. Copy the appropriate REGSVRCE.EXE to your device.

When REGSVRCE.EXE is present on your device, start it up by tapping it in the File Explorer. Enter the path, as shown in Figure 6.1, to the pimstore.dll you copied over and tap OK. The result displays in a message box. Unfortunately, the message box will "fall behind" the File Explorer, so you need to use the Start menu's Today command to find the message box.

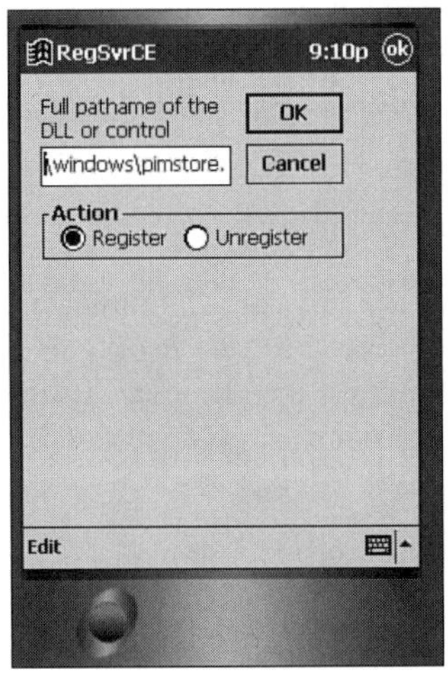

FIGURE 6.1
Using REGSVRCE.EXE to register pimstore.dll.Note:

Installation on a Development Computer

POOM doesn't really install onto the desktop computer, but places its DLL files onto your development machine. When you create a project that uses the POOM DLL (pimstore_*****.dll), you need to use the Browse button of the Project References dialog to find the DLL and select it. You can select any of the POOM DLLs as they are only used for a reference to the type library contained within. This will enable eVB to display IntelliSense functionality for POOM.

NOTE

eVB might tell you that the DLL isn't marked as useable in your current platform and ask if you want to use it anyway. Answer Yes.

Looking at Pocket Outlook's Object Model

The object model of POOM is fairly straightforward. There are several objects, but similar to many Microsoft Office automations, the object classes that are directly creatable are limited. In fact, the only directly creatable object in POOM is `PocketOutlook.Application`. All other objects in POOM need to be derived from the `Application` object.

The derivable objects in POOM:

- `AppointmentItem` is a calendar item record object.
- `CityItem` contains information about a city and is provided from the World Clock application. It may have different entries based on the manufacturer's specifications. The folder where `CityItem` persists can have custom-defined cities added, but, default cities are ROM-based and can't be modified.
- `ContactItem` is a contact item record object.
- `Exception` is a single exception to the recurrence pattern of a calendar record (`AppointmentItem`).
- `Exceptions` is a collection of the `Exception` object.
- `Folder` is a collection of items, and can contain any of four objects: Contacts, Appointments, Tasks, or Cities.
- `Recipient` is a single attendee of an Appointment. Strictly read-only in eMbedded Visual Basic.
- `Recipients` is a collection of recipients for an Appointment.
- `RecurrencePattern` represents the recurrence pattern for an appointment.
- `TaskItem` is a task, "To-Do" item record object.
- `TimeZone` represents a singular time zone. It provides information such as observation of daylight savings time and the difference between "Universal Time" (Greenwich Mean Time) and the particular time zone the object represents.

The `PocketOutlook.Application` Object

The POOM `PocketOutlook.Application` object provides interfaces to access the rest of the objects within the POOM SDK. All other objects are derived from the `PocketOutlook.Application` object.

Let's see how `PocketOutlook.Application` is created and initiated for use:

```
Public gobjPoom As PocketOutlook.Application

    ' create the PocketOutlook application once and only once....
    Set gobjPoom = CreateObject("PocketOutlook.Application")
```

```
' logon - can not use until Logon is called...
gobjPoom.Logon
```

As with all ActiveX DLL objects in eMbedded Visual Basic, the `CreateObject` memory leak needs to be minimized by creating the ActiveX object only once. In the preceding example, the variable reference to hold the `PocketOutlook.Application` object is declared `Public`. `PocketOutlook.Application` is then instantiated by using the `CreateObject` function. Next, the `Logon` method is called to initialize the object; although there's currently no security or user profiles on the PIM store, POOM follows the Microsoft Office model with the `Logon` method call. The POOM object won't operate properly without calling `Logon`.

The `PocketOutlook.Folder` Object

The `PocketOutlook.Folder` object is basically an object to access, sort, filter, and modify a collection of other POOM objects. The `Folder` object is derived by calling the `GetDefaultFolder` method of `PocketOutlook.Application`. `GetDefaultFolder` takes a single parameter of type `PocketOutlook.olDefaultFolders`. This enumeration allows access to the following folders:

Object Type	*Enumeration*	*Description*
Calendar (Appointments)	`olFolderCalendar`	All Appointments from the Calendar application.
Cities	`olFolderCities`	Collection of cities from both the World Clock application and custom-defined cities.
Contacts	`olFolderContacts`	All Contacts from the Contacts application.
Infrared	`olFolderInfrared`	"Parking lot" for any item to be beamed or received via infrared.
Tasks	`olFolderTasks`	All Tasks from the Tasks application.

A `PocketOutlook.Folder` object is derived as the return value of the `GetDefaultFolder` method. Let's look at how you can create a folder containing all the Contact objects (records):

```
Dim objFolderContacts As PocketOutlook.Folder
 ' get all contacts
 Set objFolderContacts = gobjPoom.GetDefaultFolder(olFolderContacts)
```

The first statement here declares a local variable, `objFolderContacts`, to hold the reference to the folder. The `PocketOutlook.Application`, `gobjPoom`, declared globally as discussed previously, is used to derive the Contacts folder into the variable `objFolderContacts`. This reference now allows access to all contact records within the object store.

Each ContactItem, AppointmentItem, and TaskItem object has a Category property. This property contains a comma-delimited list of the categories assigned to the item.

The PocketOutlook.Items Collection

The PocketOutlook.Items collection belongs to the PocketOutlook.Folder object. This collection allows access to each item within the folder. It is this collection that allows enumeration of the object to a derived reference for PocketOutlook.ContactItem, PocketOutlook.TaskItem, or PocketOutlook.AppointmentItem.

Enumerating the Items

Once a PocketOutlook.Folder is derived, PocketOutlook provides the Items collection of objects, which individually correlate to a PIM record. Depending on which folder was derived, the folder allows an enumeration through the Items collection to individually inspect and manipulate the object (PIM record), as shown in Listing 6.1. These objects provide a singular reference to a record existing in the native PIM object store.

Each object provides properties that correspond to a field within the PIM record. Some data is represented in a collection, such as the Recipient collection on an Appointment object.

LISTING 6.1 Enumerating Folder Objects

```
Dim objFolderContacts As PocketOutlook.Folder
Dim objContact As PocketOutlook.ContactItem

' create the application object
Set gobjPOOM = CreateObject("PocketOutlook.Application")

' logon - can not use until Logon is called...
gobjPOOM.Logon

' get all contacts
Set objFolderContacts = gobjPOOM.GetDefaultFolder(olFolderContacts)

For Each objContact In objFolderContacts.Items
    MsgBox objContact.FileAs
Next
```

In Listing 6.1, the PocketOutlook.Application is created, Logon is called, and then a Folder object (of type ContactItem) is derived from GetDefaultFolder. Each Contact object within the Items collection is then enumerated, and the FileAs property is then displayed via a message box.

Sorting Items with the `Items.Sort` Method

The `Items` collection can be sorted via the `Items.Sort` method. The `Sort` method has two parameters:

- `pwszProperty` is a string value for the field (or property) to sort on. The actual property name needs to be enclosed in brackets (for example, `[LastName]`, `[Subject]`, or `[Importance]`). The sort can be accomplished on any property except `Categories`, `Recipients`, and `ReminderTime`.
- `fDescending` is an optional Boolean, as to whether to sort descending, where `True` means to sort descending.

When the `Sort` method is called, the `Items` will present themselves in the requested sort order. It's important to remember a reference to the `Items` must be made first and then the `Sort` method called on it; if `Sort` is called directly from the `Items` collection on the folder, the sort will revert to the default sort order. Listing 6.2 shows an example of this approach.

LISTING 6.2 Sorting Items

```
Dim objFolderContacts As PocketOutlook.Folder
Dim objContact As PocketOutlook.ContactItem
Dim objItems As PocketOutlook.Items

' create the application object
Set gobjPOOM = CreateObject("PocketOutlook.Application")

' logon - can not use until Logon is called...
gobjPOOM.Logon

' get all contacts
Set objFolderContacts = gobjPOOM.GetDefaultFolder(olFolderContacts)

' get the items
Set objItems = objFolderContacts.Items

' Sort By The FirstName property
objItems.Sort "[FirstName]", False

' enumerate thru
For Each objContact In objItems
    MsgBox objContact.FirstName
Next
```

In Listing 6.2, a `PocketOutlook.Items` object is declared as `objItems`. This `objItems` holds the `Items` collection from the folder. This object reference is then populated with the collection by setting it equal to the `PocketOutlook.Items` collection, `objFolderContacts.Items`. Then it's sorted by the `FirstName` property in ascending order. Finally, it's enumerated through and each `FirstName` value is displayed in a message box.

Filtering Items with the `Items.Restrict` Method

You can filter the `Items` collection to meet certain criteria, such as a `ContactItem.LastName` starting with a certain letter, an `AppointmentItem.Start` (datetime) to be within a date range, or a `Task.Importance` (priority) being one of the enumerated values. The `Restrict` method on the `Items` collection will actually return another `Items` collection (subset) that has been filter by the supplied criteria.

The `Restrict` method takes one string parameter (`pwszRestriction`) as the criteria by which to filter. As with the `Sort` method, when specifying the property, you need to enclose it in brackets (for example, `[Start]`, `[LastName]`, or `[Importance]`). The available operators are =, <, >, >=, <=, and <>. You also can use the keywords `AND` and `OR` for multiple criteria. The criteria for filtering can be any of the properties for the object except `Recipients` and `ReminderTime`.

When specifying the actual criteria, there are some formatting requirements:

- For String Properties, enclose the criteria in quotes: `'[LastName] > "Sm"'`
- For Date Properties, leave the criteria in date format—`'[Start]>=8/1/2001'`—without the eVB date symbol `#`.
- For Enumeration Properties (for example, `TaskItem.Importance`, `Appointment.BusyStatus`), special attention needs to be given to enumeration properties for filtering. Rather than include the enumeration directly or the enumeration as string, the actual integer value needs to be specified. `'[Importance] = olImportanceHigh'` should actually be specified as `'[Importance] = 2'`.

The `Restrict` method won't return items that meet the criteria simply because the item has no value for the property. For example, a criteria of `'[LastName] <> "Smith"'` won't return `ContactItems` that have a blank (essentially `NULL`) `LastName` value. Listing 6.3 shows an example of filtering contacts with the `Restrict` method and the `LastName` value of "Smith".

LISTING 6.3 Filtering Items Using Restrict

```
Dim objFolderContacts As PocketOutlook.Folder
Dim objContact As PocketOutlook.ContactItem
Dim objItems As PocketOutlook.Items
Dim objRestrictedItems As PocketOutlook.Items

' create the application object
Set gobjPOOM = CreateObject("PocketOutlook.Application")

' logon - can not use until Logon is called...
```

LISTING 6.3 Continued

```
gobjPOOM.Logon

' get all contacts
Set objFolderContacts = gobjPOOM.GetDefaultFolder(olFolderContacts)

' get the items
Set objItems = objFolderContacts.Items

' Find all Contacts with LastName of "Smith"
Set objRestrictedItems = objItems.Restrict("[LastName] = ""Smith""")

' enumerate thru
For Each objContact In objRestrictedItems
    MsgBox objContact.FirstName
Next
```

Listing 6.3 follows the same structure as previous examples. The new functionality added is the second `PocketOutlook.Items` object reference, `objRestrictedItems`. The object `objRestrictedItems` is used as a secondary `Items` collection to receive the filtered subset of the contact `Items` collection and is populated by the `Restrict` method on the nonfiltered `Items` collection `objItems`. The criteria specifies to return a collection of Items that have the value "Smith" for the `LastName` collection. Then, the filtered `Items`, `objRestrictedItems`, is enumerated showing the values for the `FirstName` property.

Using the `Items.Find` and `Items.FindNext` Methods

The `Find` and `FindNext` methods work under the same principle as the `Restrict` method. The main difference between `Find`/`FindNext` is these methods return a singular item (`ContactItem`, `TaskItem`, or `AppointmentItem`) instead of an `Items` collection. The restriction clause syntax is the same as `Restrict`, and is passed to the `Find` method. The `Find` method returns an object for the first PIM record meeting the criteria. If no item meets the criteria, the object is set to `Nothing`. If the criteria have been met, each subsequent call to `FindNext` returns the next object meeting the criteria, until the objects meeting the criteria are exhausted and then `Nothing` is returned.

Listing 6.4 will attempt to find contacts with a CompanyName of "Rubicon Technologies" and enumerate through them.

LISTING 6.4 `Find and FindNext`

```
Dim objFolderContacts As PocketOutlook.Folder
Dim objContact As PocketOutlook.ContactItem
Dim objItems As PocketOutlook.Items
```

LISTING 6.4 Continued

```
' create the application object
Set gobjPOOM = CreateObject("PocketOutlook.Application")

' logon - can not use until Logon is called...
gobjPOOM.Logon

' get all contacts
Set objFolderContacts = gobjPOOM.GetDefaultFolder(olFolderContacts)

' get the items
Set objItems = objFolderContacts.Items

' Find all Contacts with Company Name of "Rubicon Technologies"
Set objContact = objItems.Find("[CompanyName] = ""Rubicon Technologies""")

' enumerate thru
Do While Not objContact Is Nothing
    MsgBox objContact.LastName & "," objContact.FirstName
    Set objContact = objItems.FindNext
Loop
```

Again, Listing 6.4 follows the same basic structure as previous examples. The new functionality added is that rather than enumerate directly through all `Items` or a filtered collection of `Items`, retrieval of the first object is attempted using the `Find` method. The criteria used in this example attempts to locate `ContactItem` objects that have the value `Rubicon Technologies` for their Company Name property. If a `ContactItem` meets that criteria, it's returned as a object reference to the variable `objContact`. If that reference holds a valid `ContactItem`, the `Do While` loop is entered and the contact's `LastName` and `FirstName` values are displayed in a message box.

After display, a subsequent call to `FindNext` is made. `FindNext` will continue to look for objects that meet the criteria. An object is returned from the `FindNext` method until the objects meeting the criteria are exhausted. When exhausted, the object reference `objContact` will be `Nothing` and the `Do While` loop will exit because of the test condition of `Not objContact Is Nothing`.

The PIM Objects: `ContactItem`, `TaskItem`, and `AppointmentItem`

Any of the PIM objects behave in similar ways. Each is representative of a single PIM record and has properties that correlate to a particular field in that record.

All PIM objects are derived from the `Items` collection of the `PocketOutlook.Folder` object—and each is manipulated, displayed, saved, and deleted in similar ways. Several polymorphic methods and properties are associated with these objects. These methods include, but aren't limited to, `Copy`, `Delete`, `Save`, and `Display`. A common property to each object is `OID`, the object's unique ID. Listing 6.5 shows an example of the `Display` method.

LISTING 6.5 Displaying an Object

```
Dim objFolderContacts As PocketOutlook.Folder
Dim objContact As PocketOutlook.ContactItem

' create the application object
Set gobjPOOM = CreateObject("PocketOutlook.Application")

' logon - can not use until Logon is called...
gobjPOOM.Logon

' get all contacts
Set objFolderContacts = gobjPOOM.GetDefaultFolder(olFolderContacts)

' get the first contact
Set objContact = objFolderContacts.Items(1)

' display it
objContact.Display
```

In Listing 6.5, the same initialization is completed. Then a singular `Contact` object is retrieved via the `Items` collection using a hard-coded index value. This contact is then displayed using the `Display` method.

The `PocketOutlook.ContactItem` Object

Each `ContactItem` is an object representation of a Contact record from the native Contact PIM application. It exposes several properties and methods. Each field in the native application is exposed as a property. Commonly used properties are `FirstName`, `LastName`, `CompanyName`, `BusinessTelephone`, and `Email1Address`.

The `PocketOutlook.AppointmentItem` Object

The `AppointmentItem` object is an object representation of an Appointment (Calendar) record from the native Calendar PIM application. Each field is exposed as a property. Commonly used properties are `Subject`, `Start`, and `Location`. A more unique method on the `Appointment` object is `GetRecurrencePattern`, which derives a `PocketOutlook.RecurrencePattern` object. This object is used to inspect and manipulate the recurrence of the appointment.

The `PocketOutlook.TaskItem` Object

A `TaskItem` object represents a Task record from the native Task PIM application. Again, each field in the native application is exposed as a property. Commonly used properties are `Subject`, `DueDate`, `DateCompleted`, and `StartDate`. The `Importance` property refers to an enumeration type of `PocketOutlook.olImportance`, which contains values for `Low`, `Medium`, and `High` priorities.

The `OID` Property

As mentioned earlier, each of the PIM record objects, `ContactItem`, `AppointmentItem`, and `TaskItem` have the `OID` property, a unique ID for the a particular item. It's even unique across item types. In other words, a value for a `ContactItem` can't be duplicated as an OID value for a `TaskItem` or `AppointmentItem`.

Persisting the `OID` property in another datastore isn't recommended because the value can change for an item if a backup and restore is performed on the device. This does present a problem to extend the PIM object model with a secondary datastore such as Pocket Access or SQL Server CE.

Although it's not within the scope of this chapter, it would be feasible to create an XML node within the item's `Body` property and store a second ID within the XML that your application controls. This could be a possible solution with the exception of users manipulating or deleting this information.

The `Category` Property

The `ContactItem`, `AppointmentItem`, and `TaskItem` objects all have a `Category` property. This property contains a comma-delimited list of the categories assigned to the item.

Creating the Pocket PIM Sample Application

The sample application for this chapter is Pocket PIM, a version of the native PIM applications with a few twists. Although it's not intended to replace the powerful PIM applications, it presents some interesting features.

This sample application is intended to give a detailed understanding of the more commonly used functionality of POOM. Its design is also intended to give a general understanding of the style to work with POOM.

Pocket PIM features a Contact Grid (see Figure 6.2), an Appointment Grid (see Figure 6.3), and a Task Grid (see Figure 6.4). Each grid can be sorted by any of the displayed fields.

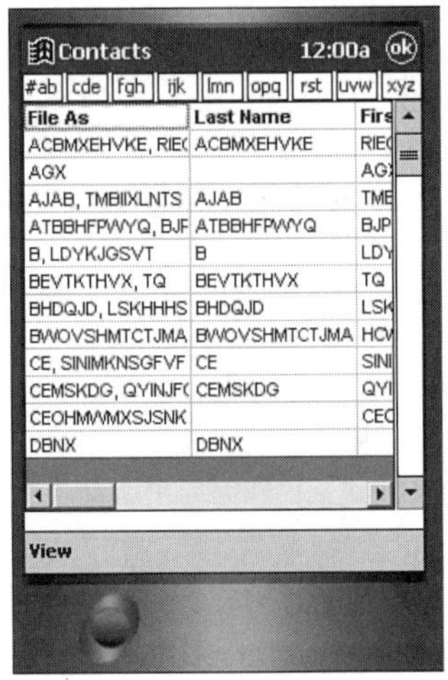

FIGURE 6.2

The Contacts Form. Notice that the vertical scroll is different from the typical vertical grid scrollbar.

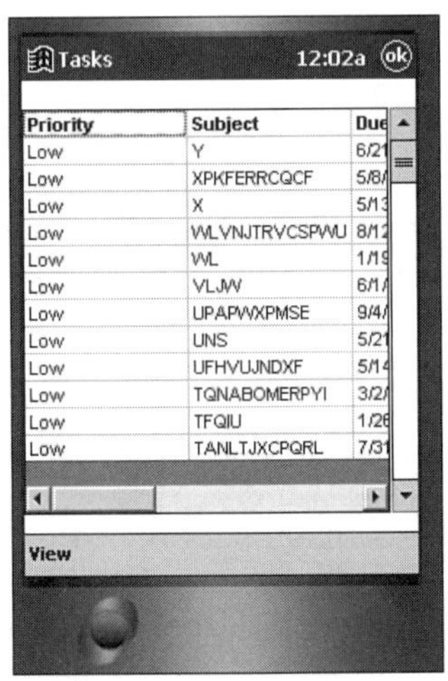

FIGURE 6.3

The Tasks Form can be sorted by any of the displayed fields.

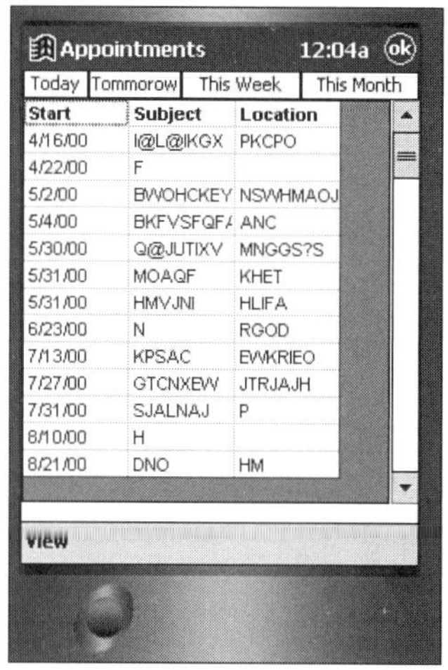

FIGURE 6.4

The Appointments Form provides a completely different view of appointments from the native PIM.

Other Technologies Demonstrated

Although not the focus of the chapter, pay attention to two other technologies or architectural styles used in the Pocket PIM application.

First, the manual paging technique used for the grids in the application. When building Pocket PIM, my device had more than 1,000 contacts present. Populating a grid with 1,000 records can be a poorly performing process. The power of the Pocket PC operating system is impressive, especially with a StrongArm processor, but there are limitations and the controls can become sluggish when consuming large amounts of data.

The grids are populated by using a manual-paging method that populates only the rows visible to users. The vertical scrollbar isn't visible, but a vertical scrollbar control is added in its place.

The second technology used is the ability to distinguish between a tap on the grid and whether the stylus is being held down to present a pop-up menu. This is accomplished by using the `AsyncKeyState` API call.

Building the Application

When first starting the project, be sure to set the reference to the PIMSTORE.DLL as instructed earlier. Let's start by creating the module modGlobal.bas.

modGlobal: Const, Global Objects, and Declares

Add a module named modGlobal to the project. The entire module is shown in Listing 6.6, but the most important aspect is to get the `gobjPoom` declared. You can create it all now, load it from the book resource files, or create it as you go.

LISTING 6.6 modGlobal.bas: Public Variables, Consts, and API Declarations

```
Option Explicit

Public gobjPoom As PocketOutlook.Application

' number of rows in the contact grid
Public Const CONTACT_CONTACTGRID_ROWS = 13

' used as the captions for the contact grid's "header" row
Public Const CONTACTGRID_HEADER_FILEAS = "File As"
Public Const CONTACTGRID_HEADER_LASTNAME = "Last Name"
Public Const CONTACTGRID_HEADER_FIRSTNAME = "First Name"
Public Const CONTACTGRID_HEADER_COMPANYNAME = "Company Name"
Public Const CONTACTGRID_HEADER_BUSINESSTELEPHONE = "Work Phone"

' used as the sort order for the contact's sort orders
Public Const CONTACTGRID_HEADER_SORT_FILEAS = "FileAs"
Public Const CONTACTGRID_HEADER_SORT_LASTNAME = "LastName"
Public Const CONTACTGRID_HEADER_SORT_FIRSTNAME = "FirstName"
Public Const CONTACTGRID_HEADER_SORT_COMPANYNAME = "CompanyName"
Public Const CONTACTGRID_HEADER_SORT_BUSINESSTELEPHONE _
            = "BusinessTelephoneNumber"

' defines the column numbers for the contact grid
Public Const CONTACTGRID_COL_FILEAS = 0
Public Const CONTACTGRID_COL_LASTNAME = 1
Public Const CONTACTGRID_COL_FIRSTNAME = 2
Public Const CONTACTGRID_COL_COMPANYNAME = 3
Public Const CONTACTGRID_COL_BUSINESSTELEPHONE = 4

' the index of the menubars for the contact grid's popup menu
Public Const CONTACTPOPUP_MENU_INDEX_NEW = 1
Public Const CONTACTPOPUP_MENU_INDEX_DELETE = 2
Public Const CONTACTPOPUP_MENU_INDEX_COPY = 3
Public Const CONTACTPOPUP_MENU_INDEX_SHOWAPPTS = 4
Public Const CONTACTPOPUP_MENU_INDEX_SAMECOMP = 5
Public Const CONTACTPOPUP_MENU_INDEX_BEAM = 6
```

LISTING 6.6 Continued

```
' captions for the menubars for the contact grid's popup menu
Public Const CONTACTPOPUP_MENU_CAPTION_NEW = "New Contact"
Public Const CONTACTPOPUP_MENU_CAPTION_DELETE = "Delete Contact"
Public Const CONTACTPOPUP_MENU_CAPTION_COPY = "Copy Contact"
Public Const CONTACTPOPUP_MENU_CAPTION_SHOWAPPTS = "Appointments for Contact"
Public Const CONTACTPOPUP_MENU_CAPTION_SAMECOMP = "New Contact-Same Company"
Public Const CONTACTPOPUP_MENU_CAPTION_BEAM = "Beam Contact"

' key for the menubars
Public Const MENU_VIEW_CONTACTS = "CONTACTS"
Public Const MENU VIEW TASKS = "TASKS"
Public Const MENU_VIEW_APPOINTMENT = "APPOINTMENT"

' key for the menubars
Public Const MENU_VIEW_CAPTION = "View"
Public Const MENU_VIEW_CONTACTS_CAPTION = "Contacts"
Public Const MENU_VIEW_TASKS_CAPTION = "Tasks"
Public Const MENU_VIEW_APPOINTMENT_CAPTION = "Appointments"

' used as the captions for the appt grid
Public Const APPTGRID_HEADER_START = "Start"
Public Const APPTGRID_HEADER_SUBJECT = "Subject"
Public Const APPTGRID_HEADER_LOCATION = "Location"

Public Const APPTGRID_HEADER_SORT_START = "Start"
Public Const APPTGRID_HEADER_SORT_SUBJECT = "Subject"
Public Const APPTGRID_HEADER_SORT_LOCATION = "Location"

Public Const APPTGRID_COL_START = 0
Public Const APPTGRID_COL_SUBJECT = 1
Public Const APPTGRID_COL_LOCATION = 2

Public Const APPT_APPTGRID_ROWS = 14

Public Const APPTPOPUP_MENU_INDEX_NEW = 1
Public Const APPTPOPUP_MENU_INDEX_DELETE = 2
Public Const APPTPOPUP_MENU_INDEX_COPY = 3

Public Const APPTPOPUP_MENU_CAPTION_NEW = "New Appt"
Public Const APPTPOPUP_MENU_CAPTION_DELETE = "Delete Appt"
Public Const APPTPOPUP_MENU_CAPTION_COPY = "Copy Appt"
```

LISTING 6.6 Continued

```
Public Const TASKGRID_COL_PRIORITY = 0
Public Const TASKGRID_COL_SUBJECT = 1
Public Const TASKGRID_COL_DUEDATE = 2

Public Const TASKGRID_HEADER_PRIORITY = "Priority"
Public Const TASKGRID_HEADER_SUBJECT = "Subject"
Public Const TASKGRID_HEADER_DUEDATE = "Due Date"

Public Const TASKGRID_HEADER_SORT_PRIORITY = "Importance"
Public Const TASKGRID_HEADER_SORT_SUBJECT = "Subject"
Public Const TASKGRID_HEADER_SORT_DUEDATE = "DueDate"

Public Const TASKPOPUP_MENU_INDEX_NEW = 1
Public Const TASKPOPUP_MENU_INDEX_DELETE = 2
Public Const TASKPOPUP_MENU_INDEX_COPY = 3
Public Const TASKPOPUP_MENU_INDEX_BEAM = 4

Public Const TASKPOPUP_MENU_CAPTION_NEW = "New Task"
Public Const TASKPOPUP_MENU_CAPTION_DELETE = "Delete Task"
Public Const TASKPOPUP_MENU_CAPTION_COPY = "Copy Task"
Public Const TASKPOPUP_MENU_CAPTION_BEAM = "Beam Task"

Public Const TASK_TASKGRID_ROWS = 13

' used to tell if the stylus is down...
Public Const ASYNCKEYSTATE_LEFTMOUSE_KEY = 1
Public Const MOUSEDOWN_RIGHTCLICK_TIMING = 0.5

Public Declare Function CreatePopupMenu Lib "Coredll" () As Long
Public Declare Function DestroyMenu Lib "Coredll" _
       (ByVal hMenu As Long) As Long

Public Declare Function AppendMenu Lib "Coredll" Alias "AppendMenuW" _
       (ByVal hMenu As Long, ByVal wFlags As Long, _
        ByVal wIDNewItem As Long, ByVal lpNewItem As String) As Long

Public Declare Function TrackPopupMenuEx Lib "Coredll" _
       (ByVal hMenu As Long, ByVal un As Long, ByVal n1 As Long, _
        ByVal n2 As Long, ByVal hWnd As Long, lpTPMParams As Long) As Long

Public Declare Function GetAsyncKeyState Lib "Coredll" _
       (ByVal vKey As Long) As Integer

Public Const MF_ENABLED = &H0&
Public Const MF_STRING = &H0&
Public Const TPM_TOPALIGN = &H0&
```

LISTING 6.6 Continued

```
Public Const TPM_LEFTALIGN = &H0&
Public Const TPM_RETURNCMD = &H100&

Public Const MF_GRAYED = &H1&
Public Const MF_CHECKED = &H8&
Public Const MF_UNCHECKED = &H0&
Public Const MF_SEPARATOR = &H800&
```

Contacts Form

Add a form to the project and name it `frmContact`. Add a grid and a vertical scrollbar. Name the grid `grdContact` and leave the scrollbar its default name of `Vscroll1`.

Add nine command buttons, sizing and placing similar to Figure 6.2. Give them captions of `#ab`, `cde`, `fgh`, `ijk`, `lmn`, `opq`, `rst`, `uvw`, and `xyz`. Name them `cmdAB`, `cmdCDE`, `cmdFGH`, `cmdIJK`, `cmdLMN`, `cmdOPQ`, `cmdRST`, `cmdUVW`, and `cmdXYZ`, respectively. To get the buttons white, you need to change the `Style` property to `vbButtonGraphical` and the `BackColor` to `WindowBackground`.

These buttons are designed to allow users to jump to a particular contact within the sort order. For example, if the current sort order is `LastName`, tapping the FGH button will locate the grid to the first contact that has a `LastName` that begins with F.

Contact Form Level Variables

There are two form level variables for the Contact form:

```
Dim gContactRowData(13) As Long
Dim gstrContactSortOrder As String
```

The array, dimensioned with 13 elements, stores the OID for each contact displayed in the grid. The current sort order for the grid is stored in the string variable `gstrContactSortOrder`.

The `Form_Load` Event

The first method to explore is the `Form_Load` event (see Listing 6.7). The Contact form should be the first form loaded, so in it, we'll create the POOM object and `Logon()` to it. For development purposes, it will check if there are any contacts and if not, prompt you to create some random ones. The rest of the code does other initialization.

LISTING 6.7 The `Form_Load` Event

```
Private Sub Form_Load()
    Dim objContacts As PocketOutlook.Items
    Dim intCol As Integer
```

LISTING 6.7 Continued

```
' create the PocketOutlook application once and only once...
Set gobjPoom = CreateObject("PocketOutlook.Application")

' logon - can not use until Logon is called...
gobjPoom.Logon

' get all contacts
Set objContacts = gobjPoom.GetDefaultFolder(olFolderContacts).Items

' check to see if there are any contacts
If objContacts.Count = 0 Then
    ' if no contacts, prompt user (developer) to create some
    If MsgBox("There are no contacts, would you like to add some?", _
              vbYesNo, "Create Contacts") = vbYes Then
                ' create dummy contacts
                MakeContacts
    End If
End If

' set the default sort order to the FileAs column
gstrContactSortOrder = CONTACTGRID_HEADER_SORT_FILEAS

' one row in grid - for the header
Me.grdContacts.Rows = 1
' five columns in grid
Me.grdContacts.Cols = 5

' set the column widths
Me.grdContacts.ColWidth(CONTACTGRID_COL_FILEAS) = 1500
Me.grdContacts.ColWidth(CONTACTGRID_COL_LASTNAME) = 1500
Me.grdContacts.ColWidth(CONTACTGRID_COL_FIRSTNAME) = 1500
Me.grdContacts.ColWidth(CONTACTGRID_COL_COMPANYNAME) = 1500
Me.grdContacts.ColWidth(CONTACTGRID_COL_BUSINESSTELEPHONE) = 1500

' set the header row captions
Me.grdContacts.TextMatrix(0, CONTACTGRID_COL_FILEAS) = _
    CONTACTGRID_HEADER_FILEAS

Me.grdContacts.TextMatrix(0, CONTACTGRID_COL_LASTNAME) = _
    CONTACTGRID_HEADER_LASTNAME

Me.grdContacts.TextMatrix(0, CONTACTGRID_COL_FIRSTNAME) = _
    CONTACTGRID_HEADER_FIRSTNAME

Me.grdContacts.TextMatrix(0, CONTACTGRID_COL_COMPANYNAME) = _
    CONTACTGRID_HEADER_COMPANYNAME
```

LISTING 6.7 Continued

```
    Me.grdContacts.TextMatrix(0, CONTACTGRID_COL_BUSINESSTELEPHONE) = _
        CONTACTGRID_HEADER_BUSINESSTELEPHONE

    ' set the row to 0 - so we can manipulate the header cells
    Me.grdContacts.Row = 0

    ' set the fonts for the header to bold
    For intCol = 0 To Me.grdContacts.Cols - 1
        Me.grdContacts.Col = intCol
        Me.grdContacts.CellFontBold = True
    Next

' set the column back to 0
    Me.grdContacts.Col = 0

End Sub
```

Let's dissect this method and look at different segments of it.

Initializing POOM

In the following code snippet, the variable `objContacts` is declared as `PocketOutlook.Items` to retain a reference to the Contacts folder items. The `POOM` object is created through the `CreateObject` statement; remember that the declaration for it, `gobjPOOM`, was declared as `Public` in the modGlobal module file. After the POOM object is created, it's initialized by called the `Logon` method.

```
Dim objContacts As PocketOutlook.Items
Dim intCol As Integer

' create the PocketOutlook application once and only once....
Set gobjPoom = CreateObject("PocketOutlook.Application")

' logon - can not use until Logon is called...
gobjPoom.Logon
```

Checking for Contacts and Creating Samples

Rather than just get a reference to a `PocketOutlook.Folder`, a reference is taken directly to the `Items` collection from the `Folder` object, as shown in the following code. This reference, set to `objContacts`, was declared in the preceding snippet as `PocketOutlook.Items`. The `Count` property is tested for zero and if so, users are prompted to create some contacts. If users answer Yes, the method `MakeContacts` is called to create the contacts. (We'll explore `MakeContacts` after discussion the `Form_Load` event.)

NOTE

If your Pocket PC creates a default contact or appointment, you may have to change the check of `Count = 0`. The HP Jornada will create a contact and a task after a hard reset.

```
' get all contacts
Set objContacts = gobjPoom.GetDefaultFolder(olFolderContacts).Items

' check to see if there are any contacts
If objContacts.Count = 0 Then
    ' if no contacts, prompt user (developer) to create some
    If MsgBox("There are no contacts, would you like to add some?", _
              vbYesNo, "Create Contacts") = vbYes Then
                  ' create dummy contacts
                  MakeContacts
    End If
End If
```

Setting the Sort Order

The default current sort order is stored to the variable `gstrContactSortOrder`. This value comes again from a Const from the modGlobal module:

```
' set the default sort order to the FileAs column
gstrContactSortOrder = CONTACTGRID_HEADER_SORT_FILEAS
```

Setting Up the Grid

Next, the grid is set up to have the correct number of rows and columns:

```
' one row in grid - for the header
Me.grdContacts.Rows = 1
' five columns in grid
Me.grdContacts.Cols = 5
```

Then the column widths are set:

```
' set the column widths
Me.grdContacts.ColWidth(CONTACTGRID_COL_FILEAS) = 1500
Me.grdContacts.ColWidth(CONTACTGRID_COL_LASTNAME) = 1500
Me.grdContacts.ColWidth(CONTACTGRID_COL_FIRSTNAME) = 1500
Me.grdContacts.ColWidth(CONTACTGRID_COL_COMPANYNAME) = 1500
Me.grdContacts.ColWidth(CONTACTGRID_COL_BUSINESSTELEPHONE) = 1500
```

The “virtual” headers are created:

```
' set the header row captions
Me.grdContacts.TextMatrix(0, CONTACTGRID_COL_FILEAS) = _
```

```
    CONTACTGRID_HEADER_FILEAS

Me.grdContacts.TextMatrix(0, CONTACTGRID_COL_LASTNAME) = _
    CONTACTGRID_HEADER_LASTNAME

Me.grdContacts.TextMatrix(0, CONTACTGRID_COL_FIRSTNAME) = _
    CONTACTGRID_HEADER_FIRSTNAME

Me.grdContacts.TextMatrix(0, CONTACTGRID_COL_COMPANYNAME) = _
    CONTACTGRID_HEADER_COMPANYNAME

Me.grdContacts.TextMatrix(0, CONTACTGRID_COL_BUSINESSTELEPHONE) = _
    CONTACTGRID_HEADER_BUSINESSTELEPHONE
```

After the headers are created, they are made bold by moving to the first row (`Row = 0`) and then cycling through the columns and setting the font to bold:

```
' set the row to 0 - so we can manipulate the header cells
Me.grdContacts.Row = 0

' set the fonts for the header to bold

    ' set the fonts for the header to bold
    For intCol = 0 To Me.grdContacts.Cols - 1
        Me.grdContacts.Col = intCol
        Me.grdContacts.CellFontBold = True
    Next

    ' set the column back to 0
    Me.grdContacts.Col = 0
```

Loading the Menu

Finally, the menu is populated:

```
' set up the menu
LoadMenu
```

Although the menu code is present in the code resources, see Chapter 4, "Working with Menu Controls for Pocket PC," for a description of menu functionality. If you don't want to implement the menu now, omit this code line or comment it out.

The `MakeContacts` Routine

The `MakeContacts` routine (see Listing 6.8) is designed to allow you to have a group of contacts that can be manipulated without affecting your actual contacts. If you plan to use `MakeContacts`, be sure that your device has been hard-reset and is configured in ActiveSync to not sync Contacts.

LISTING 6.8 Making Sample Contacts

```
Sub MakeContacts()

    Dim objContact As PocketOutlook.ContactItem
    Dim objItemsContact As PocketOutlook.Items
    Dim intContact As Integer
    Dim intProperty As Integer
    Dim intChar As Integer
    Dim strLetter As String

    ' get the contact folder
    Set objItemsContact = gobjPoom.GetDefaultFolder(olFolderContacts).Items

    ' seed the RND() function
    Rnd Timer()

    ' add 100 contacts
    For intContact = 1 To 100

        ' get the new contact
        Set objContact = objItemsContact.Add()

        ' set 3 different properties
        For intProperty = 1 To 3

            ' make a string up to 15 chars in length
            For intChar = 1 To Int(Rnd() * 15)

                ' make the letter
                strLetter = Chr((Rnd() * 26) + 63)

                ' is it alpha?
                If strLetter >= "A" And strLetter <= "Z" Then

                    ' which property are we setting
                    Select Case intProperty

                        Case 1

                            ' set the FirstName property
                            objContact.FirstName =
                                  ➥objContact.FirstName & strLetter

                        Case 2
```

LISTING 6.8 Continued

```
                            ' set the LastName property
                            objContact.LastName =
                                   ➥objContact.LastName & strLetter

                        Case 3

                            ' set the CompanyName property
                            objContact.CompanyName =
                                   ➥objContact.CompanyName & strLetter

                    End Select
                End If
            Next
        Next

        ' we need to ensure there is at least something
        ' in one of the Properties
        If Len(objContact.FirstName & objContact.LastName) = 0 Then
            objContact.FirstName = "Bob"
        End If

        ' set the email property
        objContact.Email1Address = objContact.FirstName & "@rtmobile.com"
        ' save the contact
        objContact.Save
    Next

End Sub
```

Let's dissect `MakeContacts`, covering the new ground.

First, a reference to the `ContactFolder.Items` is retrieved:

```
' get the contact folder
Set objItemsContact = gobjPoom.GetDefaultFolder(olFolderContacts).Items
```

The following snippet shows an abbreviated version of the loop that creates 100 contacts. An object reference to a newly created `ContactItem` is retrieved by calling the `Add` method from the `Items` collection. Remember that the `Items` collection is located on the Folder object.

```
' add 100 contacts
For intContact = 1 To 100
```

```
    ' get the new contact
    Set objContact = objItemsContact.Add()

...

    ' save the contact
    objContact.Save

Next
```

Next, three properties are set from a randomly created string: `FirstName`, `LastName`, and `CompanyName`.

```
Case 1

    ' set the FirstName property
    objContact.FirstName = objContact.FirstName & strLetter

Case 2

    ' set the LastName property
    objContact.LastName = objContact.LastName & strLetter

Case 3

    ' set the CompanyName property
    objContact.CompanyName = objContact.CompanyName & strLetter
```

Something important to remember before attempting to save a `ContactItem` is that one of the following properties must have a value: `FirstName`, `LastName`, `FileAs`, or `CompanyName`. A check is performed in the following code to ensure that the contact has a `FirstName` or `LastName` value set:

```
' we need to ensure there is at least something
' in one of the Properties
If Len(objContact.FirstName & objContact.LastName) = 0 Then
    objContact.FirstName = "Bob"
End If

' set the email property
objContact.Email1Address = objContact.FirstName & "@rtmobile.com"
```

After all is well, the Contact is saved via the `Save` method:

```
' save the contact
objContact.Save
```

The `Form_Activate` Event

The `Form_Activate` event is used simply to refresh the contact grid. The method to refresh the grid is `RefreshContacts`:

```
Private Sub Form_Activate()
    ' refresh ALL contacts
    RefreshContacts ""
End Sub
```

The `RefreshContacts` function (see Listing 6.9) is the Contact form's meat-and-potatoes. It's responsible for finding the correct contacts, sorting, and displaying them.

LISTING 6.9 The `RefreshContacts` Function

```
Public Function RefreshContacts(ByVal strSeek As String)

    Dim objContact As PocketOutlook.ContactItem
    Dim objItemsContact As PocketOutlook.Items
    Dim intContact As Integer
    Dim lngThisContact As Long
    Dim strRestrict As String
    Dim lngOIDFirstFound As Long
    Dim lngFirstContactDisplayed As Long

    On Error Resume Next

    ' get all contacts
    Set objItemsContact = gobjPoom.GetDefaultFolder(olFolderContacts).Items

    ' sort by the current sort order - always ascending
    objItemsContact.Sort "[" & gstrContactSortOrder & "]", False

    ' set the max for the scrollbar to be the top contact
    ' of the last "page" of contacts    Me.VScroll1.Max = objItemsContact.Count
- Me.VScroll1.LargeChange + 1
    ' if we have a seek parameter try to find
    ' the first contact meeting that parameter
    If Len(strSeek) > 0 Then
        ' setup the restrict clause to be equal to or greater than
        ' the seek parameter
        ' this will find the next contact that meets the seek
        ' parameter if one does not exactly meet it
        strRestrict = "[" & gstrContactSortOrder & _
                      "]>=""" & "" & strSeek & """"
```

LISTING 6.9 Continued

```
        ' apply the seek
        Set objContact = objItemsContact.Find(strRestrict)

        ' if we found a contact meeting the seek
        ' let's store the OID value (primary key - Outlook ID)
        If Not objContact Is Nothing Then
            ' grab the OID
            lngOIDFirstFound = objContact.oid

            ' start at the 1st contact
            lngThisContact = 1

            ' cycle thru the contacts to find the contact's
            ' place in the sort order

            ' while we still looking at a valid contact
            Do While lngThisContact <= objItemsContact.Count
                ' get the contact
                Set objContact = objItemsContact.Item(lngThisContact)

                ' if it's our contact, let's get out
                ' lngThisContact will be the correct index of
                ' the contact found
                If objContact.oid = lngOIDFirstFound Then
                    Exit Do
                End If

                lngThisContact = lngThisContact + 1
            Loop
        End If
    Else
        ' if we don't have a seek value, use the scroll bar
' current value
        lngThisContact = Me.VScroll1.Value
    End If

    ' set the rows
    Me.grdContacts.Rows = CONTACT_CONTACTGRID_ROWS

    ' save the index of the first contact displayed
    ' this is used to update the scroll bar with the correct
    ' position after we're done
    lngFirstContactDisplayed = lngThisContact
```

LISTING 6.9 Continued

```
    ' we don't clear the grid here, but just write over top of it
    ' this prevents less flickering and better performance
    ' if we don't use all the available rows, we just truncate them at the
end....

    ' we're going to cycle through the contacts
    ' and write them to the grid
    For intContact = 0 To CONTACT_CONTACTGRID_ROWS - 1

        ' if we've gone past the last contact
        ' let's get out
        ' this happens when you start displaying contacts
        ' near the bottom - or when the first contact
        ' is closer to the bottom than the number of rows in the grid
        If lngThisContact > objItemsContact.Count Then
            Exit For
        End If

        ' get the contact
        Set objContact = objItemsContact.Item(lngThisContact)

        ' display the fields
        Me.grdContacts.TextMatrix(intContact + 1, _
            CONTACTGRID_COL_FILEAS) = objContact.FileAs

        Me.grdContacts.TextMatrix(intContact + 1, _
            CONTACTGRID_COL_LASTNAME) = objContact.LastName

        Me.grdContacts.TextMatrix(intContact + 1, _
            CONTACTGRID_COL_FIRSTNAME) = objContact.FirstName

        Me.grdContacts.TextMatrix(intContact + 1, _
            CONTACTGRID_COL_COMPANYNAME) = objContact.CompanyName

        Me.grdContacts.TextMatrix(intContact + 1, _
            CONTACTGRID_COL_BUSINESSTELEPHONE) = _
            objContact.BusinessTelephoneNumber

        ' save the OID into the array
        ' this is used to do an action on the contact such as delete,
        ' copy, display, etc...
        ' we would use the Grid.RowData collection here, but there seems
        ' to be some bug that it will not take the value
        gContactRowData(intContact + 1) = objContact.oid
```

LISTING 6.9 Continued

```
        ' increment the index of the contact to be displayed
        lngThisContact = lngThisContact + 1

    Next

    ' if we displayed less contacts than the grid allows
    ' we need to truncate the dead rows
    ' the -1 and +1 accounts for the header row
    If intContact < CONTACT_CONTACTGRID_ROWS - 1 Then
        Me.grdContacts.Rows = intContact + 1
    End If

End Function
```

`RefreshContacts` takes a single string parameter, `strSeek`:

```
Public Function RefreshContacts(ByVal strSeek As String)
```

This parameter is used when one button is tapped. It provides the criteria on which to seek in the current sort order. In other words, when the grid is sorted by Last Name and the fgh button is tapped, `strSeek` will have a value of F, meaning to start displaying contacts where the Last Name begins with F.

Now let's look at the functionality of `RefreshContacts` piece by piece.

Populating and Sorting the Grid Rows

Let's jump to the main loop that displays the Contacts and look at it:

```
' we're going to cycle through the contacts
' and write them to the grid
For intContact = 0 To CONTACT_CONTACTGRID_ROWS - 1

    ' if we've gone past the last contact
    ' let's get out
    ' this happens when you start displaying contacts
    ' near the bottom - or when the first contact
    ' is closer to the bottom than the number of rows in the grid
    If lngThisContact > objItemsContact.Count Then
        Exit For
    End If

    ' get the contact
    Set objContact = objItemsContact.Item(lngThisContact)

    ' display the fields
    Me.grdContacts.TextMatrix(intContact + 1, _
```

```
        CONTACTGRID_COL_FILEAS) = objContact.FileAs

    Me.grdContacts.TextMatrix(intContact + 1, _
        CONTACTGRID_COL_LASTNAME) = objContact.LastName

    Me.grdContacts.TextMatrix(intContact + 1, _
        CONTACTGRID_COL_FIRSTNAME) = objContact.FirstName

    Me.grdContacts.TextMatrix(intContact + 1, _
        CONTACTGRID_COL_COMPANYNAME) = objContact.CompanyName

    Me.grdContacts.TextMatrix(intContact + 1, _
        CONTACTGRID_COL_BUSINESSTELEPHONE) = objContact.BusinessTelephoneNumber

    ' save the OID into the array
    ' this is used to do an action on the contact such as delete,
    ' copy, display, etc...
    ' we would use the Grid.RowData collection here, but there seems
    ' to be some bug that it will not take the value
    gContactRowData(intContact + 1) = objContact.oid

    ' increment the index of the contact to be displayed
    lngThisContact = lngThisContact + 1

Next
```

The `intContact` loop cycles through once for each nonheader row in the grid. The variable `lngThisContact` is used as an index to the contact `Items` collection. After a refresh of all contacts starting at the top of the sort order, `lngThisContact` equals 1 at the start of the loop. If you refresh starting later in the sort order, it will contain a different value. We'll investigate that later in this chapter.

The first test completed is a check to be sure the index value in `lngThisContact` hasn't exceeded the `Count` in the contact folder `Items` collection. If this index value has exceeded the `Count`, the loop is exited.

After this index value is verified to be valid, a reference to the `ContactItem` existing at that index value in the `Items` collection is retrieved to the variable `objContact`, declared as a `PocketOutlook.ContactItem`.

This `ContactItem` is then used to populate a row in the grid using the grid's `TextMatrix` array. The key to the item—the OID property of the `ContactItem`—is then stored to the respective row of the array `gContactRowData`. This creates a one-to-one relationship between the grid row and the row in the array. Typically, the grid's `RowData` array would be used for this purpose, but there seems to be an inconsistent bug with the `RowData` array when trying to store certain OID values.

Lastly, in the loop, the index value in lngThisContact is incremented by one, ready for the next ContactItem in the contact folder's Items collection.

Let's look more closely at some of the setup before the display loop and the filtering of the ContactItems:

```
' get all contacts
Set objItemsContact = gobjPoom.GetDefaultFolder(olFolderContacts).Items
```

First, objItemsContact—the object reference for a PocketOutlook.Items collection used to populate the grid—is set equal to an Items collection from the ContactItem folder via the GetDefaultFolder(olFolderContacts).Items collection. This retrieves all contacts that exist in the ContactItem folder.

Then, these items are sorted into the requested order by using the Sort method:

```
' sort by the current sort order - always ascending
objItemsContact.Sort "[" & gstrContactSortOrder & "]", False
```

Here, the public variable gstrContactSortOrder contains the currently requested sort order property name (for example FileAs, LastName, or CompanyName). Remember, the default sort order is assigned in the Form_Load event as FileAs.

Updating the Scrollbar

Because you are using manual-paging for the grid, you need to manually control the scrollbar Max property:

```
' set the max for the scrollbar to be the top contact
' of the last "page" of contacts
Me.VScroll1.Max = objItemsContact.Count - Me.VScroll1.LargeChange + 1
```

At this point, you know how many contacts exist and set the VScroll1.Max property to objItemsContact.Count (contact item count), minus the scrollbar's LargeChange value plus one. This formula allows navigation to the first contact by sliding the scrollbar completely to the top, yielding a Value of 1. Then, the LargeChange value plus 1 is subtracted from the objItemsContact.Count value to show the last page of contacts by sliding the scrollbar completely to the bottom. When the scrollbar is completely at the bottom, it's Value is the index of the first contact on the last page of contact items. If you simply set the Max value to the contact items Count value, only the last contact in the collection is displayed when the scrollbar is slid all the way to the bottom; this would waste the rest of the rows in the grid.

Seeking the First Matching Contact

Next, the control-flow checks to see whether there's a seek value (strSeek) as to where to locate the grid in the collection of contact items by the current sort order. This value can be passed by any command buttons placed above the grid control. (The following code to handle the seek value is abbreviated from the Listing 6.9.) If a seek value isn't provided, the contact index (lngThisContact) is specified by the scrollbar's Value.

```
' if we have a seek parameter try to find
' the first contact meeting that parameter
If Len(strSeek) > 0 Then

...

Else
    ' if we don't have a seek value, use the scroll bar
' current value
    lngThisContact = Me.VScroll1.Value
End If
```

Let's see what was abbreviated from the previous example that handles the seek value. Here, the code inside the If...Then control-flow block is listed (up to the Else statement):

```
If Len(strSeek) > 0 Then
    ' setup the restrict clause to be equal to or greater than
    ' the seek parameter
    ' this will find the next contact that meets the seek
    ' parameter if one does not exactly meet it
    strRestrict = "[" & gstrContactSortOrder & "]>=""" & "" & strSeek & """"

    ' apply the seek
    Set objContact = objItemsContact.Find(strRestrict)

...

Else
```

This code block handles receiving the seek value (strSeek). First, the restrict clause (used by the Find method) is constructed. It consists of the proper formatting brackets ([]) around the current sort order (provided by the public variable gstrContactSortOrder). Because the sort order can be dynamically changed, you need to seek its value. This restrict clause is completed by adding the strSeek value inside quotes. Some examples of the clause are

- [FileAs] >= "F", where the sort order is the FileAs property and the button tapped is FGH
- [LastName] >= "R", where the sort order is the LastName property and the button tapped is RST
- [CompanyName] >= " ", meaning to go to the top of the Company sort order

Then, this seek is applied by using it as the parameter for the Find method. If a contact meets this criteria, the Find method will return the first contact meeting it. If no contacts meet this criteria, objContact will be set to Nothing.

Next, let's investigate what happens when a contact is returned from the `Find` method:

```
' if we found a contact meeting the seek
' let's store the OID value (primary key - Outlook ID)
If Not objContact Is Nothing Then
    ' grab the OID
    lngOIDFirstFound = objContact.oid

    ' start at the 1st contact
    lngThisContact = 1

    ' cycle thru the contacts to find the contact's
    ' place in the sort order

    ' while we're still looking at a valid contact
Do While lngThisContact <= objItemsContact.Count
        ' get the contact
        Set objContact = objItemsContact.Item(lngThisContact)

        ' if it's our contact, let's get out
        ' lngThisContact will be the correct index of
        ' the contact found
        If objContact.oid = lngOIDFirstFound Then
            Exit Do
        End If

        lngThisContact = lngThisContact + 1
    Loop
End If
```

A check is completed to ensure that a valid `ContactItem` is returned to the object reference `objContact` from the call to the `Find` method. If `objContact` has a valid `ContactItem` reference, the value of its `OID` property is stored to a `Long` variable, `lntOIDFirstFound`. This value is kept to compare each `ContactItem` object within the collection to the first one's place within the sort order.

> **NOTE**
>
> You are *not* filtering the contacts, but just jumping to the first one that meets the criteria. This not only allows the grid to be scrolled above the contact that meets the criteria, but also to continue beyond those that do.

Next, the index variable, `lngThisContact`, is set equal to 1. This index value is incremented by 1 for each contact that you cycle through to find the index value of the first contact that met the criteria. Imagine that you have a list of contacts sorted by some property stacked from top to bottom. You know what the first contact that meets the criteria is, but you don't know where it falls in the sort order.

Through the `lngThisContact` index variable, as the test case of being less than or equal to the number of contacts, `objItemsContact.Count`, begin a `Do While` loop. Inside this loop retrieve a reference to each `ContactItem` by its index number, using `lngThisContact`. A comparison is then made between each `ContactItem` `OID` value and the one from the first contact that met the criteria (as stored in the variable `lgnOIDFirstFound`). If the `OID` is the same, you have again found the `ContactItem` in the collection and now have its position. The position is the value of `lngThisContact`, the index variable, so exit the `Do While` loop with an `Exit Do` statement.

So, whether you have a seek value or are dealing with just the value from the scrollbar, you know where to start displaying the contacts.

Resetting the Grid

The next two items before entering the display loop are straightforward, as shown in the following snippet. You reset the grid to the maximum number of rows available. This is important only after you seek a value near the bottom of the sort order and may have truncated some unused rows. Secondly, now that you know which contact (by the index value) will be displayed, store this value off to `lngFirstContactDisplayed`. This allows the scrollbar `Value` to be updated when you complete the displaying of the contacts.

```
' set the rows
Me.grdContacts.Rows = CONTACT_CONTACTGRID_ROWS

' save the index of the first contact displayed
' this is used to update the scroll bar with the correct
' position after we're done
lngFirstContactDisplayed = lngThisContact
```

After all the contacts are displayed in the grid, as presented in Listing 6.9 and repeated as follows, a simple test is completed to ensure that we aren't leaving unused rows visible. If we exit the display loop before using all the grid rows, we simply adjust the number of rows to the number of contacts displayed (`intContact`) plus one. The extra row is to accommodate the header.

```
' if we displayed less contacts than the grid allows
' we need to truncate the dead rows
' the -1 and +1 accounts for the header row
If intContact < CONTACT_CONTACTGRID_ROWS - 1 Then
    Me.grdContacts.Rows = intContact + 1
End If
```

In summary, the `RefreshContacts` method displays contacts from the Contact PIM store by using the `PocketOutlook.Items` and `PocketOutlook.ContactItem`. It can display contacts based on the scrollbar's position (`ScrollBar.Value`) or by using a seek value provided from one of the jump buttons. It uses an optimized manual-paging method to display only the number of contacts visible in the grid.

Try this code. At this point, your application should be able to display the first page of contacts.

The `Vscroll1_Change` Routine

If your application is currently functional to display the first page of contacts, let's add the capability to move through the contacts using the scrollbar:

```
Private Sub VScroll1_Change()
    ' refresh the contact grid with no seek value
    RefreshContacts ""
End Sub
```

The Jump Buttons

Having `RefreshContacts` structured to accept a seek value, you now need to implement the jump buttons (see Listing 6.10). These buttons were added to the form when you added the other controls.

LISTING 6.10 The Event Code for Jump Buttons

```
Private Sub cmdAB_Click()
    'refresh contacts using the space character as the first record to display
    RefreshContacts " "
End Sub

Private Sub cmdCDE_Click()
    ' refresh contacts using the "C" as the first record to display
    RefreshContacts "C"
End Sub

Private Sub cmdFGH_Click()
    ' refresh contacts using the "F" as the first record to display
    RefreshContacts "F"
End Sub

Private Sub cmdIJK_Click()
    ' refresh contacts using the "I" as the first record to display
    RefreshContacts "I"
End Sub

Private Sub cmdLMN_Click()
    ' refresh contacts using the "L" as the first record to display
```

LISTING 6.10 Continued

```
    RefreshContacts "L"
End Sub

Private Sub cmdOPQ_Click()
    ' refresh contacts using the "O" as the first record to display
    RefreshContacts "O"
End Sub

Private Sub cmdRST_Click()
    ' refresh contacts using the "R" as the first record to display
    RefreshContacts "R"
End Sub

Private Sub cmdUVW_Click()
    ' refresh contacts using the "U" as the first record to display
    RefreshContacts "U"
End Sub

Private Sub cmdXYZ_Click()
    ' refresh contacts using the "X" as the first record to display
    RefreshContacts "X"
End Sub
```

Listing 6.10 has all the event code for the `Click` events for all the jump buttons. Each jump button calls `RefreshContacts` with the string value of the first contact to be displayed in the sort order. In other words, if the current sort order is `LastName`, tapping the button `cmdLMN` will call `RefreshContacts "L"`, thus displaying the first contact whose `LastName` value starts with L or greater. The only unique jump button is `cmdAB`, which should start at any numbers or symbols when it calls `RefreshContacts`; a space character (`Chr(32)`) is used for this purpose, because in the sort order, all readable characters come after the space character.

Test the application again. You should now be able to jump to different contacts using the jump buttons.

The `Grid_Click` Event

You can implement two different sets of functionalities by tapping the grid:

- Implement the capability to tap the grid to re-sort the contacts or open a particular contact.
- Use some API calls to detect a held-down stylus to present a shortcut (or pop-up) menu.

Listing 6.11 presents all the code for the `grdContacts_Click` event.

LISTING 6.11 Re-sorting the Grid or Opening a Contact for Display and Edit

```
Private Sub grdContacts_Click()

    Dim objContact As PocketOutlook.ContactItem
    Dim objFolder As PocketOutlook.Folder
    Dim lngOID As Long

    On Error Resume Next

    ' if clicked on the top row, then
    ' the grid is resorted and refreshed
    If Me.grdContacts.Row = 0 Then
        ' first row clicked

        ' set the sort order
        Select Case Me.grdContacts.Col
            Case CONTACTGRID_COL_FILEAS
                gstrContactSortOrder = CONTACTGRID_HEADER_SORT_FILEAS
            Case CONTACTGRID_COL_LASTNAME
                gstrContactSortOrder = CONTACTGRID_HEADER_SORT_LASTNAME
            Case CONTACTGRID_COL_FIRSTNAME
                gstrContactSortOrder = CONTACTGRID_HEADER_SORT_FIRSTNAME
            Case CONTACTGRID_COL_COMPANYNAME
                gstrContactSortOrder = CONTACTGRID_HEADER_SORT_COMPANYNAME
            Case CONTACTGRID_COL_BUSINESSTELEPHONE
                gstrContactSortOrder = _
                    CONTACTGRID_HEADER_SORT_BUSINESSTELEPHONE
        End Select

        ' refresh the contacts
        RefreshContacts ""
    Else
        ' get the id of the contact clicked on
        lngOID = gContactRowData(Me.grdContacts.Row)

        ' get the contact clicked on
        Set objContact = gobjPoom.GetItemFromOid(lngOID)

        ' display the contact - used the actual Pocket Outlook form
        objContact.Display

        ' refresh the changes
        RefreshContacts ""
    End If

End Sub
```

One simple control-flow `If` statement determines whether the tap was on the header row (row = 0) or one of the contact rows. Let's first investigate what happens when the header row is tapped:

```
' first row clicked

' set the sort order
Select Case Me.grdContacts.Col
    Case CONTACTGRID_COL_FILEAS
        gstrContactSortOrder = CONTACTGRID_HEADER_SORT_FILEAS
    Case CONTACTGRID_COL_LASTNAME
        gstrContactSortOrder = CONTACTGRID_HEADER_SORT_LASTNAME
    Case CONTACTGRID_COL_FIRSTNAME
        gstrContactSortOrder = CONTACTGRID_HEADER_SORT_FIRSTNAME
    Case CONTACTGRID_COL_COMPANYNAME
        gstrContactSortOrder = CONTACTGRID_HEADER_SORT_COMPANYNAME
    Case CONTACTGRID_COL_BUSINESSTELEPHONE
        gstrContactSortOrder = CONTACTGRID_HEADER_SORT_BUSINESSTELEPHONE
End Select

' refresh the contacts
RefreshContacts ""
```

Here, after you have determined it was the header row tapped, a `Select Case` statement determines which column in the grid was tapped by using the Consts declared in the module `modGlobal` (as shown earlier in Listing 6.6). The sort order is then set by using the public variable that holds the current sort order, `gstrContactSortOrder`. Last, the grid is refreshed, starting at the top of the sort order (using the blank string parameter) by calling `RefreshContacts`.

The following code segment reacts to any other row, besides the header row, in the grid being tapped. It retrieves the OID value from the Public array gContactRowData, which is declared at the form level in the section "Contact Form Level Variables," and stores it to the local long variable `lngOID`. Remember that the array `gContactRowData` is populated with the corresponding `OID` from the `ContactItem.OID` property value when the grid is populated in the `RefreshContacts` method.

```
' get the id of the contact clicked on
lngOID = gContactRowData(Me.grdContacts.Row)

' get the contact clicked on
Set objContact = gobjPoom.GetItemFromOid(lngOID)

' display the contact - used the actual Pocket Outlook form
objContact.Display

' refresh the changes
RefreshContacts ""
```

The OID value is the primary key for the `PocketOutlook.Item`, and is unique even across object types. This is why the next line of code can retrieve the `ContactItem` by simply using the `GetItemFromOID()` method on the `PocketOutlook.Application` object. Next, the `Display` method on this object is called, which brings this PIM item up in its native GUI. The item is displayed semimodally, meaning that when the item is displayed, your application pauses execution.

NOTE

The PIM item displayed is modal to the point that after it's closed via the OK button in the upper-right corner, or the Delete menu on the Tools menubar, control returns to your application. Users can tap the Start icon to start any other application just as when they are directly in your application.

After control from `Display` is returned, the grid is refreshed using no seek-value; therefore, it stays as the same position within the sort order. There's room for improvement here that you could try to implement. Something not addressed is if the fields of the contact are edited that pertain to the current sort order, that contact row may disappear from the grid as it finds its new placement in the sort order.

The second tap functionality to be implemented is the held-down stylus to present a context-sensitive shortcut (pop-up) menu. This is implemented in the `Grid.MouseDown` event as presented in Listing 6.12.

LISTING 6.12 Determining Whether the Stylus Is Held Down Long Enough to Generate a Shortcut Menu

```
Private Sub grdContacts_MouseDown(ByVal Button As Long, _
        ByVal Shift As Long, ByVal x As Single, ByVal y As Single)

    Dim lngOID As Long
    Dim intRow As Integer
    Dim sngStart As Single

    On Error Resume Next

    ' start timing - used to figure out how long the
    ' stylus has been down
    sngStart = Timer()
```

LISTING 6.12 Continued

```
    ' figure out which row was clicked on
    intRow = Fix(y / Me.grdContacts.RowHeightMin)

    ' if the header row
    If intRow = 0 Then
        ' nothing to do for a "right-click" on the header row....
        Exit Sub
    End If

    ' set the grid to that row
    Me.grdContacts.Row = intRow

    ' get the OID for the row...
    lngOID = gContactRowData(Me.grdContacts.Row)

    ' while the stylus is down
    Do While GetAsyncKeyState(ASYNCKEYSTATE_LEFTMOUSE_KEY) <> 0
        If Timer() - sngStart > MOUSEDOWN_RIGHTCLICK_TIMING Then
            If GetAsyncKeyState(1) <> 0 Then
                ShowContextMenu _
                    x + Me.grdContacts.Left, _
                    y + Me.grdContacts.Top, _
                    lngOID
                Exit Do
            End If
        End If
    Loop
End Sub
```

In Listing 6.12, first the current `Timer()` value is stored to a local single variable, `sngStart`. This value determines how long the stylus has been held down. We're using a threshold of 0.5 seconds to present the shortcut menu.

Next, the row in which the stylus is present is determined by dividing the Y coordinate (a parameter of the `MouseDown` event) by the grid's `RowHeightMin`, which is essentially the `RowHeight` of all rows in this grid. The result has the decimal places dropped by using the `Fix` function and are stored to the local variable, `intRow`. If it's determined that the row where the stylus is held is the header row (row = 0), the routine is exited because there's no defined functionality for a popup from the header row.

The grid's current row is then set to this determined row (`intRow`). This is completed because the grid won't accomplish this natively until the `MouseUp` event occurs. After the grid refocuses the specified row, lngOID has the correct OID stored to it by using the array gContactRowData containing the OIDs as populated in RefreshContacts.

Next, use an API call to GetAsyncKeyState in a Do While loop to determine whether the stylus is still down. If the stylus is still down and has been down for 0.5 seconds or more, it is determined that the user desires a shortcut menu and calls ShowContextMenu. Parameters for ShowContextMenu are the x- and y-coordinates to place the menu and the OID of the currently selected contact in the grid.

The ShowContextMenu Routine

ShowContextMenu creates a shortcut (pop-up) menu with as many as six menu prompts (see Figure 6.5). It will determine if a valid OID is passed and add menu prompts that correlate only to a valid contact. After users choose one of the menu prompts, an appropriate action is taken.

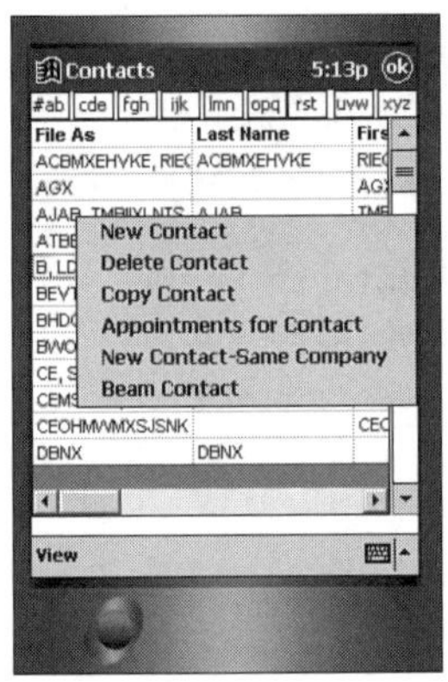

FIGURE 6.5
After holding down the stylus for more than a half second, users see a context-sensitive shortcut menu from which to choose an action to perform on the currently selected contact item.

Listing 6.13 shows the entire code for the ShowContextMenu routine.

LISTING 6.13 Showing a Pop-Up Menu

```
Private Sub ShowContextMenu(ByVal sngX As Single, _
        ByVal sngY As Single, ByVal lngOID As Long)

    Dim hMenu As Long
    Dim objContact As PocketOutlook.ContactItem
    Dim objFolderContact As PocketOutlook.Folder
    Dim objRecipient As PocketOutlook.Recipient
```

LISTING 6.13 Continued

```
Dim strCompanyName As String
Dim blnRefresh As Boolean
Dim lngMenuResult As Long
Dim objInfraredFolder As PocketOutlook.Folder

On Error Resume Next

' create the menu handle
hMenu = CreatePopupMenu()

' add prompts
AppendMenu hMenu, MF_ENABLED Or MF_STRING, _
    CONTACTPOPUP_MENU_INDEX_NEW, CONTACTPOPUP_MENU_CAPTION_NEW

' only append the following if we have a valid OID (Primary Key)
If lngOID > 0 Then

    AppendMenu hMenu, MF_ENABLED Or MF_STRING, _
            CONTACTPOPUP_MENU_INDEX_DELETE, _
            CONTACTPOPUP_MENU_CAPTION_DELETE

    AppendMenu hMenu, MF_ENABLED Or MF_STRING, _
            CONTACTPOPUP_MENU_INDEX_COPY, _
            CONTACTPOPUP_MENU_CAPTION_COPY

    AppendMenu hMenu, MF_ENABLED Or MF_STRING, _
            CONTACTPOPUP_MENU_INDEX_SHOWAPPTS, _
            CONTACTPOPUP_MENU_CAPTION_SHOWAPPTS

    AppendMenu hMenu, MF_ENABLED Or MF_STRING, _
            CONTACTPOPUP_MENU_INDEX_SAMECOMP, _
            CONTACTPOPUP_MENU_CAPTION_SAMECOMP

    AppendMenu hMenu, MF_ENABLED Or MF_STRING, _
            CONTACTPOPUP_MENU_INDEX_BEAM, _
            CONTACTPOPUP_MENU_CAPTION_BEAM

End If

' show the menu and return the choice chosen
lngMenuResult = TrackPopupMenuEx( _
                        hMenu, _
                        TPM_LEFTALIGN Or TPM_TOPALIGN Or TPM_RETURNCMD, _
                        sngX / Screen.TwipsPerPixelX, _
```

LISTING 6.13 Continued

```
                                sngY / Screen.TwipsPerPixelY, _
                                frmContact.hWnd, _
                                0)

    ' get the contacts folder collection
    Set objFolderContact = gobjPoom.GetDefaultFolder(olFolderContacts)

    ' pick the correct action
    Select Case lngMenuResult

        Case CONTACTPOPUP_MENU_INDEX_NEW

            ' Adding a contact, so let's make sure to refresh afterwards
            blnRefresh = True
            ' Create the new contact
            Set objContact = objFolderContact.Items.Add()
            ' display it for editing
            objContact.Display

        Case CONTACTPOPUP_MENU_INDEX_DELETE

            ' deleting a contact, so let's make sure to refresh afterwards
            blnRefresh = True
            ' get the contact by its id
            Set objContact = gobjPoom.GetItemFromOid(lngOID)
            ' delete the contact
            objContact.Delete

        Case CONTACTPOPUP_MENU_INDEX_COPY

            ' copying a contact, so let's make sure to refresh afterwards
            blnRefresh = True
            ' get the contact by its id
            Set objContact = gobjPoom.GetItemFromOid(lngOID)
            ' make a copy
            Set objContact = objContact.Copy()
            ' display it for editing
            objContact.Display

        Case CONTACTPOPUP_MENU_INDEX_SHOWAPPTS

            ' show the appt form - giving it the OID (primary-key)
            frmAppt.ShowApptForContact (lngOID)
```

LISTING 6.13 Continued

```
        Case CONTACTPOPUP_MENU_INDEX_SAMECOMP

            ' basically copying a contact, so let's make sure
            ' to refresh afterwards
            blnRefresh = True
            ' get the contact by its id
            Set objContact = gobjPoom.GetItemFromOid(lngOID)
            ' save the company name
            strCompanyName = objContact.CompanyName
            ' create a new contact and store back
            ' to the same object reference
            Set objContact = objFolderContact.Items.Add()
            ' set the company name
            objContact.CompanyName = strCompanyName
            ' save the contact before displaying, else error occurs
            objContact.Save
            ' display the contact
            objContact.Display

        Case CONTACTPOPUP_MENU_INDEX_BEAM

            ' get the contact by its id
            Set objContact = gobjPoom.GetItemFromOid(lngOID)
            ' create infrared folder
            Set objInfraredFolder = gobjPoom.GetDefaultFolder(olFolderInfrared)
            ' add the contact to the folder
            objInfraredFolder.AddItemToInfraredFolder olContactItem, objContact
            ' send the folder (contact)
            objInfraredFolder.SendToInfrared

    End Select

    ' release the menu resources
    DestroyMenu hMenu

    ' if we did something that requires, let's refresh
    If blnRefresh Then
        ' refresh with no find
        RefreshContacts ""
    End If

End Sub
```

Let's break down Listing 6.13 and examine it.

Using API Calls with the Pop-Up Menu

The following lists the code to create, populate, show, and return the result from the pop-up menu. For reference on all APIs used in the shortcut menu, see Chapter 9, "Harnessing the Windows CE API." All these API functions are declared in the module modGlobal (refer to Listing 6.5). `CreatePopupMenu` returns a long handle to the menu, which is stored to the local variable `hMenu`.

```
' create the menu handle
hMenu = CreatePopupMenu()

' add prompts
AppendMenu hMenu, MF_ENABLED Or MF_STRING, _
    CONTACTPOPUP_MENU_INDEX_NEW, CONTACTPOPUP_MENU_CAPTION_NEW

' only append the following if we have a valid OID (Primary Key)
If lngOID > 0 Then

    AppendMenu hMenu, MF_ENABLED Or MF_STRING, _
        CONTACTPOPUP_MENU_INDEX_DELETE, CONTACTPOPUP_MENU_CAPTION_DELETE

    AppendMenu hMenu, MF_ENABLED Or MF_STRING, _
        CONTACTPOPUP_MENU_INDEX_COPY, CONTACTPOPUP_MENU_CAPTION_COPY

    AppendMenu hMenu, MF_ENABLED Or MF_STRING, _
        CONTACTPOPUP_MENU_INDEX_SHOWAPPTS, CONTACTPOPUP_MENU_CAPTION_SHOWAPPTS

    AppendMenu hMenu, MF_ENABLED Or MF_STRING, _
        CONTACTPOPUP_MENU_INDEX_SAMECOMP, CONTACTPOPUP_MENU_CAPTION_SAMECOMP

    AppendMenu hMenu, MF_ENABLED Or MF_STRING, _
        CONTACTPOPUP_MENU_INDEX_BEAM, CONTACTPOPUP_MENU_CAPTION_BEAM

End If

' show the menu and return the choice chosen
lngMenuResult = TrackPopupMenuEx( _
                        hMenu, _
                        TPM_LEFTALIGN Or TPM_TOPALIGN Or TPM_RETURNCMD, _
                        sngX / Screen.TwipsPerPixelX, _
                        sngY / Screen.TwipsPerPixelY, _
                        frmContact.hWnd, _
                        0)
```

The first prompt, for a New Contact, is always added to the pop-up menu, because it doesn't depend on a contact row being selected.

If the `OID` is valid, the additional prompts are added that are context-sensitive: Delete Contact, Copy Contact, Show Appointments For Contact, New Contact–Same Company, and Beam.

Lastly, the shortcut menu is shown and its results are returned and stored to the local long variable `lngMenuResult`.

Reacting to User Selection

Next, let's examine the actions taken when the user chooses one of the menu options. The following code sets the object reference variable to a `PocketOutlook.Folder` by using the public `gobjPoom PocketOutlook.Application's GetDefaultFolder`. This folder contains all contacts and is created here because most of the actions in the `Select Case` structure below it will take advantage of it.

```
' get the contacts folder collection
Set objFolderContact = gobjPoom.GetDefaultFolder(olFolderContacts)
```

Next, let's examine the actions taken when users choose one of the menu options. Each of the following actions are taken via a `Select Case` structure that you can review in Listing 6.13.

Working with Contacts

The following code segment is associated with adding a new contact and displaying it:

```
' Adding a contact, so let's make sure to refresh afterwards
blnRefresh = True
' Create the new contact
Set objContact = objFolderContact.Items.Add()
' display it for editing
objContact.Display
```

The `Boolean` variable `blnRefresh` is set to `True`, letting you know that an action has taken place that may affect the grid's contents. A new contact is created by calling the `Add` method of the `PocketOutlook.Items` collection object `objFolderContact`. This reference is held by the local `PocketOutlook.ContactItem` variable `objContact`. Lastly, the contact is displayed by using the native Contact application GUI by calling the `Display` method. (Remember, calling `Display` is semimodal and your application pauses execution until the user closes the native PIM form.)

The following code deletes the contact:

```
' deleting a contact, so let's make sure to refresh afterwards
blnRefresh = True
' get the contact by its id
Set objContact = gobjPoom.GetItemFromOid(lngOID)
' delete the contact
objContact.Delete
```

Again, you want to set the refresh so it happens. Next, the contact is retrieved with the public `PocketOutlook.Application` object variable reference `gobjPoom`. `GetItemFromOid` is called with the `OID` to return a single `PocketOutlook` item, whether it's a `ContactItem`, `TaskItem`, or `AppointmentItem`. This item is then deleted by calling the `Delete` method on the item itself.

The following code snippet demonstrates copying a contact:

```
' copying a contact, so let's make sure to refresh afterwards
blnRefresh = True
' get the contact by its id
Set objContact = gobjPoom.GetItemFromOid(lngOID)
' make a copy
Set objContact = objContact.Copy()
' display it for editing
objContact.Display
```

Again, the refresh flag is set and the contact is retrieved from `GetItemFromOid`. With the valid contact object, the `Copy` method is called returning a new `ContactItem` object with the same values. A different variable could be used here, but it's not necessary because you are done with the original object. This newly created copy is then displayed for viewing and editing via `Display` on the object itself.

The following code segment is for a user choosing Show Appts For Contact. This simple call to `frmAppt.ShowApptForContact` passes the `OID` as the parameter. Although the Appointment form isn't published in this chapter, it's part of the sample application downloadable from `www.samspublising.com` (enter this book's ISBN in the Search field).

```
' show the appt form - giving it the OID (primary-key)
frmAppt.ShowApptForContact (lngOID)
```

In the following code, as with previous actions, set the refresh `Boolean` and retrieve the contact from the `OID`. Then the `CompanyName` value is stored to a local variable. Again, as before, we create a new `ContactItem` by calling the `Add` method of the `Items` collection. Because we have set values on the properties, we need to save the contact first by calling the `Save` method on the object. Then, the contact is displayed via the `Display` method.

```
' basically copying a contact, so let's make sure to refresh afterwards
blnRefresh = True
' get the contact by its id
Set objContact = gobjPoom.GetItemFromOid(lngOID)
' save the company name
strCompanyName = objContact.CompanyName
' create a new contact and store back
' to the same object reference
```

```
Set objContact = objFolderContact.Items.Add()
' set the company name
objContact.CompanyName = strCompanyName
' save the contact before displaying, else error occurs
objContact.Save
' display the contact
objContact.Display
```

The following snippet demonstrates how to beam a single contact via infrared. You can use this methodology to beam any POOM objects.

```
' get the contact by its id
Set objContact = gobjPoom.GetItemFromOid(lngOID)
' create infrared folder
Set objInfraredFolder = gobjPoom.GetDefaultFolder(olFolderInfrared)
' add the contact to the folder
objInfraredFolder.AddItemToInfraredFolder olContactItem, objContact
' send the folder (contact)
objInfraredFolder.SendToInfrared
```

In this code, a `ContactItem` object is obtained via `GetItemFromOid`. Then, a reference is created to a folder used as a repository for the beaming. This folder appears the same as any of the other folders, but is obtained using the `olFolderInfrared` enumeration as the parameter for folder type to the `GetDefaultFolder` method.

After an infrared folder is created, items can be prepared for beaming by adding them to the folder. To add items to the infrared folder, use `AddItemToInfraredFolder`. The first parameter is the object type (`olItemType`); here, the enumeration `olContactItem was used`. The second parameter for the `AddItemToInfraredFolder` method is the object itself—`objContact`. When all items are added to the folder, initiate the beaming by calling the `SendToInfrared` method.

Cleaning Up and Refreshing the Grid

After all actions are taken, the following code is what remains of `ShowContextMenu`. The menu resources are released using the `DestroyMenu` API with the menu handle `hMenu`. Then, if an action was taken that needs to refresh the contact grid, it's refreshed in place by using `RefreshContacts` without a seek value.

```
' release the menu resources
DestroyMenu hMenu

' if we did something that requires, let's refresh
If blnRefresh Then
    ' refresh with no find
    RefreshContacts ""
End If
```

The `Form_Unload` Routine

Listing 6.14 logs off POOM and cleans up the object by setting it to `Nothing`.

LISTING 6.14 Logging Off and Cleaning Up

```
Private Sub Form_Unload(Cancel As Integer)
    ' logoff
    gobjPoom.Logoff

    ' clear reference to POOM
    Set gobjPoom = Nothing
End Sub
```

Summary

We've thoroughly investigated the contacts aspects of the POOM. This chapter discussed the contacts aspects of the POOM. The `Application` object and folders were also thoroughly explained. The sample downloadable application code source presents similar forms for Tasks and Appointments—you can investigate them as well.

The sample application gives you a good template to create your own PIM application that extends or enhances the native versions.

Storing and Retrieving Data with ActiveX Data Objects CE

CHAPTER

7

Microsoft publishes ActiveX Data Objects for Windows CE (ADOCE) in the platform SDKs. ADOCE allows eVB applications to access data. Historically, ADOCE was an object model that allowed an application to use data in the CE Object Store. Its intention wasn't actually to access data currently stored in the CE Object Store, such as the native PIM contacts, the calendar, and so on, but it did allow applications to define their own data in the CE Object Store and manipulate these structures and data.

With the introduction of ADOCE 3.0, ADOCE could access Microsoft Pocket Access files. *Pocket Access* is a lightweight version of Microsoft Access that ships with its Office product. This was a welcome change, because tables in the CE Object Store had to be uniquely named. This meant that no two applications could have a table named "contacts," "accounts," or so on. Also, an application had to manually delete the tables from the object, a task most eVB programmers didn't bother with. This meant that an application using the Object Store that was removed from the machine could leave behind tons of obsolete data.

Interestingly enough, Microsoft doesn't publish a Pocket Access application for the Pocket PC, nor is there one for the Palm-size PC. But, ActiveSync allows users to sync a Microsoft Access database to a Pocket PC. Allowing ActiveSync to sync a Microsoft Access database to the device with no software to access must be extremely confusing to nonprogrammer users. But, after placing a Pocket Access database (or creating it programmatically as we do in our sample application), eVB can utilize ADOCE to store and query data.

With SQL Server CE, came ADOCE 3.1 and the capability to actually use a powerful data engine. SQL Server CE runs on top of OLEDBCE, a implementation of OLEDB for Windows CE. This means that third-party vendors can publish OLEDBCE drivers for data stores—local and remote—and ADOCE can access them. (SQL Server CE is discussed in Chapter 8, "Using SQL Server CE in a Mobile Environment.")

Although ADOCE presents a similar object model, there are differences between it and the ADO model for Win32 MDAC kit.

ADOCE has limitations that you need to be aware of when designing an application for Windows CE, as discussed in Chapter 2, "Introducing eMbedded Visual Basic." This chapter presents a sample application that uses an architecture that works well with ADOCE. The sample application's design probably wouldn't be the best for operating on a desktop or server, but it is well-suited for CE and ADOCE. With a Windows CE application and Pocket Access, remember that the data access is local, like applications before client/server or three-tier applications. Keep this in mind when developing Windows CE applications.

This chapter doesn't cover remote data access available with technologies such as SQL Server CE, ViaXML, or CEFusion. This chapter instead presents an application that's best for a single user due to its nature of working standalone or with a single Microsoft Access database residing on a desktop machine. With that in mind, in this chapter you will

- Gain an understanding of the ADOCE object model
- Create a Pocket Access database, as well as tables and indexes
- Use ADO methods to retrieve and manipulate data
- Use SQL via ADO to retrieve and manipulate data

Storing Windows CE Data

Outside of third-party products, ADOCE can access data stored in one of three places:

- The original data store for ADOCE was the Windows CE Object Store.
- Improved versions of ADOCE could access a Pocket Access File.
- The introduction of ADOCE 3.1 allows access to Microsoft SQL Server CE or other OLEDBCE providers.

When designing an ADOCE application, you need to determine which data store to use. The CE Object Store choice is probably no longer desirable for an eVB application, so its discussion isn't included here.

NOTE

The CE Object Store limitation of requiring unique table names across applications is a good enough reason to not use it anymore. Also, the Object Store is difficult to maintain remotely, performs slower, and is more prone to corruption.

Using Pocket Access is fairly easy. A Pocket Access database is file-based, similar to the desktop version, and can exist anywhere in the file structure of a CE device. Its extension is .cdb.

There are two ways to create a Pocket Access database:

- Use ActiveSync to create a Pocket Access database with a similar structure to a companion database on the desktop.
- You can programmatically create a Pocket Access database through the `ADOCE.Connection` object.

Introducing ADOCE Objects

The first task in using ADOCE is to understand the object model. ADOCE is comprised of the `Connection`, `Recordset`, `Field`, `Error`, and `Property` objects and `Errors`, `ErrorParameters`,

Fields, and Properties collections. The most commonly used are Connection, Recordset, Field, and Fields. The remaining objects have limited implementation and functionality in ADOCE.

The Connection Object

The Connection object is the root of using ADOCE. It's the means to getting to all the other objects and creating data definitions. The Connection object allows you to specify which data source to create and use.

The three most important methods and properties of the Connection object are ConnectionString, Open, and Execute.

The Recordset Object

The Recordset object contains the actual data. A Recordset object is populated via a couple of different methods:

- The Connection.Execute method can create a new, already populated Recordset object. To create and populate a Recordset object using the Connection.Execute method, a SQL statement is issued to the Execute method as the source.
- Use the Open method of the Recordset itself. Once a Recordset object is open, you can cycle through records, and access values of the fields.

The Recordset object allows programmatic control of moving forward and backward through the records, deleting records, adding records, and saving and setting bookmarks. The most important properties of the Recordset object are State and EOF. The Fields collection is widely used as well. The commonly used methods of the Recordset object are Open, MoveNext, Add, Delete, and Update.

The Fields Collection

The Fields collection is a collection of all columns within a Recordset. There is one Field object in the collection for each corresponding column in the data source. A Field object is also created within the Fields collection for each computed column in the SQL statement.

The Field Object

The Field object is a member of the Fields collection that allows access to the data column's value and properties. It allows the ability to read and write values to the column using the Value property, which in turn can be updated to the data store. Information about the column and the values of the Field object also can be determined via the object's Name, Type, and UnderlyingValue properties.

Creating the CD Library Sample Application

In this chapter, we'll use a sample application that allows users to keep an inventory of musical compact discs. Two friends of mine, whose CD collection numbers more than 6,000 CDs, inspired this application.

The CD Library allows the storage of artists, genres, and CDs. On the initial form, CD Library displays a grid of all artists sorted alphabetically and a grid of each artist's CDs (see Figure 7.1). Users can then select a CD from the grid and the application enables editing of the CD information. To enter a new CD, users tap the New button on the menu.

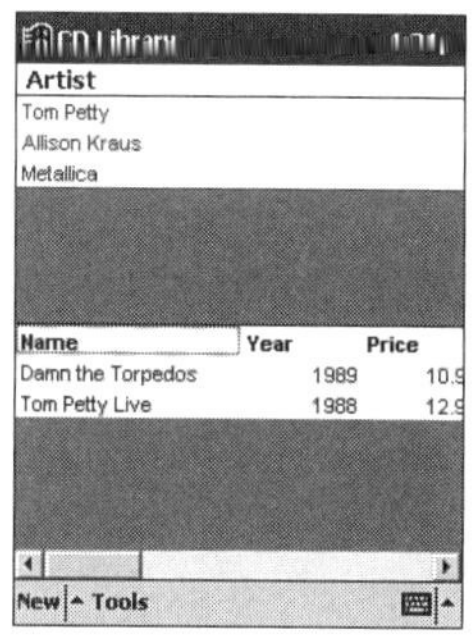

FIGURE 7.1

The initial form for the sample application CD Library. In the upper grid, a listing of all artists is displayed. The lower grid displays all the CDs for the currently selected artist.

Understanding Some Issues

Before you get started with ADOCE, you must become familiar with a few caveats. The first issue centers on the different versioning that ADOCE uses in comparison to the desktop ADO. The second issue centers on the `CreateObject` memory leak (as discussed in Chapters 2 and 3). These two issues alone dramatically change the architecture of how an application that uses ADOCE should be designed as compared to a desktop Visual Basic application.

ADOCE Versioning Implementation

To use ADOCE in an eVB application, your project needs to have a reference to the ADOCE library. Interestingly enough, there seems to be a design flaw in the way Microsoft implemented the ADOCE library in comparison to ADO for the desktop or other ActiveX libraries. There is no methodology incorporated in the type libraries for an eVB application to gracefully "upgrade" to a newer version of ADOCE.

So, you can't reference an older ADOCE library and use a newer version installed on the machine. For example, you create an eVB application using a reference to ADOCE version 3.0 and this application is installed on a device. Now, a newer version (ADOCE 3.1) is installed on the machine. The older application will continue to use ADOCE 3.0, because the names of the ActiveX classes for ADOCE must be referenced with a version number. For example,

```
CreateObject( "ADOCE.Connection.3.0" )
```

will work properly, but

```
CreateObject( "ADOCE.Connection" )
```

won't work. Issuing

```
CreateObject( "ADOCE.Connection" )
```

will result in an error that the ActiveX object can't be found.

For maintainability of an eVB application, I have found it best to define a `Const` with the ADOCE class names defined as a string. In an application, you can define the version of ADOCE that should be used in one place, utilizing this `Const` wherever `CreateObject` is called for an ADOCE object. Then, when you need to upgrade the ADOCE version that the application should utilize, simply edit these `Consts`.

`Consts` define the version of ADOCE classes used in CD Library:

```
' constants for the ADOCE classes
Const ADOCE_CLASS_CONNECTION = "ADOCE.Connection.3.0"
Const ADOCE_CLASS_RECORDSET = "ADOCE.Recordset.3.0"
```

The following is an example of `Consts` being used:

```
Set gobjArtist = CreateObject(ADOCE_CLASS_RECORDSET)
```

Impact of `CreateObject` Memory Leak on ADOCE Applications

Before building Windows CE applications, I built Web applications. Typically, these applications used the Microsoft Windows DNA design, a three-tier architecture. In a three-tier architecture, the typical design utilizes a methodology to open a connection, retrieve a recordset resource locally, and then use and dispose of it. This is a good design to keep applications modular, scalable, maintainable, and consume less resources. If you have built three-tier applications, your instincts to build Windows CE applications similarly might follow three-tier design, as my experience did. But, there is a problem with this methodology—the `CreateObject` memory leak put a stop to this.

In eVB, if your application constantly creates new `ADOCE.Connection` or `ADOCE.Recordset` objects, the device eventually runs out or runs low on memory. This happens because of a bug in the `CreateObject` function and its garbage collection. The `CreateObject` function slowly, yet surely, leaks memory.

Therefore, when designing ADOCE applications, it's best to define all your ADOCE objects globally, instantiate them at application startup, and leave them there until your application closes. This goes against many design rules, but really is one of the better workarounds for ADOCE applications. One reason this isn't such a large problem is that all data is local and typically there is only one connection to the database.

The CD Library application declares all ADOCE objects in a module file so that they are available globally within the application:

```
' global objects for all ADOCE objects
Public gobjConnection As ADOCE.Connection
Public gobjArtist As ADOCE.Recordset
Public gobjCD As ADOCE.Recordset
Public gobjPKEY As ADOCE.Recordset
Public gobjGenre As ADOCE.Recordset
```


The CD Library application initializes the ADOCE at the startup of the application during the `Form.Load` event (see Listing 7.1).

LISTING 7.1 modGlobal.bas: Initializing the Global ADOCE Objects

```
Function InitializeGlobals() As Boolean

    On Error Resume Next

    InitializeGlobals = False

    ' initialize globals - this needs to take place
    ' only once, due to CreateObject memory leak

    ' ADOCE_CLASS_CONNECTION & ADOCE_CLASS_RECORDSET
    ' are used because ce references these classes
    ' by their version numbers, create Consts allows
    ' changing of these version quickly and accurately

    Set gobjConnection = CreateObject(ADOCE_CLASS_CONNECTION)
    Set gobjArtist = CreateObject(ADOCE_CLASS_RECORDSET)
    Set gobjCD = CreateObject(ADOCE_CLASS_RECORDSET)
    Set gobjGenre = CreateObject(ADOCE_CLASS_RECORDSET)
    Set gobjPKEY = CreateObject(ADOCE_CLASS_RECORDSET)

    If Err.Number = 0 Then
        InitializeGlobals = True
    End If

End Function
```

Understanding the Project Components

The CD Library contains the following three components:

- The modGlobal.bas module serves to declare the global variables and hold common routines.
- The `frmMain` form serves as the main form for the Artist and CD grids.
- The `frmCD` form enables users to edit existing and new CD records.

Defining Data Structures for the Application

The data for the CD Library application is created and stored in a Pocket Access database named cd.cdb. Table 7.1 lists the definitions of the four tables used in the CD Library Application. The first three—Artist, Genre, and CD—are entities displayed and edited by users.

TABLE 7.1 Table Definitions

Column	*Type*	*Description*
	Artist Table	
ArtistId	`Int`	Unique Id for the Artist record.
ArtistName	`VarChar(64)`	Name of the artist.
DefaultGenre	`Int`	Foreign Key to the Genre table. Default Genre when adding a new CD for the Artist.
	Genre Table	
GenreId	`Int`	Unique Id for the Genre record.
GenreName	`VarChar(64)`	Name of the genre.
	CD Table	
CDId	`Int`	Unique Id for the CD record.
CDName	`VarChar(64)`	Name of the CD.
Year	`Int`	Year the CD was released.
Price	`Float`	Price paid for the CD.
GenreId	`Int`	Foreign Key to the Genre table.
	Primary Key Table (PKey)	
TableName	`VarChar(20)`	Name of the table.
KeyValue	`Int`	Last value used for the primary key for the table.

The fourth table, PKey, serves as a repository for the last value used as a primary key in each of the other tables. This is necessary because Pocket Access doesn't support AutoNumber. This table is referenced each time a new record is added to one of the three other tables. When a record is added to a table, a record corresponding to the table is looked up in the PKey table. The value of the Value field is incremented by one and updated in the PKey table. This takes place in the function `GetNewPK`, which resides in the `modGlobal` module.

Setting Up the CD Library Project

Create a new Pocket PC project.

To add a reference to ADOCE for the project, choose Project, References. As discussed previously, there are multiple versions of ADOCE. Each version installed on the development machine will be present in the Project References dialog.

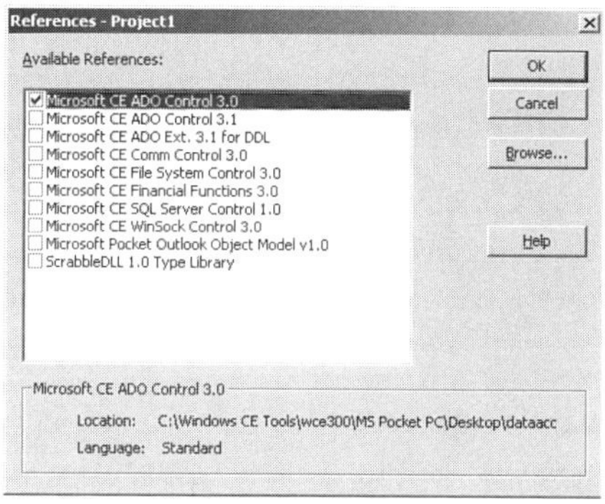

FIGURE 7.2
On this particular install of eVB, both versions of ADOCE—3.0 and 3.1—are available. This application requires only ADOCE 3.0, but is compatible with both ADOCE 3.0 and 3.1.

Check a reference to ADOCE by checking Microsoft CE ADO Control 3.0. Notice that Microsoft CE ADO Control 3.1 might be available if SQL Server CE was installed.

Adding References to Additional Controls

Three additional controls are used in the CD Library: Grid, Menu, and File System. Add these components as shown in Figure 7.3.

Adding the `frmCD` Form to the Project

Add a form to the project, and rename it to `frmCD`. Set the `caption` of frmCD to `"CD"`.

Adding the `modGlobal` Module to the Project

Add a module to the project, and name it `modGlobal`.

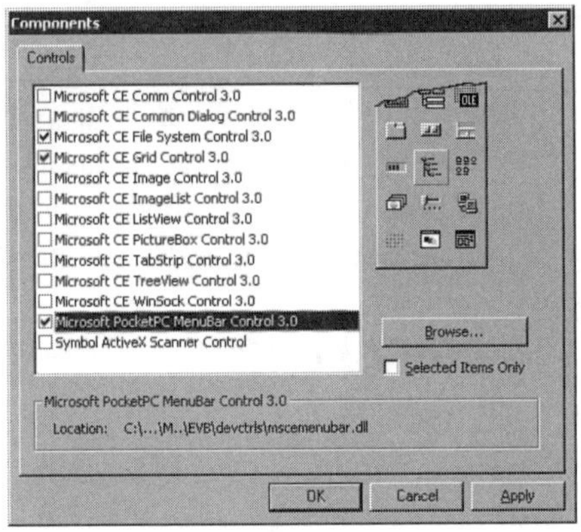

FIGURE 7.3
Components used in CD Library application are checked on in the Components dialog.

Setting Up `frmMain`

First, rename the form to `frmMain`. Also, set the value of the `Caption` property to `CD Library`.

Add one instance of the Pocket PC menu bar control to the form. No attention needs to be placed to the `Top`, `Left`, `Width` or `Height` properties as the actual control is invisible at runtime. For more information on the menu bar control, see Chapter 4, "Working with Menu Controls for Pocket PC."

Next, add the File System control to the form. Again, no attention needs to be given to the `Top`, `Left`, `Width`, or `Height` properties as the File System control is invisible at runtime. This allows you to delete the database file when you call the sub to re-create the database. For more information about the File System control, see Chapter 3, "Manipulating Files."

Finally, let's add two instances of the grid control to the form. These grids should be arranged as shown earlier in Figure 7.1. The top grid should be named `grdArtist` and the lower grid `grdCD`.

Setting Up `modGlobal`'s `Consts` and `Public` Variables

Now set up the code for `modGlobal as shown in Listing 7.2`. First, set up the `Consts` and global variables.

LISTING 7.2 modGlobal.bas: Defining `Consts` and Global Objects

```
' constants for mode that the
' cd form can operate in
Const CDFORM_MODE_EDIT = 0
```

LISTING 7.2 Continued

```
Const CDFORM_MODE_NEW = 1

' contstants for the ADOCE classes
Const ADOCE_CLASS_CONNECTION = "ADOCE.Connection.3.0"
Const ADOCE_CLASS_RECORDSET = "ADOCE.Recordset.3.0"

' contstant for database path and name
Const CD_CDB_PATH_FILENAME = "\cd.cdb"

' global objects for all ADOCE objects
Public gobjConnection As ADOCE.Connection
Public gobjArtist As ADOCE.Recordset
Public gobjCD As ADOCE.Recordset
Public gobjPKEY As ADOCE.Recordset
Public gobjGenre As ADOCE.Recordset
```

In Listing 7.2, the first two `Consts` are used when calling `frmCD`, to inform it of the mode in which it should operate, editing an existing or new record.

The next two `Consts` define the ActiveX class name (and version) that will be used throughout the application for the ADOCE classes that will be instantiated directly. These `Consts` assist in maintainability for the version problem as discussed earlier.

The last `Const` defines the path and name of the CD database. The backslash denotes to put the database into the root directory of the device. You can change this to meet your needs.

The five `Public` variables declared are used throughout the application to access data. Remember that these objects being global (`Public`) is a workaround that diminishes the `CreateObject` memory leak as discussed earlier.

Secondly, stub out all the subs and functions for `modGlobal`. These functions serve as application-level functions. Enter the code in Listing 7.3 into `modGlobal`.

LISTING 7.3 modGlobal.bas: Stubbing Out the Global Functions

```
Function InitializeGlobals() As Boolean
End Function

Function ReleaseGlobals()
End Function

Function OpenDatabase() As Boolean
End Function
```

LISTING 7.3 Continued

```
Function EnsureDatabaseExists() As Boolean
End Function

Function CreateTables() As Boolean
End Function

Function GetNewPK(ByVal strTable As String) As Long
End Function

Function AddGenre(ByVal strGenre As String) As Long
End Function

Function AddArtist( ByVal strArtist As String, _
                    ByVal lngDefaultId As Long) As Long
End Function

Function AddCD( _
    ByVal lngArtistId As Long, _
    ByVal lngGenreId As Long, _
    ByVal strCDName As String, _
    ByVal lngYear As Long, _
    ByVal curPrice As Currency) As Long

End Function

Function CreateData() As Boolean
End Function

Function RecreateDatabase() As Boolean
End Function

Function DeleteDataBase() As Boolean
End Function
```

Setting Up `frmMain`'s `Consts` and `Public` Variables

First, set up all form-level `Consts` and `Public` variables as shown in Listing 7.4.

LISTING 7.4 Consts and Public Variables

```
Const MENU_ROOTPROMPT_TOOLS_KEY = "TOOLS"
Const MENU_TOOLS_RECREATEDB_KEY = "TOOLSRECREATEDB"

' stores the column names and
```

LISTING 7.4 Continued

```
' captions for the cd grid
Public gstrCDCols(1, 3) As String
' used to store the current sort
' order for the cd grid
Public glngCDSortCol As Long
' stores the current artist id
Public glngArtistId As Long
```

The two constants define unique key values for the menu. This follows the same methodology used in Chapter 4.

Next, the three `Public` variables are to hold form-level values that will be used. The first is a two-dimensional array that holds the column names and their respective captions to display in the first row of the CD grid.

The second `Public` variable is an index to the row of the array for the current sort order of the CD grid. The CD grid allows users to re-sort by tapping the first row; when a column in the first row of the CD grid is tapped, the grid is refreshed and sorted by that column.

The last `Public` variable is used to store the ID value of the last artist selected from the grid. This value is used when the CD grid is refreshed to filter the records to that artist. It's also used when the new button is pressed to inform the CD form of the default artist for the new CD record.

Stubbing Out All `frmMain` Subs and Functions

The functions in Listing 7.5 are defined and implemented in `frmMain`. Each is a function returning a Boolean type. Although there shouldn't be any errors when calling these stub functions, the return values still need to be `True` for the application to function in limited capacity while we're still creating it. So, include the code to check for errors and set the return value into the stubs for now. We'll implement the rest later.

LISTING 7.5 Stubbing Out Common Functions

```
Function PopulateArtistGrid() As Boolean

    ' check for errors, if none, return True
    If Err.Number = 0 Then
        PopulateArtistGrid = True
    End If

End Function

Function RefreshCDGrid() As Boolean
```

LISTING 7.5 Continued

```
    ' check for errors, if none, return True
    If Err.Number = 0 Then
        RefreshCDGrid = True
    End If
End Function

Function PopulateMenus() As Boolean

    ' check for errors, if none, return True
    If Err.Number = 0 Then
        PopulateMenus = True
    End If

End Function

Function InitializeGridVariables() As Boolean

    ' check for errors, if none, return True
    If Err.Number = 0 Then
        InitializeGridVariables = True
    End If

End Function
```

The following code snippet is the template used in the stub functions to ensure that each is returning `True` (the non-error return value), until you implement them later:

```
If Err.Number = 0 Then
    ' set return value for function
    ' to True here
End If
```

Using the `Form.Load` Event

Let's look at what happens in the `Form.Load` event (see Listing 7.6).

LISTING 7.6 Implementing `frmMain`'s Load Event

```
Private Sub Form_Load()

    On Error Resume Next

    ' initialize all global variables
    If Not InitializeGlobals() Then
```

LISTING 7.6 Continued

```
        MsgBox "Error initializing global objects."
        Exit Sub
    End If

    ' open the database
    If Not OpenDatabase() Then
        MsgBox "Error opening the database."
        Exit Sub
    End If

    ' set up the menus
    If Not PopulateMenus() Then
        MsgBox "Error populating the menu object."
        Exit Sub
    End If

    ' initialize the column array and other
    ' grid variables
    If Not InitializeGridVariables() Then
        MsgBox "Error initializing the grid variables."
        Exit Sub
    End If

End Sub
```

Using the `InitializeGlobals` Function

In Listing 7.7, the `InitializeGlobals` function is called from the `Form.Load` event. `InitializeGlobals` instantiates all the global ADOCE objects. Remember, `InitializeGlobals` exists in the module `modGlobal`.

LISTING 7.7 modGlobal.bas: Creating the ADOCE Objects

```
Function InitializeGlobals() As Boolean

    On Error Resume Next

    InitializeGlobals = False

    ' initialize globals - this needs to take place
    ' only once, due to CreateObject memory leak

    ' ADOCE_CLASS_CONNECTION & ADOCE_CLASS_RECORDSET
```

Listing 7.7 Continued

```
    ' are used because ce references these classes
    ' by their version numbers, create Consts allows
    ' changing of these version quickly and accurately

    Set gobjConnection = CreateObject(ADOCE_CLASS_CONNECTION)
    Set gobjArtist = CreateObject(ADOCE_CLASS_RECORDSET)
    Set gobjCD = CreateObject(ADOCE_CLASS_RECORDSET)
    Set gobjGenre = CreateObject(ADOCE_CLASS_RECORDSET)
    Set gobjPKEY = CreateObject(ADOCE_CLASS_RECORDSET)

    If Err.Number = 0 Then
        InitializeGlobals = True
    End If

End Function
```

> **Note**
>
> All the ADOCE objects are created here and only here, once and only once. This minimizes the `CreateObject` memory leak. This, as discussed earlier, diverges completely from the architecture that should be used in a three-tier application.

The first object created is `ADOCE.Connection`. There is only one `Connection` object in the application. The next four objects are `ADOCE.Recordset` objects. Each `Recordset` object corresponds to a table within the application. The first three correspond to an entity within the CD Library that appears as an entity with the application.

Using the `OpenDatabase` Function

Next, look at `OpenDatabase as shown in Listing 7.8`. The `OpenDatabase` function opens the connection for the entire application. It first calls `EnsureDatabaseExists`, which makes sure that \cd.cdb, the Pocket Access file, exists. `EnsureDatabaseExists` also creates the tables, indexes, and populates some sample data.

> **Note**
>
> This sample application places cd.cdb in the device's root directory. More robust applications should use the App.Path or a registry to locate the database.

LISTING 7.8 modGlobal.bas: Opening the Pocket Access Database

```
Function OpenDatabase() As Boolean

    On Error Resume Next

    ' set the return value to an error
    ' condition, so we can exit early
    ' if an error occurs
    OpenDatabase = False

    ' make sure the database exists
    If Not EnsureDatabaseExists() Then
        Exit Function
    End If

    ' we need to check if the connection is
    ' open or close, because EnsureDatabaseExists may
    ' opened the database

    If gobjConnection.State = adStateClosed Then
        ' opens the pocket access database
        gobjConnection.Open CD_CDB_PATH_FILENAME
    End If

    If Err.Number = 0 Then
        OpenDatabase = True
    End If

End Function
```

Using the `EnsureDatabaseExists` Function

Let's look at `EnsureDatabaseExists` in Listing 7.9, where the CD database (cd.cdb), its tables, and its sample data are created.

LISTING 7.9 modGlobal.bas: Checking for the Existence of the Database

```
Function EnsureDatabaseExists() As Boolean

    Dim strDir As String

    On Error Resume Next

    ' set the return value to an error
    ' condition, so we can exit early
    ' if an error occurs
```

LISTING 7.9 Continued

```
    EnsureDatabaseExists = False

    ' check to see if the database exists
    strDir = frmMain.FileSystem1.Dir( CD_CDB_PATH_FILENAME )
    ' if it doesn't let's create it
    If Len(strDir) = 0 Then
        ' prepares the connection for use
        gobjConnection.Open

        ' creates a pocket access database
        gobjConnection.Execute "CREATE DATABASE '" & CD_CDB_PATH_FILENAME & "'"

        ' closes the connection - can not open
        ' the database while the connection is open
        gobjConnection.Close

        ' reopen the database (using the cd.cdb)
        If Not OpenDatabase() Then
            MsgBox "Can not open database."
            Exit Function
        End If

        ' create the tables and indexes
        If Not CreateTables() Then
            MsgBox "Can not create tables."
            Exit Function
        End If

        ' create test data
        If Not CreateData() Then
            MsgBox "Error occurred in creating sample data."
            Exit Function
        End If

    End If

    ' if no errors have occurred, we
    ' have successfully completed this
    ' function, so let's return a
    ' successful return value
    If Err.Number = 0 Then
        EnsureDatabaseExists = True
    End If

End Function
```

In Listing 7.9, `EnsureDatabaseExists` first checks to see if the database exists. It uses the File System control that resides on `frmMain`. It uses the `Dir` method to get the file path (\cd.cdb) to the database. If the file exists, the `Dir` method will return this path, if it doesn't exist, the `Dir` method will return an empty string. For more information about the File System control, see Chapter 3.

Next in Listing 7.9, the `ADOCE.Connection` object (`gobjConnection`) is opened. This must be done to execute any statements. Even though no `ConnectionString` is specified, the `ADOCE.Connection` opens. It actually is opening a connection to the Windows CE Object Store; this doesn't hamper our effort to create a database by executing the SQL command `CREATE DATABASE '\cd.cdb'`. `CREATE DATABASE 'cd.cdb'` actually creates the Pocket Access database.

Then, the `Connection` object (`gobjConnection`) is closed. This allows the object to be reopened, this time opening the Pocket Access database (\cd.cdb). This is accomplished by making a recursive call to `OpenDatabase` method.

Using the `CreateTables` Function to Create Tables and Indexes, and to Insert Data

After the database is open, you need to create the tables. The `CreateTables` function in Listing 7.10 creates all four tables and indexes for those tables.

LISTING 7.10 modGlobal.bas: Creating the Tables for the CD Library

```
Function CreateTables() As Boolean

    On Error Resume Next

    CreateTables = False

    ' creates the table artist
    gobjConnection.Execute "CREATE TABLE Artist " _
        & "(ArtistId int, ArtistName varchar(64), DefaultGenre int)"
    ' creates the table CD
    gobjConnection.Execute "CREATE TABLE CD " _
        & "(CDId int, ArtistId int, CDName varchar(64), " _
        & "Year int, Price float, GenreId int)"
    ' creates the Genre table
    gobjConnection.Execute "CREATE TABLE Genre " _
        & "(GenreID int, GenreName varchar(64))"
    ' creates the PKey table (primary key)
    gobjConnection.Execute "CREATE TABLE PKey " _
        & "(TableName varchar(20), KeyValue int)"
```

LISTING 7.10 Continued

```
    ' creates an index on ArtistId on table CD
    gobjConnection.Execute "CREATE INDEX ArtistId ON CD (ArtistId)"

    ' creates an index on TableName on table PKey
    gobjConnection.Execute "CREATE INDEX TableName ON PKey (TableName)"

    ' creates an index on GenreId on table Genre
    gobjConnection.Execute "CREATE INDEX Genre ON Genre (GenreId)"

    ' populates the PKey table with a record for the Artist table
    gobjConnection.Execute "INSERT INTO PKey VALUES (""Artist"", 0 )"
    ' populates the PKey table with a record for the cd table
    gobjConnection.Execute "INSERT INTO PKey VALUES (""CD"", 0 )"
    ' populates the PKey table with a record for the Genre table
    gobjConnection.Execute "INSERT INTO PKey VALUES (""Genre"", 0 )"

    If Err.Number = 0 Then
        CreateTables = True
    End If

End Function
```

Creating Tables by Using `CREATE TABLE`

The first four lines in `CreateTables` each execute a standard SQL statement that creates the four tables:

```
' creates the table artist
gobjConnection.Execute "CREATE TABLE Artist " _
    & "(ArtistId int, ArtistName varchar(64), DefaultGenre int)"
' creates the table cd
gobjConnection.Execute "CREATE TABLE CD " _
    & "(CDId int, ArtistId int, CDName varchar(64), " _
    & "Year int, Price float, GenreId int)"
' creates the genre table
gobjConnection.Execute "CREATE TABLE Genre " _
    & "(GenreID int, GenreName varchar(64))"
' creates the PKey table (primary key)
gobjConnection.Execute "CREATE TABLE PKey " _
    & "(TableName varchar(20), KeyValue int)"
```

These statements use SQL directly to perform data-definition. Each SQL statement complies with standard Data Definition Language (DDL).

Creating Indexes by Using CREATE INDEX

The next three statements (repeated here) use SQL to create indexes, directly executed through the connection object. The syntax of the CREATE INDEX statement is standard DDL.

```
' creates an index on ArtistId on table CD
gobjConnection.Execute "CREATE INDEX ArtistId ON CD (ArtistId)"

' creates an index on TableName on table PKey
gobjConnection.Execute "CREATE INDEX TableName ON PKey (TableName)"

' creates an index on GenreId on table Genre
gobjConnection.Execute "CREATE INDEX Genre ON Genre (GenreId)"
```


The index on the Genre table is absolutely necessary, because there is a JOIN condition in the application between the CD and Genre tables (see Figure 7.4). With ADOCE, at least one of the tables needs to be indexed on the field(s) used for the JOIN.

The remaining two indexes are created for performance reasons when selecting filter data from their tables using the WHERE clause.

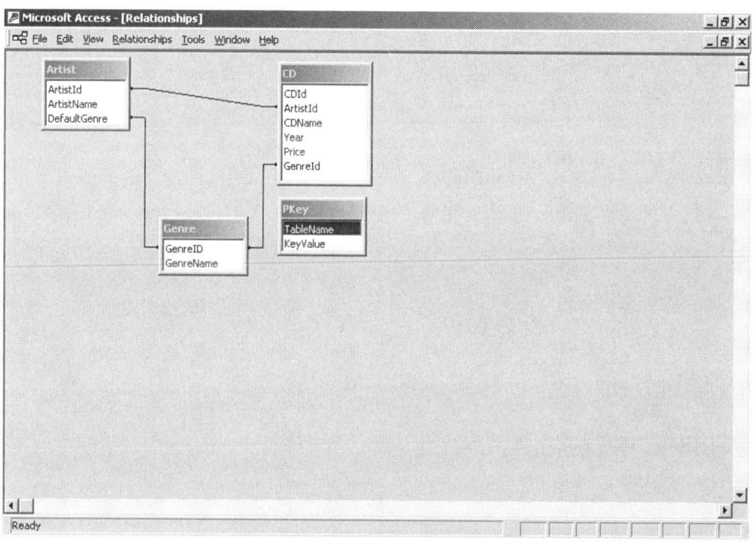

FIGURE 7.4
A relation diagram shows the tables and their relationships to each other.

Inserting Records by Using INSERT

The last three statements are the first statements called in the application that manipulate data. These use standard SQL to insert records into the PKey table. Each record corresponds to one of the other three tables. These records are used to store the last value for the primary key column.

```
' populates the PKey table with a record for the Artist table
gobjConnection.Execute "INSERT INTO PKey VALUES (""Artist"", 0 )"
' populates the PKey table with a record for the cd table
gobjConnection.Execute "INSERT INTO PKey VALUES (""CD"", 0 )"
' populates the PKey table with a record for the Genre table
gobjConnection.Execute "INSERT INTO PKey VALUES (""Genre"", 0 )"
```

Using the `CreateData` Function

The `CreateData` function creates sample data. The code in Listing 7.11 creates three genres. Later you will add code to create three artists and two CDs for each artist.

LISTING 7.11 modGlobal.bas: Creating Sample Genre Records

```
Private Function CreateData() As Boolean

    Dim lngRockId As Long
    Dim lngBlueGrassId As Long
    Dim lngHeavyMetalId As Long

    On Error Resume Next

    ' set the return value to an
    ' error condition, this allows
    ' early exit if an error occurs
    CreateData = False

    ' let's add genres
    lngRockId = AddGenre("Rock")

    ' check the return value, should be
    ' greater than zero
    If lngRockId < 0 Then
        Exit Function
    End If

    lngBlueGrassId = AddGenre("Bluegrass")
    ' check the return value, should be
    ' greater than zero
    If lngBlueGrassId < 0 Then
        Exit Function
    End If
```

LISTING 7.11 Continued

```
    lngHeavyMetalId = AddGenre("Heavy Metal")
    ' check the return value, should be
    ' greater than zero
    If lngHeavyMetalId < 0 Then
        Exit Function
    End If

    If Err.Number = 0 Then
        CreateData = True
    End If

End Function
```

Each Genre has a corresponding variable of type `Long` declared. The primary key values for each of these Genre records are retained to these variables. These primary key values are used when creating CD records.

Using the `AddGenre` Function

Listing 7.12 calls the `AddGenre` function from the `CreateData` function (it's also called from the CD form, as you will see later). The `AddGenre` function inserts records but uses the `ADOCE.Recordset` method to accomplish this. This is different from the SQL direct method used to insert the records into PKey in the `CreateTables` function. After a successful insert of the genre record, `AddGenre` returns the value of the primary key of the newly inserted record.

LISTING 7.12 modGlobal.bas: Encapsulating Adding a Genre Record

```
Function AddGenre(ByVal strGenre As String) As Long

    ' adds an genre to the table and returns
    ' its primary key value

    Dim lngGenreId As Long

    On Error Resume Next

    ' set the return value to error code
    ' in case we need to exit early
    AddGenre = -1

    ' get a new primary key value
    lngGenreId = GetNewPK("Genre")
```

LISTING 7.12 Continued

```
    ' check the return value for the new primary key
    If lngGenreId < 0 Then
        Exit Function
    End If

    ' if the recordset is open
    ' let's check if it supports addnew
    If gobjGenre.State = adStateOpen Then
        ' if the current recordset does not
        ' support adding new records, let's close
        ' it and reopen it
        If Not gobjGenre.Supports(adAddNew) Then
            gobjGenre.Close
        End If
    End If

    ' if the recordset is closed above
    ' or closed before we get into this
    ' function, let's open it with the
    ' proper support for adding
    If gobjGenre.State = adStateClosed Then
         gobjGenre.Open "genre", gobjConnection, _
            adOpenForwardOnly, adLockOptimistic, adCmdTableDirect
    End If

    ' add a new record
    gobjGenre.AddNew

    ' set the values
    gobjGenre.Fields("GenreId").Value = lngGenreId
    gobjGenre.Fields("GenreName").Value = strGenre

    ' update the recordset
    gobjGenre.Update

    ' set the return value
    AddGenre = lngGenreId

    ' if there was an error, let's set the return
    ' value to a negative value
    If Err.Number <> 0 Then
        AddGenre = -1 * Abs(Err.Number)
    End If

End Function
```

Getting a New Primary Key Value

First, `AddGenre` does some routine setup, but then calls the function `GetNewPK` (as repeated in the code that follows). `GetNewPK` will be explained later, but for now, know that it will return the next key for the table that's passed as a string. The value returned from `GetNewPK` is retained into a local variable.

```
' get a new primary key value
lngGenreId = GetNewPK("Genre")

' check the return value for the new primary key
If lngGenreId < 0 Then
    Exit Function
End If
```

Also, it's important to note the methodology of a quick exit and the preset error-condition return value. This is a methodology found to work well for a few reasons. This presetting of the return value and quick exit on any error works well in Visual Basic, but even better in eVB. Because there is no error handler in eVB, except for `On Error Resume Next`, it's nice to assume an error return value unless the function makes it to the end without an error. This allows an `Exit Function` to be issued on every error condition without having to set the return value each time. It also prevents arrowheads, as demonstrated in this pseudocode:

```
If everything Is Ok Then
    ' do something
    If That Went OK Then
        'do something else
        If This 3rd Thing Went OK Then
            'do a 3rd thing
            and so on and so on....
        End If
    End If
End If
```

This methodology is in several places within the application, so familiarize yourself with it. Also, at the end of the function, the `Err` object's `Number` property's value is checked. If it's not zero, the return value is set to the negative of the absolute value of the error number. For example, let's say you have a native eVB of 1200. Taking –1 and multiplying it by the absolute value of 1200, gives you –1200; because this value is less than 0, it's an error condition. Use the absolute value in case the error is an ActiveX error—for example, –800096007. This returns –1 times the absolute value of –80096007, which is still the negative value –80096007.

```
If Err.Number <> 0 Then
    GetNewPK = -1 * Abs(Err.Number)
End If
```

Checking the Recordset State

Once the value returned from `GetNewPK` is verified, the state of the Genre recordset object is verified. The verification first checks to see if the recordset object is open by inquiring its `State` property. If the Genre recordset is open, a check is made to ensure that the recordset currently supports adding a new record by using the `Supports` method and the `adAddNew` enumeration. If the recordset doesn't currently support adding new records, it's closed, reopen by:

```
' if the recordset is open
' let's check if it supports addnew
If gobjGenre.State = adStateOpen Then
    ' if the current recordset does not
    ' support adding new records, let's close
    ' it and reopen it
    If Not gobjGenre.Supports(adAddNew) Then
        gobjGenre.Close
    End If
End If
```

Opening the Recordset for Adding (or Updating/Deleting)

To open the recordset for adding new, and updating or deleting records, the recordset must have certain attributes. The most important attribute for the recordset to be modifiable is the `LockType` assigned to it. The `LockType` property can be set directly:

```
Recordset.LockType = adLockOptimistic
```

Or, the `LockType` can be set via the `LockType` parameter of the `Open` method:

```
Recordset.Open "(Source for records)", connection, cursortype, _
        adLockOptimistic
```

In `AddGenre`, if the recordset was closed on entry to `AddGenre` or closed in `AddGenre` because it didn't currently support adding new records, the recordset is opened. It's opened with *table direct*, a preferable method for using ADOCE recordsets. The table direct performs better with SQL Server CE. To open a recordset directly, notice the `adCmdTableDirect` enumeration value as the optional parameter to the `Recordset.Open` method. Table direct opens the table directly without using SQL; it's equivalent to `SELECT * FROM table`.

```
' if the recordset is closed above
' or closed before we get into this
' function, let's open it with the
' proper support for adding
If gobjGenre.State = adStateClosed Then
        gobjGenre.Open "genre", gobjConnection, _
            adOpenForwardOnly, adLockOptimistic, adCmdTableDirect
End If
```

Adding the Record

After the recordset supports adding records, issue the statement AddNew. The AddGenre function issues the AddNew method to the recordset.

```
' add a new record
gobjGenre.AddNew
```

Setting the Values for the Recordset's Columns

After the new record is appended to the recordset, the values for that new record are assigned using the Recordset.Fields collection.

The AddGenre function uses a verbose method to assign the values:

```
' set the values
gobjGenre.Fields("GenreId").Value = lngGenreId
gobjGenre.Fields("GenreName").Value = strGenre
```

Because the Field object's default property is Value, the column's values can be assigned as follows:

```
' set the values
gobjGenre.Fields("GenreId") = lngGenreId
gobjGenre.Fields("GenreName") = strGenre
```

Each Field in the collection can be referenced by the column name or its index in the collection. An example of using the index value is as follows:

```
' set the values
gobjGenre.Fields(0) = lngGenreId
gobjGenre.Fields(1) = strGenre
```

And, because the recordset's default property is actually the Fields collection, an even shorter method of assigning the values can be used:

```
' set the values
gobjGenre(0) = lngGenreId
gobjGenre(1) = strGenre
```

Committing the Update

To send the update back to the data store, call the Update method:

```
' update the recordset
gobjGenre.Update
```

Returning the Primary Key Value

Because the AddGenre function is called from various places within the application to add a new genre on-the-fly, the primary key value of the newly created record is returned:

```
' set the return value
AddGenre = lngGenreId
```

Ensuring a New Record's Validity

To ensure that the record has correctly inserted, the eVB error object Err is checked to be sure that no errors occurred throughout the entire function:

```
' if there was an error, let's set the return
' value to a negative value
If Err.Number <> 0 Then
    AddGenre = -1 * Abs(Err.Number)
End If
```

If an error occurred, the return value is set to the negative value of the Err.Number. Any method that calls AddGenre should check the return value to be zero or greater.

Using the GetNewPK Function to Control Primary Keys

Pocket Access does not support automatically incrementing key values; eVB applications need to control their own primary keys. Typically this is accomplished by using a control table. The CD Library application uses the PKey table to achieve this. Each time a new record is added to any of the other tables (Artist, Genre, CD), GetNewPK finds the appropriate record and increments the value (KeyValue) by one, updates the record, and returns this new value (see Listing 7.13).

Listing 7.13 modGlobal.bas: Getting a New Primary Key Value

```
Function GetNewPK(ByVal strTable As String) As Long

    ' gets a new pk for a particular table

    On Error Resume Next

    ' set the return value in case we exit early
    GetNewPK = -1

    ' if the table is open, let's close it
    If gobjPKEY.State = adStateOpen Then
        gobjPKEY.Close
    End If
```

LISTING 7.13 Continued

```
    ' open the table with the correct record
    gobjPKEY.Open "SELECT KeyValue FROM PKey WHERE TableName = " _
        & """" & strTable & """", gobjConnection, _
        adOpenForwardOnly, adLockOptimistic

    ' if there is no record for this table
    ' we have an error
    If gobjPKEY.EOF Then
        Exit Function
    End If

    ' set the value to itself plus one
    gobjPKEY.Fields("KeyValue").Value = gobjPKEY.Fields("KeyValue").Value + 1

    ' update the record
    gobjPKEY.Update

    ' set the return value
    GetNewPK = gobjPKEY.Fields("KeyValue").Value

    ' if we had an error, let's set the
    ' return value to a negative return
    If Err.Number <> 0 Then
        GetNewPK = -1 * Abs(Err.Number)
    End If

End Function
```


Give It a Whirl

At this point, your CD Library application is ready for testing. It should be able to

- Check if the database exists
- Create the database if it doesn't exist
- Create the tables
- Add a record to the PKey control table for each entity
- Create a new primary key value for each entity
- Add three genre records

To test your CD Library application in its current state, place a breakpoint on the first executable line of the Form.Load event. This allows you to walk through the entire application's codebase in one debugging session.

Using the `AddArtist` Function

Now, let's implement the `AddArtist` function (see Listing 7.14). Just as `AddGenre` adds a record to the Genre table, `AddArtist` adds a record to the Artist table. `AddArtist` follows the exact same template as `AddGenre`.

LISTING 7.14 modGlobal.bas: Adding a New Artist

```
Function AddArtist(ByVal strArtist As String, _
                   ByVal lngDefaultId As Long) As Long

    ' adds an artist to the table and returns
    ' its primary key value
    ' if there is an error, returns a negative value

    Dim lngArtistId As Long

    On Error Resume Next

    ' set the return value to an error value
    ' in case we exit early
    AddArtist = -1

    ' returns a new id for the new artist
    lngArtistId = GetNewPK("Artist")

    ' checks the return value
    If lngArtistId < 0 Then
        Exit Function
    End If

    ' needs to test the recordset to see if
    ' it currently supports adding new records

    ' let's see if recordset is open
    If gobjArtist.State = adStateOpen Then
        ' if it currently does not support
        ' adding new, let's close it and reopen
        ' it below
        If Not gobjArtist.Supports(adAddNew) Then
            ' close the recordset
            gobjArtist.Close
        End If
    End If

    ' if it was closed before we got into this
```

LISTING 7.14 Continued

```
    ' function or closed in this function, let's
    ' reopen it with the correct support (AddsNew)
    If gobjArtist.State = adStateClosed Then
        gobjArtist.Open _
            "artist", _
            gobjConnection, _
            adOpenForwardOnly, _
            adLockOptimistic, _
            adCmdTableDirect
        ' "artist" - open the table direct
        ' gobjConnection - the global connection object
        ' adOpenForwardOnly - we're only going to add,
        '   so no need to have scrollable cursor
        ' adLockOptimistic - quick updates
        ' adCmdTableDirect - optional parameter that
        ' informs the recordset to open the table directly
        ' allowing the quickest manipulation
    End If

    ' append a new record
    gobjArtist.AddNew

    ' set values
    gobjArtist.Fields("ArtistId").Value = lngArtistId
    gobjArtist.Fields("ArtistName").Value = strArtist

    ' if we have a genre, let's set it
    If Not IsEmpty(lngDefaultId) Then
        gobjArtist.Fields("DefaultGenre").Value = lngDefaultId
    End If

    ' update the recordset - commits the record
    gobjArtist.Update

    ' set the return value
    AddArtist = lngArtistId

    ' if we had an error, let's set the
    ' return value to a negative value
    ' so we know that it failed
    If Err.Number <> 0 Then
        AddArtist = -1 * Abs(Err.Number)
    End If

End Function
```

Using the AddCD Function

The final function to be implemented that adds a record to a table is AddCD (see Listing 7.15). Again, AddCD follows the same template.

LISTING 7.15 modGlobal.bas: Adding a New CD

```
Function AddCD( _
    ByVal lngArtistId As Long, _
    ByVal lngGenreId As Long, _
    ByVal strCDName As String, _
    ByVal lngYear As Long, _
    ByVal curPrice As Currency) As Long

    Dim lngCDId As Long

    On Error Resume Next

    ' let's set the return value to
    ' an error code, so if we exit early
    AddCD = -1

    ' get a new primary key value
    lngCDId = GetNewPK("CD")

    ' check the value to make sure it valid
    If lngCDId < 0 Then
        Exit Function
    End If

    ' if the CD recordset is open, let's
    ' check to make sure it can support
    ' adding a new record
    If gobjCD.State = adStateOpen Then
        ' check to see if the current
        ' recordset supports adding a new record
        If Not gobjCD.Supports(adAddNew) Then
            gobjCD.Close
        End If
    End If

    ' if the recordset is closed, either
    ' before we entered the function
    ' or if we closed it above
    If gobjCD.State = adStateClosed Then
```

LISTING 7.15 Continued

```
        gobjCD.Open "cd", gobjConnection, adOpenForwardOnly, _
            adLockOptimistic, adCmdTableDirect
    End If

    ' add a new record
    gobjCD.AddNew
    ' set the values
    gobjCD.Fields("CDId").Value = lngCDId

    ' let's set the Artist value
    gobjCD.Fields("ArtistId").Value = lngArtistId

    ' let's set the Genre value
    gobjCD.Fields("GenreId").Value = lngGenreId

    ' if we have an cd name, let's set the value
    If Not IsEmpty(strCDName) Then
       gobjCD.Fields("CDName").Value = strCDName
    End If

    ' if we have an year, let's set the value
    If Not IsEmpty(lngYear) Then
       gobjCD.Fields("Year").Value = lngYear
    End If

    ' if we have an price, let's set the value
    If Not IsEmpty(curPrice) Then
       gobjCD.Fields("Price").Value = curPrice
    End If

    ' update the recordset
    gobjCD.Update

    ' set the return value
    AddCD = lngCDId

    ' if we had an error, let's set
    ' the return value to a negative value
    If Err.Number <> 0 Then
        AddCD = -1 * Abs(Err.Number)
    End If

End Function
```

The only structural difference between AddCD and AddGenre or AddArtist is that validation is completed on the values of Year and Price. These fields are checked as to whether they have values. If these fields have valid values, the recordset's field values are set. If not, they are left empty, resulting in a NULL.

Updating the CreateData Function to Add Artists and CDs

Now that the AddArtist and AddCD functions are implemented, the CreateData function in Listing 7.16 can add artists and CDs to the database when it's creating the sample data.

LISTING 7.16 modGlobal.bas: Adding Artists and CDs

```
Private Function CreateData() As Boolean

    Dim lngRockId As Long
    Dim lngBlueGrassId As Long
    Dim lngHeavyMetalId As Long

    Dim lngTomPettyId As Long
    Dim lngAllisonKrausId As Long
    Dim lngMetallicaId As Long

    On Error Resume Next

    ' set the return value to an
    ' error condition, this allows
    ' early exit if an error occurs
    CreateData = False

    ' let's add genres
    lngRockId = AddGenre("Rock")

    ' check the return value, should be
    ' greater than zero
    If lngRockId < 0 Then
        Exit Function
    End If

    lngBlueGrassId = AddGenre("Bluegrass")
    ' check the return value, should be
    ' greater than zero
    If lngBlueGrassId < 0 Then
        Exit Function
    End If
```

LISTING 7.16 Continued

```
lngHeavyMetalId = AddGenre("Heavy Metal")
' check the return value, should be
' greater than zero
If lngHeavyMetalId < 0 Then
    Exit Function
End If

' let's add some artists
lngTomPettyId = AddArtist("Tom Petty", lngRockId)
' check the return value, should be
' greater than zero
If lngTomPettyId < 0 Then
    Exit Function
End If

lngAllisonKrausId = AddArtist("Allison Kraus", lngBlueGrassId)
' check the return value, should be
' greater than zero
If lngAllisonKrausId < 0 Then
    Exit Function
End If

lngMetallicaId = AddArtist("Metallica", lngHeavyMetalId)
' check the return value, should be
' greater than zero
If lngMetallicaId < 0 Then
    Exit Function
End If

' add cds for Tom Petty
If AddCD(lngTomPettyId, lngRockId, _
    "Damn the Torpedos", 1989, 10.99) < 0 Then
        Exit Function
End If

If AddCD(lngTomPettyId, lngRockId, _
    "Tom Petty Live", 1988, 12.99) < 0 Then
        Exit Function
End If

' add cds for Allison Kraus
If AddCD(lngAllisonKrausId, lngBlueGrassId, _
    "Best Of Allison Kraus", 1998, 12.99) < 0 Then
        Exit Function
```

Listing 7.16 Continued

```
    End If

    If AddCD(lngAllisonKrausId, lngBlueGrassId, _
        "Long and Blue", 1999, 15.99) < 0 Then
            Exit Function
    End If

    ' add cds for Metallica
    If AddCD(lngMetallicaId, lngHeavyMetalId, _
        "Master Of The Puppets", 1986, 9.99) < 0 Then
            Exit Function
    End If

    If AddCD(lngMetallicaId, lngHeavyMetalId, _
        "Metallica", 1983, 12.99) < 0 Then
            Exit Function
    End If

    If Err.Number = 0 Then
        CreateData = True
    End If

End Function
```

The first new section of code simply `Dims` some new variables to store the artist's primary keys. This follows the same methodology as when `CreateData` retained the primary key values from the added Genre records:

```
Dim lngTomPettyId As Long
Dim lngAllisonKrausId As Long
Dim lngMetallicaId As Long
```

The next change adds the three artists of the sample data, "Tom Petty," "Allison Kraus," and "Metallica." It accomplishes this by calling the `AddArtist` function. It checks the return value of the `AddArtist` function. If it's an invalid key, it exits the function, returning the default return value, which was set at the top of the function.

Notice the local variable for the Genre primary key as the second parameter to `AddArtist`. This stores the GenreId in the Artist table; this is used to set the default genre in the CD form (`frmCD`) when creating a new CD for the artist.

```
' let's add some artists
lngTomPettyId = AddArtist("Tom Petty", lngRockId)
' check the return value, should be
```

```
' greater than zero
If lngTomPettyId < 0 Then
    Exit Function
End If

lngAllisonKrausId = AddArtist("Allison Kraus", lngBlueGrassId)
' check the return value, should be
' greater than zero
If lngAllisonKrausId < 0 Then
    Exit Function
End If

lngMetallicaId = AddArtist("Metallica", lngHeavyMetalId)
' check the return value, should be
' greater than zero
If lngMetallicaId < 0 Then
    Exit Function
End If
```


Another Trip Around the Block

Your application should be ready for another test—after all, it should now create all the sample data. There's one catch, because your database is already created, the `CreateData` function won't automatically execute. `CreateData` is called from `EnsureDatabaseExists` and `RecreateDatabase` (which isn't implemented yet). Your options include placing a call to `CreateData` at the end of the `Form.Load` event (this will create duplicate genres and can eventually create errors) or deleting the cd.cdb from your emulator or device. Or, you can jump ahead and complete `PopulateMenus`, the `Menu.Click` event, and `RecreateDatabase`.

Using the `InitializeGridVariables` Function

Recall the `InitializeGridVariables` function that we stubbed out early on. Here it is in Listing 7.17. A few things happen here, none that are really important to ADOCE.

LISTING 7.17 modGlobal.bas: Setting Up the Grid's Variables

```
Function InitializeGridVariables() As Boolean

    On Error Resume Next

    ' set the return value to error condition
    InitializeGridVariables = False

    ' set the column width of the
    ' artist grid to the grid width
```

LISTING 7.17 Continued

```
    grdArtist.ColWidth(0) = grdArtist.Width

    ' set up the cd grid variables
    gstrCDCols(0, 0) = "CDName"      ' field name
    gstrCDCols(1, 0) = "Name"        ' caption

    gstrCDCols(0, 1) = "Year"        ' field name
    gstrCDCols(1, 1) = "Year"        ' caption

    gstrCDCols(0, 2) = "Price"       ' field name
    gstrCDCols(1, 2) = "Price"       ' caption

    gstrCDCols(0, 3) = "GenreName"   ' field name
    gstrCDCols(1, 3) = "Genre"       ' caption

    ' set the grid's first column width to half
    ' of the grid's width
    grdCD.ColWidth(0) = grdCD.Width / 2

    ' set the current sort order to the first column (CDName)
    glngCDSortCol = 0

    ' check for errors, if none, return True
    If Err.Number = 0 Then
        InitializeGridVariables = True
    End If

End Function
```

Set the `ColWidth` of the first column in the artist grid to the full width of the grid.

```
' set the column width of the
' artist grid to the grid width
grdArtist.ColWidth(0) = grdArtist.Width
```

Then an array is initialized. This array serves two purposes: it provides the captions for the header (first row) of the CD grid and the names of the respective column from the CD table. The CD field name is used for sorting the CD records by different columns. This re-sorting occurs when the user taps the caption (header) of the CD grid.

```
' set up the cd grid variables
gstrCDCols(0, 0) = "CDName"      ' field name
gstrCDCols(1, 0) = "Name"        ' caption
```

```
gstrCDCols(0, 1) = "Year"       ' field name
gstrCDCols(1, 1) = "Year"       ' caption

gstrCDCols(0, 2) = "Price"      ' field name
gstrCDCols(1, 2) = "Price"      ' caption

gstrCDCols(0, 3) = "GenreName"  ' field name
gstrCDCols(1, 3) = "Genre"      ' caption
```

The CD grid's first column is set to half the width of the CD grid. This can only be accomplished at runtime.

```
' set the grid's first column width to half
' of the grid's width
grdCD.ColWidth(0) = grdCD.Width / 2
```


The public variable (`glngCDSortCol`) that retains the current sort column of the CD is set to the first column (CDName). This variable is really an index to the array (`gstrCDCols`).

```
' set the current sort order to the first column (CDName)
glngCDSortCol = 0
```

Using the `PopulateArtistGrid` Function to See the Data

Now that there is data to display, let's get it into that artist grid (see Listing 7.18).

LISTING 7.18 Displaying the Artists

```
Function PopulateArtistGrid() As Boolean

    On Error Resume Next

    PopulateArtistGrid = False

    ' if the artist table is open, let's close
    ' it so we can reopen it under the right conditions
    If gobjArtist.State = adStateOpen Then
        gobjArtist.Close
    End If

    ' open the table
    ' ordering by the artistname
    gobjArtist.Open "SELECT * FROM artist ORDER BY ArtistName", _
        gobjConnection, adOpenForwardOnly, adLockReadOnly
```

LISTING 7.18 Continued

```
    ' clear the grids
    grdArtist.Rows = 0
grdCD.Rows = 0
    grdArtist.Clear
    grdCD.Clear

    ' go top in artist table
    gobjArtist.MoveFirst

    Do While Not gobjArtist.EOF
        ' add the artist to the grid
        grdArtist.AddItem gobjArtist.Fields("ArtistName")
        ' next record
        gobjArtist.MoveNext
    Loop

    ' check for errors, if none, return True
    If Err.Number = 0 Then
        PopulateArtistGrid = True
    End If

End Function
```

`PopulateArtistGrid` does the standard setup with the `Error` trap and sets the return value:

```
On Error Resume Next

PopulateArtistGrid = False
```

Then, the function closes the artist `Recordset` object if it's open:

```
' if the artist table is open, let's close
' it so we can reopen it under the right conditions
If gobjArtist.State = adStateOpen Then
    gobjArtist.Close
End If
```

Next, the artist `Recordset` is reopened using a standard SQL statement that has an `ORDER BY` clause. This orders the artist data by the ArtistName column. Notice, the recordset specifies a forward-only (`adOpenForward`) cursor for the `CursorType` parameter. This recordset is only scrolled through from top to bottom, so any other cursor would consume unnecessary resources. The recordset is also specified to be read-only by including `adLockReadOnly` for the

LockType parameter. There is no update from the artist grid, so again, it's using resources efficiently.

```
' open the table
' ordering by the artistname
    gobjArtist.Open "SELECT * FROM artist ORDER BY ArtistName", _
        gobjConnection, adOpenForwardOnly, adLockReadOnly
```

The next segment of code deals directly with the grids. It's not the scope of this chapter to go into the grids, but basically the grids are both cleared. There is a bug in the grid control that if the rows aren't set to zero before calling Clear, sometimes the device locks up.


```
' clear the grids
grdArtist.Rows = 0
grdCD.Rows = 0
grdArtist.Clear
grdCD.Clear
```

Before the grid is populated, the recordset is ensured to be on the first record by issuing the MoveFirst method. Then, the recordset is cycled through and each record's ArtistName value is added to the grid, using the grid's AddItem method. AddItem adds a row to the grid and sets the first column of that row to the value of the parameter passed to it.

After adding the ArtistName to the grid, you need to store the primary key value of the artist record with the row. The grid's RowData collection provides this functionality. The artist record's primary key value allows the application to display the respective CDs in the CD grid. This is implemented in the next two steps.

After the record is processed, the recordset moves to the next record by using the MoveNext method:

```
' go top in artist table
gobjArtist.MoveFirst

Do While Not gobjArtist.EOF
    ' add the artist to the grid
    grdArtist.AddItem gobjArtist.Fields("ArtistName")
    ' set the RowData to the primary key of the artist
        grdArtist.RowData(grdArtist.Rows - 1) = _
            gobjArtist.Fields("ArtistID").Value
    ' next record
    gobjArtist.MoveNext
Loop

' check for errors, if none, return True
If Err.Number = 0 Then
    PopulateArtistGrid = True
End If
```

Once More Around the Block: Let's See Those Artists

At this point, execute your application. You should see the artists populated in the grid.

What Artist? Which CDs?

Now that the artist grid displays the artists, let's get their respective CDs into the CD grid. The functionality of displaying all the CDs for an artist is implemented when a row in the artist grid is tapped. Let's implement the `Grid.Click` event, `grdArtist_Click`:

```
Private Sub grdArtist_Click()
    ' each time the artist
    glngArtistId = grdArtist.RowData(grdArtist.Row)

    ' refreshes the cd grid for the currently select artist
    RefreshCDGrid

End Sub
```

Remember that public variable `glngArtistId` declared for the form (`frmMain`)? This is where the application stores the "current artist." The "current artist" is the artist that has been tapped. The `RefreshCDGrid` function uses `glngArtistId` (refer to Listing 7.4) to filter the CD recordset to the CD records that have the ArtistId foreign key value that matches.

Using the `RefreshCDGrid` Function: Finally, Those CDs!

The `RefreshCDGrid` function refreshes the CD grid with the CDs that belong to the "current artist." Remember, "current artist" is stored as the primary key value of the artist record in the public variable `glngArtistId`.

The `RefreshCDGrid` function in Listing 7.19

- Closes the CD recordset.
- Builds a SQL string (that includes a `JOIN`).
- Opens the CD recordset using the SQL string.
- Clears the CD grid.
- Sets the number of columns in the grid to the number of columns in the recordset that should be displayed. The primary key column, CDId, isn't displayed.
- Adds a header row to the grid, sets the captions, and makes them bold.
- Cycles through the CD recordset and adds the CD records to the grid, while setting the `RowData` to the primary key value of the CD record.

LISTING 7.19 Displaying the CDs

```
Function RefreshCDGrid() As Boolean

    Dim strSortField As String
    Dim i As Long
    Dim strSQL As String

    On Error Resume Next

    RefreshCDGrid = False

    ' close the cd recordset if it is open
    If gobjCD.State = adStateOpen Then
        gobjCD.Close
    End If

    ' build a sql string
    strSQL = "SELECT "

    ' add the columns
    For i = 0 To UBound(gstrCDCols, 2)
        strSQL = strSQL & gstrCDCols(0, i) & ","
    Next

    ' add the id for the RowData
    strSQL = strSQL & "CDId"

    ' select the data
    ' sort by the current sort order
    strSQL = strSQL & " FROM cd INNER JOIN " _
        & " Genre ON cd.GenreId = genre.GenreID "

    ' let's filter that data to the current artist
    strSQL = strSQL & "WHERE ArtistId = " & CStr(glngArtistId)

    ' and sort that data by the current sort order
    strSQL = strSQL & " ORDER BY " & gstrCDCols(0, glngCDSortCol)

    ' open the recordset, forward only - read only
    gobjCD.Open strSQL, gobjConnection, adOpenForwardOnly, adLockReadOnly

    ' clear the grid
    grdCD.Clear

    ' set the rows to one to cover the column name cells
```

LISTING 7.19 Continued

```
    grdCD.Rows = 1

    ' set the col count to the field count
    ' minus one for the CDId (PK field)
    grdCD.Cols = gobjCD.Fields.Count - 1

    ' set up the header row
    ' move to the first row - 0 based
    grdCD.Row = 0
    For i = 0 To UBound(gstrCDCols, 2)
        'add the label to the grid
        grdCD.TextMatrix(0, i) = gstrCDCols(1, i)
        ' bold the labels
        grdCD.Col = i
        grdCD.CellFontBold = True
    Next

    ' put the col back to the left
    grdCD.Col = 0

    ' add the records
    Do While Not gobjCD.EOF
        ' add the cd name and row at the same time
        grdCD.AddItem gobjCD.Fields("CDName").Value

        ' set each of the columns values
        For i = 0 To UBound(gstrCDCols, 2)
            grdCD.TextMatrix(grdCD.Rows - 1, i) = _
                gobjCD.Fields(gstrCDCols(0, i)).Value
        Next

        ' set the rowdata to the primary key
        grdCD.RowData(grdCD.Rows - 1) = gobjCD.Fields("CDId").Value

        ' move to next record
        gobjCD.MoveNext
    Loop

    ' check for errors, if none, return True
    If Err.Number = 0 Then
        RefreshCDGrid = True
    End If
End Function
```

The first block of code to examine builds a standard SQL string that retrieves the data from the CD table. The array `gstrCDCols` is used as the repository of the CD table's displayed columns. The fields are stored in the 0 element of the array. The CD table's primary key is added to the SQL string as well. Although it won't be displayed, it's added to the column list so it can be used to populate the `RowData` collection of the CD grid. The CD primary key value is used to open the CD edit form if the user taps the CD record.

```
' build a sql string
strSQL = "SELECT "

' add the columns
For i = 0 To UBound(gstrCDCols, 2)
    strSQL = strSQL & gstrCDCols(0, i) & ","
Next

' add the id for the RowData
strSQL = strSQL & "CDId"
' select the data
' sort by the current sort order
    strSQL = strSQL & " FROM cd INNER JOIN " _
        & " Genre ON cd.GenreId = genre.GenreID "
```

The SQL string is then appended with the proper syntax to filter the recordset to the "current artist." Remember, current artist is stored in the public variable `glngArtistId` and is set from the artist grid's `RowData` when the user select an artist record.

```
' let's filter that data to the current artist
strSQL = strSQL & "WHERE ArtistId = " & CStr(glngArtistId)
```

Next, to sort the recordset, an `ORDER BY` clause is added to the SQL string. The particular sort order is determined by the current value of the public variable `glngCDSortCol`, which is an index to a row of the array `gstrCDCols`.

```
' and sort that data by the current sort order
strSQL = strSQL & " ORDER BY " & gstrCDCols(0, glngCDSortCol)
```

The CD recordset is then opened using this SQL string. Notice that again, like the recordset for the artist grid, it's opened forward only and read-only. These options are specified by using the ADOCE enumeration values `adOpenForwardOnly` and `adLockReadOnly` for the `CursorType` and `LockType` parameters, respectively.

```
' open the recordset, forward only - read only
gobjCD.Open strSQL, gobjConnection, adOpenForwardOnly, adLockReadOnly
```

The grid is then cleared and the column count (`Cols`) is set to the number of fields in the recordset minus one (so that it doesn't display the primary key field CDId).

```
' clear the grid
grdCD.Clear
```

```
' set the rows to one to cover the column name cells
grdCD.Rows = 1

' set the col count to the field count
' minus one for the CDId (PK field)
grdCD.Cols = gobjCD.Fields.Count - 1
```

The header row is then added to the grid. The current row is set to be the first row of the grid by setting the `Row` property to 0 (the grid's rows are zero-based). A loop cycles through the columns and sets the text of each cell in that first row. The current column is set so that the `CellFontBold` property will apply, and the cell is set to be bold. The current column is then restored to the first column by using the `Col` property.

```
' set up the header row
' move to the first row - 0 based
grdCD.Row = 0
For i = 0 To UBound(gstrCDCols, 2)
    'add the label to the grid
    grdCD.TextMatrix(0, i) = gstrCDCols(1, i)
    ' bold the labels
    grdCD.Col = i
    grdCD.CellFontBold = True
Next
' put the col back to the left
grdCD.Col = 0
```

Lastly, the data is populated onto the grid. As with the artist grid, you cycle through the records. For each record, you append a new row to the grid by using the `AddItem` method of the grid. The call to `AddItem` also sets the value of the first column equal to `CDName`. Moving across the grid, each row of the `gstrCDCols` array is queried for its column name and the value of the corresponding `Field` in the recordset is applied to the row. And, the `RowData` is set to the primary key value of the record. Last, the recordset is advanced by using the `MoveNext` method.

```
' add the records
Do While Not gobjCD.EOF
    ' add the cd name and row at the same time
    grdCD.AddItem gobjCD.Fields("CDName").Value

    ' set each of the columns values
    For i = 0 To UBound(gstrCDCols, 2)
            grdCD.TextMatrix(grdCD.Rows - 1, i) = _
                gobjCD.Fields(gstrCDCols(0, i)).Value
    Next
```

```
    ' set the rowdata to the primary key
    grdCD.RowData(grdCD.Rows - 1) = gobjCD.Fields("CDId").Value

    ' move to next record
    gobjCD.MoveNext
Loop
```

Are We There Yet?

Start your application and tap the different rows in the artist grid. Does the grid refresh? Does it have the correct records in it?

Tapping the CD Grid

When the user taps a particular CD record in the CD grid, the application should display that CD record for editing. To accomplish this, implement the `Grid.Click` event (see Listing 7.20) for the CD grid.

LISTING 7.20 Implementing the `Grid.Click` Event

```
Private Sub grdCD_Click()
    If grdCD.Row = 0 Then
        ' the user clicked the first row
        ' let's change the sort order and
        ' refresh the cd grid
        glngCDSortCol = grdCD.Col
        RefreshCDGrid
    Else
        ' if the user clicked on a cd
        ' let's open the cd form
        frmCD.CDOpen grdCD.RowData(grdCD.Row), glngArtistId, CDFORM_MODE_EDIT
    End If
End Sub
```

First, the subroutine checks the current row of the CD grid (`grdCD`). When the grid control is tapped, it sets the current `Row` (and `Col`) to the row and column tapped.

If the header row is tapped, the `Row` value will be 0. If `Row = 0`, the value of `glngCDSortCol` (the current sort order for the grid) is set. Then, the CD grid is refreshed to reflect this new sort order.

If any other `Row` is tapped, the CD form (`frmCD`) is opened using a custom subroutine, `CDOpen`. The primary key value, the "current artist" and the `Const CDFORM_MODE_EDIT` are passed as parameters. For this to work, you need to implement the CD form.

Implementing the CD Form

Now, build the CD form that you added at the beginning of the project. The CD form allows the user to edit an existing CD record or add a new CD record.

Designing the CD Form

The CD form (`frmCD`) has the following controls and nondefault property values:

Control	*Property Setting(s)*
Label	Caption = "Artist"
ComboBox	Name = "cboArtist"
Label	Caption = "Genre"
ComboBox	Name = "cboGenre"
Label	Caption = "CD Name"
Textbox	Name = "txtCDName", MaxLength = 64
Label	Caption = "Year Released"
Textbox	Name = "txtYear", MaxLength = 4
Label	Caption = "Price"
Textbox	Name = "txtPrice"
Menu	Name = "MenuBar1", NewButton = True (default value, but ensure)

Visually design the CD form to look similar to Figure 7.5.

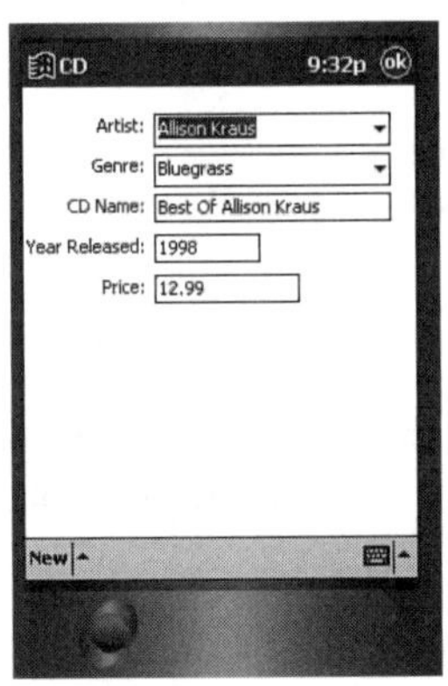

FIGURE 7.5

The CD form (`frmCD`) has a control for each user-editable column in the CD table. The menu control is added to allow the creation of a new CD record.

Setting Up `frmCD`

The CD form (`frmCD`) uses two module-level variables:

```
Dim mlngCDId As Long      'stores the current CD primary key
Dim mlngArtistId As Long  'stores the current Artist primary key
```

Implementing `CDOpen`: The Entry Point to `frmCD`

Because the only function called from the main form (`frmMain`) is `CDOpen`, implement it first (see Listing 7.21).

LISTING 7.21 Opening the CD Form

```
Public Function CDOpen( _
    ByVal lngCDId As Long, _
    ByVal lngArtistId As Long, _
    lngFormMode As Long) As Boolean

    On Error Resume Next

    ' set the default error return
    CDOpen = False

    ' check to see if a CDId was received
    If IsNumeric(lngCDId) Then
        ' set the module variable
        mlngCDId = lngCDId
    End If

    ' check to see if an artist was received
    If IsNumeric(lngArtistId) Then
        ' set the module variable
        mlngArtistId = lngArtistId
    End If

    ' which mode are we in?
    Select Case lngFormMode

        Case CDFORM_MODE_EDIT
            ' Edit Mode

            ' Close this up so we can get an
            ' updatable version of just this record
            If gobjCD.State = adStateOpen Then
                gobjCD.Close
            End If
```

LISTING 7.21 Continued

```
            ' get the record
            gobjCD.Open _
                "SELECT * FROM cd WHERE CDId = " & mlngCDId, _
                gobjConnection, _
                adOpenForwardOnly, _
                adLockOptimistic

            ' did we find it?
            If gobjCD.EOF Then
                Exit Function
            End If

            ' let's refresh the form
            If Not RefreshFormCD() Then
                ' something went wrong
                MsgBox "Error refreshing form"
                Exit Function
            End If

        Case CDFORM_MODE_NEW

            ' New CD
            If Not CdNew() Then
                MsgBox "Can not create a new CD."
                Exit Function
            End If

    End Select

    ' show the form
    Me.Show

End Function
```

`CDOpen` does the usual setup, and then checks the value of the CDId parameter (`lngCDId`). If a numeric value was passed, it sets the module variable to it. This value is used to retrieve and save the record.

```
' check to see if a CDId was received
If IsNumeric(lngCDId) Then
    ' set the module variable
    mlngCDId = lngCDId
End If
```

A similar action is taken with the contents of the ArtistId parameter (`lngArtistId`). If the New button on the Menu is tapped, the new CD record will default to this artist.

```
' check to see if an artist was received
If IsNumeric(lngArtistId) Then
    ' set the module variable
    mlngArtistId = lngArtistId
End If
```

A decision is then made via a `Select Case` statement as to whether the form should behave in “edit” or “add new” mode. Remember, the `Const CDFORM_MODE_EDIT` and `CDFORM_MODE_NEW` are defined in `modGlobal`.


```
' which mode are we in?
Select Case lngFormMode

    Case CDFORM_MODE_EDIT
        ' Edit Mode

        ' Close this up so we can get an
        ' updatable version of just this record
        If gobjCD.State = adStateOpen Then
            gobjCD.Close
        End If

        ' get the record
        gobjCD.Open _
            "SELECT * FROM cd WHERE CDId = " & mlngCDId, _
            gobjConnection, _
            adOpenForwardOnly, _
            adLockReadOnly

        ' did we find it?
        If gobjCD.EOF Then
            Exit Function
        End If

        ' let's refresh the form
        If Not RefreshFormCD() Then
            ' something went wrong
            MsgBox "Error refreshing form"
            Exit Function
        End If

    Case CDFORM_MODE_NEW
```

```
        ' New CD
        If Not CdNew() Then
            MsgBox "Can not create a new CD."
            Exit Function
        End If

End Select
```

In edit mode, the CD Recordset (`gobjCD`) is immediately closed. Then, the particular record being edited is retrieved into the CD recordset.

The recordset `LockType` is still read-only (via `adLockReadOnly` enumeration value for the `LockType` parameter of the `Open` method). This would seem like an obvious place to open the recordset as an updatable `LockType`, but, in the `SaveCD` function, the record is retrieved again before updating.

I have found in my experience with eVB, it's best to count on maintaining the state of as few items as I can. In other words, there is currently no design reason here to not open the recordset as updatable (`adLockOptimistic`). But, knowing eVB's encapsulation limitations, I find that it leads to more robust, maintainable codebase if the application never counts on that recordset to be in the same state when attempting to update the recordset. The recordset objects are constantly being reused. The application design might change in the sense that the CD recordset is manipulated in some manner that's not harmonious to the goals of opening the recordset updatable in the `CDOpen` function. This is one limitation to the encapsulation model of eVB and using global objects.

```
' Close this up so we can get an
' updatable version of just this record
If gobjCD.State = adStateOpen Then
    gobjCD.Close
End If

' get the record
gobjCD.Open _
    "SELECT * FROM cd WHERE CDId = " & mlngCDId, _
    gobjConnection, _
    adOpenForwardOnly, _
    adLockReadOnly
```

`CDOpen` verifies the record was retrieved. If not, it exits the function returning an error value. If all is well, the `RefreshFormCD` function is called.

```
' did we find it?
If gobjCD.EOF Then
    MsgBox "Error finding CD record."
    Exit Function
End If
```

```
' let's refresh the form
If Not RefreshFormCD () Then
    ' something went wrong
    MsgBox "Error refreshing form"
    Exit Function
End If
```

Implementing the `RefreshFormCD` Function

`RefreshFormCD` is generic to handle both an edit of a record and new record (see Listing 7.22). It populates both the Artist and Genre comboboxes. If the artist or genre is known, it sets the combobox to the appropriate record. Then, it populates all the textboxes with the known values.

LISTING 7.22 Setting the Values on the CD Form

```
Private Function RefreshFormCD() As Boolean

    Dim lngIndex As Long

    On Error Resume Next

    RefreshFormCD = False

    ' add all artist records to
    ' the artist combobox
    PopulateArtistCombo

    ' add all genre records to
    ' genre combobox
    PopulateGenreCombo

    ' set the artist combo to no selected item
    Me.cboArtist.ListIndex = -1

    ' check for valid value
    If Not IsNull(gobjCD.Fields("ArtistId").Value) Then
        If gobjCD.Fields("ArtistId").Value > 0 Then
            ' set the artist combobox
            For lngIndex = 0 To Me.cboArtist.ListCount - 1

                ' is this the artist?
                If Me.cboArtist.ItemData(lngIndex) = _
                    gobjCD.Fields("ArtistId").Value Then
```

Listing 7.22 Continued

```
                        ' set the selected item
                        Me.cboArtist.ListIndex = lngIndex
                        ' get out of here
                        Exit For

                End If
            Next
        End If
    End If

    ' set the genre combo to no selected item
    Me.cboGenre.ListIndex = -1

    ' check for valid value
    If Not IsNull(gobjCD.Fields("GenreId").Value) Then
        If gobjCD.Fields("GenreId").Value > 0 Then

            ' set the genre combobox
            For lngIndex = 0 To Me.cboGenre.ListCount - 1
                If Me.cboGenre.ItemData(lngIndex) = _
                    gobjCD.Fields("GenreId").Value Then
                        Me.cboGenre.ListIndex = lngIndex
                        Exit For
                End If
            Next
        End If
    End If

    ' clear the textboxes
    Me.txtCDName.Text = ""
    Me.txtYear.Text = ""
    Me.txtPrice.Text = ""

    ' do we have a CD name?
    If Not IsNull(gobjCD.Fields("CDName").Value) Then
        ' set the name
        Me.txtCDName.Text = gobjCD.Fields("CDName").Value
    End If

    ' do we have a valid year?
    If Not IsNull(gobjCD.Fields("Year").Value) Then
        If gobjCD.Fields("Year").Value <> 0 Then
            ' set the year
            Me.txtYear.Text = gobjCD.Fields("Year").Value
```

LISTING 7.22 Continued

```
        End If
    End If

    ' valid price
    If Not IsNull(gobjCD.Fields("Price").Value <> 0) Then
        If gobjCD.Fields("Price").Value <> 0 Then
            ' set the price
            Me.txtPrice.Text = gobjCD.Fields("Price").Value
        End If
    End If

    If Err.Number = 0 Then
        RefreshFormCD = True
    End If

End Function
```


Implementing the `PopulateArtistCombo` Function

The `PopulateArtistCombo` function closes, then opens the artist table with the artist recordset object (`gobjArtist`). After clearing the artist combobox (`cboArtist`), it repopulates it (see Listing 7.23). The artist recordset is scanned, adding an entry to the combobox for each artist record. After adding the record, it sets the appropriate item in the `ItemData` collection to the primary key value of the artist record.

LISTING 7.23 Adding the Choices to the Artist Combobox

```
Private Function PopulateArtistCombo() As Boolean

    On Error Resume Next

    ' set the error state for early exit
    PopulateArtistCombo = False

    ' close the artist recordset
    If gobjArtist.State = adStateOpen Then
        gobjArtist.Close
    End If

    ' open artist
    gobjArtist.Open "artist", _
        gobjConnection, _
        adOpenForwardOnly, _
```

LISTING 7.23 Continued

```
        adLockReadOnly, _
        adCmdTableDirect

    ' clear the current contents
    ' of the combobox
    Me.cboArtist.Clear

    ' scan the recordset
    Do While Not gobjArtist.EOF
        ' add the artist
        Me.cboArtist.AddItem gobjArtist.Fields("ArtistName").Value
        ' set the ItemData to the primary key of the artist record
        Me.cboArtist.ItemData(Me.cboArtist.NewIndex) = _
            gobjArtist.Fields("ArtistId").Value
        ' next record
        gobjArtist.MoveNext
    Loop

    ' check for errors
    If Err.Number = 0 Then
        PopulateArtistCombo = True
    End If

End Function
```

Implementing the `PopulateGenreCombo` Function

The `PopulateGenreCombo` function works exactly like the `PopulateArtistCombo` function, except it uses the genre table (see Listing 7.24).

LISTING 7.24 Adding the Choices to the Genre Combo Box

```
Private Function PopulateGenreCombo() As Boolean
    On Error Resume Next

    ' set the error state for early exit
    PopulateGenreCombo = False

    ' close the genre recordset
    If gobjGenre.State = adStateOpen Then
        gobjGenre.Close
    End If

    ' open genre
```

LISTING 7.24 Continued

```
    gobjGenre.Open "genre", _
        gobjConnection, _
        adOpenForwardOnly, _
        adLockReadOnly, _
        adCmdTableDirect

    ' clear the current contents
    ' of the combobox
    Me.cboGenre.Clear

    ' scan the recordset
    Do While Not gobjGenre.EOF
        ' add the artist
        Me.cboGenre.AddItem gobjGenre.Fields("genreName").Value
        ' set the ItemData to the primary key of the artist record
        Me.cboGenre.ItemData(Me.cboGenre.NewIndex) = _
            gobjGenre.Fields("genreId").Value
        ' next record
        gobjGenre.MoveNext
    Loop

    If Err.Number = 0 Then
        PopulateGenreCombo = True
    End If

End Function
```

Viewing the CD

At this point, your CD form should operate minimally. Start the application up and tap a CD record in the grid of the main form (`frmMain`). Does it bring up the CD form? Are the comboboxes populated?

Implementing the New Button on the Main Form

At this point, let's take a step back and implement the New button of the menu bar from the main form (`frmMain`):

```
Private Sub MenuBar1_NewClick()
    ' open the cd form with the current artist in new mode
    frmCD.CDOpen Null, glngArtistId, CDFORM_MODE_NEW
End Sub
```

Implementing a New CD in the CD Form

In the CDOpen function (refer to Listing 7.21), there was a case of the Select Case block we didn't examine. Part of the functionality of creating a new CD from the main form is implemented in CDOpen within that Case statement:

```
Case CDFORM_MODE_NEW

    ' New CD
    If Not CdNew() Then
        MsgBox "Can not create a new CD."
        Exit Function
    End If
```

In the Case CDFORM_MODE_NEW statement, a call is made to the CdNew function, whose duty it is to temporarily append a record to the CD recordset object (see Listing 7.25),. A peculiar looking approach might be to append a new record, canceling it only a few lines later. This is just a "trick" to give RefreshFormCD the ability to generically handle new and edit records.

LISTING 7.25 frmCD: Creating a New CD Record

```
Private Function CdNew() As Boolean

    On Error Resume Next

    ' a bit different, since we have
    ' cleanup to do, we'll assume no
    ' error return value and set it at
    ' the end if there is an error
    CdNew = True

    ' since it's a new record, it has no primary key
    mlngCDId = Null

    ' if it currently does not adding
    ' new records, let's close it, so
    ' we can reopen it with AddNew support
    If gobjCD.State = adStateOpen Then
        If Not gobjCD.Supports(adAddNew) Then
            gobjCD.Close
        End If
    End If

             adOpenForwardOnly, adLockOptimistic, adCmdTableDirect
    End If

    ' add a new record
```

LISTING 7.25 Continued

```
    gobjCD.AddNew
    ' set the artist id foreign key
    gobjCD.Fields("ArtistId") = mlngArtistId

    ' we're going to refresh the form
    ' while we have this blank record
    ' on hand, this is a good way to
    ' keep that RefreshFormCD generic
    If Not RefreshFormCD() Then
        ' error
        CdNew = False
    End If

    ' now that we refreshed the form, we
    ' need to cancel the update
    gobjCD.CancelUpdate

    ' everything go ok?
    If Err.Number <> 0 Then
        ' something did not go ok
        CdNew = False
    End If
End Function
```

Go Ahead, Make My CD

Your application should be able to not only display a particular record from the CD table, but be able to mimic creating a new one. Start your application and tap the New button on the main form. It should display a blank record, with the exception of setting the artist combobox (`cboArtist`) to the "current artist."

Implementing the `SaveCD` Function

The CD Library application saves CD records when users tap the OK button on the top-right of the form. By default, there is an OK button on every eVB form. Typically, on first edit of a form's code, eVB will put template code in the `Form.OKClick` event to stop execution of the application:

```
Private Sub Form_OKClick()
    App.End
End Sub
```

You need to override this behavior in the CD form. The code in Listing 7.26 enables the CD form to call `SaveCD` on an `OKClick` event of the form.

LISTING 7.26 Saving the CD Record

```
Private Sub Form_OKClick()

    On Error Resume Next

    ' save the cd
    If SaveCD() Then
        ' it's saved, let's get back
        frmMain.Show
    Else
        ' error - do not close form
        MsgBox "Error saving record."
    End If

End Sub
```

The `OKClick` event in Listing 7.26 calls the `SaveCD` function in Listing 7.27.

LISTING 7.27 Committing the Record

```
Private Function SaveCD() As Boolean

    Dim lngArtistId As Long
    Dim lngGenreId As Long

    On Error Resume Next

    ' because we may have some cleanup
    ' work to do, let's set the
    ' default return value to true
    SaveCD = True

    ' do we have an existing or new genre
    If Me.cboGenre.ListIndex >= 0 Then
        ' existing genre
        ' get the pk value
        lngGenreId = Me.cboGenre.ItemData(Me.cboGenre.ListIndex)
    Else
        ' new genre
        ' ask user to add new genre
        If MsgBox("Would you like to add the genre: " _
            & Me.cboGenre.Text, vbYesNo) = vbYes Then
                ' get a new genre pk value
                lngGenreId = AddGenre(Me.cboGenre.Text)
                ' is it valid?
```

LISTING 7.27 Continued

```
            If lngGenreId < 0 Then
                ' outta here
                MsgBox "Error adding genre."
                SaveCD = False
                Exit Function
            End If
        Else
            ' can't save without a genre
            SaveCD = False
            MsgBox "You can not save a CD without a genre."
            Exit Function
        End If
    End If

    ' do we have an existing or new artist
    If Me.cboArtist.ListIndex >= 0 Then
        ' existing genre
        ' get the pk value
        lngArtistId = Me.cboArtist.ItemData(Me.cboArtist.ListIndex)
    Else
        ' new genre

        ' ask user to add new genre
              If MsgBox("Would you like to add the artist: " _
            & Me.cboArtist.Text, vbYesNo) = vbYes Then
             ' get a new artist pk value
             lngArtistId = AddArtist(Me.cboArtist.Text, lngGenreId)
             ' is it valid?
             If lngArtistId < 0 Then
                 ' outta here
                 SaveCD = False
                 MsgBox "Error adding artist."
                 Exit Function
            End If
        Else
            ' can't save without a artist
            SaveCD = False
            MsgBox "You can not save a CD without a artist."
            Exit Function
        End If
    End If

    ' close the CD recordset, we're about to update
    If gobjCD.State = adStateOpen Then
```

LISTING 7.27 Continued

```
        gobjCD.Close
    End If

    ' check mode
    If Not IsNull(mlngCDId) Then
        'edit mode - let's get the record
        gobjCD.Open "SELECT * FROM cd WHERE CDId = " _
            & mlngCDId, gobjConnection, _
            adOpenForwardOnly, adLockOptimistic
    Else
        ' new mode, no primary key value
        gobjCD.Open "cd", gobjConnection, adOpenForwardOnly, _
            adLockOptimistic, adCmdTableDirect
        ' get a new pk value
        mlngCDId = GetNewPK("CD")
        ' add the record
        gobjCD.AddNew
        ' set the pk value
        gobjCD.Fields("CDId").Value = mlngCDId
    End If

    ' are we at the end of the
    ' recordset (no record added
    ' or no record retrieved)
    If gobjCD.EOF Then
        Exit Function
    End If

    ' assign the values
    gobjCD.Fields("ArtistID").Value = lngArtistId
    gobjCD.Fields("CDName").Value = Me.txtCDName.Text
    gobjCD.Fields("Year").Value = CLng(Me.txtYear.Text)
    gobjCD.Fields("Price").Value = CCur(Me.txtPrice.Text)
    gobjCD.Fields("GenreID").Value = lngGenreId

    ' update the recordset
    gobjCD.Update

    ' check for errors
    If Err.Number <> 0 Then
        Exit Function
    End If
```

LISTING 7.27 Continued

```
    ' everything's cool, return true
    SaveCD = True

End Function
```

Now examine `SaveCD`. This function determines whether the genre combobox is an existing or new genre. If the current genre combobox displays an existing genre, the `ListIndex` property of the combobox will be => 0. If `ListIndex` is < 0, it must be a genre not in the genre table.

If the genre already exists, the primary key value of that genre record is retained from the `ItemData` collection of the combobox:

```
' do we have an existing or new genre
If Me.cboGenre.ListIndex >= 0 Then
    ' existing genre
    ' get the pk value
    lngGenreId = Me.cboGenre.ItemData(Me.cboGenre.ListIndex)
Else
    ' new genre
    ' ask user to add new genre
        If MsgBox("Would you like to add the genre: " _
            & Me.cboGenre.Text, vbYesNo) = vbYes Then
                ' get a new genre pk value
                lngGenreId = AddGenre(Me.cboGenre.Text)
                ' is it valid?
                If lngGenreId < 0 Then
                    ' outta here
                    MsgBox "Error adding genre."
                    SaveCD = False
                    Exit Function
                End If
    Else
        ' can't save without a genre
        SaveCD = False
        MsgBox "You can not save a CD without a genre."
        Exit Function
    End If
End If
```

If the genre doesn't exist, the user is prompted by a MsgBox to add it. If the user agrees to add the genre, `AddGenre` is called with the value of the combobox's `Text` property. The return value of `AddGenre` (the new primary key value) is retained and checked for validity.

```
' do we have an existing or new genre
If Me.cboGenre.ListIndex >= 0 Then
```

```
    ' existing genre
    ' get the pk value
    lngGenreId = Me.cboGenre.ItemData(Me.cboGenre.ListIndex)
Else
    ' new genre
    ' ask user to add new genre
        If MsgBox("Would you like to add the genre: " _
            & Me.cboGenre.Text, vbYesNo) = vbYes Then
                ' get a new genre pk value
                lngGenreId = AddGenre(Me.cboGenre.Text)
                ' is it valid?
                If lngGenreId < 0 Then
                    ' outta here
                    MsgBox "Error adding genre."
                    SaveCD = False
                    Exit Function
                End If
    Else
        ' can't save without a genre
        SaveCD = False
        MsgBox "You can not save a CD without a genre."
        Exit Function
    End If
End If
```

If the genre doesn't exist and the user doesn't choose to add the genre, the return value for the `SaveCD` function is set to `False` and the function exits.

```
' do we have an existing or new genre
If Me.cboGenre.ListIndex >= 0 Then
    ' existing genre
    ' get the pk value
    lngGenreId = Me.cboGenre.ItemData(Me.cboGenre.ListIndex)
Else
    ' new genre
    ' ask user to add new genre
        If MsgBox("Would you like to add the genre: " _
            & Me.cboGenre.Text, vbYesNo) = vbYes Then
        ' get a new genre pk value
        lngGenreId = AddGenre(Me.cboGenre.Text)
        ' is it valid?
        If lngGenreId < 0 Then
            ' outta here
            MsgBox "Error adding genre."
            SaveCD = False
            Exit Function
        End If
```

```
    Else
        ' can't save without a genre
        SaveCD = False
        MsgBox "You can not save a CD without a genre."
        Exit Function
    End If
End If
```

The same structure of checking the combobox values and prompting the user takes place for the artist combobox:

```
' do we have an existing or new artist
If Me.cboArtist.ListIndex >= 0 Then
    ' existing genre
    ' get the pk value
    lngArtistId = Me.cboArtist.ItemData(Me.cboArtist.ListIndex)
Else
    ' new genre

    ' ask user to add new genre
        If MsgBox("Would you like to add the artist: " _
            & Me.cboArtist.Text, vbYesNo) = vbYes Then
             ' get a new artist pk value
             lngArtistId = AddArtist(Me.cboArtist.Text, lngGenreId)
             ' is it valid?
             If lngArtistId < 0 Then
                 ' outta here
                 SaveCD = False
                 MsgBox "Error adding artist."
                 Exit Function
            End If
    Else
        ' can't save without a artist
        SaveCD = False
        MsgBox "You can not save a CD without a artist."
        Exit Function
    End If
End If
```

Now, `SaveCD` should have all the values needed to save the CD record. The CD recordset object is closed.

```
' close the CD recordset, we're about to update
If gobjCD.State = adStateOpen Then
    gobjCD.Close
End If
```

The check of mlngCDId for Null determines whether the record to save is a new CD record or a CD record edit. If the value of mlngCDId is Not Null, the record being saved is an edit, otherwise it's a new record.

```
' check mode
If Not IsNull(mlngCDId) Then
        'edit mode - let's get the record
        gobjCD.Open "SELECT * FROM cd WHERE CDId = " _
            & mlngCDId, gobjConnection, _
            adOpenForwardOnly, adLockOptimistic
Else
        ' new mode, no primary key value
        gobjCD.Open "cd", gobjConnection, adOpenForwardOnly, _
            adLockOptimistic, adCmdTableDirect
        ' get a new pk value
        mlngCDId = GetNewPK("CD")
        ' add the record
        gobjCD.AddNew
        ' set the pk value
        gobjCD.Fields("CDId").Value = mlngCDId
End If
```

If the record is an edit, the CD recordset object is opened via a SQL statement. The table is filtered down to one record using the WHERE clause and the value of mlngCDId. The LockType is adLockOptimistic.

```
'edit mode - let's get the record
gobjCD.Open "SELECT * FROM cd WHERE CDId = " _
        & mlngCDId, gobjConnection, _
        adOpenForwardOnly, adLockOptimistic
```

If the record is a new record, the CD table is opened directly, again using LockType of adLockOptimistic. Also, notice the optional parameter of adCmdTableDirect. This is why the source is only the table name.

```
' new mode, no primary key value
gobjCD.Open "cd", gobjConnection, adOpenForwardOnly, _
        adLockOptimistic, adCmdTableDirect
```

Because this is new CD record, it needs a primary key value. GetNewPK provides this new primary key value:

```
' get a new pk value
mlngCDId = GetNewPK("CD")
```

A new record is added:

```
' add the record
gobjCD.AddNew
```

Set the primary key value on this new record:

```
' set the pk value
gobjCD.Fields("CDId").Value = mlngCDId
```

Now that the different actions have been taken for a new or edited CD record, the rest of the function to save the record is the same, for both Add and Edit.

A check is made to ensure you have a record, whether that record should be an appended record (for new) or a single record (for an edit):

```
' are we at the end of the
' recordset (no record added
' or no record retrieved)
If gobjCD.EOF Then
    Exit Function
End If
```

The values are assigned to the `Field` objects of the `Fields` collection:

```
' assign the values
gobjCD.Fields("ArtistID").Value = lngArtistId
gobjCD.Fields("CDName").Value = Me.txtCDName.Text
gobjCD.Fields("Year").Value = CLng(Me.txtYear.Text)
gobjCD.Fields("Price").Value = CCur(Me.txtPrice.Text)
gobjCD.Fields("GenreID").Value = lngGenreId
```

The recordset object is updated, sending the data back to the data store. A check for errors and `SaveCD` is done:

```
' update the recordset
gobjCD.Update

' check for errors
If Err.Number <> 0 Then
    Exit Function
End If

' everything's cool, return true
SaveCD = True
```

Summary

In this chapter we've investigated ADOCE, which provides easy access to Pocket Access databases. When you use ADOCE, remember to keep the limitations in mind; test your application frequently as you built it.

The sample application's design is a good template for an ADOCE application, although you can implement some enhancements. First, you could implement allowing the CD form to track whether changes have been made and commit the record only when changes are made. Moreover, validation can be done on the year and price fields.

Another enhancement to the application would be to automatically populate the genre combobox to the artist's default genre when a new CD is created for the artist. Lastly, you could implement the `Recordset.Delete` function for deleting a CD.

Using SQL Server in a Mobile Environment

CHAPTER **8**

IN THIS CHAPTER

SQL Server CE is the first Microsoft product for enterprise data access for Windows CE. SQL Server CE provides a high-performance data engine that runs on all Windows CE platforms. The SQL Server CE provides access to both local and remote data.

Local data is accessed via ADOCE, the same as Pocket Access data. This local data can be defined locally or retrieved from a remote source. In other words, you can use SQL Server CE just as you would Pocket Access. But, the power of SQL Server CE comes from the capability to communicate with a Microsoft SQL Server to exchange data. SQL Server CE can pull data to the device and push updates back to the enterprise SQL Server.

Remote data is accessed in one of two ways using SQL Server CE:

- SQL Server CE can subscribe to publications from Microsoft SQL Server 2000.
- SQL Server CE provides a Remote Data Access (RDA) technology that allows dynamic access to remote data.

Other features SQL Server CE provides over Pocket Access include higher performance, more robustness, encryption, and security. In this chapter, you will learn about

- The SQL Server CE object, replication, and remote data access models
- How to install and configure SQL Server CE on your server, as well as on your Pocket PC or emulator
- How to choose between SQL Server CE merge replication and Remote Data Access
- How to create a publication for replication to a Windows CE device
- How to subscribe to and use a publication from Windows CE in the sample application

Installing and Configuring SQL Server CE on Your Server

SQL Server CE uses Internet Information Services (IIS) to communicate with the enterprise SQL Server. Because Windows CE devices are predominantly mobile, this allows secured access to the SQL Server using any TCP/IP connection to the IIS server. SQL Server CE allows even more secure access to the server by using HTTPS as the protocol.

To install SQL Server CE on the server, use the SQL Server CE installation package, which you can obtain from Microsoft's Web site at `www.microsoft.com/sql/downloads`.Once downloaded, run the installation package on the server that will provide the SQL Server CE services. You will also need to run the installation on the development machine and choose the Development Tools option during the install.

NOTE

The SQL Server CE development tools will install only on a machine having SQL Server 2000 Developer Edition installed on it or within its intranet. Or, you can use the 120-day trial version of SQL Server CE.

When installation is complete, you need to register the two server-side DLLs, sscerp10.dll and sscesa10.dll, by using RegSvr32.exe. In a typical install, these DLLs are installed to C:\Program Files\Microsoft SQL Server CE\Server, but can be moved or copied before registering. RegSvr32.exe is located in the System32 directory.

After these DLLs are registered, start the IIS administration tool. Create a new virtual directory by using the folder where the DLLs reside. Be sure to set Execute Permissions to Scripts and Executables. Your Virtual Directory properties should be similar to those in Figure 8.1.

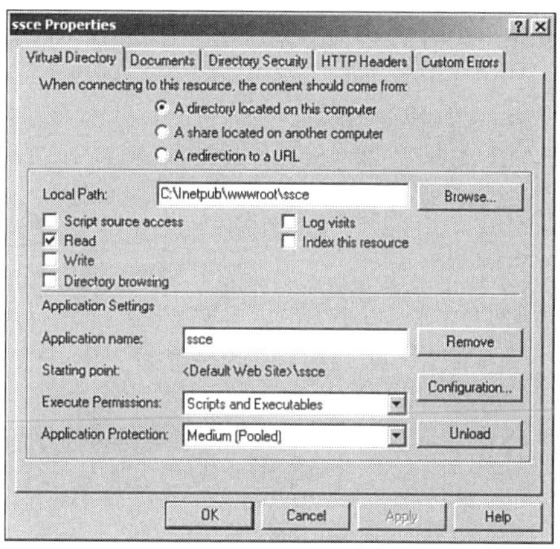

FIGURE 8.1

Properties for the virtual directory where the SQL Server CE DLLs are registered. In this example, the DLLs were relocated to C:\Inetpub\wwwroot\ssce.

As soon as your Virtual Directory is created, you can change the security settings to meet your needs; SQL Server CE allows the device to pass authentication credentials to IIS. So, if necessary in your environment, you can configure Basic Authentication and/or Integrated Windows Authentication.

To test the installation, you can navigate an Internet browser to the URL for the DLL sscesa10.dll (for example, `http://localhost/ssce/sscesa10.dll`). If the DLL is configured and working properly, the browser should display the text `Body`. If it doesn't seem to work properly, check the permission in both the virtual directory and the NTFS permissions on the folder and DLL files.

Installing and Configuring SQL Server CE on Your Device or Emulator

Although there is no installation package to install SQL Server CE onto a Windows CE device, you need to pay special attention when running SQL Server CE for the first time from eVB.

Click the Browse button from the Project References dialog to set a reference to the type library ca_mergex.tlb. This file is installed in the default installation to C:\Program Files\Microsoft SQL Server CE\Lib\ca_mergex.tlb.

SQL Server CE exists as set of ActiveX DLLs on the Windows CE device. Unlike typical ActiveX DLLs, SQL Server CE must be forced down to the device. When running an eVB project that uses SQL Server CE for the first time, you need to set the project's Update Component's Frequency setting to Always, as shown in Figure 8.2.

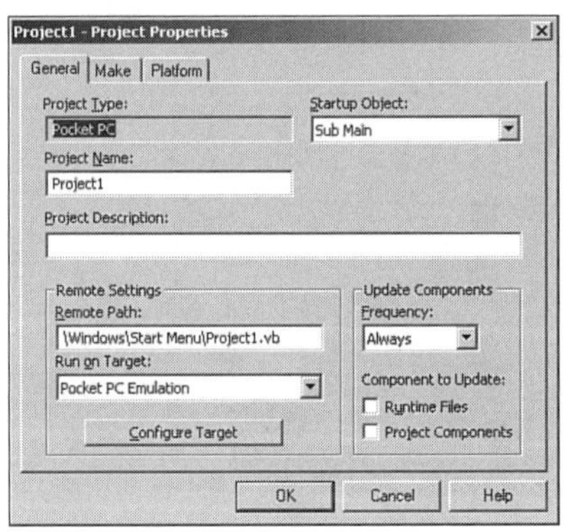

FIGURE 8.2
Set the Frequency to Always for an eVB project to force the SQL Server CE DLLs to the device or emulator.

After successfully pushing the SQL Server CE DLL files to the device or emulator, you can reset your project properties to their previous values. Repeat this process for each new device or emulator on which you want to use SQL Server CE. When distributing SQL Server CE, the install wizard should sense the SQL Server CE DLLs and include them.

After the DLLs are forced down to the device, no configuration is needed. There's no GUI application to SQL Server CE, unlike the SQL Server's Enterprise Manager or ISQL/W. All configuration takes place during runtime. SQL Server CE should now be available for use on the device.

Establishing Connectivity for SQL Server CE

SQL Server CE works over TCP/IP to communicate with the IIS server providing the SQL Server CE services. A device or emulator using SQL Server CE to communicate with the remote SQL Server, whether using replication or remote data access, must have some means to communicate with the server. This can be accomplished in a variety of ways:

- Direct connection to the IIS server over ActiveSync, meaning the device is connected directly to the same machine providing the SQL Server CE services. This is only practical for development purposes as you would not want to run IIS and SQL Server CE on every user's machine.
- A device can use an Ethernet card or modem (wired or wireless) to establish a TCP/IP connection to the IIS Server providing the SQL Server CE services.
- Using ActiveSync as a proxy, users can run SQL Server CE Relay on their desktop machines. When a Windows CE devices connects with ActiveSync, SQL Server CE Relay will intercept SQL Server CE transport communications and forward to the IIS Server providing the SQL Server CE services. For more information about SQL Server CE Relay, see the documentation that comes with SQL Server CE.

Understanding the SQL Server CE Object Model

You can create three object classes in the SQL Server CE library:

- `SSCE.Replication` enables bidirectional access to SQL Server publications residing within a Microsoft SQL Server.
- `SSCE.RemoteDataAccess` provides the ability to pull data manually with SQL statements and to push back changes.
- `SSCE.Engine` allows compacting of a SQL Server CE database.

Using SQL Server CE Data

To use SQL Server CE data, your application uses ADOCE, just as Pocket Access does. The major difference in consuming SQL Server CE data versus Pocket Access data is in the

ConnectionString value structure. Here is an example of opening an ADOCE.Connection object using SQL Server CE:

```
Dim objConnection As ADOCE.Connection

Set objConnection = CreateObject("ADOCE.Connection.3.1")

objConnection.ConnectionString = _
    "Provider=Microsoft.SQLServer.OLEDB.CE.1.0;" _
    & "Data Source=\Program Files\My Program\MySSCEDb.sdf"

objConnection.Open
```

Notice the difference from Pocket Access—the Provider element of the ConnectionString value is required for SQL server CE.

Updating SQL Server CE Recordsets

One of the most surprising limitations of SQL Server CE is that recordsets created from a SQL statement aren't updatable. When I first started working with SQL Server CE, I found this mind-boggling. The workaround isn't incredibly familiar to Visual Basic programmers, but far too familiar to former FoxPro programmers, so it came as second nature to me and will to you soon.

Let's investigate the workaround necessary to mimic SELECTing a single record and updating it (see Listing 8.1). What is accomplished here is similar to that used with ActiveX Data Objects (from desktop and server PCs).

LISTING 8.1 Typical UPDATE in Place for Non-SQL Server CE Recordset

```
Dim objConnection As New ADODB.Connection
Dim objRecordset As New ADODB.Recordset

objConnection.ConnectionString = _
    "Provider=SQLOLEDB.1;Password=;" _
    & "User ID=sa;Initial Catalog=CD;Data Source=MyServer"

objConnection.Open

objRecordset.Open _
    "SELECT * FROM MyTable WHERE MyPrimaryKey = 1001", _
    objConnection, _
    adOpenDynamic, _
    adLockOptimistic
```

LISTING 8.1 Continued

```
objRecordset.Fields("MyField").Value = "MyValue"

objRecordset.Update
```

You may remember in Chapter 7, "Storing and Retrieving Data with ActiveX Data Objects CE," that areas of the application used the table name instead of a SQL statement as the `Source` parameter to the `Open` method of the `ADOCE.Recordset` object. This table name was paired with `adCmdTableDirect` enumeration as the `Options` parameter. This may have seemed like a difficult or unnecessary methodology with Pocket Access, but is a great primer to creating updateable recordsets with SQL Server CE. Listing 8.2 reviews creating an updateable recordset using this approach.

LISTING 8.2 Opening a SQL Server CE for an UPDATE in Place

```
Dim objADOCEConnection As ADOCE.Connection
Dim objRecordset As ADOCE.Recordset

Set objADOCEConnection = CreateObject("ADOCE.Connection.3.1")
Set objRecordset = CreateObject("ADOCE.Recordset.3.1")

objADOCEConnection.ConnectionString = _
    "Provider=Microsoft.SQLServer.OLEDB.CE.1.0;" _
    & "Data Source=\CD.sdf"

objRecordset.Open "MyTable", _
    objADOCEConnection, adOpenDynamic, adLockOptimistic
```


Now that you have an updateable recordset, let's investigate how you can do an in-place update (see Listing 8.3).

LISTING 8.3 Creating an Updateable Recordset from SQL Server CE Data

```
Dim objADOCEConnection As ADOCE.Connection
Dim objRecordset As ADOCE.Recordset

Set objADOCEConnection = CreateObject("ADOCE.Connection.3.1")
Set objRecordset = CreateObject("ADOCE.Recordset.3.1")

objADOCEConnection.ConnectionString = _
    "Provider=Microsoft.SQLServer.OLEDB.CE.1.0;" _
    & "Data Source=\CD.sdf"
```

LISTING 8.3 Continued

```
objRecordset.Open "MyTable", _
    objADOCEConnection, adOpenDynamic, adLockOptimistic

objRecordset.Index = "MyPrimaryKeyIndex"

objRecordset.Seek 1001

objRecordset.Fields("MyField").Value = "MyValue"

objRecordset.Update
```

After you have an updateable recordset, the `Index` property is set to the name of index from the data definition. In other words, this is the name of the index created on the primary key field. Next, the `Seek` method is called with the primary value of the record to be updated. Then, things return to normal with the updates to the record and the `Update` method is called.

SQL Server CE Merge Replication and Remote Data Access

Whether your application uses SQL Server CE replication data, RDA data or data defined directly on the device, the data is stored in a file with the default extension of .sdf (for example, \Program Files\My Program\MySSCEDb.sdf). All types of SQL Server CE data (replication data, RDA data, and data defined on the device) can coexist in a single database. Distinct databases are maintained in separate files.

SQL Server CE Merge Replication

SQL Server CE merge replication allows SQL Server CE to subscribe to Microsoft SQL Server 2000 publications; replication isn't compatible with previous versions of Microsoft SQL Server. *Publications* are a collection of articles that reside within a SQL server. *Articles* are simply tables that can have both horizontal and vertical filtering applied. *Horizontal filtering* is the process of filtering rows by static or dynamic criteria. *Vertical filtering* is the process of defining a subset of available table columns. When defining the article, you specify which columns to include in the replication.

You can filter rows in an article based on static or dynamic attributes. In the sample application, dynamic filtering is accomplished by using the `HOST_NAME()` value to filter rows to the current subscriber. This is a potential strategy for applications such as an order entry system where the salesperson should only subscribe to customer records that belong to him or her. Also, you can filter records in subsequent articles based on filtered rows in other articles. In other words, if a horizontal filter is applied to one article, subsequent articles can be filtered by using a `JOIN` condition on the originally filtered article. In the salesperson example, a dynamic filter is applied to a customer table and then propagated to an orders or sales table with a `JOIN` from customers to orders and a `JOIN` from customers to sales leads.

At the same time horizontal filters are being applied to articles, vertical filters can be applied to the articles. When defining the article, you define which column(s) are available or not available. Both horizontal and vertical filtering can be an important strategy to limit the amount of data being exchanged with the enterprise SQL Server. Limiting the data can be an important aspect to a Windows CE solution, ensuring effective use of limited memory on the device and minimizing time to exchange data via a slower or less reliable wireless connection.

Using replication with SQL Server CE allows for automatic identity column management. SQL Server CE replication provides an easy integration into those existing SQL Server solutions using identity columns. To manage identity columns, you configure "blocks" of keys for each article to be downloaded to the subscriber device.

To use merge replication, you must specify articles for a SQL Server CE publication. Merge replication allows a record updated in two locations (two mobile devices or a mobile device and the server) to be merged back together. Microsoft SQL Server merge replication provides a default merge handler, other various merge handlers (see Microsoft SQL Server documentation), and the capability to write a custom COM merge handler.

Tables published as articles for merge replication have certain requirements:

- Any identity columns must be set to Not For Replication (that choice of words seems completely counterintuitive to me, too).
- When completing publication of a table as an article, a column named `ROWGUID` will be added of type `uniqueidentifier` if there's currently no column of type `uniqueidentifier` (there can be only one column of this type per table). This column is a 128-bit data type uniquely identifying a record, even across tables and databases.

These database changes shouldn't be taken lightly because any application(s) currently accessing the data may not be compatible with these changes. (Remember all those warnings from senior-level developers and DBAs to not use `SELECT * FROM` *`table`*?)

SQL Server CE Remote Data Access

SQL Server CE remote data access (RDA) allows for direct SQL queries to Microsoft SQL Server databases, including versions 6.5, 7.0, and 2000. If your solution needs to use version 6.5 or 7.0, remote data access is the only choice in which to integrate SQL Server CE.

With SQL Server CE RDA, a standard SQL query is sent to the server and a table is created in the SQL Server CE database from the resultset. The table created from this resultset can be configured to allow updates to be sent back to the server or to essentially be read-only using what is known as the tracking option.

A key difference between replication and RDA is that your application doesn't get automatic primary key management features with RDA. But, RDA does allow a higher degree of management and flexibility from the client side. Replication must be defined and managed from the server, yet RDA allows the management to be dynamically defined and configured from the client side. Also, you can use RDA to send data definition language (DDL) statements directly to the server to be executed on the server.

Using Replication with SQL Server CE

The following sections discuss the process to convert the CD Library application from Chapter 7 into an enterprise solution that uses SQL Server replication.

Creating the CD Library Database on the Server

Before you can use SQL Server CE replication, you must create a publication on the server to subscribe to. You can create a SQL Server publication programmatically or through the Enterprise Manager. Obviously, before you can create a publication, you need to have a database. Figure 8.3 represents a model of the CD library data before the publishing as a replication. Listing 8.4 is the T-SQL that creates this database on the server.

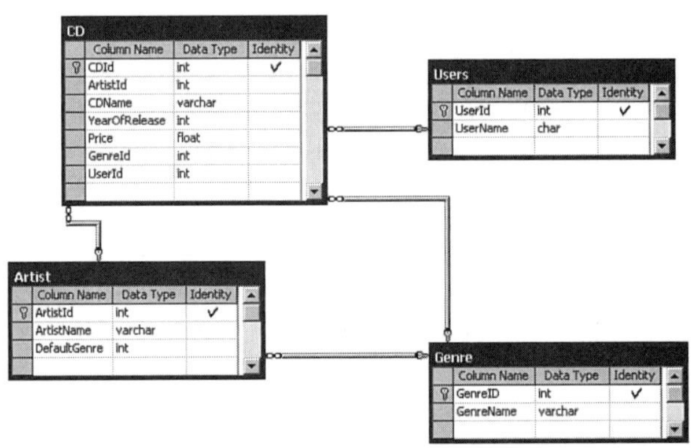

FIGURE 8.3

An entity relation diagram for CD library database before publication takes place.

LISTING 8.4 CreateCDDatabase.sql: Creating the CD Database on the Server

```
CREATE TABLE [dbo].[Artist] (
    [ArtistId] [int] IDENTITY (1, 1) NOT NULL ,
    [ArtistName] [varchar] (64) ,
    [DefaultGenre] [int] NULL
)
GO

CREATE TABLE [dbo].[CD] (
    [CDId] [int] IDENTITY (1, 1) NOT NULL ,
    [ArtistId] [int] NULL ,
    [CDName] [varchar] (64) ,
    [YearOfRelease] [int] NULL ,
    [Price] [float] NULL ,
    [GenreId] [int] NULL ,
    [UserId] [int] NULL
)
GO

CREATE TABLE [dbo].[Genre] (
    [GenreID] [int] IDENTITY (1, 1) NOT NULL ,
    [GenreName] [varchar] (64)
)
GO

CREATE TABLE [dbo].[Users] (
    [UserId] [int] IDENTITY (1, 1) NOT NULL ,
    [UserName] [char] (20)
)
GO

ALTER TABLE [dbo].[Artist] WITH NOCHECK ADD
    CONSTRAINT [PK_Artist] PRIMARY KEY  CLUSTERED
    (
       [ArtistId]
    )  ON [PRIMARY]
GO

ALTER TABLE [dbo].[CD] WITH NOCHECK ADD
    CONSTRAINT [PK_CD] PRIMARY KEY  CLUSTERED
    (
       [CDId]
    )  ON [PRIMARY]
GO
```

LISTING 8.4 Continued

```
ALTER TABLE [dbo].[Genre] WITH NOCHECK ADD
    CONSTRAINT [PK_Genre] PRIMARY KEY  CLUSTERED
    (
       [GenreID]
    )  ON [PRIMARY]
GO

ALTER TABLE [dbo].[Users] WITH NOCHECK ADD
    CONSTRAINT [PK_Users] PRIMARY KEY  CLUSTERED
    (
       [UserId]
    )  ON [PRIMARY]
GO

ALTER TABLE [dbo].[Artist] ADD
    CONSTRAINT [FK_Artist_Genre] FOREIGN KEY
    (
        [DefaultGenre]
    ) REFERENCES [dbo].[Genre] (
        [GenreID]
    )
GO

ALTER TABLE [dbo].[CD] ADD
    CONSTRAINT [FK_CD_Artist] FOREIGN KEY
    (
        [ArtistId]
    ) REFERENCES [dbo].[Artist] (
        [ArtistId]
    ),
    CONSTRAINT [FK_CD_Genre] FOREIGN KEY
    (
        [GenreId]
    ) REFERENCES [dbo].[Genre] (
        [GenreID]
    ),
    CONSTRAINT [FK_CD_Users] FOREIGN KEY
    (
        [UserId]
    ) REFERENCES [dbo].[Users] (
        [UserId]
    )
GO
```

After you complete your data definitions, create some data in the tables. Listing 8.5 shows the T-SQL to insert some sample data. Using ISQL/W from the SQL Server Tools, open MakeData.sql in ISQL/W and execute it.

LISTING 8.5 MakeData.sql: Creating Sample Data in the CD Database

```
SET IDENTITY_INSERT Users ON

INSERT INTO Users ( UserId, UserName ) VALUES ( 1, 'mobileuser1' )
INSERT INTO Users ( UserId, UserName ) VALUES ( 2, 'mobileuser2' )
INSERT INTO Users ( UserId, UserName ) VALUES ( 3, 'mobileuser3' )

SET IDENTITY_INSERT Users OFF

GO

SET IDENTITY_INSERT Genre ON

INSERT INTO Genre ( GenreID, GenreName ) VALUES ( 1, 'Pop' )
INSERT INTO Genre ( GenreID, GenreName ) VALUES ( 2, 'Rock' )
INSERT INTO Genre ( GenreID, GenreName ) VALUES ( 3, 'Bluegrass' )

SET IDENTITY_INSERT Genre OFF

GO

SET IDENTITY_INSERT Artist ON

INSERT INTO Artist ( ArtistId, ArtistName, DefaultGenre )
    VALUES ( 1, 'Britney Spears', 1 )

INSERT INTO Artist ( ArtistId, ArtistName, DefaultGenre )
    VALUES ( 2, 'Dave Matthews Band', 2 )

INSERT INTO Artist ( ArtistId, ArtistName, DefaultGenre )
    VALUES ( 3, 'Allison Krauss', 3 )

SET IDENTITY_INSERT Artist OFF

GO

SET IDENTITY_INSERT CD ON
```

LISTING 8.5 Continued

```
INSERT INTO CD ( CDId, ArtistId, CDName, YearOfRelease,
       Price, GenreId, UserId ) VALUES
       ( 1, 1, 'Oops...', 2000, 15.99, 1, 1 )

INSERT INTO CD ( CDId, ArtistId, CDName, YearOfRelease,
       Price, GenreId, UserId ) VALUES
       ( 2, 1, 'Best Of Britney', 2001, 18.99, 1, 1 )

INSERT INTO CD ( CDId, ArtistId, CDName, YearOfRelease,
       Price, GenreId, UserId ) VALUES
       ( 3, 2, 'Under the Table and Dreaming', 1998, 10.99, 2, 3 )

INSERT INTO CD ( CDId, ArtistId, CDName, YearOfRelease,
       Price, GenreId, UserId ) VALUES
       ( 4, 2, 'Everyday', 2001, 15.99, 2, 2 )

INSERT INTO CD ( CDId, ArtistId, CDName, YearOfRelease,
       Price, GenreId, UserId ) VALUES
       ( 5, 3, 'Union Station', 1996, 12.99, 3, 1 )

INSERT INTO CD ( CDId, ArtistId, CDName, YearOfRelease,
       Price, GenreId, UserId ) VALUES
       ( 6, 3, 'Best Of...', 1999, 13.99, 3, 1 )

SET IDENTITY_INSERT CD OFF

GO
```

Creating a Publication for Replication to a Windows CE Device

Now that you have the CD database created, you can create the publication for replication. This publication uses horizontal filtering to filter the User table with the `HOST_NAME()` function. The CD table records are then horizontally filtered by using `JOIN` to join the User table to the CD table.

To invoke the Create Publication Wizard, right-click the CD database in the Enterprise Manager and choose New, Publication. When the wizard opens (see Figure 8.4), leave Show Advanced Options in this Wizard unchecked and click Next because you won't be modifying any advanced options in this publication.

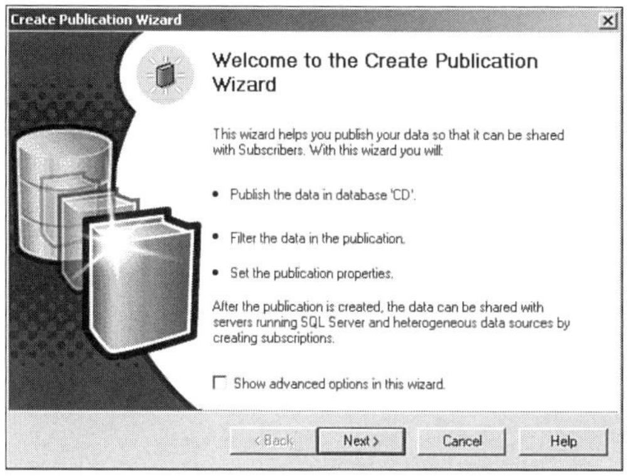

FIGURE 8.4

Creating a new publication is accomplished through the Create Publication Wizard.

Next, select the CD database in the Choose Publication Database step (see Figure 8.5) and click Next.

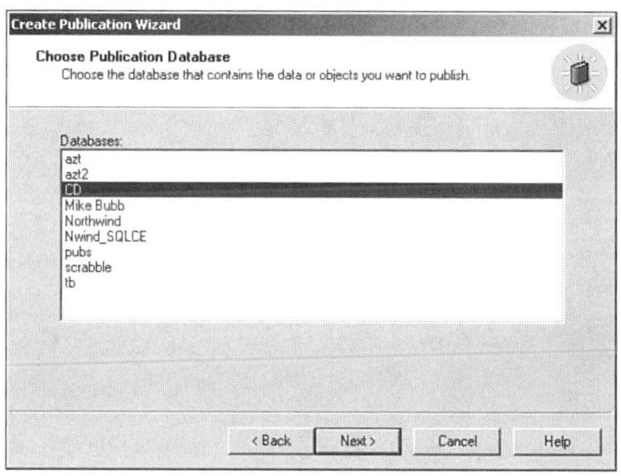

FIGURE 8.5

Selecting the database from which the publication originates.

After selecting the correct database, you need to select the correct publication type. Select the only publication compatible with SQL Server CE, Merge Publication, as shown in Figure 8.6.

Next, specify what types of subscribers will subscribe to the publication. You can select any subscriber type, but you need to select Devices Running SQL Server CE as shown in Figure 8.7.

In the Specify Articles step, include all the tables by selecting them. If no tables are displayed, ensure that Show Unpublished Objects is selected. Your settings should resemble Figure 8.8.

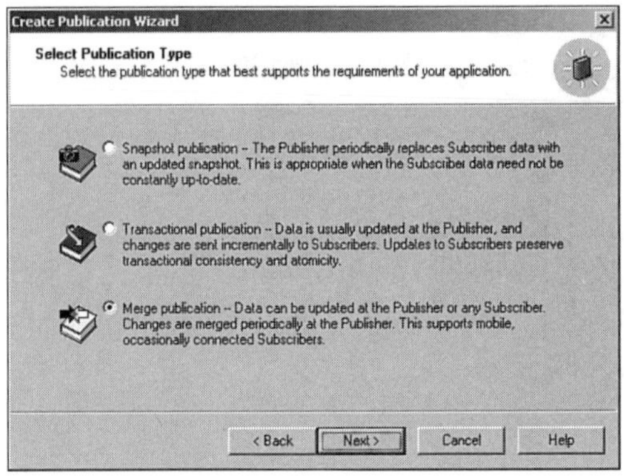

FIGURE 8.6

The only publication type compatible with Windows CE is Merge Publication.

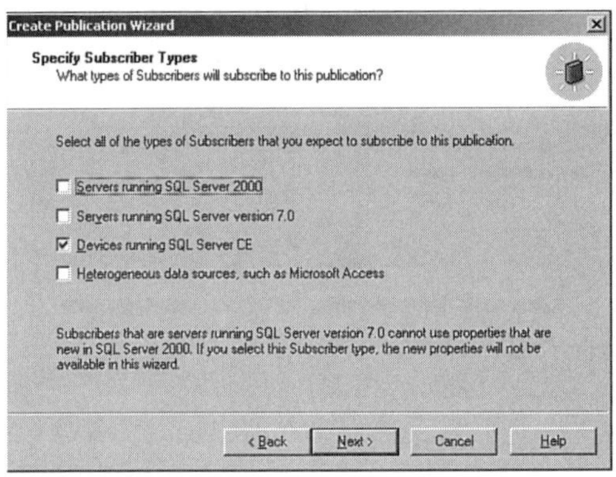

FIGURE 8.7

You can choose the other options without adversely effecting the publication for SQL Server CE.

An identity range needs to be defined for each article whose data will be modifiable on the subscriber. This identity range is a "block" of available primary keys for new records. Managing the identity range allows a subscriber to "block out" a range of identity column values each time it synchronizes with the publication.

Identity ranges are managed on an article basis. To manage the identity range, click the ellipsis (…) right of the article name to open an article's properties dialog box. To create an identity range, display the Identity Range tab (see Figure 8.9). Select Automatically Assign and Maintain a Unique Identity Range for Each Subscription to enable the rest of the tab's controls. The defaults are an identity range size of 100 at both the publisher and the subscriber. This allows the subscriber to attempt 100 inserts for the article. Also, a default threshold of 80 percent is set for the publisher to start a new range when 80 percent of the range is exhausted. You can adjust these values to meet the needs of your solution. When the identity range for an article is exhausted on the subscriber, no more records may be added to the article until the subscriber syncs with the publisher.

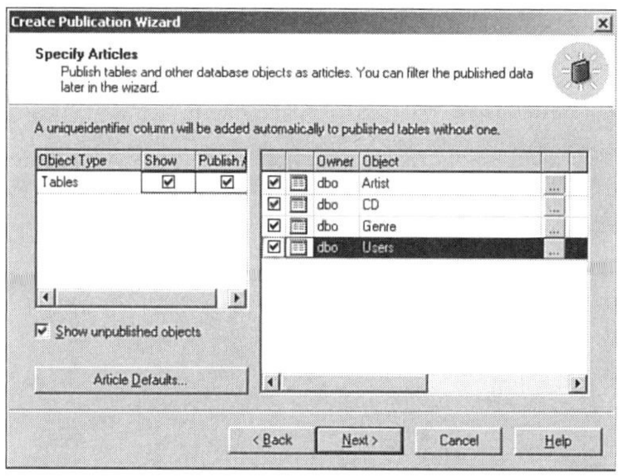

FIGURE 8.8
Specify the articles to be published in the publication. In this sample, all tables are published as articles.

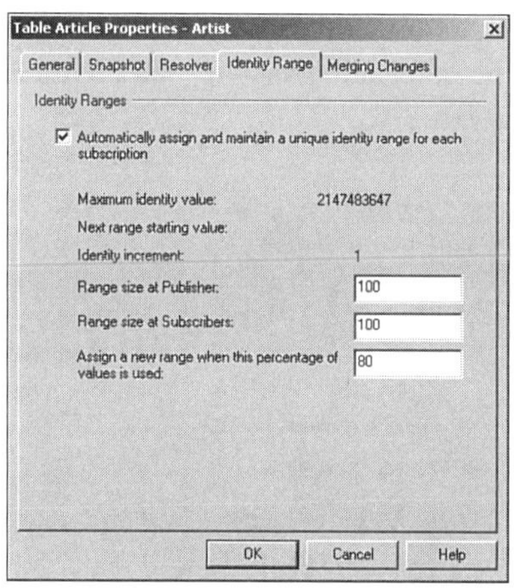

FIGURE 8.9
Managing an identity range for an article is specified under the Identity Range tab of the article's properties.

You need to create an identity range for each article: Artist, Genre, and CD. No identity range is needed for the Users table because the application won't be modifying records in that table.

After going to the next step, the wizard informs you of any problems with the database for the type of publication you are creating. In this example, there are two problems:

- The absence of an `uniqueidentifier` column in each article
- The identity columns not set to Not For Replication

The wizard displays these problems, how it will fix them, and the implications of the fixes (see Figure 8.10).

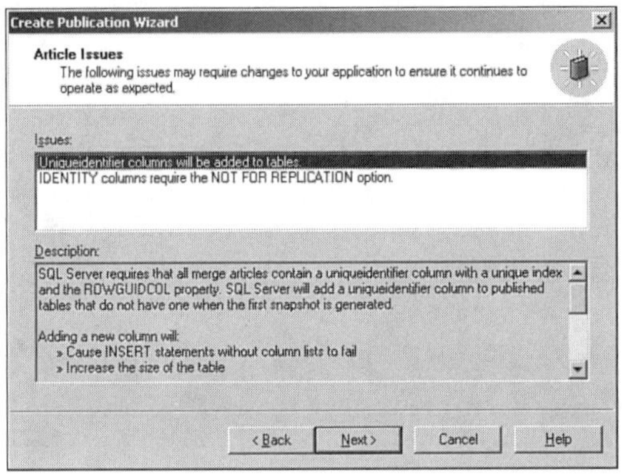

FIGURE 8.10

The Create Publication Wizard analyzes all publication articles for problems, resolves each problem, and explains implications of its resolution(s).

The wizard now prompts for the publication's name (see Figure 8.11). For this example, name the `CDPublication` and click Next.

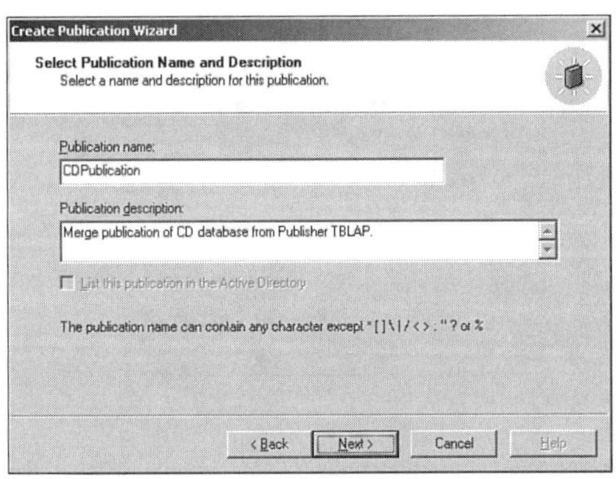

FIGURE 8.11

Naming the publication.

To do some filtering, choose Yes in the customize properties step (see Figure 8.12) and click Next. Because subscriptions from SQL Server CE are always anonymous, you need a method to inform the server which user is subscribing or synching. Using the `HostName` property on the SSCE.Replication object provides the server with the ability to query that value using the `HOST_NAME()` function. The publication is filtered to include only the Users table record (as created in MakeData.sql from Listing 8.5) with the UserName field matching the return value from the `HOST_NAME()` function. Also, the CD records are filtered by `JOIN`ing the filtered Users table to the CD table.

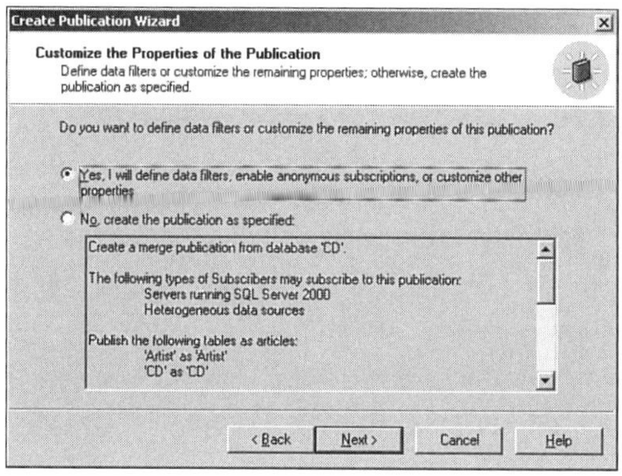

FIGURE 8.12
The wizard has collected enough information to create the publication, but you can define further information before the publication is created.

To filter the articles, the publication needs to have a horizontal filtering set, as shown in Figure 8.13.

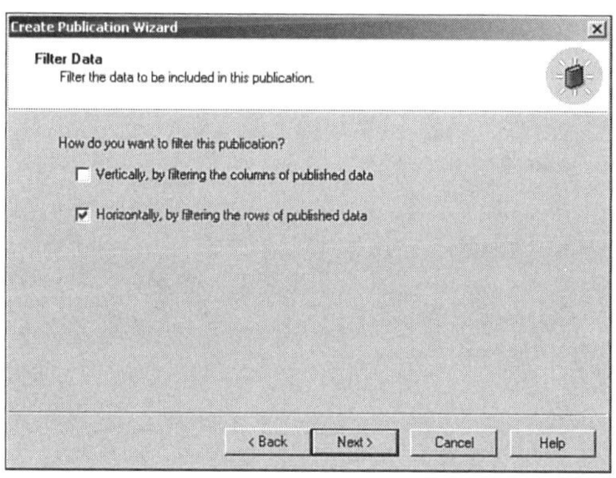

FIGURE 8.13
To filter article rows for subscribers, use horizontal filtering. Vertical filtering applied to articles eliminates columns from the article.

After specifying either type of filtering, the wizard asks whether the filtering will be dynamic or static. The sample application uses dynamic filtering to minimize network bandwidth, so select Yes, Enable Dynamic Filters (see Figure 8.14).

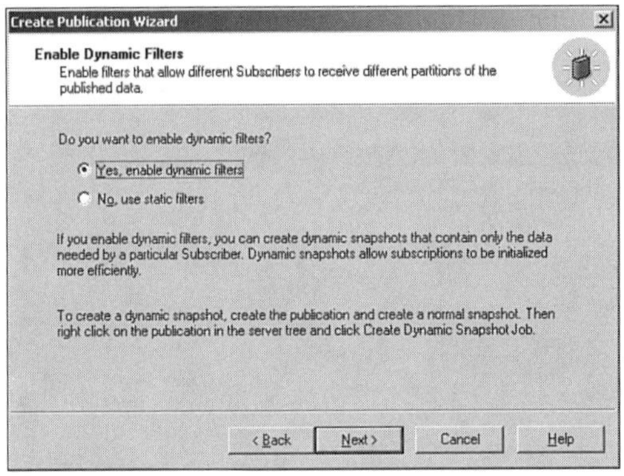

FIGURE 8.14

The sample application uses dynamic filtering.

The sample application sets the `HostName` property to the current user allowing the `HOST_NAME()` function to return the value. This value is compared to the Users.UserName column to filter the Users table to a single record. This record is then `JOIN`ed to the CD table to allow only the CD records for that user to be subscribed to.

Select the Users table in the Table to Filter dropdown and add

```
UserName = HOST_NAME()
```

to the `WHERE` clause in the text box, as shown in Figure 8.15. Click Next.

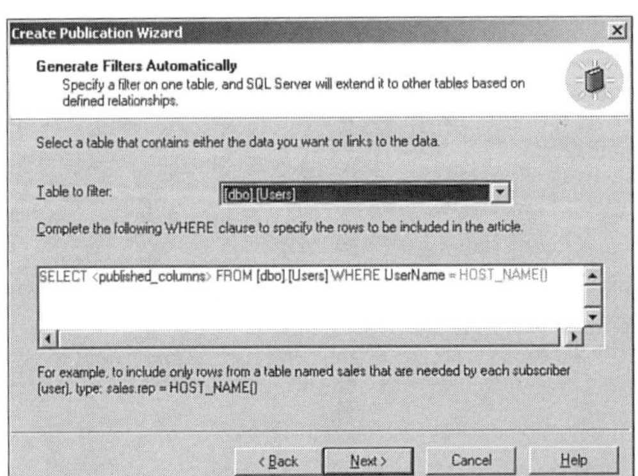

FIGURE 8.15

Filtering the Users article to the current user by using the `HOST_NAME()` function.

In the Filter Table Rows step, you can specify more filtering to take place on articles. The filter can be specified by adding a `WHERE` clause to any table (see Figure 8.16). This is accomplished by clicking the ellipsis next to the article name in the top grid. The second type of row filtering that you can apply to the articles is a `JOIN` condition specified in the lower grid.

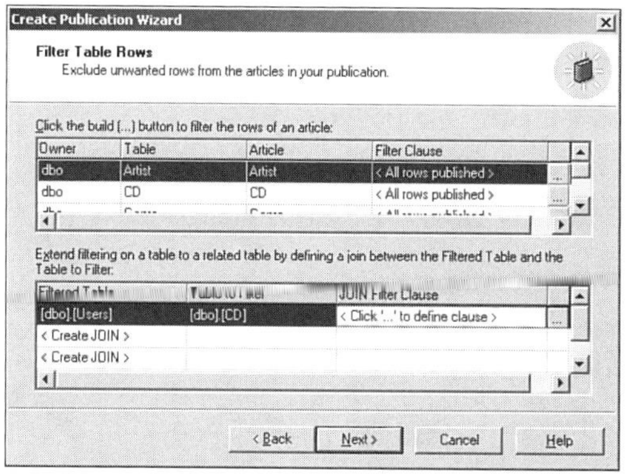

FIGURE 8.16

The Create Publication Wizard allows for horizontal filtering of any articles using a `WHERE` *clause (top grid) or a* `JOIN` *clause (lower grid).*

The sample application needs to filter the CD article by the UserId foreign key. This is accomplished by adding a `JOIN` condition to the CD article in the lower grid. As shown in Figure 8.16, choose the Users table (dbo.Users) in the lower grid's Filtered Table column. Next, in the Table to Filter column, choose the CD table (dbo.CD). The JOIN Filter Clause column then informs you to click the ellipsis to open a dialog box, as shown in Figure 8.17.

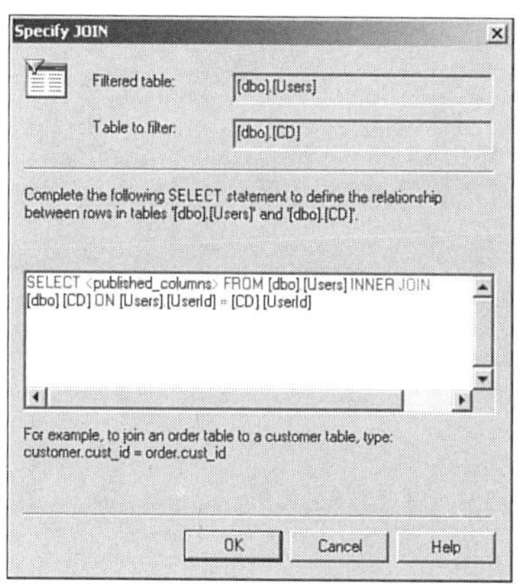

FIGURE 8.17

The Specify Join dialog allows you to create the `JOIN` *clause between a filtered table and any other table in the publication.*

Enter the `JOIN` condition between the Users table and the CD table as

```
[Users].[UserId] = [CD].[UserId]
```

This causes the publication to publish only CD records that belong to the subscriber. After completing this step, your wizard should look like Figure 8.18. Click Next.

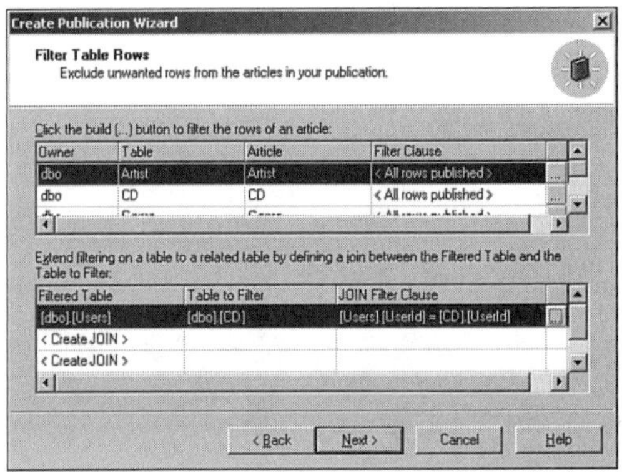

FIGURE 8.18

The CD table is filtered to only publish records that match the User by specifying a `JOIN` *to the filtered Users table.*

The next step asks if you want to validate the subscriber information. Because SQL Server CE doesn't support this validation, choose No (see Figure 8.19).

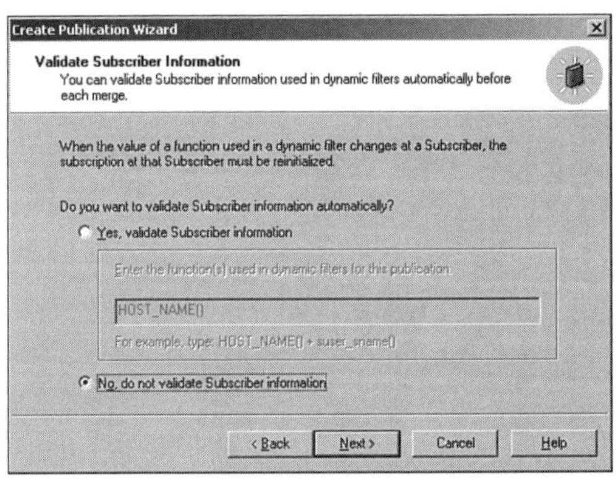

FIGURE 8.19

You don't need to specify validation of subscriber information because SQL Server CE doesn't validate it.

The next option provides the opportunity to minimize data sent over the network. This sounds like a great option for Windows CE, so choose Yes as shown in Figure 8.20.

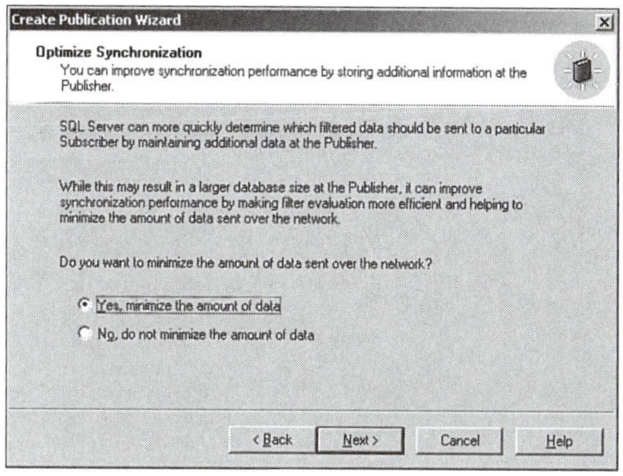

FIGURE 8.20

SQL Server can minimize network traffic for subscriptions by maintaining more sophisticated snapshots of the data at the server.

In the next step (see Figure 8.21), the wizard presents a single choice of Yes for allowing anonymous subscriptions. Because SQL Server CE supports only anonymous subscription, the No option is disabled. Click Next.

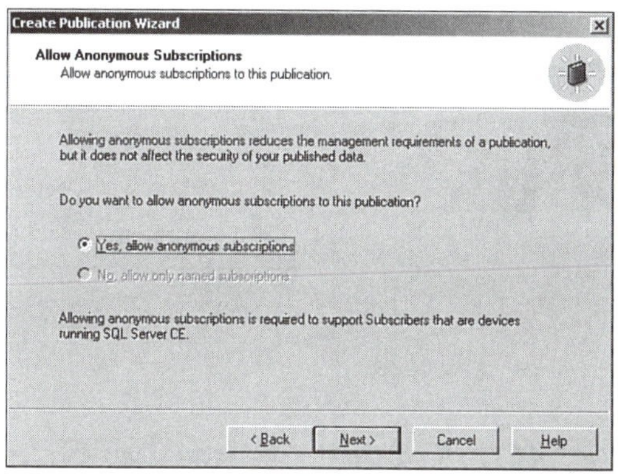

FIGURE 8.21

SQL Server CE only allows for anonymous subscription.

The next step allows for the scheduling of the snapshots for new subscribers. Leaving the default schedule is fine, but be sure Create the First Snapshot Immediately is checked (see Figure 8.22). Click Next.

Lastly, the publication is created as the last step of the wizard, as shown in Figure 8.23.

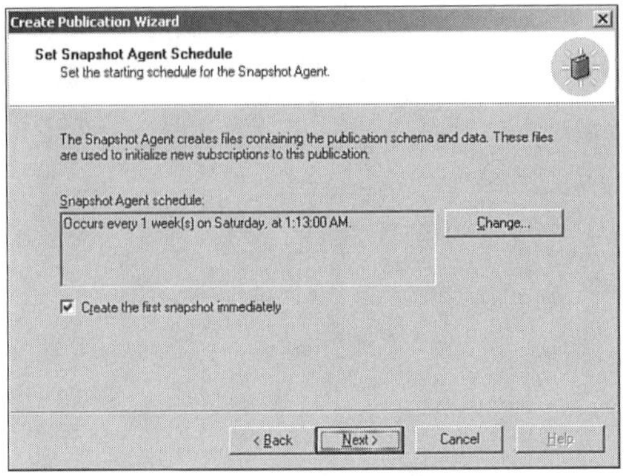

FIGURE 8.22
The default schedule is weekly for the snapshot agent to run, but be sure the initial snapshot is created immediately.

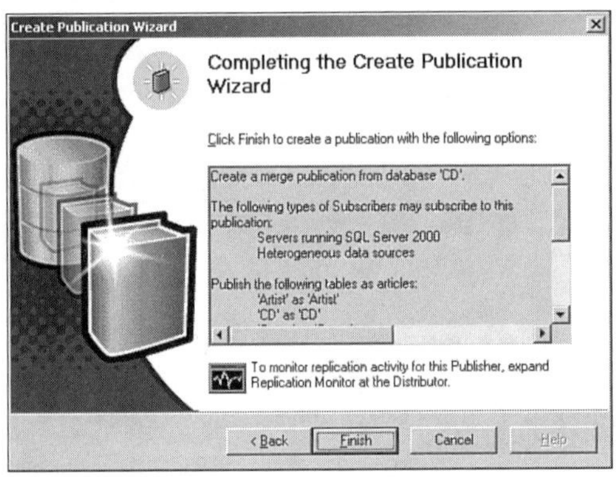

FIGURE 8.23
The publication is created after clicking the Finish button.

Investigating the SQL Server CE Replication Object

Now that you are more familiar with the Microsoft SQL Server replication model, let's look at the SQL Server CE replication object. To use SQL Server CE replication, your application will use the `SSCE.Replication` ActiveX DLL server. `SSCE.Replication` is one of three creatable SQL Server CE objects. `SSCE.Replication` provides access to a Microsoft SQL Server 2000 publisher. It requires quite a few properties configured to properly establish a subscription from the publisher.

Table 8.1 shows the minimal properties that should be set to initialize a publication on SQL Server CE.

TABLE 8.1 Minimal SQL Server CE Properties to Subscribe to a SQL Server Publication

Property	*Description and Example*
`InternetURL`	URL of the sscesa10.dll: *`object`*`.InternetURL = "http://www.myserver.com/ssce/sscesa10.dll"`
`Publication`	Name of the publication published on the publisher: *`object`*`.Publication = "MyPublication"`
`Publisher`	Name of the Publisher (SQL Server Name): *`object`*`.Publisher = "MySQLServer"`
`PublisherAddress`	Network address of the SQL Server publisher; the publisher can exist on a different server than the IIS server: *`object`*`.PublisherAddress = "sql.myserver.com"` or *`object`*`.PublisherAddress = "192.0.0.1"`
`PublisherDatabase`	Name of the database where the publication resides; the database where the publication resides isn't necessarily the same as the name of the database where the publication originated: *`object`*`.PublisherDatabase = "MyPublishedDB"`
`PublisherLogin`	User ID for the publisher. Depending on the security mode (`PublisherSecurityMode`) for the publisher, this can be either a SQL Server login or a Windows NT login: *`object`*`.PublisherSecurityMode = "MyUserId"`
`PublisherNetwork`	Network configuration for the SQL Server serving as the publisher. Valid values are `DEFAULT_NETWORK`, `MULTI_PROTOCOL`, and `TCPIP_SOCKETS`: *`object`*`.PublisherNetwork = TCPIP_SOCKETS`
`PublisherPassword`	Password for the user ID. Works in tandem with the `PublisherLogin` value: *`object`*`.PublisherPassword = "MyPassword"`
`PublisherSecurityMode`	Security mode for the publisher, SQL, or Windows NT. Valid values are `DB_AUTHENTICATION` and `NT_AUTHENTICATION`: *`object`*`.PublisherSecurityMode = DB_AUTHENTICATION`
`Subscriber`	Name of the subscriber. Although the publication may allow anonymous subscribers, a value is required: *`object`*`.Subscriber = "MySubscriberName"`
`SubscriberConnectionString`	Connection string to the SQL Server CE database the subscription will be placed: *`object`*`.SubscriberConnectionString = "Provider=Microsoft.SQLServer.OLEDB.CE.1.0;Data Source=\MySSCEDb.sdf"`

After you properly set all the properties in Table 8.1, three different methods are called in the order listed here to create the subscription database (`AddSubscription`), initialize a subscription (`Initialize`), and synchronize the data (`Run`). After these methods are called, the subscriber should call the `Terminate` method.

`AddSubscription` marks or creates a database that subscribes to a Microsoft SQL Server publication. It takes a single parameter of type `SSCE.REPL_DBADDOPTION`. The two different values are `CREATE_DATABASE` and `EXISTING_DATABASE`. Using `CREATE_DATABASE` actually creates a new SQL Server CE database based on the values in the `SubscriberConnectionString` value. If `CREATE_DATABASE` is used and the SQL Server CE database specified in the `SubscriberConnectionString` already exists, an error occurs. `AddSubscription` is called only once for each database and subscription. If the database already exists, whether created with the `AddSubscription` method or otherwise, call `AddSubscription` with the `EXISTING_DATABASE` value for the parameter.

`Initialize` prepares for synchronization. It must always be called before the `Run` method is called.

NOTE

The database specified must not be open from any ADOCE objects.

Next, `Run` initiates the communication with the server and then retrieves the subscription. Each time `Run` is called, all data structures for the subscription are created or modified. If a structure change has occurred in any article of the publication, all modified data is uploaded first, and then the structure changes are implemented before the data comes down to the device.

Lastly, `Terminate` is called to complete the merge process.

In Listing 8.6, a simple example is given. This example creates a SQL Server CE database, `Initializes` a subscription, synchronizes with the `Run` method, and then completes the process by calling `Terminate`.

LISTING 8.6 Creating a SQL Server CE Database that Subscribes to a Publication

```
Dim objSSCEReplication As SSCE.Replication

' create the SSCE.Replication object
Set objSSCEReplication = CreateObject("SSCE.Replication.1.0")
```

LISTING 8.6 Continued

```
' the URL for the SSCE dll running on IIS
objSSCEReplication.InternetURL "http://192.0.0.1/ssce/sscesa10.dll"

' the SQL server network library setting
objSSCEReplication.PublisherNetwork = TCPIP_SOCKETS

' name of the Publisher for replication
objSSCEReplication.Publisher = "tblap"

' name of the database
objSSCEReplication.PublisherDatabase = "CD"
' name of the publication
objSSCEReplication.Publication = "CDPublication"

' security mode to authenticate to the SQL server
objSSCEReplication.PublisherSecurityMode = DB_AUTHENTICATION

' sql server login
objSSCEReplication.PublisherLogin = "sa"

' sql server password
objSSCEReplication.PublisherPassword = ""

' IP address of the publisher
objSSCEReplication.PublisherAddress = "192.0.0.1"

' Set connection properties
objSSCEReplication.SubscriberConnectionString = "Data Source=\CD.sdf"

' set the subscriber name
objSSCEReplication.Subscriber = "mobileuser1"

' if the first time, we need to create the DB
' while we're adding a subscription
objSSCEReplication.AddSubscription CREATE_DATABASE

' initialize the subscription on the device
objSSCEReplication.Initialize

' sync the subscription
objSSCEReplication.Run

' close out and complete
objSSCEReplication.Terminate
```

Let's examine Listing 8.3 line by line. First, an object reference is declared as an `SSCE.Replication` object:

```
Dim objSSCEReplication As SSCE.Replication
```

The `SSCE.Replication` object is then created:

```
Set objSSCEReplication = CreateObject("SSCE.Replication.1.0")
```

Next, the `InternetURL` property is set to the URL of the SQL Server CE DLL residing on the server:

```
objSSCEReplication.InternetURL "http://192.0.0.1/ssce/sscesa10.dll"
```

Remember, this is the virtual directory you created, copied the DLLs into, and registered by using `RegSrv32`.

The `PublisherNetwork` property is set to the value on which the server-side SQL Server listens:

```
objSSCEReplication.PublisherNetwork = TCPIP_SOCKETS
```

The `Publisher` property is set to the named instance of the SQL server that serves as the publication's publisher:

```
objSSCEReplication.Publisher = "tblap"
```

The `PublisherDatabase` property is set to the name of the database from which the publication originates:

```
objSSCEReplication.PublisherDatabase = "CD"
```

The `Publication` property is set to the name of the publication:

```
objSSCEReplication.Publication = "CDPublication"
```

The publication name can vary from the database from which it originates. There can even be multiple publications for a individual database.

The `PublisherSecurityMode` property is set to the type of authentication the subscriber (devices) desires to use as its authentication method:

```
objSSCEReplication.PublisherSecurityMode = DB_AUTHENTICATION
```

The SQL Server must be configured to use the specified security mode.

The `PublisherLogin` property is set to the SQL Server login that has access to the publication. In this example, the `sa` login is used; your security policies may dictate a different policy.

```
objSSCEReplication.PublisherLogin = "sa"
```

The PublisherPassword property is set to the valid password that corresponds to the value for PublisherLogin:

```
objSSCEReplication.PublisherPassword = ""
```

The PublisherAddress property is set to the network address of the publisher SQL Server:

```
objSSCEReplication.PublisherAddress = "192.0.0.1"
```

Remember, the publisher might be in a different location than the IIS server hosting the SQL Server CE DLLs.

The SubscriberConnectionString property is set with the Data Source syntax for the location of the SQL Server database in which the subscription should be created:

```
objSSCEReplication.SubscriberConnectionString = "Data Source=\CD.sdf"
```

The Subscriber property is set to the subscriber's name:

```
objSSCEReplication.Subscriber = "mobileuser1"
```

The AddSubscription method is called by using the CREATE_DATABASE enumeration value:

```
objSSCEReplication.AddSubscription CREATE_DATABASE
```

If the SQL Server CE database exists, as specified as the Data Source in the SubscriberConnectionString property, the EXISTING_DATABASE enumeration value should be used instead.

The Initialize method is called, preparing the object and database to synchronize:

```
objSSCEReplication.Initialize
```

The Run method is called to actually subscribe to the subscription, and receive the structures and data:

```
objSSCEReplication.Run
```

The Terminate method is called to perform cleanup and complete the merging process:

```
objSSCEReplication.Terminate
```


Converting the CD Library Application to Use SQL Server CE Replication

At this point, you should have the CD database created, a publication ready, and a good understanding of the SQL Server CE replication object. Let's get started converting that application. If you didn't create the CD Library application, you can use the sample code from Chapter 7. This chapter presents only added and modified code from the material presented in Chapter 7.

Project-Level Changes

The application needs to reference three new ActiveX libraries. The first is SQL Server CE itself. To reference SQL Server CE, you need to actually reference a type library instead of a DLL. By using the Browse button in the project references dialog, navigate to type library file ca_merge.tlb. The location of this file using a default install is C:\Program Files\Microsoft SQL Server CE\Lib\ca_merge.tlb. You may be prompted that the selected library isn't for your current platform; add it anyway. SQL Server CE appears in the dialog box as Microsoft SQL Server CE Control 1.0, even if it's version 1.1, the most current version at the time of this writing.

The second and third libraries that need a reference set should be available in your project references list already. The second library is Microsoft CE ADO Control 3.1, ADOCE version 3.1. SQL Server CE requires version 3.1 (versus Pocket Access compatibility to earlier versions) and should have been installed when you installed the developer tools for SQL Server CE from the install package. The third library needed is Microsoft CE ADO Ext 3.1 for DDL. This library is the CE version of ADOX, used for creating databases, tables, indexes, and other data structures in a SQL Server CE database. We will use this ADOXCE library to create a table for the storage of configuration parameters. Your project references dialog should now look similar to Figure 8.24.

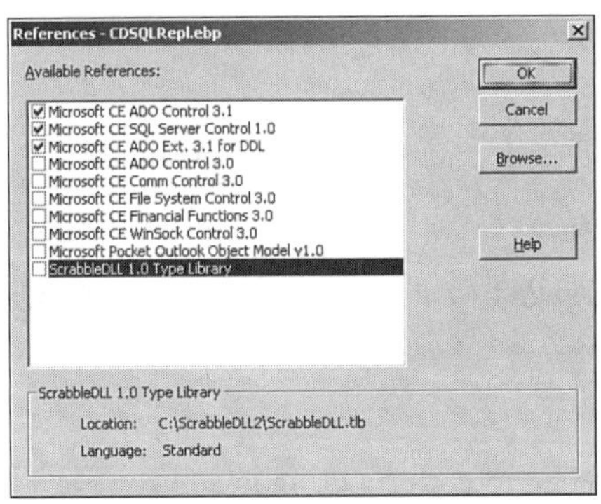

FIGURE 8.24

The CD Library Replication Application should have project references to Microsoft CE ADO Control 3.1, SQL Server CE Control 1.0 and Microsoft CE ADO Ext. for DDL 3.1.

Other project-level changes that you need to accomplish before digging in are to add a new module file named modSQLRepl.bas and a form named `frmSQLProperties`. After adding the module file, stub out a `Sub Main` in it, so you can change the Startup Object to `Sub Main` (see Figure 8.25). Also, add a FileSystem control named `frmSQLProperties`. Notice in Figure 8.25 that the project's Update Components settings are set to force down the SQL Server CE DLLs to a device as discussed for Figure 8.2.

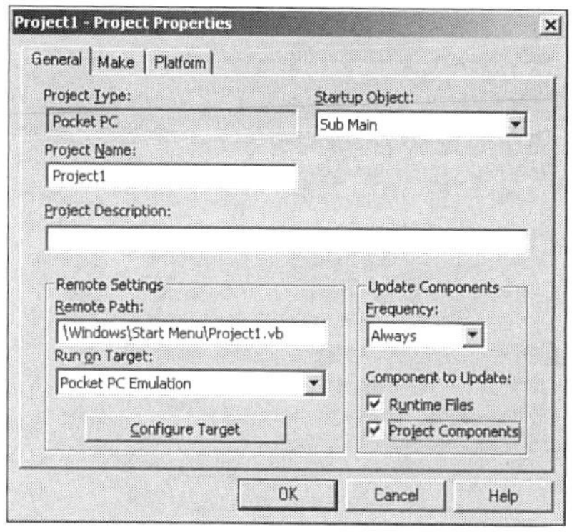

FIGURE 8.25

The CD Library Replication project needs to use `Sub Main` as its Startup Object.

Digging In: New `Consts` and `Public` Variables

Some new `Consts` and `Public` variables need to be declared to make the CD Library application compliant to SQL Server CE. These are places in the general section of module file modSQlRepl.bas, as shown in Listing 8.7.

LISTING 8.7 modSQLRepl.bas: `Consts` and `Public` Variables

```
' the database path and name
Public Const DB_PATH = "\CD.sdf"
' the config parms table
Public Const CONFIG_PARAMS_TABLE = "ConfigParms"

Public gblnFirstStartUp As Boolean
Public gstrInternetURL As String
Public gstrPublisherAddress As String
Public gstrPublisherNetwork As SSCE.REPL_NETWORK_TYPE
Public gstrPublisher  As String
Public gPublisherSecurityMode As SSCE.REPL_SECURITY_TYPE
Public gstrPublisherLogin As String
Public gstrPublisherPassword As String
Public gstrSubscriberConnectionString  As String
Public gstrSubscriber  As String
Public gstrHostName  As String
Public gstrPublication As String
Public gstrPublisherDatabase As String
Public gstrIPAddress As String
Public glngCurrentUser As Long
```

LISTING 8.8 Continued

```
' the SQL Server CE replication object
Public gSQLReplication As SSCE.Replication
' ADOXCE Catalog - Used to check for the
' config table's existence
Public gobjADOXCatalog As ADOXCE.Catalog
' configuration recordset
Public gConfigRecord As ADOCE.Recordset
' used to retrieve user id
Public gobjUser As ADOCE.Recordset

' class names
Public Const SSCE_REPLICATION_CLASS = "SSCE.Replication.1.0"
Public Const ADOXCE_CATALOG_CLASS = "ADOXCE.Catalog.3.1"

' AddSubscription Consts
Public Const EXISTING_DATABASE = 0
Public Const CREATE_DATABASE = 1

' NetworkType Consts
Public Const DEFAULT_NETWORK = 0
Public Const TCPIP_SOCKETS = 1
Public Const MULTI_PROTOCOL = 2

' Authentication Consts
Public Const DB_AUTHENTICATION = 0
Public Const NT_AUTHENTICATION = 1
```

Examining Listing 8.7 by sections, the first two `Consts` are the database path name and a table name for the configuration parameters table, ConfigParams. The configuration parameters table stores the property settings (`SSCE.Replication` object) used for a successful subscription initialization or synchronization. This allows ease of use for the user without having to manually configure the settings every time a synchronization is desired.

The second section (starting `Public gstrInternetURL As String`) is a collection of `Public` variables that store the `SSCE.Replication` configuration settings from the initial hard-coded values, the configuration form (`frmSQLProperties`), or as retrieved from the ConfigParams table.

The third section declares the references for the `SSCE.Replication` object, an `ADOXCE.Catalog` to check for the existence of the ConfigParams table, an `ADOCE.Recordset` to retrieve and update the configuration values in the ConfigParams table, and another recordset to retrieve the primary key value for the current user.

The fourth section, labeled class names, declares two `Consts` for the `SSCE.Replication` and `ADOXCE.Catalog` class names and versions. These are present for maintainability; for more information about this strategy, please see Chapter 7.

The final three sections declare `Consts` used as values for various `SSCE.Replication` properties.

NOTE

The `Consts` declared in the final three sections may not be necessary in your development environment. I've experienced some environments that require them and some that don't. I've included them here for you; if you receive errors when trying to access them, simply comment them out or remove them.

modSQLRepl.bas: `Sub Main`, Where the Journey Begins

Because application initialization takes quite a bit of configuration before the subscription arrives, a `Sub Main` (see Listing 8.8) is implemented to decide where to go.

LISTING 8.8 modSQLRepl.bas: Initializing the Application

```
Sub Main()

    On Error Resume Next

    ' initialize all global variables
    If Not InitializeGlobals() Then
        MsgBox "Error initializing global objects."
        Exit Sub
    End If

    ' default to first startup
    gblnFirstStartUp = True

    ' if the database exists then set first start up to false
If Len(frmSQLProperties.FileSystem1.Dir(DB_PATH)) > 0 Then
        gblnFirstStartUp = False
    End If
```

LISTING 8.8 Continued

```
    ' if we can't load the configs, then inform the
    ' user and exit
    If Not LoadConfigs() Then
        MsgBox "Error loading configuration."
    End If

    ' if first startup
    If gblnFirstStartUp Then
        ' let's show the sql form
        ' allow user to check/set the values
        frmSQLProperties.Show
    Else
        ' we're all set, show the main form
        frmMain.Show
    End If

End Sub
```

The code in Listing 8.8 starts by creating all the objects the application uses by calling `InitializeGlobals`. Code has been added to `InitializeGlobals` to create the objects added to CD Library Replication, as shown shortly in Listing 8.9.

Next, a global Boolean flag, `gblnFirstStartUp`, is set to `True`, indicating this is the first time the application has been run on the device. This flag determines the first form to show and whether the subscription needs to be created.

Next, the `FileSystem` object checks for the existence of the SQL Server CE database file used by the application. If the database file exists, the flag `gblnFirstStartUp` is set to `False`, indicating the application can proceed with a normal startup.

`LoadConfigs` (coming up soon in Listing 8.10) is then called to populate all the `Public` variables that hold the configuration values for synchronizing the subscription to the publication on the SQL server. These values are used by the `SSCE.Replication` object, `gSQLReplication`. When `LoadConfigs` is called without a current subscription (the first time), it will populate the values from hard-coded values; otherwise, it will load them from the ConfigParams table.

After the configuration parameters are loaded, `Sub Main` will display one of two forms. If the application is currently in a "first-run" state, as designated by the variable `gblnFirstStartUp`, the form `frmSQLProperties` is shown. If the application is a normal state, the form `frmMain` is shown.

modGlobal.bas: `InitializeGlobals`, Where All Objects Are Created

`InitializeGlobals` in Listing 8.9 creates all the ActiveX objects used in the CD Library Replication application. This function is the same with four new objects being created. For the original discussion of `InitializeGlobals`, see Listing 7.1 in Chapter 7.

LISTING 8.9 modGlobal.bas: Changes to `InitializeGlobals`

```
Function InitializeGlobals() As Boolean

    On Error Resume Next

    InitializeGlobals = False

    ' initialize globals - this needs to take place
    ' only once, due to CreateObject memory leak

    ' ADOCE_CLASS_CONNECTION & ADOCE_CLASS_RECORDSET
    ' are used because ce references these classes
    ' by their version numbers, create Consts allows
    ' changing of these version quickly and accurately
    Set gobjConnection = CreateObject(ADOCE_CLASS_CONNECTION)

    Set gobjArtist = CreateObject(ADOCE_CLASS_RECORDSET)
    Set gobjCD = CreateObject(ADOCE_CLASS_RECORDSET)
    Set gobjGenre = CreateObject(ADOCE_CLASS_RECORDSET)
    Set gobjPKEY = CreateObject(ADOCE_CLASS_RECORDSET)

    Set gConfigRecord = CreateObject(ADOCE_CLASS_RECORDSET)
    Set gSQLReplication = CreateObject(SSCE_REPLICATION_CLASS)
    Set gobjADOXCatalog = CreateObject(ADOXCE_CATALOG_CLASS)
    Set gobjUser = CreateObject(ADOCE_CLASS_RECORDSET)

    If Err.Number = 0 Then
        InitializeGlobals = True
    End If

End Function
```

`InitializeGlobals` creates four new objects to support CD Library Replication.

modSQLRepl.bas: `LoadConfigs`, Finding the Server

`LoadConfigs` (see Listing 8.10) populates the `Public` variables used to configure the `SSCE.Replication` object `gSQLReplication`. On the application's first run, the values are populated from hard-coded values. Subsequent execution of CD Library Replication will retrieve these values from the ConfigParams table. These values are saved to the ConfigParams table using the function `SaveConfiguration` after a successful initialization of the subscription.

LISTING 8.10 modSQLRepl.bas: Populating the Configuration Parameters for Creating or Synchronizing the Subscription

```
Public Function LoadConfigs() As Boolean

    On Error Resume Next

    ' set to error condition for early exit
    LoadConfigs = False

    ' are we here the first time
    ' if so, let's set the values
    If gblnFirstStartUp Then

        ' ip address of the web server
        gstrIPAddress = "192.0.0.1"

        ' URL for the SSCE dll
        gstrInternetURL = "http://" _
            & gstrIPAddress & "/ssce/sscesa10.dll"

        ' name of the Publisher (SQL)
        gstrPublisher = "tblap"

        ' security mode that the publisher uses
        gPublisherSecurityMode = DB_AUTHENTICATION

        ' login id for the publisher
        gstrPublisherLogin = "sa"

        ' password
        gstrPublisherPassword = ""

        ' network library for the publisher
        gstrPublisherNetwork = TCPIP_SOCKETS

        ' name of the database for the publication (on the publisher)
        gstrPublisherDatabase = "CD"

        ' name of the subscriber
gstrSubscriber = "mobileuser1"
```

LISTING 8.10 Continued

```
        ' host name - used to filter the data
        gstrHostName = "mobileuser1"

        ' name of the publication
        gstrPublication = "CDPublication"
    Else

        ' open the database to get the SQL CE Replication configurations
        If Not OpenDatabase() Then
            ' error - get out
            Exit Function
        End If

        ' open the config table
        gConfigRecord.Open CONFIG_PARAMS_TABLE, gobjConnection, _
            adOpenForwardOnly, adLockReadOnly, adCmdTableDirect

        ' get the values
        gstrInternetURL = gConfigRecord.Fields("InternetURL").Value
        gstrPublisherNetwork = gConfigRecord.Fields("PublisherNetwork").Value
        gstrPublisher = gConfigRecord.Fields("Publisher").Value
        gPublisherSecurityMode = _
            gConfigRecord.Fields("PublisherSecurityMode").Value
gstrPublisherLogin = gConfigRecord.Fields("PublisherLogin").Value
        gstrPublisherPassword = gConfigRecord.Fields("PublisherPassword").Value
        gstrSubscriber = gConfigRecord.Fields("Subscriber").Value
        gstrHostName = gConfigRecord.Fields("HostName").Value
        gstrPublication = gConfigRecord.Fields("Publication").Value
        gstrIPAddress = gConfigRecord.Fields("IPAddress").Value
        gstrPublisherDatabase = gConfigRecord.Fields("PublisherDB").Value

        ' close it
        gConfigRecord.Close
    End If

    ' set the return value to True if there
    ' was no error
    LoadConfigs = Err.Number = 0

End Function
```


Outside the error handling and setting of the return value for the function, `LoadConfigs` is basically two code blocks. The code block to run is determined by an `If` statement as to status of the flag `gblnFirstStartUp`. If it's the first run of the application (`gblnFirstStartUp` =

`True`), the configuration variables are set by the execution of the hard-coded code block. When entering the hard-coded code block, you can change the values to match your configuration, or enter them as they appear here. We'll be creating a form that displays all of them for configuration. After modifying their contents and receiving a valid subscription, they will be saved, so you shouldn't have to make the changes repeatedly.

The second code block (after the `Else`) opens a recordset from the ConfigParams table and populates the values from this recordset.

`frmSQLProperties`: Setting Configuration Properties at Runtime

With the first startup, `Sub Main` shows the `frmSQLProperties` form, which allows configuration of the values for the `SSCE.Replication` object `gSQLReplication`. This form works by using a multiframe wizardlike interface. There are three frames to this wizard, as shown in Figures 8.26, 8.27, and 8.28. The form uses Next and Back buttons to navigate through the three frames.

FIGURE 8.26

The first frame of `frmSQLProperties` allows for configuration of the IIS SQL Server CE URL, the publisher address, the name of the publisher, and the publisher login and password.

The form `frmSQLProperties` is only one form, with three different frames placed onto it. This methodology provides speedy performance and was quite necessary in the days of the 70MHz MIPS processor. The performance need for this trick may no longer be needed with the 206MHz StrongArm processors out there, but if you ever create an application with a tab set, you'll want to pull it out of your Windows CE programming toolbox. Look at the form at design time in Figure 8.29; the three frames are randomly placed on the form and are shaded so that you can see their borders clearly.

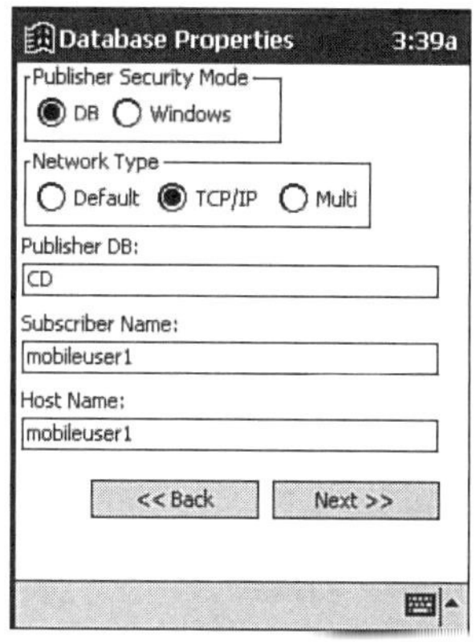

FIGURE 8.27

The second frame allows for configuration of the security mode for authentication on the publisher, the network protocol to communicate with the publisher, the name of the database on the publisher, the subscriber name, and the host name.

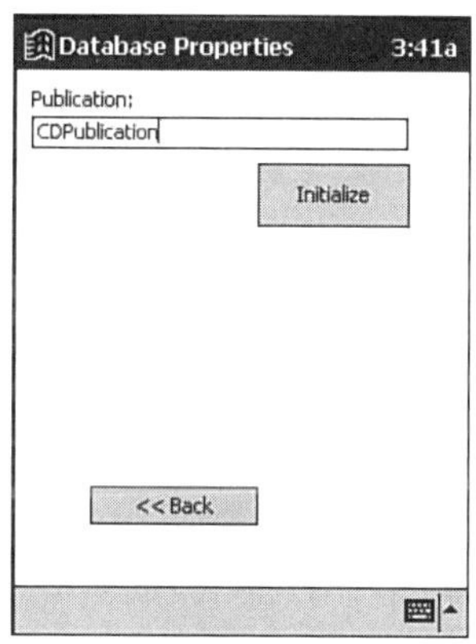

FIGURE 8.28

The third and last frame allows for configuration of the publication name and a button to initialize or synchronize the subscription.

It should be easiest for you to retrieve the visual portions of the form from the sample code files, but let's look at the code behind this form that makes it work.

One `Public` variable, `CurrentFrame`, is declared to keep track of which frame should be currently displayed:

```
' currently displayed frame
Public CurrentFrame As Integer
```

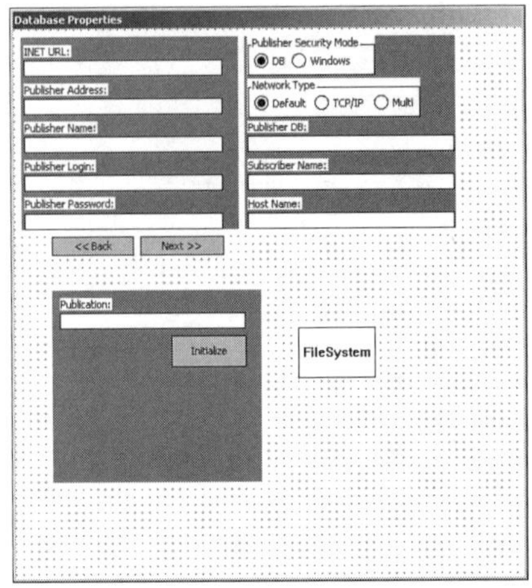

FIGURE 8.29

Form `frmSQLProperties` at design time shows all three frames clearly by shading their backgrounds.

`Form.Load`: Moving the Frames to Their Correct Positions

In the `Form.Load` event of `frmSQLProperties` (see Listing 8.11), all the frames are moved to the form's upper-left corner.

LISTING 8.11 frmSQLProperties.frm: Moving the Frames

```
Private Sub Form_Load()

    ' move all frames to proper position
    Me.Frame1.Top = 0
    Me.Frame1.Left = 0

    Me.Frame2.Top = 0
    Me.Frame2.Left = 0

    Me.Frame3.Top = 0
    Me.Frame3.Left = 0

End Sub
```

`Form.Activate`: Initializing the Controls

In the `Form.Activate` event of `frmSQLProperties` (see Listing 8.12), all the controls are initialized to the current values of the `Public` replication configuration values.

LISTING 8.12 frmSQLProperties.frm: Initializing the Controls' Values

```
Private Sub Form_Activate()

    ' set the current frame to 1
    CurrentFrame = 1

    ' Refresh the frames
    RefreshFrames

    ' set the values from the globals
    Me.txtURL.Text = gstrInternetURL
    Me.txtPublisherAddress.Text = gstrIPAddress
    Me.txtPublisherName.Text = gstrPublisher
    Me.txtPublisherLogin.Text = gstrPublisherLogin
    Me.txtPublisherPassword.Text = gstrPublisherPassword
    Me.txtDB.Text = gstrPublisherDatabase
    Me.txtSubscriberName.Text = gstrSubscriber
    Me.txtHostName.Text = gstrHostName
    Me.txtPublication.Text = gstrPublication

    ' set security mode radio buttons
    If gPublisherSecurityMode = DB_AUTHENTICATION Then
        Me.optSecDB = True
    Else
        Me.optSecWin = True
    End If

    ' set network protocol radio buttons
    Select Case gstrPublisherNetwork
        Case TCPIP_SOCKETS
            Me.optNetTCPIP = True
        Case MULTI_PROTOCOL
            Me.optNetMulti = True
        Case DEFAULT_NETWORK
            Me.optNetworkDef = True
    End Select

End Sub
```


The first item accomplished in `Form.Activate` is to set the `Public` variable `CurrentFrame` to 1 to ensure that the first frame is shown when the form displays. Then `RefreshFrames` (see Listing 8.13) is called to make the proper frame and buttons visible.

Next, all controls on all three frames are set to the current values from their corresponding `Public` variables. First, all the textboxes are set, and then the two sets of option buttons are set.

RefreshFrames: Displaying the Correct Frame and the Next/Back Buttons

RefreshFrames (see Listing 8.13) uses three simple formulas to set the Visible property for the current frame to be displayed based on the value of CurrentFrame. It then sets the Enabled property of both the Next and Back buttons also from the value of CurrentFrame.

LISTING 8.13 frmSQLProperties.frm : Displaying the Correct Frame and Buttons

```
Private Sub RefreshFrames()

    ' set each frames visible to true or
    ' false as to whether it is the current frame
    Me.Frame1.Visible = (CurrentFrame = 1)
    Me.Frame2.Visible = (CurrentFrame = 2)
    Me.Frame3.Visible = (CurrentFrame = 3)

    ' next should only be visible if frame 2 or 3
    Me.cmdBack.Enabled = (CurrentFrame > 1)
    ' back should only be visible if frame 1 or 2
    Me.cmdNext.Enabled = (CurrentFrame < 3)End Sub
```

cmdBack.Click and cmdNext.Click: Navigating Through the Frames

Both the cmdNext.Click and cmdBack.Click events (see Listing 8.14) change the value of CurrentFrame and refresh the form with RefreshFrames. Sub cmdNext.Click increments CurrentFrame by 1, whereas Sub cmdBack.Click decrements it by 1.

LISTING 8.14 frmSQLProperties.frm: Navigating Through the Frames Using cmdBack.Click and cmdNext.Click

```
Private Sub cmdNext_Click()
    If CurrentFrame < 3 Then
        ' move forward one frame
        CurrentFrame = CurrentFrame + 1
        ' refresh the frames
        RefreshFrames
    End IfEnd Sub

Private Sub cmdBack_Click()
    If CurrentFrame > 1 Then
        ' move back one frame
        CurrentFrame = CurrentFrame - 1
        ' refresh the frames
        RefreshFrames
    End IfEnd Sub
```

`cmdInitialize.Click`: Initializing the Subscription

In Listing 8.15, `cmdInitialize.Click` retrieves all the values from all controls located within the three frames and sets these values to the appropriate configuration `Public` variables. It then calls the `Sync` function to create the subscription. With a successful call to `Sync`, the current state of the configuration is saved to the ConfigParams table using the `SaveConfiguration` function.

LISTING 8.15 frmSQLProperties.frm: Setting the Configuration Values, Initializing the Subscription, and Saving the Configuration

```
Private Sub cmdInitialize_Click()

    ' set the global properties from the
    ' form's values
    gstrInternetURL = Me.txtURL.Text
    gstrPublisherAddress = Me.txtPublisherAddress.Text
    gstrPublisher = Me.txtPublisherName.Text
    gstrPublisherLogin = Me.txtPublisherLogin.Text
    gstrPublisherPassword = Me.txtPublisherPassword.Text
    gstrSubscriber = Me.txtSubscriberName.Text
    gstrHostName = Me.txtHostName.Text
    gstrPublication = Me.txtPublication.Text
    gstrPublisherDatabase = Me.txtDB.Text
    gstrIPAddress = Me.txtPublisherAddress.Text

    ' radio button set
    Select Case True
        Case Me.optNetMulti.Value
            gstrPublisherNetwork = MULTI_PROTOCOL
        Case Me.optNetTCPIP.Value
            gstrPublisherNetwork = TCPIP_SOCKETS
        Case Me.optNetworkDef.Value
            gstrPublisherNetwork = DEFAULT_NETWORK
    End Select

    ' radio button set
    Select Case True
        Case Me.optSecDB.Value
            gPublisherSecurityMode = DB_AUTHENTICATION
        Case Me.optSecWin.Value
            gPublisherSecurityMode = NT_AUTHENTICATION
    End Select
```

LISTING 8.5 Continued

```
    ' Sync
    If Not Sync() Then
        MsgBox "Errors occurred in creating subscription."
Exit Sub
    End If

    If Not SaveConfiguration() Then
        MsgBox "Could not save configuration."
        Exit Sub
    End If

    ' show the main form
    frmMain.Show
End Sub
```

The majority of `cmdInitialize.Click` (up to the `Sync` call) sets the configuration values, which is basically a reversal of the `Form.Activate` event (refer to Listing 8.12), which sets the control values from the configuration values.

Next, the `Sync` Function (shown soon in Listing 8.16) is called. If `Sync` isn't successful, a message box informs users of the failure and the routine is exited.

Continuing on (`Sync` was successful), the configuration is saved using the `SaveConfiguration` function.

modSQLRepl.bas: `Sync`, Getting at That Data

The `Sync` function uses the `SSCE.Replication` object, `gSQLReplication`, to create the database and initialize the subscription (see Listing 8.16).

LISTING 8.16 modReplSQL.bas: Initializing the Subscription

```
Function Sync() As Boolean

    On Error Resume Next

    'set the error state so we can leave quickly
    Sync = False

    ' we have to close the database
    ' before we Sync to the remote server
    If Not CloseDatabase() Then
        ' problem closing - let's exit with
        ' an error condition
```

LISTING 8.16 Continued

```
        Exit Function
    End If

    ' the URL for the SSCE dll running on IIS
    gSQLReplication.InternetURL = gstrInternetURL

    ' the SQL server network library setting
    gSQLReplication.PublisherNetwork = TCPIP_SOCKETS

    ' name of the Publisher for replication
    gSQLReplication.Publisher = gstrPublisher

    ' name of the database
    gSQLReplication.PublisherDatabase = gstrPublisherDatabase

    ' name of the publication
    gSQLReplication.Publication = gstrPublication

    ' security mode to authenticate to the SQL server
    gSQLReplication.PublisherSecurityMode = gPublisherSecurityMode

    ' login
    gSQLReplication.PublisherLogin = gstrPublisherLogin

    ' password
    gSQLReplication.PublisherPassword = gstrPublisherPassword

    ' IP address of the publisher
    gSQLReplication.PublisherAddress = gstrIPAddress

    ' Set Subscriber properties
    gSQLReplication.SubscriberConnectionString = "Data Source=" & DB_PATH

    ' set the subscriber name
    gSQLReplication.Subscriber = gstrSubscriber

    ' set the host name
    gSQLReplication.HostName = gstrSubscriber

    ' if the first time, we need to create the DB
    ' while we're adding a subscription
    If gblnFirstStartUp Then
        gSQLReplication.AddSubscription CREATE_DATABASE
    End If
```

LISTING 8.16 Continued

```
    ' initialize the subscription on the device
    gSQLReplication.Initialize

    ' check for errors
    If gSQLReplication.ErrorRecords.Count > 0 Then
        ' display any errors
        ConnErrRoutine gSQLReplication
    Else
        ' Sync with server
        gSQLReplication.Run
        ' check for errors
        If gSQLReplication.ErrorRecords.Count > 0 Then
            ' display errors
            ConnErrRoutine gSQLReplication
        End If
    End If

    ' close out and complete
    gSQLReplication.Terminate

    ' open or reopen the database
If Not OpenDatabase() Then
        Exit Function
    End If

    ' set the return value to true if no error
    Sync = Err.Number = 0

    ' check the status
    If Sync Then
        MsgBox "Sync completed successfully.", , "CD Library"
    Else
        MsgBox "Sync completed with errors.", , "CD Library"
    End If

End Function
```

Let's break down the `Sync` function and investigate it. Setup is completed in Listing 8.17.

LISTING 8.17 Setting the Error Condition and Closing the Database

```
'set the error state so we can leave quickly
Sync = False
```

LISTING 8.17 Continued

```
' we have to close the database
' before we Sync to the remote server
If Not CloseDatabase() Then
    ' problem closing - let's exit with
    ' an error condition
    Exit Function
End If
```

First, in Listing 8.17, the return value is set to an error condition so that you can make a quick exit. Then the database is closed using the `CloseDatabase` function. The database needs to be closed to successfully complete a synchronization process with the publication on the server. Although you don't have a database at this point (if this is the first synchronization), `CloseDatabase` is constructed in such a way that it won't error, but should still return a success value of `True`.

Listing 8.18 sets all the configuration variables on the `SSCE.Replication` object `gSQLReplication`. It also uses the `Const DB_PATH` to set the `Data Source` attribute of the `SubscriberConnectionString` property.

LISTING 8.18 Transferring the Configuration Values to the Replication Object

```
' the URL for the SSCE dll running on IIS
gSQLReplication.InternetURL = gstrInternetURL

' the SQL server network library setting
gSQLReplication.PublisherNetwork = gstrPublisherNetwork

' name of the Publisher for replication
gSQLReplication.Publisher = gstrPublisher

' name of the database
gSQLReplication.PublisherDatabase = gstrPublisherDatabase

' name of the publication
gSQLReplication.Publication = gstrPublication

' security mode to authenticate to the SQL server
gSQLReplication.PublisherSecurityMode = gPublisherSecurityMode

' login
gSQLReplication.PublisherLogin = gstrPublisherLogin
```

LISTING 8.18 Continued

```
' password
gSQLReplication.PublisherPassword = gstrPublisherPassword

' IP address of the publisher
gSQLReplication.PublisherAddress = gstrIPAddress

' Set Subscriber properties
gSQLReplication.SubscriberConnectionString = "Data Source=" & DB_PATH

' set the subscriber name
gSQLReplication.Subscriber = gstrSubscriber

' set the host name
gSQLReplication.HostName = gstrSubscriber
```

Listings 8.18 and 8.19 correlate to the mandatory values to create a subscription to a publication or synchronize the subscription with the publication.

LISTING 8.19 Initializing the Subscription

```
' if the first time, we need to create the DB
' while we're adding a subscription
If gblnFirstStartUp Then
    gSQLReplication.AddSubscription CREATE_DATABASE
End If
```

If it's determined that this is a first time initialization with the publication, you need to call `AddSubscription` to properly initialize the `SSCE.Replication` object. Also, the `CREATE_DATABASE` parameter is used for the `AddSubscription` method because you currently shouldn't have a SQL Server CE database file (if this is the first time you have attempted to subscribe to the publication).

Listing 8.20 finally retrieves the subscription from the publication.

LISTING 8.20 Retrieving the Subscription

```
' initialize the subscription on the device
gSQLReplication.Initialize

' check for errors
If gSQLReplication.ErrorRecords.Count > 0 Then
    ' display any errors
    ConnErrRoutine gSQLReplication
Else
```

LISTING 8.20 Continued

```
    ' Sync with server
    gSQLReplication.Run
    ' check for errors
    If gSQLReplication.ErrorRecords.Count > 0 Then
        ' display errors
        ConnErrRoutine gSQLReplication
    End If
End If
```

Before a subscription can actually be initialized or synchronized using the `Run` method, the `Initialize` method needs to be called as shown in Listing 8.20. `Initialize` prepares the `SSCE.Replication` for synchronizing with the publication. At this point, the SQL Server CE database is created.

If there are no `ErrorRecords` after calling the `Initialize` method, the `Run` method is called to actually retrieve the subscription or synchronize it. If there are `ErrorRecords`, `ConnErrRoutine` is called passing the `SSCE.Replication` object `gSQLReplication`.

Listing 8.21 starts the cleanup for the `Sync` function.

LISTING 8.21 Finishing the Merge Replication and Cleaning Up

```
' close out and complete
gSQLReplication.Terminate

' open or repopen the database

If Not OpenDatabase() Then
    Exit Function
End If
```

The call to the `Terminate` method actually finishes the merging of data in the SQL Server CE database (if the database existed and had previously subscribed to the publication).

Also in Listing 8.21, the database is opened, or reopened in the case that it was previously present and open using the `OpenDatabase` Function.

In Listing 8.22, the return value is set to `True` if there were no errors. Also, the status of the sync process is displayed to users based on the return value.

LISTING 8.22 Setting the Return Value and Informing Users of the Synchronization's Status

```
' set the return value to true if no error
Sync = (Err.Number = 0)

' check the status
If Sync Then
    MsgBox "Sync completed successfully.", , "CD Library"
Else
    MsgBox "Sync completed with errors.", , "CD Library"
End If
```

modSQLRepl.bas: `SaveConfiguration`, Saving the Configuration Information to Synchronize with the Publisher

`SaveConfiguration` in Listing 8.23 allows any changes made at runtime to the hard-coded values in `LoadConfigs` (see Listing 8.10) to be saved. This allows quick and easy synchronization to occur without significant effort on the user's behalf.

LISTING 8.23 modReplSQL.bas: Storing the Replication Configuration for Future Syncs

```
Function SaveConfiguration() As Boolean

    Dim objADOXTable As ADOXCE.Table
    Dim blnTableFound As Boolean

    On Error Resume Next

    ' set error condition so we can exit early
    SaveConfiguration = False

    ' set the ADOX catalog connection to the db connection
    Set gobjADOXCatalog.ActiveConnection = gobjConnection

    ' set flag that we have not found
' the configuration table
    blnTableFound = False

    ' cycle through each table in the DB
    For Each objADOXTable In gobjADOXCatalog.Tables
        ' check if it is the ConfigParams Table
        If objADOXTable.Name = CONFIG_PARAMS_TABLE Then
            ' if we found it, set the flag and get out
            blnTableFound = True
```

LISTING 8.23 Continued

```
            Exit For
        End If
    Next

    ' if we did not find the table, let's create it
    If Not blnTableFound Then
        ' create the table
        gobjConnection.Execute "CREATE TABLE " _
            & CONFIG_PARAMS_TABLE _
            & " ( InternetURL nvarchar(255), PublisherNetwork tinyint, " _
            & "Publisher nvarchar(255), PublisherDB nvarchar(255), " _
            & "PublisherSecurityMode tinyint, PublisherLogin nvarchar(255), " _
            & "PublisherPassword nvarchar(255), Subscriber nvarchar(255), " _
            & "HostName nvarchar(255), Publication nvarchar(255), " _
            & "IPAddress nvarchar(255))"
    End If

    ' open it for adding/updating
    gConfigRecord.Open CONFIG_PARAMS_TABLE, gobjConnection, _
        adOpenForwardOnly, adLockOptimistic, adCmdTableDirect

    ' there should only be one record, so if there
    ' are not, add a record
    If gConfigRecord.EOF Then
        ' add the record
        gConfigRecord.AddNew
    End If

    ' save all the configuration data
    gConfigRecord.Fields("InternetURL") = gstrInternetURL
    gConfigRecord.Fields("PublisherNetwork") = gstrPublisherNetwork
    gConfigRecord.Fields("Publisher") = gstrPublisher
    gConfigRecord.Fields("PublisherSecurityMode") = gPublisherSecurityMode
    gConfigRecord.Fields("PublisherLogin") = gstrPublisherLogin
    gConfigRecord.Fields("PublisherPassword") = gstrPublisherPassword
    gConfigRecord.Fields("Subscriber") = gstrSubscriber
    gConfigRecord.Fields("HostName") = gstrHostName
    gConfigRecord.Fields("Publication") = gstrPublication
    gConfigRecord.Fields("IPAddress") = gstrIPAddress
    gConfigRecord.Fields("PublisherDB") = gstrPublisherDatabase

    ' send the changes
    gConfigRecord.Update
```

LISTING 8.23 Continued

```
    ' if we're done with no errors let's
    ' clear the first time flag and set
    ' return value to success
    If Err.Number = 0 Then
        gblnFirstStartUp = False
        SaveConfiguration = True
    End If

End Function
```

Let's break down `SaveConfiguration`. Listing 8.24 declares a local `ADOXCE.Table` object and `Boolean`. The `ADOXCE.Table` object `objADOXTable` is used with the global `ADOXCE.Catalog` object `gobjADOXCatalog` to determine whether the configuration parameters table ConfigParams is present. Next, the `gobjADOXCatalog` is given a reference to the database using its `ActiveConnection` property. Lastly, the `Boolean` variable `blnTableFound` is explicitly set to `False`, making the assumption that ConfigParams doesn't exist.

LISTING 8.24 Getting Set Up and Setting the Catalog's Connection

```
Dim objADOXTable As ADOXCE.Table
Dim blnTableFound As Boolean

On Error Resume Next

' set error condition so we can exit early
SaveConfiguration = False

' set the ADOX catalog connection to the db connection
Set gobjADOXCatalog.ActiveConnection = gobjConnection

    ' set flag that we have not found ' the configuration table
blnTableFound = False
```

Listing 8.25 first presents a `For...Each` loop that enumerates through each table contained within the `ADOXCE.Catalog`'s `Tables` collection. Each enumerated `ADOXCE.Table` object is checked to see if it's the ConfigParams table. If it is, the `Boolean` is set to `True` and the `For...Each` loop is exited.

Next in Listing 8.25, if the table hasn't been found, a SQL DDL statement is issued to create it.

LISTING 8.25 Searching for the ConfigParams Table and Creating It If Not Found

```
' cycle through each table in the DB
For Each objADOXTable In gobjADOXCatalog.Tables
    ' check if it is the ConfigParams Table
    If objADOXTable.Name = CONFIG_PARAMS_TABLE Then
        ' if we found it, set the flag and get out
        blnTableFound = True
        Exit For
    End If
Next

' if we did not find the table, let's create it
If Not blnTableFound Then
    ' create the table
    gobjConnection.Execute "CREATE TABLE " _
        & CONFIG_PARAMS_TABLE _
        & " ( InternetURL nvarchar(255), PublisherNetwork tinyint, " _
        & "Publisher nvarchar(255), PublisherDB nvarchar(255), " _
        & "PublisherSecurityMode tinyint, PublisherLogin nvarchar(255), " _
        & "PublisherPassword nvarchar(255), Subscriber nvarchar(255), " _
        & "HostName nvarchar(255), Publication nvarchar(255), " _
        & "IPAddress nvarchar(255))"
End If
```


In Listing 8.26, whether the table previously existed or was just created, the `ADOCE.Recordset` object `Opens` the table. If there's no record within the recordset, by testing the `EOF` property, a record is appended using the `AddNew` method of the `ADOCE.Recordset` object.

LISTING 8.26 Opening the ConfigParams Table and Ensuring a Record for Saving Values

```
' open it for adding/updating
    gConfigRecord.Open CONFIG_PARAMS_TABLE, gobjConnection, _
        adOpenForwardOnly, adLockOptimistic, adCmdTableDirect

' there should only be one record, so if there
' are not, add a record
If gConfigRecord.EOF Then
    ' add the record
    gConfigRecord.AddNew
End If
```

Listing 8.27 simply transfers the values from the global variables to the record and `Updates` the table.

LISTING 8.27 Setting the Record's Values and Updating the Table

```
' save all the configuration data
gConfigRecord.Fields("InternetURL") = gstrInternetURL
gConfigRecord.Fields("PublisherNetwork") = gstrPublisherNetwork
gConfigRecord.Fields("Publisher") = gstrPublisher
gConfigRecord.Fields("PublisherSecurityMode") = gPublisherSecurityMode
gConfigRecord.Fields("PublisherLogin") = gstrPublisherLogin
gConfigRecord.Fields("PublisherPassword") = gstrPublisherPassword
gConfigRecord.Fields("Subscriber") = gstrSubscriber
gConfigRecord.Fields("HostName") = gstrHostName
gConfigRecord.Fields("Publication") = gstrPublication
gConfigRecord.Fields("IPAddress") = gstrIPAddress
gConfigRecord.Fields("PublisherDB") = gstrPublisherDatabase

' send the changes
gConfigRecord.Update
```

Listing 8.28 does the cleanup. If there are no errors, the return value is set to a success value of `True`. Also, the first time run flag is set to `False` now that you have the subscription synchronized.

LISTING 8.28 Cleaning Up

```
' if we're done with no errors let's
' clear the first time flag and set
' return value to success
If Err.Number = 0 Then
    gblnFirstStartUp = False
    SaveConfiguration = True
End If
```

Changing the CD Form and Supporting Functions for SQL Server CE Compatibility

The CD form `frmCD` needs some changes to be compatible with SQL Server CE. There are two key differences in `frmCD` for Pocket Access and SQL Server CE:

- Because SQL Server CE subscriptions offer identity columns, you need to remove the manual primary key generating function, `GetNewPK`, and any calls made to it.
- You need to modify any code that did in-place updates to recordsets created through SQL statements. (For more information about in-place updating, refer to "Updating SQL Server CE Recordsets" earlier in this chapter.)

Go ahead and remove the function `GetNewPK` from the project as well as any calls to it. Then, let's investigate the changes for `SaveCD` function in Listing 8.29.

LISTING 8.29 frmCD.frm: Changes for SQL Server CE Compatibility

```
Private Function SaveCD() As Boolean

    Dim lngArtistId As Long
    Dim lngGenreId As Long

    On Error Resume Next

    ' because we may have some cleanup
    ' work to do, let's set the
    ' default return value to true
    SaveCD = True

    ' do we have an existing or new genre
    If Me.cboGenre.ListIndex >= 0 Then
        ' existing genre
        ' get the pk value
        lngGenreId = Me.cboGenre.ItemData(Me.cboGenre.ListIndex)
    Else
        ' new genre
        ' ask user to add new genre
        If MsgBox("Would you like to add the genre: " _
            & Me.cboGenre.Text, vbYesNo) = vbYes Then
                ' get a new genre pk value
                lngGenreId = AddGenre(Me.cboGenre.Text)
                ' is it valid?
                If lngGenreId < 0 Then
                    ' outta here
                    MsgBox "Error adding genre."
                    SaveCD = False
                    Exit Function
                End If
        Else
            ' can't save without a genre
            SaveCD = False
            MsgBox "You cannot save a CD without a genre."
Exit Function
        End If
    End If

    ' do we have an existing or new artist
    If Me.cboArtist.ListIndex >= 0 Then
```

Listing 8.29 Continued

```
        ' existing genre
        ' get the pk value
        lngArtistId = Me.cboArtist.ItemData(Me.cboArtist.ListIndex)
    Else
        ' new genre

        ' ask user to add new genre
        If MsgBox("Would you like to add the artist: " _
            & Me.cboArtist.Text, vbYesNo) = vbYes Then
             ' get a new artist pk value
             lngArtistId = AddArtist(Me.cboArtist.Text, lngGenreId)
             ' is it valid?
             If lngArtistId < 0 Then
                 ' outta here
                 SaveCD = False
                 MsgBox "Error adding artist."
                 Exit Function
            End If
        Else
            ' can't save without a artist
            SaveCD = False
            MsgBox "You cannot save a CD without a genre."
            Exit Function
        End If
    End If

    ' close the CD recordset, we're about to update
    If gobjCD.State = adStateOpen Then
        gobjCD.Close
    End If

    ' check mode
    If Not IsNull(mlngCDId) Then
        'edit mode - let's get the record
        gobjCD.Open "CD", gobjConnection, _
            adOpenForwardOnly, adLockOptimistic, adCmdTableDirect

        ' set the index so we can seek
        gobjCD.Index = "PK_CD"

        ' seek the value
        gobjCD.Seek mlngCDId
```

LISTING 8.29 Continued

```
    Else
        ' new mode, no primary key value
        gobjCD.Open "cd", gobjConnection, adOpenForwardOnly, _
            adLockOptimistic, adCmdTableDirect

        ' add the record
        gobjCD.AddNew

    End If

    ' are we at the end of the
    ' recordset (no record added
    ' or no record found )
    If gobjCD.EOF Then
        Exit Function
    End If

    ' assign the values
    gobjCD.Fields("ArtistID").Value = lngArtistId
    gobjCD.Fields("CDName").Value = Me.txtCDName.Text
    gobjCD.Fields("YearOfRelease").Value = CLng(Me.txtYear.Text)
    gobjCD.Fields("Price").Value = CCur(Me.txtPrice.Text)
    gobjCD.Fields("GenreID").Value = lngGenreId

    ' set the UserId
    gobjCD.Fields("UserId").Value = glngCurrentUser

    ' update the recordset
    gobjCD.Update

    ' check for errors
    If Err.Number <> 0 Then
        Exit Function
    End If

    ' everything's cool, return true
    SaveCD = True

End Function
```

Changes made to SaveCD are boldfaced in Listing 8.29. Let's investigate the first change in Listing 8.30.

LISTING 8.30 Updating an Existing CD Record

```
'edit mode - let's get the record
gobjCD.Open "CD", gobjConnection, _
    adOpenForwardOnly, adLockOptimistic, adCmdTableDirect

' set the index so we can seek
gobjCD.Index = "PK_CD"

' seek the value
gobjCD.Seek mlngCDId
```

Listing 8.30 should accomplish finding a single CD record based on a primary key value. It uses the methodology to create an updateable recordset from SQL Server CE data. First, the recordset is opened using the `adCmdTableDirect` value for the `Open` method's `Options` parameter. Next, the `Index` property is set to the name of the primary key index for the table, allowing you to perform a `Seek` on the recordset. The `Seek` method is called using the primary key value for the record to update.

The next change to `SaveCD` is setting the UserId field's value for the current user. Having this value set allows the server side SQL Server to filter the CD table by users. The `Public` variable `glngCurrentUser` is set in the `OpenDatabase` function, shown in Listing 8.32.

```
' set the UserId
gobjCD.Fields("UserId").Value = glngCurrentUser
```

The two changes that take place to make CD Library work with SQL Server CE occur in the modGlobal.bas functions `AddGenre` and `AddArtist`. Listing 8.31 indicates boldfaced changes to `AddGenre`. `AddArtist` follows the exact same changes; if necessary, retrieve it from the sample source code.

LISTING 8.31 modGlobal.bas: Changes for SQL Server CE Compatibility

```
Function AddGenre(ByVal strGenre As String) As Long

    ' adds a genre to the table and returns
' its primary key value

    On Error Resume Next

    ' set the return value to error code
    ' in case we need to exit early
    AddGenre = -1

    ' if the recordset is open
```

LISTING 8.31 Continued

```
    ' let's check if it supports addnew
    If gobjGenre.State = adStateOpen Then
        ' if the current recordset does not
        ' support adding new records, let's close
        ' it and reopen it
        If Not gobjGenre.Supports(adAddNew) Then
            gobjGenre.Close
        End If
    End If

    ' if the recordset is closed above
    ' or closed before we get into this
    ' function, let's open it with the
    ' proper support for adding
    If gobjGenre.State = adStateClosed Then
        gobjGenre.Open "genre", gobjConnection, _
            adOpenDynamic, adLockOptimistic, adCmdTableDirect
    End If

    ' add a new record
    gobjGenre.AddNew

    ' set the values
    gobjGenre.Fields("GenreName").Value = strGenre

    ' update the recordset
    gobjGenre.Update

    ' set the return value
    gobjGenre.Close

    gobjGenre.Open "SELECT MAX( GenreId ) AS GenreId FROM Genre", _
        gobjConnection, adOpenStatic, adLockOptimistic

    AddGenre = CLng(gobjGenre.Fields("GenreId").Value)

End Function
```

The `GetNewPK` function has been removed. In the first boldfaced change in Listing 8.31, the `CursorType` parameter for the `Open` method has been changed to `adOpenDynamic`. The second highlighted change made adds code to close the recordset, so it can be reused to find the identity value used for the record in the GenreId field. The identity value is retrieved using the `MAX` function, and then the return value is set from this result.

Let's look at the last supporting function for `frmCD` that was changed, `OpenDatabase` (see in Listing 8.32). `OpenDatabase` is modified to use the SQL Server CE `ConnectionString` syntax used in the `Open` method of the `ADOCE.Connection gobjConnection`. It also makes a call to `SetUserId` when it opens the database.

LISTING 8.32 modGlobal.bas: Changes to the OpenDatabase Function for SQL Server CE Compatibility

```
Function OpenDatabase() As Boolean

    On Error Resume Next

    ' set the return value to an error
    ' condition, so we can exit early
    ' if an error occurs
    OpenDatabase = False

    ' we need to check if the connection is
    ' open or close, because EnsureDatabaseExists may
    ' opened the database

    If gobjConnection.State = adStateClosed Then
        ' opens the SQL Server CE database
        gobjConnection.Open "Provider=Microsoft.SQLServer.OLEDB.CE.1.0;" _
            & "Data Source=" & DB_PATH

        ' if we're opening the db
        ' let's set the UserId
        If Not SetUserId() Then
            Exit Function
        End If
    End If

    If Err.Number = 0 Then
        OpenDatabase = True
    End If

End Function
```

modSQLRepl.bas: `SetUserId`, Setting the User ID

The `SetUserId` function opens the Users table and retrieves the single record in it. Remember, we used the `HOST_NAME()` function in the publication to filter down the Users table to one record. The `Public` variable `glngCurrentUser` is then set equal to the UserId field value. This variable is used when creating new CD records to specify which user they belong to.

LISTING 8.33 modSQLRepl.bas: Knowing Which User Data Is Being Used

```
Function SetUserId() As Boolean

    On Error Resume Next

    ' set to error condition
    SetUserId = False

    ' close the record set
    If gobjUser.State = adStateClosed Then
        gobjUser.Open "Users", gobjConnection, _
            adOpenForwardOnly, adLockReadOnly, adCmdTableDirect    End If

    ' if end of file, there's a problem
    If gobjUser.EOF Then
        Exit Function
    End If

    ' set the current user - used to populate UserId in cd table
    glngCurrentUser = CLng(gobjUser.Fields("UserId").Value)

    ' set the return value
    SetUserId = Err.Number = 0

End Function
```


`frmMain`: Wrapping Up the Last Changes

There are a few more changes made to the CD Library Replication application. First, remove the call to `InitializeGlobals` from the `frmMain.Load` event.

Next, add menu commands to the menu to call the synchronization routine and show the `frmSQLProperties` form.

The following `Consts` are added to the general section of `frmMain` to support the new menu commands:

```
Const MENU_TOOLS_SYNC_KEY = "TOOLSSYNC"
Const MENU_TOOLS_SETTINGS_KEY = "SETTINGS"
```

In Listing 8.34, two highlighted lines of code are added to create a menu command for Sync and Settings. Next, in the `MenuBar1.Menu_Click` event, you respond to these new prompts.

LISTING 8.34 frmMain.frm: Adding Menu Commands to the Menu for Sync and Settings

```
Function PopulateMenus() As Boolean

    Dim objMenu As MenuBarLib.MenuBarMenu
    Dim objPrompt As MenuBarLib.Item

    On Error Resume Next

    PopulateMenus = False

    ' add tools menu
    Set objMenu = MenuBar1.Controls.AddMenu("Tools", MENU_ROOTPROMPT_TOOLS_KEY)
    ' add Sync prompt
    Set objPrompt = objMenu.Items.Add(, MENU_TOOLS_SYNC_KEY, "Sync")
    ' add settings prompt
    Set objPrompt = objMenu.Items.Add(, MENU_TOOLS_SETTINGS_KEY, "Settings")

    ' check for errors, if none, return True
    If Err.Number = 0 Then
        PopulateMenus = True
    End If
```

```
End Function
```

Listing 8.35 provides the new code to support the new menu commands. For the Sync menu command, the `Sync` method is called. After the synchronization is complete, the form is refreshed (there is potentially new data) by calling the `PopulateArtistGrid` function.

The Settings menu command displays the `frmSQLProperties` form by calling the `Show` method.

LISTING 8.35 frmMain.frm: Adding Code to Respond to the New Menus

```
Private Sub MenuBar1_MenuClick(ByVal Item As MenuBarLib.Item)

    Select Case Item.Key
        Case MENU_TOOLS_SYNC_KEY
            Sync
            PopulateArtistGrid
        Case MENU_TOOLS_SETTINGS_KEY
            frmSQLProperties.Show
        Case Else
```

LISTING 8.35 Continued

```
            MsgBox "Unknown Menu!"
    End Select

End Sub
```

Summary

SQL Server CE provides flexibility to create enterprise Windows CE applications. Replication can be a bit overwhelming at first, but after you get the hang of it, it becomes second nature. Remember to frequently script your publications using the SQL generation tools of SQL Server Enterprise Manager.

SQL Server replication identity range management is a powerful tool, a technology that could be envied by all types of distributed data applications and devices.

For further sample applications using SQL Server CE, check out the samples provided with its installation. Check the SQL Server CE help file for installation and file locations.

Harnessing the Windows CE API

CHAPTER

9

IN THIS CHAPTER

This chapter isn't meant to be the definitive source for API programming in Windows CE. In fact, it covers only a small part of the available Win32 API functions. Although you will get a good understanding of *how* to call just about any API from any library, trying to cover even a majority of what the APIs can be used for is beyond the scope of a single book, let alone this chapter.

If you want more information and practice on what can be done with the API set, from graphics to menus to window behavior modifications, you can find plenty of information online as well as at bookstores. API calls in eVB are almost identical to API calls in Visual Basic 6, so any VB API source will be of use. To really get into the depths of the API, I recommend Dan Appleman's definitive *Visual Basic Programmer's Guide to the Win32 API* (Sams Publishing, ISBN 0-672-31590-4).

If you've gone through every chapter of the book so far, you should have a strong understanding of how to write most any type of application for the PocketPC. However, undoubtedly sometimes eVB just doesn't expose the function or ability to do what you want. This chapter looks at how to go beyond the native eVB functions and call some of the C++ functions in the Windows CE Application Programming Interface (API). We'll look at how you declare API calls, where you can get the declaration prototypes, and how you can use them from within your eVB application. Because many API calls require User-Defined Data types (UDTs) and eVB doesn't support them, we'll also look at a workaround that will allow you to still use them.

In this chapter you'll see

- What API calls are and how to declare them in eVB
- How to use the API Text Viewer tool that comes with eVB
- Some of the non-UDT requiring API calls
- What UDTs are at memory level and how to work around eVB's lack of support for them
- Some of the UDTs requiring API calls

In this chapter you won't be writing a sample application, but instead looking at many of the utility functions that you can use in other projects. By no means will we cover all the API calls, but this chapter should give you the know-how to look up and use most functions defined in the Windows CE API set.

NOTE

Unless otherwise noted, all code samples in this chapter can be found in the file modUtil.bas, which you can download from `www.samspublishing.com` (enter this book's ISBN in the Search field).

The Application Programming Interface

Most of the functionality of any Windows operating system lies in dynamic link libraries (DLLs). It's also true that most of those DLLs aren't COM compliant and therefore can't be added to your eVB project as a reference or component. You can, however make calls to functions within almost all the DLLs available if you know the function's method signature—that is, the function's name as well as all its parameters and parameter types.

These functions are exposed in APIs and, as I said, most DLLs have one. The challenge is determining what functions are exposed through the API and what the method signatures look like. Making incorrect API calls is a good way to cause application or even system failures, potentially causing the user a data loss; therefore care should always be taken when declaring and calling API functions.

Using API functions requires that you follow three rules:

- All API declarations must be in a module (.bas file) and must occur in the General Declarations section before any application functions are declared.
- All API declarations must follow correct declaration syntax.
- You must distribute pvbdecl.dll with your application.

The first rule is simple and straightforward. API declarations aren't valid in form code pages. They must be made in modules, and they must be at the top.

The second rule of using an API function is that the declaration must follow a specific syntax, which can be generally written like this:

```
[Scope] Declare Function|Sub {FunctionName} Lib "{Library File Name}" _
      [Alias "Library Function Name"] _
      ({Function Parameter List}) As {Function Return}
```


First, you can optionally declare a scope for the function. If you don't explicitly declare scope, it will be assumed to be `Public`.

Next, use the keywords `Declare Function` (or `Declare Sub` if the API has no return value), followed by the name used in the eVB code to call the function. Most often this is either the exact name of the function in the library file or something very close, as you'll soon see.

After the function name, you must tell the compiler where to find the function—that is, in what library (DLL) file. This is accomplished with `Lib` and the filename, without the extension.

Next, you can optionally have an alias for the function. This is where you must put the exact function name if you didn't use it previously. The reasoning behind this is that many APIs in Windows have two versions, one for ANSI, usually suffixed with an `A`, and one for Unicode, usually suffixed with a W. Because it would be uncommon to need both versions in a program, the functions are usually aliased to remove the suffix.

Finally, provide the function's parameter list and return values.

A full API declaration, then, would look something like this:

```
Public Declare Function CharLower Lib "Coredll" Alias "CharLowerW" _
       (ByVal lpsz As String) As String
```

The API Text Viewer

Determining the contents of an API is made significantly easier with the use of the API Text Viewer, which is automatically installed with eMbedded Visual Tools in the \Windows CE Tools\BIN folder of your installation drive as APILOAD.EXE. The API Text Viewer can be used to open, browse, and seek through an API declaration file, which is simply a formatted text file that lists all an API's functions, constants, and structures (UDTs).

In Windows CE, most of the core Windows functionality is contained in the file Coredll.dll, and eVB comes with a API declaration file that covers most of Coredll.dll. The file is WINCEAPI.TXT and the default installation places it also in the \Windows CE Tools\BIN folder of your installation drive.

Running APILOAD.EXE presents you with the simple interface shown in Figure 9.1.

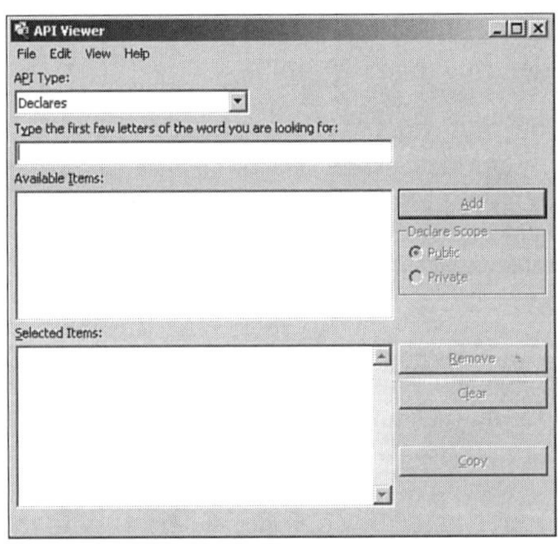

FIGURE 9.1
The API Viewer application.

Choosing Open from the File menu displays the Windows Open File dialog, which you can then use to navigate to and open WINCEAPI.TXT. Opening the API declaration file will immediately populate the Available Items list box in the middle of the form. This is the list of all functions, or declares, listed in the opened file. By changing the API Type combo box, you can also list all the defined constants.

NOTE

The combo box has Types as an option as well, but selecting Types gives you nothing in the Available Items list. This is because eVB doesn't natively support Types, which are simply UDTs or structures. We'll look at getting past this inconvenience later in the chapter. For now, just get used to using the API viewer to get function and constant declarations into an eVB project.

If you choose Declares and select a function to copy by either double-clicking its name or highlighting the name and clicking Add, you will see that the API declaration will be added to the Selected Items text box at the bottom of the form. The same can be done for Constants (see Figure 9.2).

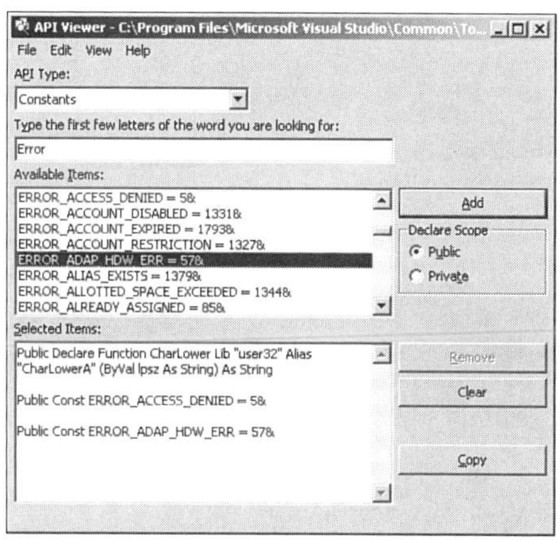

FIGURE 9.2

The API Viewer after selecting the `CharLower` *API declare and the* `ERROR_ACCESS_DENIED` *and* `ERROR_ADAP_HDW_ERR` *constants.*

You can select any number and any combination of declares or constants, and when you've selected all the APIs you need, press Ctrl+C or click Copy to move the contents of the Selected Items to your Clipboard.

From there, simply paste the declarations into the top of your code module by choosing Paste from the Edit menu in the eVB IDE.

Non-UDT API Examples

Now that we've covered how to declare APIs, let's look at something a bit more interesting: their use. We'll start by looking at some simple APIs that I find provide useful functionality beyond what eVB exposes and that don't require any workarounds, such as the UDT workaround covered later, to use.

BringWindowToTop

Declare Function BringWindowToTop Lib "Coredll" (ByVal hwnd As Long) As LongA common annoyance in Windows CE is the inability to show forms modally. This can lead to users sending your application behind another form, often by accidentally clicking just outside your form or by pressing one of their device's hardware buttons.

To bring the form back to the top of the z-order, simply call the `BringWindowToTop` API with the target window's `hWnd`. For example, if your application has a form named `frmMain`, to bring it to the top, and therefore make it visible to users, you would call

```
BringWindowToTop(frmMain.hWnd)
```

CompareString

```
Declare Function CompareString Lib "Coredll" Alias "CompareStringW"  _
                                             (ByVal Locale As Long, _
                                             ByVal dwCmpFlags As Long, _
                                             ByVal lpString1 As String, _
                                             ByVal cchCount1 As Long, _
                                             ByVal lpString2 As String, _
                                             ByVal cchCount2 As Long) As Long
```

Comparing strings for exact equality is a simple task in eVB. For example, you can compare `apples` and `oranges` as in Listing 9.1's code.

LISTING 9.1 The Non-API Way of Comparing Strings

```
Private Sub TestCompareString()
    Dim strString1 As String
    Dim strString2 As String
    Dim bEqual As Boolean

    strString1 = "apples"
    strString2 = "oranges"

    bEqual = strString1 = strString2

    If bEqual Then
```

LISTING 9.1 Continued

```
        MsgBox "They're Equal"
    Else
        MsgBox "They're Not Equal"
    End If
End Sub
```

And you would get a message box telling users that `They're Not Equal`.

But what if you wanted to compare `Apples` to `apples`? Or `AppLes` to `aPplEs`? One option would be to change the case on both to all uppercase or all lowercase and then make the comparison, but then you lose the original string.

A faster, more elegant solution is to use the `CompareString` API. With `CompareString`, you can make comparisons without worrying about the case..

Look at the parameters to `CompareString`. First, you need to provide a *locale*, which is simply a regional setting for the device that may affect the comparison. For example, comparisons in Chinese would be different than in U.S. English. It's simplest to use 0, which equates to `LANG_NEUTRAL`, `SUBLANG_NEUTRAL`, and `SORT_DEFAULT`.

Next you need to provide comparison flag(s). Here the following two flags are useful, and either or both can be used: `NORM_IGNORECASE` and `NORM_IGNORESYMBOLS`. The first ignores case; the second ignores any symbols and punctuation. The constants are defined as

```
Const NORM_IGNORECASE = &H1
Const NORM_IGNORESYMBOLS = &H4
```

The next two parameters are the first string to compare and its length in character, and the last two parameters are the second string to compare and its length in characters.

Rather than return `true` or `false`, this function returns one of three values, defined as

```
Const CSTR_LESS_THAN = 1          ' string 1 less than string 2
Const CSTR_EQUAL = 2              ' string 1 equal to string 2
Const CSTR_GREATER_THAN = 3       ' string 1 greater than string
```

So using the previous example, you could create the code shown in Listing 9.2 and you would get a message box declaring that `They're Equal`, even though the cases vary and both have symbols in them.

LISTING 9.2 Comparing Strings with an API Call to Ignore Case as Well as Punctuation and Symbols

```
Private Sub TestCompareString()
    Dim strString1 As String
    Dim strString2 As String
```

LISTING 9.2 Continued

```
    Dim iCompare As Integer

    strString1 = "AppLes?"
    strString2 = "[aPp.lEs]"

    iCompare = CompareString(0, NORM_IGNORECASE Or NORM_IGNORESYMBOLS, _
            strString1, Len(strString1), strString2, Len(strString2))

    If iCompare = CSTR_EQUAL Then
        MsgBox "They're Equal"
    ElseIf iCompare = CSTR_GREATER_THAN Then
        MsgBox strString1 & " is greater than " & strString2
    Else
        MsgBox strString1 & " is less than " & strString2
    End If
End Sub
```

CopyFile

```
Declare Function CopyFile Lib "Coredll" Alias "CopyFileW" _
                                        (ByVal lpExistingFileName As String, _
                                        ByVal lpNewFileName As String, _
                                        ByVal bFailIfExists As Long) As Long
```

Occasionally I find that I need to copy a file in an application, but don't necessarily want to deal with the overhead of creating a full `CEFileSystem` object to do so. The `CopyFile` API works great for this situation. The first parameter is the name of the file to be copied, including path. The second parameter is the name of the new file to be created. The third is a flag to tell it whether to overwrite any existing file with the same name.

So if I wanted to make a copy of my application's error log file, ERRLOG.TXT, to a different directory and mark it with the app name and date, I could use the code in Listing 9.3.

LISTING 9.3 A Simple File Copy Operation

```
Private Sub MoveErrLog()
    Dim strSource As String
    Dim strDestination As String
    Dim lReturn As Long

    strSource = App.Path & "\ERRLOG.TXT"
    strDestination = "\ErrLogs\MyApp" & DatePart("yyyy", Now) _
                                      & DatePart("m", Now) _
```

LISTING 9.3 Continued

```
                                            & DatePart("d", Now) _
                                            & ".TXT"
    lReturn = CopyFile(strSource, strDestination, True)
    If lReturn = 0 Then
        MsgBox "File Copy Failed!", vbExclamation, "Error"
    End If
End Sub
```

CreateProcess

```
Declare Function CreateProcess Lib "Coredll" Alias "CreateProcessW" _
                                           (ByVal lpImageName As String, _
                                           ByVal lpCmdLine As String, _
                                           ByVal psaProcess As Long, _
                                           ByVal psaThread As Long, _
                                           ByVal bInheritSec As Boolean, _
                                           ByVal lCreate As Long, _
                                           ByVal lEnviron As Long, _
                                           ByVal lpDirectory As Long, _
                                           ByVal psaStartInfo As Long, _
                                           ByVal psaProcInfo As Long) As Long
```

Because the VB `Shell()` function doesn't exist in eVB, running another program from eVB can be done only through an API call. `CreateProcess` isn't in the WINCEAPI.TXT API declaration file, and therefore doesn't show up in the API Text Viewer, which is surprising because it's a very useful function.

While the declaration looks a bit daunting, and a quick glance in the eMbedded Visual Tools Help file shows that it takes a lot of UDTs as parameters, most of them are unsupported and can simply be passed as zero.

The only three parameters that you need to be concerned with are `lpImageName`, which is the name of the file you want to run; `lpCmdLine`, which contains any command-line parameters you want to pass the application; and `lpDirectory`, which is the application's startup directory.

Launching something like the Windows CE Calculator is as simple as this:

```
Private Sub LaunchCalculator()
    Dim lReturn As Long

    lReturn = CreateProcess("\Windows\calc.exe ", "", 0, 0, 0, 0, 0, 0, 0, 0)

    If lReturn = 0 Then
        MsgBox "Error launching application!", vbExclamation, "Error"
    End If
End Sub
```

Remember that an eVB application is actually interpreted, and therefore hosted within pvbload.exe, so launching another eVB app would be correctly done like this:

```
lReturn = CreateProcess("\Windows\pvbload.exe ", _
          "\MyeVBApp.vb", 0, 0, 0, 0, 0, 0, 0, 0)
```

Creating Your Own `DoEvents`

`DoEvents` is probably one of the most misunderstood and maligned functions in Visual Basic, and I somehow think that the eVB team left it out for that reason. All too often I've read threads in discussion forums warning new programmers about the evils and perils that `DoEvents` wreaks and that there is never any good cause to call it.

If you worked through Chapter 5, "Using the Windows CE WinSock for IR Communication," you may recall when you had to poll the WinSock control waiting for it to close after an error. This often takes a fraction of a second, but it's a good idea to wait, and we don't want to inconvenience users by locking up their devices while we do. This is a good example of when `DoEvents` is helpful, and therefore we need to do what Microsoft didn't and write one.

Regardless of its reputation, `DoEvents` isn't terribly arcane or mysterious. Its function, simply, is to check the Windows message queue, if a message is waiting, `DoEvents` then translates and sends, or dispatches the message, removing it from the queue as it does.

To do this, you make three API calls: `PeekMessage`, `TranslateMessage`, and `DispatchMessage`.

So the entire implementation, with API declarations, is shown in Listing 9.4.

LISTING 9.4 Implementing `DoEvents` in eVB

```
Declare Function PeekMessage Lib "coredll.dll" Alias "PeekMessageW" _
    (ByVal MSG As String, ByVal hWnd As Long, ByVal wMsgFilterMin As Integer, _
    ByVal wMsgFilterMax As Integer, ByVal wRemoveMsg As Integer) As Boolean

Declare Function TranslateMessage Lib "coredll.dll" (ByVal MSG As String) _
    As Boolean
Declare Function DispatchMessage Lib "coredll.dll" Alias "DispatchMessageW" _
    (ByVal MSG As String) As Boolean

Public Const PM_REMOVE = 1
Public MSG  As String

Public Sub DoEventsCE()
    MSG = String(18, Chr(0))
    ' Get message from queue and dispatch it
    If PeekMessage(MSG, 0, 0, 0, PM_REMOVE) Then
```

LISTING 9.4 Continued

```
        TranslateMessage (MSG)
        DispatchMessage (MSG)
    End If
End Sub
```

NOTE

I've called this function `DoEventsCE` because the eVB IDE will throw an error if it's named `DoEvents`, thinking that it's a reserved word.

Shutting Down the Device

```
Public Declare Sub GwesPowerOffSystem Lib "Coredll" ()
```

Unfortunately, Windows CE doesn't support the `ExitWindowsEx` API that Windows 98/NT/2000 support, so you can't use it to reset the device. In fact, there are no direct code APIs to reset the device. There is, however, an undocumented API that can be used to shut down a PocketPC, and presumably any Windows CE 3.0, device.

Calling `GwesPowerOffSystem` is straightforward, but rude to users if you don't confirm that it should happen (unless you shut down due to inactivity):

```
Private Sub ShutDown()
    If MsgBox("Shutdown device now?", vbYesNo, "Shutdown") = vbNo Then Exit Sub

    GwesPowerOffSystem
End Sub
```

Keep in mind that this just takes the device to power save mode just as if you physically pressed the power button. Although the CPU will be idle, preventing any actual processing, your app will remain in the current task list unless you specifically shut it down.

GetActiveWindow

```
Declare Function GetActiveWindow Lib "Coredll" () As Long
```

A large number of API calls require a window handle, or `hWnd`, as a parameter. Unfortunately, most eVB controls don't expose their `hWnd` as a property like they do in VB 6.

`GetActiveWindow` returns the `hWnd` or the currently active control or window, so getting the `hWnd` of any control is simple as long as you can set the application focus to that control.

Here's a simple example. If you have a form that contains many controls, including a TextBox called `txtName`, you can get that control's `hWnd` using this code snippet:

```
Dim hWnd As Long

txtName.SetFocus
hWnd = GetActiveWindow()
```

You can then use that `hWnd` for any other API calls you want to make to change the look or behavior of `txtName`.

GetAsyncKeyState

```
Declare Function GetAsyncKeyState Lib "Coredll" (ByVal vKey As Long) _
                                                As Integer
```

Determining if a key is down at any given time isn't straightforward in eVB, but the `GetAsyncKeyState` function easily provides this functionality. You simply call the function with the virtual key value for the key in which you're interested, which for the alphanumeric is just the key's ASCII value.

The function has more use when you use it to detect whether other keys are down, such as if the stylus is onscreen or if user is tapping a hardware directional button.

To determine if the stylus is onscreen, simply call `GetAsyncKeyState` with `VK_LBUTTON`, which is defined as `&H01`, like this:

```
Dim bStylusIsDown As Boolean

bStylusIsDown = GetAsyncKeyState(VK_LBUTTON)
```

All the virtual key codes can be found in the eVB Toolkit's Help files under Virtual Key Codes.

By itself, `GetAsyncKeyState` doesn't seem to have much utility, but later in the chapter under "Putting It All Together" you'll see how it is crucial for implementing a popup menu workaround.

GetTickCount

```
Declare Function GetTickCount Lib "Coredll" () As Long
```

The best way to test function or code segment performance is to time the code's execution. You can use the timer, but it really isn't designed to determine the length of time something takes to happen. It's designed to make something happen after a certain period of time. A subtle difference, but one that makes using it for performance testing a challenge.

`GetTickCount`, on the other hand, returns the number of milliseconds elapsed since the device was started—at least in theory. The actual resolution is based on the device's hardware and therefore may not be down to the millisecond. Also, because `GetTickCount` returns a `Long` instead of something like a `Double`, after about 50 days, it will wrap back to zero and begin counting again.

To time a section of code, simply store the result from `GetTickCount` before you enter the code, and then again after you exit. The difference between the two values is the time elapsed in milliseconds. Of course, it's always a good idea to run several iterations of the test and average the results. Listing 9.5 gives an example of testing the performance of a `For...Next` loop.

LISTING 9.5 Timing the Performance of Code Pieces

```
Private Sub TestGetTickCount()
    Dim i As Integer
    Dim j As Integer
    Dim strBuffer As String
    Dim lStart As Long
    Dim lStop As Long
    Dim lElapsed As Long
    Dim lAverage As Long

    ' Get the start time
    lStart = GetTickCount()
    For i = 1 To 10 ' Do 10 tests
        For j = 1 To 500
            strBuffer = strBuffer & "A"
        Next j
    Next i

    ' Get the stop time
    lStop = GetTickCount()

    ' calculate the elapsed time
    lElapsed = lStop - lStart

    ' calculate the average
    lAverage = lElapsed / 10

    MsgBox "The average execution time was " & lAverage & " ms"
End Sub
```

PlaySound

```
Declare Function PlaySound Lib "Coredll" Alias "PlaySoundW" _
                                          (ByVal lpszName As String, _
                                          ByVal hModule As Long, _
                                          ByVal dwFlags As Long) As Long
```

Being able to notify users audibly that something has happened is often a nice feature. In VB 6, you can use the `Beep` function, but even with Windows NT, which does allow pitch changes that Windows 98 doesn't, the functionality is somewhat limited.

eVB doesn't support `Beep`, but the `PlaySound` API is far better anyway. It allows you to play any system sound or sound file on the device with a single call. That means that you can deploy your own sounds and not have to have a separate control to play them. You simply call `PlaySound` with the `SND_FILENAME` constant, which is defined as `&H20000`.

For example, if I want to play the exclamation sound on my device, I simply call `PlaySound` with the name of the sound file (`Exclam`). Here I've wrapped it in a `Beep` function:

```
Public Sub Beep()
    PlaySound "Exclam", 0, SND_FILENAME
End Sub
```

You device should have several sound files in the Windows directory from which to choose, but be sure that you always distribute your sound files with your application, as not all devices have the same sound files included with them.

RegQueryValueEx and RegSetValueEx

```
Declare Function RegQueryValueEx Lib "Coredll" Alias "RegQueryValueExW" _
                                          (ByVal hKey As Long, _
                                          ByVal lpValueName As String, _
                                          ByVal lpReserved As Long, _
                                          lpType As Long, _
                                          ByVal lpData As String, _
                                          lpcbData As Long) As Long

Declare Function RegSetValueEx Lib "Coredll" Alias "RegSetValueExW" _
                                          (ByVal hKey As Long, _
                                          ByVal lpValueName As String, _
                                          ByVal Reserved As Long, _
                                          ByVal dwType As Long, _
                                          ByVal lpData As String, _
                                          ByVal cbData As Long) As Long

Declare Function RegCreateKeyEx Lib "Coredll" Alias "RegCreateKeyExW" _
                                          (ByVal hKey As Long, _
```

```
                                        ByVal lpSubKey As String, _
                                        ByVal Reserved As Long, _
                                        ByVal lpClass As String, _
                                        ByVal dwOptions As Long, _
                                        ByVal samDesired As Long, _
                                        lpSecurityAttributes As Long, _
                                        phkResult As Long, _
                                        lpdwDisposition As Long) As Long
Declare Function RegOpenKeyEx Lib "Coredll" Alias "RegOpenKeyExW" _
                                        (ByVal hKey As Long, _
                                        ByVal lpSubKey As String, _
                                        ByVal ulOptions As Long, _
                                        ByVal samDesired As Long, _
                                        phkResult As Long) As Long
Declare Function RegCloseKey Lib "Coredll" Alias "RegCloseKey" _
                                        (ByVal hKey As Long) As Long
```

Data persistence between successive runs of an application are important in almost any application. From user preferences to server names, usernames and passwords, users expect to have a lot of information to supply only once.

One option is to use the `File` object and create a configuration file for your application. Another more elegant, as well as more common, option is to use the device registry.

The registry on a Windows CE device is very similar to the Registry on a desktop machine, and contains only the following three root keys: `HKEY_CLASSES_ROOT`, `HKEY_CURRENT_USER`, and `HKEY_LOCAL_MACHINE`.

Unlike desktop Visual Basic's `SaveSetting` and `GetSetting` methods, eVB has no native methods to access even part of the registry, so any registry manipulation must be done with API calls. We will cover both reading a value with `RegQueryValueEx` and writing a value with `RegSetValueEx` by writing functions that mimic the desktop functions. They are named `SaveSettingCE` and `GetSettingCE` and we will try to preserve their original behavior.

To test and debug the functions it will be extremely helpful to be able to view a device's registry. Fortunately, eMbedded Visual Tools installs a registry editor by default, which can be accessed through the eVB Tools, Remote Tools, Registry Editor menu. In fact, you can use the Windows CE Remote Registry Editor to view and modify the local desktop registry as well.

If you launch the Windows CE Remote Registry Editor and select Connection, Add Connection, you will be prompted with the Select a Windows CE Device dialog (see Figure 9.3). From here you can select either your physical device or an emulator.

Initially, the editor presents a root node in the TreeView for the local desktop machine. Selecting a device will add to the TreeView a parent node for the connected device, as you can see in Figure 9.4.

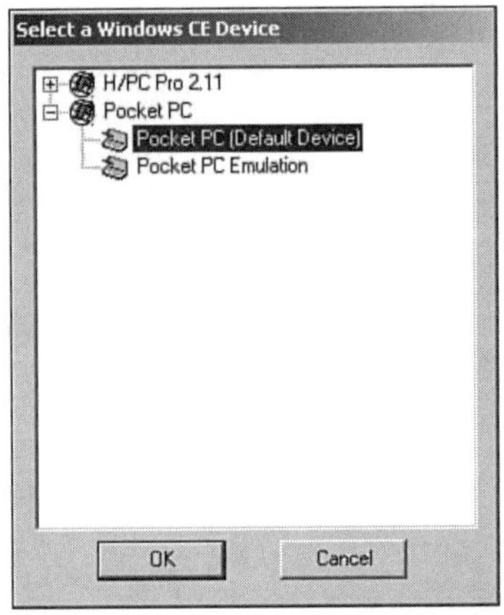

FIGURE 9.3
Selecting the locally connected PocketPC for registry editing.

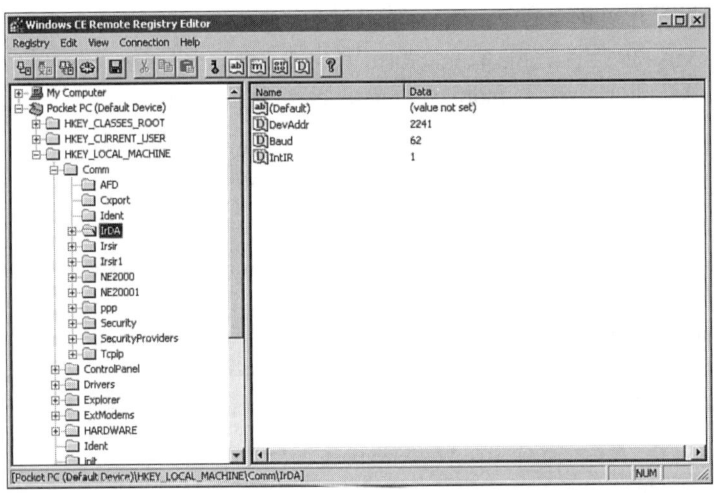

FIGURE 9.4
The Windows CE Remote Registry Editor connected to a PocketPC device.

Because Visual Basic 6's `SaveSetting` and `GetSetting` functions read and write from the `HKEY_CURRENT_USER/Software/Microsoft` key, we'll maintain that functionality.

SaveSettingCE

First, to save a value to the registry, open the desired key. If the key isn't there, you must create it. Both actions are handled by `RegCreateKeyEx`. Although `RegCreateKeyEx` has many parameters, Reserved, lpClass, dwOptions, samDesired, and lpSecurityAttributes are unsupported in Windows CE and simply take zero as a value. Also, lpdwDisposition returns a value of whether the key existed or was created, and in this case it's irrelevant so you can pass zero for it as well.

This leaves three parameters that you need to be concerned with: hKey, lpSubkey, and phkResult. Because we've decided to emulate the desktop functions, hKey will be set to HKEY_CURRENT_USER, which is defined as &H80000001, and lpSubKey will be a concatenation of Software\Microsoft and the passed-in AppName and Key parameters.

The remaining parameter, phkResult, is a Long that the handle to the opened key. You will need to pass it to RegSetValueEx.

All registry functions that you will be using return zero for success, so check the return of each call, and inform users if you fail. In production code, you would probably want to handle this more elegantly, but for these purposes, a simple error message box is sufficient.

After you have an open key, call RegSetValueEx to set whatever value you want. The parameters are: the key's handle, the ValueName (or section) within the key to set (which users provide), a reserved Long that you pass zero, the type of key that you pass REG_SZ (meaning a Unicode string and defined as 1), the value you want to set it to, and the value's length in bytes. Remember, a Unicode character is 2 bytes, so you need to use LenB instead of Len.

Next, check for success and notify users if there's a problem and end by closing the key you've opened.

To make this API easy to use, we can wrap it in a function named SaveSettingCE that mimics VB6's SaveSetting function (see Listing 9.6).

LISTING 9.6 A Registry-Writing Function That Mimics VB6's SaveSetting Function

```
Public Function SaveSettingCE(AppName As String, Key As String, _
                                                  Section As String, _
                                                  Setting As String)

    Dim lKey As Long
    Dim lRet As Long

    ' Open the key, creating if necessary
    lRet = RegCreateKeyEx(HKEY_CURRENT_USER, "Software\Microsoft\" & _
           AppName & "\" & Key, 0, 0, 0, 0, 0, lKey, 0)

    ' Check for success
    If lRet <> 0 Then
        MsgBox "Error opening key", vbExclamation, "Error"
        Exit Function
```

LISTING 9.6 Continued

```
    End If

    ' Set the key value
    ' Value length is bytes, not characters
    lRet = RegSetValueEx(lKey, Section, 0, REG_SZ, Setting, LenB(Setting))

    ' Check for success
    If lRet <> 0 Then
        MsgBox "Error saving value", vbExclamation, "Error"
        Exit Function
    End If

    ' Close the key
    RegCloseKey lKey
End Function
```

Now saving a value to the registry is as simple as calling `SaveSettingCE` like this:

```
SaveSettingCE "Test App", "My Key", "My Section", "My Setting"
```

Use the Registry Editor to confirm that it worked (see Figure 9.5).

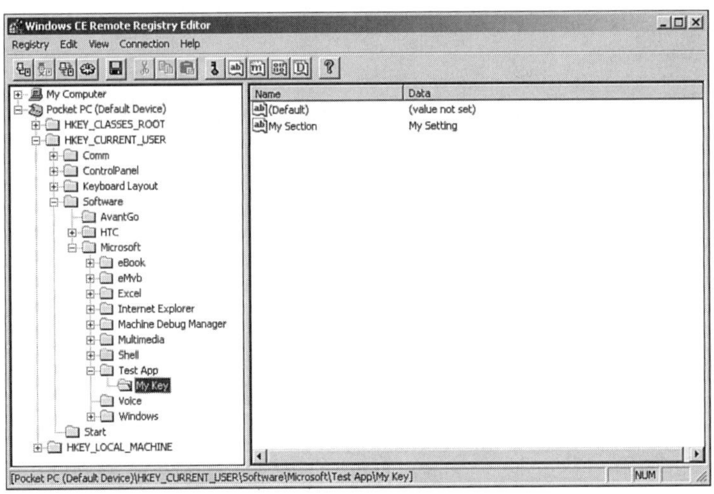

FIGURE 9.5
The device registry after inserting your value with `SaveSettingCE`.

GetSettingCE

Reading a registry setting is similar to saving one. You open the key, retrieve the value, and finally close the key. There are a few other things to be aware of, as you'll see in Listing 9.7.

LISTING 9.7 A Registry-Reading Function That Mimics VB6's `GetSetting` Function

```
Public Function GetSettingCE(AppName As String, Key As String, _
                             Section As String)
    Dim lKey As Long
    Dim lRet As Long
    Dim strValue As String
    Dim iValueLength As Integer
    Dim lType As Long

    ' Allocate space for the value, setting it to zero
    strValue = String(128, Chr(0))

    ' Initialize our length variable
    iValueLength = Len(strValue) * 2
    ' Open the key
    lRet = RegOpenKeyEx(HKEY_CURRENT_USER, "Software\Microsoft\" & _
           AppName & "\" & Key, 0, 0, lKey)

    ' Check for success
    If lRet <> 0 Then
        MsgBox "Error opening key", vbExclamation, "Error"
        Exit Function
    End If

    ' Get the key value
    lRet = RegQueryValueEx(lKey, Section, 0, lType, strValue, iValueLength)

    ' Check for success
    If lRet <> 0 Then
        MsgBox "Error getting value", vbExclamation, "Error"
        Exit Function
    End If

    ' Close the key
    RegCloseKey lKey

    ' Set return value
    ' Value length is bytes, not characters
    GetSettingCE = LeftB(strValue, iValueLength)
End Function
```

Because eVB variables are `Variants`, you must first be sure you have enough space to hold the value the API call will be returning. I simply call the `String` function to create a 128-character (256 byte) string. This is arbitrary and you can adjust it to your needs—just be sure you have enough space for the longest value you will retrieve.

Next, set a variable to the byte length of the value buffer. This will tell the `RegQueryValueEx` API how many bytes you can accept in the buffer. If a key value is longer than what you state the buffer length is, the API call will fail.

Next, open the desired key, passing in the `hKey`, the `ValueName`, and a variable that the API will populate with the newly opened key's handle. Again you have some unsupported parameters—`dwOptions` and `samDesired`—that you pass zero to.

After checking for success, call `RegQueryValueEx` to retrieve your value. You need to pass the API a variable for the key type, which will come back as `REG_SZ (1)` for any of the values you set. You also pass it the buffer variable and the length variable. The API call will change the length variable to the length, in bytes, of the returned key value.

Again, check for success and close the key. Before returning, though, you need to trim the buffer variable to the length of the actual key value returned. `LeftB` returns a specific number of bytes instead of characters, so use it to grab the data and assign it as your function's return value.

You can now retrieve the value you set in the previous section like this:

```
GetSettingCE "Test App", "My Key", "My Section"
```

Sleep

```
Declare Sub Sleep Lib "Coredll" (ByVal dwMilliseconds As Long)
```

If you need your program to wait for a period of time without processing, such as when you display a splash screen, rather than use a timer control, you can simply call the `Sleep` API. `Sleep` simply pauses execution for the number of milliseconds passed in. Sleep also has the distinct advantage over something like an empty `For...Next` loop in that it uses no CPU cycles.

To pause for three seconds, you would call `Sleep` with 3000 like this:

```
Sleep 3000
```

Putting It All Together

Now that you've seen some code snippets for several API calls, let's look at how you can use API calls in an application. One significant functionality not supported by eVB is context-sensitive pop-up menus. When users tap and hold a control, it's a PocketPC standard that, if applicable, a pop-up menu should appear.

There is a way around this, though, that provides eVB developers the pop-ups available in eVC.

Basically you'll use API calls to determine if users have held the stylus down for a set period of time. If they have, you then programmatically create a pop-up menu with additional API calls and display it.

First, create a PocketPC project with a single form, `frmPopupTest`, and single module, `modMain`.

Next, add two Labels, `lblPopupTestA` and `lblPopupTestA`, to `frmMain`. The header for `frmPopupTest` should now look something like this:

```
Begin VB.Form frmPopupTest
   Caption         =   "Popup Menu Test"
   ClientHeight    =   3615
   ClientLeft      =   60
   ClientTop       =   840
   ClientWidth     =   3480
   Begin VBCE.Label lblPopupTestB
      Height          =   855
      Left            =   960
      Top             =   1560
      Width           =   1455
      Caption         =   "Tap and Hold for Menu B"
      BeginProperty Font {0BE35203-8F91-11CE-9DE3-00AA004BB851}
         Size            =   11.25
      EndProperty
      Alignment       =   2
   End
   Begin VBCE.Label lblPopupTestA
      Height          =   855
      Left            =   960
      Top             =   420
      Width           =   1455
      Caption         =   "Tap and Hold for Menu A"
      BeginProperty Font {0BE35203-8F91-11CE-9DE3-00AA004BB851}
         Size            =   11.25
      EndProperty
      Alignment       =   2
   End
End
```

In modMain, add the declarations for PeekMessage, TranslateMessage, DispatchMessage, GetAsyncKeyState, GetTickCount, CreatePopupMenu, DestroyMenu, AppendMenu and TrackPopupMenuEx.

Add the following API constants: PM_REMOVE, VK_LBUTTON, MF_ENABLED, MF_STRING, MF_GRAYED, MF_CHECKED, MF_UNCHECKED, MF_SEPARATOR, TPM_TOPALIGN, TPM_LEFTALIGN, TPM_RETURNCMD, a global MSG string, and the DoEventsCE implementation.

modMain should look like the code in Listing 9.8.

LISTING 9.8 API Declarations and Routines Needed for Implementing Pop-Up Menus

```
Option Explicit

' API Declarations
Declare Function PeekMessage Lib "coredll.dll" Alias "PeekMessageW" _
    (ByVal MSG As String, _
     ByVal hWnd As Long, _
     ByVal wMsgFilterMin As Integer, _
     ByVal wMsgFilterMax As Integer, _
     ByVal wRemoveMsg As Integer) As Boolean
Declare Function TranslateMessage Lib "coredll.dll" _
    (ByVal MSG As String) As Boolean
Declare Function DispatchMessage Lib "coredll.dll" _
    Alias "DispatchMessageW" _
    (ByVal MSG As String) As Boolean
Public Declare Function GetAsyncKeyState Lib "Coredll" _
    (ByVal vKey As Long) As Integer
Public Declare Function GetTickCount Lib "Coredll" () As Long
Public Declare Function CreatePopupMenu Lib "Coredll" () As Long
Public Declare Function DestroyMenu Lib "Coredll" _
    (hMenu As Long) As Integer
Public Declare Function AppendMenu Lib "Coredll" _
    Alias "AppendMenuW" (ByVal hMenu As Long, _
    ByVal wFlags As Long, _
    ByVal wIDNewItem As Long, _
    ByVal lpNewItem As String) As Long
Public Declare Function TrackPopupMenuEx Lib "Coredll" _
    (ByVal hMenu As Long, _
     ByVal un As Long, _
     ByVal n1 As Long, _
     ByVal n2 As Long, _
     ByVal hWnd As Long, _
     lpTPMParams As Long) As Long
```

LISTING 9.8 Continued

```
' API Constants
Public Const PM_REMOVE = &H1
Public Const VK_LBUTTON = &H1
Public Const MF_ENABLED = &H0&
Public Const MF_STRING = &H0&
Public Const MF_GRAYED = &H1&
Public Const MF_CHECKED = &H8&
Public Const MF_UNCHECKED = &H0&
Public Const MF_SEPARATOR = &H800&
Public Const TPM_TOPALIGN = &H0&
Public Const TPM_LEFTALIGN = &H0&
Public Const TPM_RETURNCMD = &H100&

Public MSG  As String

Public Sub DoEventsCE()
    MSG = String(18, Chr(0))
    ' Get message from queue and dispatch it
    If PeekMessage(MSG, 0, 0, 0, PM_REMOVE) Then
        TranslateMessage (MSG)
        DispatchMessage (MSG)
    End If
End Sub
```

To determine when to pop up the menu, you need to determine that the stylus is on your control *and* has been down for a certain period of time. This sample waits one second. This can all be done in the `MouseDown` event of a specific control. Listing 9.9 shows the `MouseDown` event handler for `lblPopupTestA`. The handler for `lblPopupTestB` is almost identical.

LISTING 9.9 Determining Whether Users Have Held the Stylus Down for More Than a Second

```
Private Sub lblPopupTestA_MouseDown(ByVal Button As Integer, _
                                    ByVal Shift As Integer, _
                                    ByVal X As Single, _
                                    ByVal Y As Single)
    Dim lKey As Long
    Dim lStart As Long
    Dim lDuration As Long

    ' store the start time of the click
    lStart = GetTickCount
```

LISTING 9.9 Continued

```
    Do While GetAsyncKeyState(VK_LBUTTON)
        ' determine how long the stylus has been down
        lDuration = GetTickCount - lStart

        ' Allow the system to handle any other app events
        DoEventsCE

        ' If the user has held it for 1 second, show the popup
        If lDuration > 1000 Then
            ' display the menu
            ShowMenuA Me.hWnd, lblPopupTestA.Left + X, _
                                lblPopupTestA.Top + Y
            Exit Do
        End If
    Loop

End Sub
```

You can check the stylus state with a call to `GetAsyncKeyState`. As long as the stylus is down, keep checking, calling `DoEventsCE` with each loop iteration so that the device doesn't lock up. In the loop, keep checking the elapsed time since the stylus was first pressed down. When the elapsed time reaches 1 second, or 1000 milliseconds, show the pop-up menu.

The last item you need to add is the actual menu handler that will create, display and handle the user's selection, all of which can be done in one function.

Listing 9.10 shows two different menu handlers: `ShowMenuA` and `ShowMenuB`. Both follow the same basic logic: create a popup menu, append items to it, display it, handle the user's selection and then destroy the menu. The only difference is that `ShowMenuB` shows a few different menu item attributes such as the divider and a grayed item.

LISTING 9.10 Creating, Displaying, and Handling User Selections on a Pop-Up Menu

```
Public Sub ShowMenuA(hWnd As Long, X As Long, Y As Long)
    Dim hMenu As Long

    'Create a popup menu
    hMenu = CreatePopupMenu

    ' Append our menu items
    AppendMenu hMenu, MF_ENABLED Or MF_STRING, 1, "Menu Item 1"
    AppendMenu hMenu, MF_ENABLED Or MF_STRING, 2, "Menu Item 2"
```

LISTING 9.10 Continued

```
    ' display the popup and handle the user's selection
    Select Case TrackPopupMenuEx(hMenu, _
                                 TPM_LEFTALIGN Or TPM_TOPALIGN _
                                 Or TPM_RETURNCMD, _
                                 X / Screen.TwipsPerPixelX, _
                                 Y / Screen.TwipsPerPixelY, _
                                 hWnd, 0)

        Case 1
            MsgBox "You selected Item 1"
        Case 2
            MsgBox "You selected Item 2"
    End Select

    ' destroy the menu when we're done
    DestroyMenu hMenu

End Sub

Public Sub ShowMenuB(hWnd As Long, X As Long, Y As Long)
    Dim hMenu As Long

    'Create a popup menu
    hMenu = CreatePopupMenu

    ' Append our menu items
    AppendMenu hMenu, MF_ENABLED Or MF_STRING, 1, "&Open"
    AppendMenu hMenu, MF_ENABLED Or MF_STRING, 2, "&New"
    AppendMenu hMenu, MF_SEPARATOR Or MF_STRING, 3, "-"
    AppendMenu hMenu, MF_GRAYED Or MF_STRING, 4, "E&xit"

    ' display the popup and handle the user's selection
    Select Case TrackPopupMenuEx(hMenu, _
                                 TPM_LEFTALIGN Or TPM_TOPALIGN _
                                 Or TPM_RETURNCMD, _
                                 X / Screen.TwipsPerPixelX, _
                                 Y / Screen.TwipsPerPixelY, _
                                 hWnd, 0)

        Case 1
            MsgBox "You selected Open"
        Case 2
            MsgBox "You selected New"
        Case 4
```

LISTING 9.10 Continued

```
            MsgBox "You selected Exit"
    End Select

    ' destroy the menu when we're done
    DestroyMenu hMenu

End Sub
```

User-Defined Data Type Workaround

As I mentioned earlier, eVB is somewhat hindered even in the API calls it can make because it doesn't support callback functions or User-Defined Types (UDTs). While there really isn't anything to be done about the lack of callback support, you can work around the lack of UDT support.

> **NOTE**
>
> We will be doing a lot of bit manipulation throughout this section and therefore will be looking at most numbers in hexadecimal format. Numbers in hexadecimal are prefixed in VB and eVB with `&H`, so 255 in hexadecimal would be `&HFF`.
>
> Bit manipulation can be confusing, especially if you've never worked at a binary level before, so I highly recommend researching decimal, hexadecimal, and binary numbers if you're not comfortable with it.
>
> The source for this section is available from `www.samspublishing.com`. Although you can easily cut and paste the code from this section and it will work fine, understanding what the code is doing will allow you to take advantage of the techniques in other situations.

User-Defined Data Types

You first need to understand that simply put, a UDT is a single, contiguous block of memory that contains linear data.

For example, let's look at the `RECT` UDT, which will be used in the `ClipCursor` sample later. A `RECT` is the definition of a rectangle. If you look in the eMbedded Tools Help, a `RECT` is defined like this:

```
typedef struct RECT {
        LONG left;
        LONG top;
```

```
        LONG right;
        LONG bottom;
} RECT;
```

Because a RECT can be used in only eMbedded Visual C++, the help file gives the C++ declaration. If it were written in Visual Basic 6, it would look like this:

```
Public Type RECT
        Left As Long
        Top As Long
        Right As Long
        Bottom As Long
End Type
```

If you looked at this in memory, there would be 16 contiguous bytes (a Long is 32 bits, so it takes up 4) like this:

Bytes 1–4	*Bytes 5–8*	*Bytes 9–12*	*Bytes 13–16*
Left	Top	Right	Bottom

To make things even trickier, the bytes aren't in the order you would expect, because x86 type processors (386, 486, Pentium, Athlon, and so on), and therefore all Windows desktop operating systems, use what's known as *Little Endian architecture*. This means that the little, or least significant bits are stored first. For example, if you had the short (VB Integer) number &H9832, it would be stored in memory like this:

Byte 1	*Byte 2*
&H32	&H98

It works similarly with Longs, so &H12345678 would be stored in memory like this:

Byte 1	*Byte 2*	*Byte 3*	*Byte 4*
&H78	&H56	&H34	&H12

Notice I said that all Windows *desktop* operating systems use Little Endian architecture. This is simply because the processors used for desktop PCs, and servers for that matter, dictate this. It should also hold true for Windows CE devices, providing the processor uses Little Endian architecture.

NOTE

Macintosh architecture is Big Endian, so the large end is stored first, and this is why there are no Windows clones for Mac or MacOS for x86 machines.

Looking back at the `RECT` UDT, if you define a `RECT` with the following:

```
Left = 100
Top = 50
Right = 1200
Bottom = 175
```

It would look like this in memory:

Bytes 1–4	*Bytes 5–8*	*Bytes 9–12*	*Bytes 13–16*	
Left	*Top*	*Right*	*Bottom*	
Decimal	100	50	1200	1175
Hex	&H00000064	&H00000032	&H000004B0	&H00000497
Little Endian	&H64000000	&H32000000	&HB0040000	&H97040000

Strings

Now you know what a UDT looks like in memory, but how does it help you work around eVB's lack of UDT support? Well, the key is that a `String` is also a single, contiguous block of memory that contains linear data. What this means is that if you place the data from a UDT into a `String`, you can pass it as a parameter to an API and the receiver will handle it all the same. You simply need to figure out how to transfer the binary data into a binary string.

You need to be aware of one more thing. PocketPCs—and, in fact, all Windows CE devices—use Unicode for storing strings, which means that each character takes up two bytes, not just one. The reason behind this is that many languages of the world can't be fully represented in 256 characters, but 2 bytes allows for more than 65,000 characters.

What this means is that you can't use standard character manipulation functions to handle binary strings. `Left(strMyString, 1)` would return 2 bytes, and you need to be able to manipulate one byte at a time to achieve the Little Endian format.

Fortunately, you have binary versions of the `String` methods `Mid`, `Left`, `Right`, and `Asc`, which are `MidB`, `LeftB`, `RightB`, and `AscB`, respectively, and they all work just like their non-binary counterparts.

Getting a Byte Value

To build a binary string in Little Endian format, the first thing you need to be able to do is to extract a single byte from your numeric data. If you consider the previous example and you have `&H12345678`, you need to extract each byte right to left and append them to a string left to right.

The first step is to isolate the byte you're after. This can be accomplished by simply doing a bitwise `And` with a number that has only the desired byte's bits turned on. This number is called a *mask*. In essence, this means if you want to extract `&H34` from your number, you would perform the following:

```
&H12345678 And &H00FF0000
```

This results in `&H00340000`. The only exception is that the most significant bit, position 31 in our example, isn't used for holding a value in Windows, but is used instead to hold the sign. If the bit is on, the number is negative, if it's off, the number is positive. This means that if you want the first byte, `&H12` in the example, you turn on all bits in that byte except bit 7 (which is bit 31 in our 4 byte number). This means you `And` it with `&H7F000000`.

You can then divide the resulting number by a number with all the bits of lower significance (those to the right of the desired byte) turned on. So in this example of getting the `&H34`, you would do the following:

```
&H00340000 / &H0000FFFF
```

This results in `&H00000034` or simply `&H34`.

So you need a function that performs this. You can make a single function that works both for Integers or Longs, and it looks like the code in Listing 9.11.

LISTING 9.11 Extracting the Value at a Specific Byte Position in a Binary String

```
Public Function GetByteValue(Number As Variant, BytePos As Integer) As Long
    Dim mask As Long

    On Error Resume Next

    ' cannot check byte positions other than 0 to 3
    If BytePos > 3 Or BytePos < 0 Then Exit Function

    If BytePos < 3 Then
        ' build a mask of all bits on for the desired byte
        mask = &HFF * (2 ^ (8 * BytePos))
    Else
        ' the last bit is reserved for sign (+/-)
        mask = &H7F * (2 ^ (8 * BytePos))
    End If

    ' turn off all bits but the byte we're after
    GetByteValue = Number And mask
    ' move that byte to the end of the number
    GetByteValue = GetByteValue / (2 ^ (8 * BytePos))
End Function
```

Now to get our `&H34` value out of `&H12345678`, you could call `GetByteValue` with a `BytePos` of 2 (you wrote the function zero-based, and you count from the right) like this:

```
MsgBox(GetByteValue(&H12345678, 2)) 'remember we've number 0 to 3
```

And you would get a MessageBox with 52, the decimal equivalent of `&H34`, as its text.

Building a Binary String

Now that you have a function to pull the byte value at a specific position, you need another function that takes the `Long` or `Integer`, steps through its bytes, and builds a binary string.

If you could strongly type the variable, you could just check the length in the function, but because all eVB variables are really Variants trying to get the correct length of the variable is unreliable. Instead you'll need to tell the function how long the input number really is.

To make things a little more readable in the calling code, you can declare constants for the only two values you'll ever use, 2 for `Integers` and 4 for `Longs`, like this:

```
Public Const CE_INTEGER = 2
Public Const CE_LONG = 4
```

The function itself is quite short. The major work is done in a `For...Next` loop that just iterates through the bytes of the passed in number and appends them to the binary string.

One thing you must do before you start building the string is to handle negative numbers. Negative numbers are easily recognizable because, as I mentioned before, the most significant byte is turned on. In fact, a negative number is stored in memory as the binary complement of the number's absolute value, plus 1. A binary complement is achieved by reversing the values of all the bits in a number, turning off those that are on and vice versa. This is done easily by `Xor`ing the number with a mask number with all bits on.

Look at the number –10 as an example. First, you need the absolute value, which is 10 (`&H0A`, or `00001010` in binary). We get the complement by `Xor`ing with `&HFF` to get `11110101` in binary and then add 1 to get `11110110` or `&HF6`.

"10" in hex	`&H0A`
"10" in binary	`0000 1010`
Mask with `&HFF`	`1111 1111`
`Xor` result	`1111 0101`
Add 1	`1111 0110`
Back to hex	`&HF6`

To make things a bit more complex, if you try Xoring the most significant bit of a Long, you get an overflow error, so you have to Xor it as you build the string so that you're Xoring only a single byte.

The resulting function, ToBinaryString, looks like Listing 9.12.

LISTING 9.12 Iterating Through the Bytes of an Integer or Long and Returning a Binary String Equivalent

```
Public Function ToBinaryString(Number As Variant, Bytes As Integer) As String
    Dim i As Integer
    Dim bIsNegative As Boolean

    ' cannot check byte positions other than 0 to 3
    If Bytes > 4 Or Bytes < 1 Then Exit Function

    ' If the number is negative, we need to handle it last, _
    '  so we'll set a flag
    If Number < 0 Then
        bIsNegative = True

        ' get the absolute value
        Number = Number * -1

        ' get the binary complement (except the most sign. bit)
        Number = Number Xor ((2 ^ (8 * Bytes - 1)) - 1)

        ' add one
        Number = Number + 1
    End If

    ' start at the least significant bit (0) and work backwards
    For i = 0 To Bytes - 1
        If i = Bytes - 1 And bIsNegative Then
            ' If the number is negative we must turn on the most
            '  significant bit and then and append it to the string
            ToBinaryString = ToBinaryString _
                    & (ChrB(GetByteValue(Number, i) + &H80))
        Else
            ' just append the byte to our string
            ToBinaryString = ToBinaryString & ChrB(GetByteValue(Number, i))
        End If
    Next i
End Function
```

Converting from a Binary String

Now that you can generate a binary string from a number, you can call any API that has UDTs that contain `Integers` or `Longs` as well as `Strings`, but if you need to retrieve a value set by an API in a UDT, you will need `ToBinaryString`'s complementary function.

Here, you can reliably check the length of the variable because it has been strongly typed by the C++ API, so you only need to pass the function the binary string.

Again, this is just reverse engineering the `ToBinaryString` function. We step through the string, pulling each character (which is actually a byte), determining its numeric value, and adding it to the resulting number. Remember, the rightmost character contains the most significant, or sign, bit, so you have to check for it and if it's on, you have to `Xor` each byte with `&HFF`, add one to get the absolute value of the actual number, and then multiply by –1 to make it negative.

Listing 9.13 shows my implementation of `FromBinaryString`.

LISTING 9.13 Iterating Through a Binary String's Bytes and Converting It Back to a Usable Number Format

```
Public Function FromBinaryString(BString As String) As Variant
    Dim i As Integer
    Dim bIsNegative As Boolean

    bIsNegative = False

    ' start at the end of the string and work backwards
    For i = LenB(BString) - 1 To 0 Step -1
        If i = LenB(BString) - 1 And (AscB(MidB(BString, i + 1, 2)) _
                  And &H80) Then
            ' check the signigicant bit
            ' If it's negative, set a flag
            bIsNegative = True
        End If

        If bIsNegative = True Then
            ' extract the binary complement of the byte
            FromBinaryString = FromBinaryString + _
                ((AscB(MidB(BString, i + 1, 2)) Xor &HFF) * (2 ^ (8 * i)))
        Else
            ' extract the byte
            FromBinaryString = FromBinaryString + _
                AscB(MidB(BString, i + 1, 2)) * (2 ^ (8 * i))
        End If
```

LISTING 9.13 Continued

```
    Next i

    ' if it is supposed to be negative, make it so
    If bIsNegative Then
        ' Subtract one
        FromBinaryString = FromBinaryString + 1

        ' make it negative
        FromBinaryString = FromBinaryString * -1
    End If

End Function
```

UDT API Examples

Now that you have functions to generate binary strings from numbers, you need to look at exactly how to use them.

I said before that both UDTs and `Strings` are just contiguous, linear memory blocks, so let's look at our initial example UDT, the `RECT`.

Again a `RECT`, if written in VB, would look like this:

```
Public Type RECT
        Left As Long
        Top As Long
        Right As Long
        Bottom As Long
End Type
```

Because eVB doesn't support types, you need to create a binary string that just concatenates the four members in this fashion:

```
Left & Top & Right & Bottom
```

Our initial example has the following values:

```
Left = 100
Top = 50
Right = 1200
Bottom = 175
```

So you could write code to generate this as a binary string like this:

```
Dim binaryStringAs String
```

```
binaryString= ToBinaryString(100, CE_LONG)
binaryString= binaryString& ToBinaryString (50, CE_LONG)
binaryString= binaryString& ToBinaryString (1200, CE_LONG)
binaryString= binaryString& ToBinaryString (175, CE_LONG)
```

The last thing you need to know before diving into some examples is that when using a byte string, *you must change the API declaration* from what the API viewer gives you. You must declare any UDT parameter as a `String` instead of the UDT type.

For example, the API viewer defines `ClipCursor` as

```
Declare Function ClipCursor Lib "Coredll" Alias "ClipCursor" _
    (lpRect As Long) As Long
```

This is misleading. It looks like the parameter should be a `Long`, but if you look in the eMbedded Help you see this:

```
BOOL ClipCursor(CONST RECT *lpRect);
```

What it's actually looking for is a pointer to a `RECT` structure or UDT. You need to modify the API declaration to take a `String` then, so its declaration in the project would be

```
Declare Function ClipCursor Lib "Coredll"(ByVal lpRect As String) As Long
```

The rest of the API declarations I give will already be modified to take `String` parameters, so what you see in the samples will differ from the definitions in the API viewer.

SetLocalTime

```
Declare Function SetLocalTime Lib "Coredll" (ByVal lpSystemTime As String) _
    As Long

Type SYSTEMTIME
        Integer wYear;
        Integer wMonth;
        Integer wDayOfWeek;
        Integer wDay;
        Integer wHour;
        Integer wMinute;
        Integer wSecond;
        Integer wMilliseconds;
End Type
```

Surprisingly, eVB doesn't expose any methods that allow you to easily set the device's clock programmatically. There are a few API calls that allow you to set and read the clock in both local time and GMT. Let's look at `SetLocalTime`.

`SetLocalTime` takes a single input parameter, a `SYSTEMTIME` UDT, which you can see defined previously. It's simply 8 Integers, one for each portion of the date. To set the time, you need to create a binary string of desired settings and pass it to this function. To make it both simple and reusable, create a wrapper function called `SetDeviceTime` (see Listing 9.14) that takes each of the UDT members as parameters, builds the binary string, and makes a call to `SetLocalTime`.

LISTING 9.14 Setting the Device Time Using the `SetLocalTime` API

```
Public Function SetDeviceTime(Year As Integer, Month As Integer, _
                              DayOfWeek As Integer, Day As Integer, _
                              Hour As Integer, Minute As Integer, _
                              Second As Integer, Millisecond As Integer) _
                              As Boolean

    Dim binaryString As String
    Dim lRet As Long

    binaryString = ToBinaryString(Year, CE_INTEGER)
    binaryString = binaryString & ToBinaryString(Month, CE_INTEGER)
    binaryString = binaryString & ToBinaryString(DayOfWeek, CE_INTEGER)
    binaryString = binaryString & ToBinaryString(Day, CE_INTEGER)
    binaryString = binaryString & ToBinaryString(Hour, CE_INTEGER)
    binaryString = binaryString & ToBinaryString(Minute, CE_INTEGER)
    binaryString = binaryString & ToBinaryString(Second, CE_INTEGER)
    binaryString = binaryString & ToBinaryString(Millisecond, CE_INTEGER)

    lRet = SetLocalTime(binaryString)

    ' check for success
    If lRet = 0 Then
        SetDeviceTime = False
    Else
        SetDeviceTime = True
    End If
End Function
```

To build the binary string, convert each input parameter with `ToBinaryString` and concatenate them onto the larger string, which you then pass to `SetLocalTime`.

GetLocalTime

```
Declare Sub GetLocalTime Lib "Coredll" (ByVal lpSystemTime As String)

Type SYSTEMTIME
        Integer wYear;
        Integer wMonth;
        Integer wDayOfWeek;
```

```
    Integer wDay;
    Integer wHour;
    Integer wMinute;
    Integer wSecond;
    Integer wMilliseconds;
End Type
```

Retrieving data from a long, concatenated binary string isn't difficult either, provided you know where each data piece starts and how long it is, and if you're writing the code that creates the binary string, you've got that information.

To demonstrate this, write `SetDeviceTime`'s complement, `GetDeviceTime` (see Listing 9.15). While the inherent `Now()` function will also provide the current time, the function will provide each piece of the date and time separately, making manipulation easy.

LISTING 9.15 Extracting Each Piece of the Current Time into Separate Numeric Variables

```
Public Function GetDeviceTime(ByRef Year As Integer, _
                              ByRef Month As Integer, _
                              ByRef DayOfWeek As Integer, _
                              ByRef Day As Integer, _
                              ByRef Hour As Integer, _
                              ByRef Minute As Integer, _
                              ByRef Second As Integer, _
                              ByRef Millisecond As Integer) As Boolean

    Dim binaryString As String
    Dim lRet As Long

    ' Allocate space for the variable
    binaryString = String(8, Chr(0))

    ' Call the API
    GetLocalTime(binaryString)

    ' Extract the values from the binary string
    ' Remember, we must use MidB to extract bytes
    Year = FromBinaryString(MidB(binaryString, 1, CE_INTEGER))
    Month = FromBinaryString(MidB(binaryString, 3, CE_INTEGER))
    DayOfWeek = FromBinaryString(MidB(binaryString, 5, CE_INTEGER))
    Day = FromBinaryString(MidB(binaryString, 7, CE_INTEGER))
    Hour = FromBinaryString(MidB(binaryString, 9, CE_INTEGER))
    Minute = FromBinaryString(MidB(binaryString, 11, CE_INTEGER))
    Second = FromBinaryString(MidB(binaryString, 13, CE_INTEGER))
    Millisecond = FromBinaryString(MidB(binaryString, 15, CE_INTEGER))
    GetDeviceTime = True
End Function
```

In eVB, VB, or even C for that matter, a function can have only one return value. To return all the members of `SYSTEMTIME`, you will pass the parameters in `ByRef`. This allows the called function to modify the variable and when execution returns to the caller, the changes remain.

Because eVB variables are all `Variants`, they aren't initialized with any size information. To avoid stepping on memory that you haven't yet laid claim to, you must actually allocate space for the UDT data coming back from the API call.

`GetLocalTime` returns a `SYSTEMTIME` structure, which is 8 `Integers`, or 16 bytes long, so the variable `binaryString` needs to be initialized to 16 bytes. Because Windows CE uses Unicode, each character in a `String` takes up 2 bytes, so you need 8 characters. You could reasonably set `binaryString` to any 8 characters—8 spaces, ABCDEFGH, a name—but I prefer to set all the bits to zero using the `String` function. `String` simply creates a string of a specified length—in this case, 8—using the specified character or characters—in this case, `Chr(0)`, or all bits off. This also ensures that the string is properly terminated by the C language standard.

Next make the API call, which fills the `binaryString` variable.

Next, extract each member from the binary string. Again, remember that each integer is 2 bytes, so use `MidB` to extract them, starting at bytes 1 and 2 for the year and finishing at 15 and 16 for the millisecond.

Finally, set the actual return value, which simply indicates we succeeded, and exit the function. Again, because all the parameters were passed in `ByRef`, the caller will still be able to see the values we set.

Transferring Data to and from a PC

One of the bigger challenges facing Windows CE developers, whether using eVB or eVC, is getting data to and from the device. Stand-alone applications have their uses and merit, but to truly integrate with an enterprise solution, some method of data transfer must be used.

All the code for handling data transfer is in the D2D project for Chapter 9.

There are several commercially available tools, and numerous ways to roll-your-own solution, from socket and serial communication to ActiveSync plug-ins and custom RAPI DLLs. One of the easiest methods to move data between a PC and a device is to use two API calls available through ActiveSync: `DESKTOPTODEVICE` and `DEVICETODESKTOP`. As their names suggest, one transfers data from the desktop to the device, and the other vice versa.

`DESKTOPTODEVICE` and `DEVICETODESKTOP` also have some limitations that include the following:

- Because they are ActiveSync APIs, they only work with ActiveSync installed *and running*. This means that transferring data requires the device be connected to the ActiveSync host.

- The API calls must be made from the desktop. This means that the sync can only be initiated from the desktop and not the device.
- The API doesn't throw an error, so debugging can be very challenging. A non-zero return is an error, but determining the cause of the error is difficult at best.
- The API calls only work with Access databases.
- You can vertically partition data (selectively choose columns to transfer) but you can't horizontally partition data (selectively choose rows to transfer). In SQL terms, this means you can use any column name in your SQL statement, but you can't use a `WHERE` clause.

Even with these limitations, `DESKTOPTODEVICE` and `DEVICETODESKTOP` can be useful. A little programming creativity may be required to get around the last limitation, but it isn't an insurmountable hurdle. Building temporary tables that are already horizontally partitioned is my usual method.

NOTE

Because `DESKTOPTODEVICE` and `DEVICETODESKTOP` are ActiveSync APIs, they must be declared in your VB application. The declarations here state that the Lib is in the Program Files\Microsoft ActiveSync directory, but it's a good idea to change the declaration for production code just in case the user has installed ActiveSync somewhere other than the default location.

DESKTOPTODEVICE

```
Declare Function DESKTOPTODEVICE _
   Lib "\Program files\Microsoft ActiveSync\adofiltr.dll" _
   (ByVal DesktopLocn As String, _
    ByVal TableList As String, _
    ByVal Sync As Boolean, _
    ByVal Overwrite As Boolean, _
    ByVal DeviceLocn As String) As Long
```

As its name suggests, `DESKTOPTODEVICE` transfers data from a desktop PC (specifically, the ActiveSync host) and a connected device.

Let's first look at what each of the parameters are for:

- `DesktopLocn` is the full path to the desktop database, including the filename.
- `TableList` is more than the name implies. It's both a list of tables and fields to transfer. If it's not an empty string (which means copy all columns and all tables), it must be a string in the general form

  `Tablename.Fieldname..`

NOTE

Because parameter 2 can be a bit confusing, let's look at a few examples. The following are samples for parameter 2 only (not the entire API call) and what data will be transferred.

- `"Contacts..Customers..Notes.."` All columns from the Contacts, Customers, and Notes tables will be transferred.
- `"Contacts.Name.Phone.Fax.Email.CompanyID.."` The Name, Phone, Fax, Email, and CompanyID columns (fields) will be transferred from the Contacts table.
- `"Contacts.Name.Phone..Customers.Address..Notes.Description.."` The Name and Phone columns from Contacts, the Address column from Customers and the Description column from Notes will be transferred.

Notice that in all cases, the final table is terminated with a pair of periods (`..`). If these are omitted, the API call will fail.

- `Sync` determines whether ActiveSync will continue to synchronize the table(s) transferred. This is just like selecting a database for sync through the ActiveSync program itself.
- `Overwrite` determines whether the operation will overwrite the database on the device if it already exists.
- `DeviceLocn` is the path and filename for the database on the device. If this parameter is left as an empty string, the tables will be created in the native data store.

Assume that you have a simple Access database on your desktop called D2D.mdb, and it contains two tables, Customers, and States, with the table definitions in Listing 9.16.

LISTING 9.16 Table Definitions for the `DESKTOPTODEVICE` and `DEVICETODESKTOP` API Samples

```
<Table>
<Name>Customers</Name>
        <Field>
        <Name>CustomerID</Name>
        <Type>AutoNumber</Type>
        <Size>4</Size>
        </Field>
```

LISTING 9.16 Continued

```
        <Field>
        <Name>FirstName</Name>
        <Type>Text</Type>
        <Size>50</Size>
        </Field>

        <Field>
        <Name>LastName</Name>
        <Type>Text</Type>
        <Size>50</Size>
        </Field>

        <Field>
        <Name>Phone</Name>
        <Type>Text</Type>
        <Size>50</Size>
        </Field>

        <Field>
        <Name>Email</Name>
        <Type>Text</Type>
        <Size>50</Size>
        </Field>

        <Field>
        <Name>Company</Name>
        <Type>Text</Type>
        <Size>50</Size>
        </Field>
</Table>

<Table>
<Name>States</Name>
        <Field>
        <Name>ID</Name>
        <Type>AutoNumber</Type>
        <Size>4</Size>
        </Field>

        <Field>
        <Name>Name</Name>
        <Type>Text</Type>
        <Size>50</Size>
        </Field>
```

LISTING 9.16 Continued

```
        <Field>
        <Name>Abbreviation</Name>
        <Type>Text</Type>
        <Size>2</Size>
        </Field>
</Table>
```

Now say you want to transfer some of the data from this database to your device, but not all of it. You want FirstName, LastName, Email from Customers, and the entire States table. We simply make a single call to DESKTOPTODEVICE like this:

```
Private Sub cmdDesktopToDevice_Click()
    Dim lRet As Long

    ' get the Customers and States tables
' Get Firstname, Lastname and Email from Customers
    ' Get all columns in States
    ' put the data in the root directory of the device
    ' NOTE: if you supply table names, you MUST terminate with ".."

    lRet = DESKTOPTODEVICE("C:\Book\Chapter 9\D2D\D2D.mdb", _
      "Customers.FirstName.LastName.Email..States..", False, True, "\D2D.cdb")

    If lRet <> 0 Then
        MsgBox "And error occurred transferring data"
    End If
End Sub
```

Notice that I gave both the full source path and destination path. You will likely have to use a different source path.

If you look on the device at this point, you should have a file called D2D in the root directory (PocketPC hides the extension).

Another nice feature ActiveSync provided here is a log of data transfers, and it provides it automatically. Any time DESKTOPTODEVICE (or DEVICETODESKTOP) is called, a log file is created in the device's Profile directory, which can be found as a subdirectory of ActiveSync. If your device is called PocketPC, for instance, and you installed ActiveSync in the default location, the profile directory will be

```
C:\Program Files\Microsoft ActiveSync\Profiles\Pocket_PC
```

The file created will be db2ce.txt. In this example, it will look something like Listing 9.17.

LISTING 9.17 A Log File Automatically Generated by ActiveSync

```
Monday, July 09, 2001 4:54:50 PM, User: ctacke, synchronization started.

Database:

option: 255 - Overwrite existing tables
option: 0 - Keep this database synchronized

Monday, July 09, 2001 4:54:50 PM, Database transfer begun.

  Copying table Customers

    Processing indexes:
    Index processing has been stopped. There are no more indexes available.
    SQL: SELECT `FirstName`,`LastName`,`Email` FROM `Customers`
    Copying of 4 record(s) completed.

  Copying table States

    Processing indexes:
    Index processing has been stopped. There are no more indexes available.
    1 index(es) were successfully created.

    SQL: SELECT `ID`,`Name`,`Abbreviation` FROM `States`
    Copying of 6 record(s) completed.

Monday, July 09, 2001 4:54:51 PM, Database transfer complete.
Transfer Statistics:
          2 Table(s)
         10 Record(s)
          6 Packet(s)
       5594 Bytes
```

This can provide at least some help for debugging problems you may encounter when testing or deploying your applications. Notice that it provides the exact SQL statements it runs to extract the data.

DEVICETODESKTOP

```
Declare Function DEVICETODESKTOP Lib _
   "\Program files\Microsoft ActiveSync\adofiltr.dll" _
   (ByVal DesktopLocn As String, _
    ByVal TableList As String, _
    ByVal Sync As Boolean, _
    ByVal Overwrite As Boolean, _
    ByVal DeviceLocn As String) As Long
```

DEVICETODESKTOP is the complementary function of DESKTOPTODEVICE and works very similarly. Even their parameter lists are identical.

Let's continue the example from the previous section and transfer the database back to the desktop, this time transferring the whole thing (at least as far as the device is concerned). This confirms that the call to DESKTOPTODEVICE worked properly.

```
Private Sub cmdDeviceToDesktop_Click()
    Dim lRet As Long
    ' Get the entire D2D database (as it exists on the device)
    ' Change the local name

    lRet = DEVICETODESKTOP("C:\Book\Chapter 9\D2D\D2Dsmall.mdb", "", _
           False, True, "\D2D.cdb")

    If lRet <> 0 Then
        MsgBox "And error occurred transferring data"
    End If
End Sub
```

Summary

One of the biggest complaints I've heard about eVB is its lack of robustness; its inability to achieve things that have been available in desktop Visual Basic for several versions. Through the API, you can re-create and use a large amount of the functionality that Windows CE offers and produce applications that are not only robust, but also elegant and user friendly as well.

As I said at the start of the chapter, this chapter isn't meant to be the definitive resource on API programming. In fact we only scratched the surface. But you now have the foundation to apply nearly all the API programming techniques that you will find discussed in books, magazines, and online. Short of functions requiring callbacks or UDTs within UDTs, there are no APIs that, given the method signature, you can't now implement.

It's difficult to make pointed suggestions for further work with the API. API programming is usually driven by a specific project, a need, or simply interest. To get a better feel for the amount of things you can do with API calls, I suggest looking through the help files that come with eMbedded Visual Tools. All the functions referenced in WINCEAPI.TXT are there, along with some documentation that should help you sort out how to use them. Beware, though, the help files aren't always correct.

Another way to learn more is to work through an API programming book or through API sample applications. There are volumes of information available online, from declaration lists to sample code snippets to full applications using APIs. Find some of these that interest you and try porting them to Windows CE. Above all, enjoy yourself.

Control Reference

APPENDIX

A

IN THIS APPENDIX

Pocket PC MenuBar Control Reference

The Pocket PC MenuBar control allows eVB applications to display a standard Pocket PC menu. The control is selectable from the Project/Components dialog as Microsoft PocketPC MenuBar Control 3.0. The library file is mscemenubar.dll.

TABLE A.1 MenuBar Control Properties

Property	*Type*	*Description*
`Controls`	`Collection`	Collection of all first-level children objects on the menu control. Use this collection to enumerate through the first-level objects owned by the menu control. Calling methods on this collection allow the manipulation of the control itself, changing its appearance and behavior.
`Enabled`	`Boolean`	No effect on control.
`ImageList`	`Handle (Long)`	Used as a handle to an ImageList control to add graphics to menu.
`Name`	`String`	Name assigned to menu object.
`NewButton`	`Boolean`	Whether New button should be displayed. Is available only to set at design time, read-only at runtime. The actual new button object can't be programmatically referenced; doesn't appear in Controls collection.
`Parent`	`Object`	Parent object of menu bar. Should always refer to `Form` object.
`Tag`	`String`	Used for user-defined values.

TABLE A.2 MenuBar Control Events

Event	*Description*
`NewClick`	Occurs when a user clicks New button. Available only when `NewButton = True` (at design time).
`ButtonClick`	Occurs when a button is clicked on the menu bar. Passes a reference to the button clicked as a parameter.
`MenuClick`	Occurs when a menu bar is clicked. Passes a reference to the menu bar clicked as a parameter.

TABLE A.3 MenuBar Controls Collection Methods

Method	*Parameter(s)*	*Returns*	*Description*
`AddButton`	`[Key](string)` Unique value that identifies the item (button)	Reference to a button object (`MenuBarButton`)	Adds a button to the menu (or parent object).
`AddMenu`	`Caption(string)` *Caption* for menu bar `[Key](string)` Unique value that identifies the item (button)	Reference to menu object (`MenuBar`)	Adds a menu bar to the menu (or parent object).
`Clear`	None	Nothing	Removes all items from the menu bar (or parent object).

TABLE A.4 MenuBar Controls Collection Properties

Property	*Type*	*Description*
`Count`	`Integer`	Number of items in the collection.
`Item`	`Menu` object (button or menu bar)	An individual item from the collection (by `Key` or `Index`).

TABLE A.5 `MenuBarMenu` Properties

Property	*Type*	*Description*
`Caption`	`String`	Caption of menu bar. If menu bar is placed on root menu, can't be modified after being assigned.
`Enabled`	`Boolean`	Whether the menu bar is accessible to the user. Ignored if menu bar is placed on root menu.
`Index`	`Long`	Index of item within its parent's collection.
`Items`	`Collection (Item—` either `MenuBarButton` or `MenuBarMenu)`	Collection of items contained on object. On a menu bar, this can only be other menu bars and can't only be used from a menu bar on the root menu.

TABLE A.5 Continued

Property	*Type*	*Description*
`Key`	`String`	Unique identifier of object in its parent's collection.
`Tag`	`String`	User property able to hold a string value.
`Type`	`MenuBarControlType`	Read-only. Always equal to `mbrMenuBar` for menu bars.
`Visible`	`Boolean`	Whether or not the menu bar is visible to users.

TABLE A.6 `MenuBarMenu` Items Collection Properties

Property	*Type*	*Description*
`Count`	`Long`	Not implemented in eVB.
`Item`	`Collection`	Object of subitems on item.

TABLE A.7 `MenuBarMenu` Items Methods

Method	*Parameters*	*Returns*	*Description*

`Add`	`[index](Long)` Index value to position item. If the index value already exists in collection, the item is inserted before it.
	`[key](String)`
	Unique value t identify item in collection.
	`[caption](String)`
	Caption of objectto be added
	`[style](MenuStyleConstant)`
		`Object(Item)`	Adds a menu bar the `Items` to collection.

`Clear`	None	None	Clears all menu bars from `Items` collection.
`Remove`	Index	None	Removes individual menu from `Items` collection.

TABLE A.8 `MenuBarMenu Items` Properties

Property	*Type*	*Description*
`Count`	`Long`	Number of menu bars in `Items` collection.
`Item`	`MenuBar` object	Returns an individual menu bar object from the `Items` collection.

TABLE A.9 `MenuBarButton` Properties

Property	*Type*	*Description*
`Caption`	`String`	Caption of button.
`Enabled`	`Boolean`	Whether or not button is enabled.
`Image`	`Long`	Index to collection of images in ImageList control. Must set `ImageList` property on `MenuBarControl` object.
`Index`	`Long`	Index of button in collection.
`Key`	`String`	Unique identifier of button object in collection.
`MixedState`	`Boolean`	Causes button to be shaded.
`Style`	`ButtonStyleConstants`	Allows button to be a check box button, radio button, default, or separator.
`Tag`	`String`	User property able to hold a string value.
`ToolTip`	`String`	Text that pops up as a ToolTip when the user does a tap-and-hold action on the control.
`Type`	`MenuBarControlType`	Denotes whether the control is a Button or a Menu.
`Value`	`ButtonValueConstants`	Denotes the current value of the control.
`Visible`	`Boolean`	Denotes whether or not the control is visible to the User.
`Width`	`Long`	The screen-based width of the control.

TABLE A.10 `Items` Properties

Property	*Type*	*Description*
`Count`	`Long`	Number of items in the `Items` collection.
`Item`	`Enumerator`	Allows access to an individual item within the collection. Accepts either the index or the key as the value as to which item to return.

TABLE A.11 Items Methods

Method	*Parameters*	*Returns*	*Description*
Add	[*index*](Long) Value as to where to add to the collection. [*key*](String) Unique value to identify the item within the collection. [*caption*](String) Caption of the menu bar or the button. [*style*](MenuStyleConstants) Allows defining whether a menu is a menu bar or a separator.	Item	Adds a MenuBarMenu to the collection.
Clear	None	None	Removes all items from the collection.
Remove	*Index*(String|Long) Correlates to the Index or Key value of the Item in the collection.	None	Clears an individual Item from the collection.

TABLE A.12 Item Properties

Property	*Type*	*Description*
Caption	String	Caption of the button or the menu.
Checked	Boolean	Implemented only for MenuBarMenu. Allows the menu bar to display a check mark. If used with a button, returns an error.
Enabled	Boolean	If Item is MenuBarMenu, will have no effect if MenuBarMenu is on root menu. If item is MenuBarButton, setting Enabled to False causes unexpected behavior.
Index	Long	Unique value of item in its parent collection. Assigned as count of items when added to collection.

TABLE A.12 Continued

Property	Type	Description
Key	String	Unique value of item in its parent collection.
Parent	Object	Reference to the object in which the Item is contained as part of parent collection.
Style	MenuStyleConstants	Applies only to MenuBarMenu class. Allows MenuBarMenu to be a menu (mbrMenuDefault) or a separator (mbrMenuSeparator). Ignored if Item is MenuBarButton.
SubItems	Collection	Collection of items contained by the Item. This applies only to the root MenuBarMenu object as the collection of MenuBarMenu as bars on the root MenuBarMenu.
Tag	String	User-defined value.
Visible	Boolean	Whether the Item is visible to users. If the Item is a MenuBarMenu on the root MenuBar, setting has no effect.

TABLE A.13 ButtonStyleContants Constants

Constant	Value	Description
mbrAutoSize	5	Not necessary; buttons resize automatically.
mbrButtonGroup	2	Creates a group of buttons similar to a radio-button group.
mbrCheck	1	Creates a button that acts like a check box.
mbrDefault	0	Regular button.
mbrSeparator	3	Spaceholder between buttons or menu bars. Can be used to separate more than one group of button groups.

TABLE A.14 ButtonValueConstants Constants

Constant	Value	Description
mbrPressed	1	Button is pressed.
mbrUnPressed	0	Button is not pressed.

TABLE A.15 `MenuBarControlType` Constants

Constant	*Value*	*Description*
`mbrButton`	0	Button type
`mbrMenuBar`	1	Menu type

TABLE A.16 `MenuStyleConstants` Constants

Constant	*Value*	*Description*
`MbrMenuDefault`	0	Default menu type
`MbrMenuSeparator`	1	Menu separator type

ADOCE Control Reference

The ADOCE control is used to create and manipulate data residing in Pocket Access or SQL Server CE databases. The control is added to an eVB project via the Project/References dialog. Depending on version, it will display as "Microsoft CE ADO Control x.x", where "x.x" is the version number. The latest available version at the time of publication is 3.1. The file for the ADOCE control is adocedt30.dll or adocedt31.dll, depending on version.

TABLE A.17 `ADOCE.Connection` Properties

Property	*Type*	*Description*
`Attributes`	`Long`	Implemented only with OLEDBCE providers.
`ConnectionString`	`String`	Information on where and how the connection object should open the data source. With Pocket Access, merely provide the Pocket Access file path and name. For example, `ConnectionString = "\Program Files\My Application\MyPocketAccess.cdb"`. Note: Make sure to localize the "Program Files" directory according to the application's needs.
`Errors`	`Collection`	Collection of all `ADOCE.Errors` on `Connection` object since `Connection` was opened or `Connection.Errors.Clear` was called. See `ADOCE.Error`.

TABLE A.17 `ADOCE.Connection` Properties

Property	*Type*	*Description*
`Properties`	`Collection`	Provides collection of properties about the Connection. See provider documentation as to properties available. Not implemented with Pocket Access.
`Provider`	`String`	Name of the provider for the data. Pocket Access is `"CEDB"`.
`State`	`ADOCE.ObjectStateEnum`	Provides the open or closed state of the `Connection` object.
`Version`	`String`	Version number of ADOCE server DLL(s).

TABLE A.18 `ADOCE.Connection` Methods

Method	*Parameters*	*Description*
`BeginTrans`	None	Begins a database transaction that supports an atomic unit of work. Not implemented with Pocket Access.
`Close`	None	Closes the current connection.
`CommitTrans`	None	Commits changes to data since last `BeginTrans`. Not implemented with Pocket Access.
`Execute`	`CommandText; String` `[RecordsAffected]; Long` (`ByRef`) Number of records affected by data manipulation statement (Not implemented with Pocket Access) `[Options]; Long` Not implemented with Pocket Access.	Executes a SQL Statement statement and returns the resulting recordset.

TABLE A.18 Continued

Method	*Parameters*	*Description*
`Open`	`[ConnectionString]; String` `ConnectionString` to access the data store. If left blank in ADOCE, the connection will open the Windows CE Object Store. `[UserId]; String` User ID for access to data store. Not implemented in Windows CE Object Store or Pocket Access. `[Password]; String` provided Password for user ID for access to data store. Not implemented in Windows CE Object Storeor Pocket Access.	Opens a data source for access to data.
`RollbackTrans`	None	Discards changes made to data since `BeginTrans` was invoked. Not implemented in Windows CE Object Store or Pocket Access.

TABLE A.19 `ADOCE.Field` Properties

Property	*Type*	*Description*
`ActualSize`	`Integer`	Length of the field in the data store. This can be confusing for string types, because Windows CE strings are *always* UNICODE; therefore, the `ActualSize` of the field will be twice the character length.
`Attributes`	`Long`	Bit-shifted value for information about the field. It contains information such as whether the field may be updated in its current state, whether it allows NULLs, and whether it is a primary key. Refer to ADOCE documentation for these values.

ABLE A.19 Continued

Property	*Type*	*Description*
`DefinedSize`	`Integer`	Length of the field as defined when it was created. This yields the capacity of the field in length.
`Name`	`String`	Name of the field.
`NumericScale` (`Float`).	`Byte`	Number of digits to the left of the decimal
`Precision`	`Integer`	Number of total digits available in the field.
`Type`	`ADOCE.DataTypeEnum`	Value that relates to a member of the `DataTypeEnum`. The actual type of the field. For example, `adDate`, `adInt`, `adVarChar`.
`UnderlyingValue`	`Variant`	The value of the field before it was changed (if changed). Can be useful for auditing and dirty record detection.

TABLE A.20 `ADOCE.Field` Methods

Method	*Parameters*	*Description*
`AppendChunk`	*`Data`*; `Variant` Information to be appended to the field.	Appends data to a binary or text field. Implemented only with an OLEDBCE provide. Version 3.1 and higher.
`GetChunk`	*`Size`*; `Long` Number of bytes to be returned.	Returns data from a binary or text field. Implemented only with an OLEDBCE provider. Version 3.1 and higher.

TABLE A.21 `ADOCE.Recordset` Properties

Property	*Type*	*Description*
`AbsolutePage`	`Long`; Read/Write	Position of the record within the data pages.
`AbsolutePosition`	`Long`; Read/Write	The position of the current record within the recordset.

TABLE A.21 Continued

Property	*Type*	*Description*
ActiveConnection	Object; ADOCE.Connection	Returns a reference to the connection used to open the recordset. If queried directly, will return the connection. ConnectionString, as ConnectionString is the default property for the ADOCE.Connection object.
BOF	Boolean; Read-only	Returns True if the AbsolutePosition is before the first record in the recordset.
Bookmark	Variant; Read/Write	If queried, returns a unique variant that if set onto the recordset will return the recordset to the same record. If set, locates the AbsolutePosition to the record where the value of Bookmark was queried from.
CursorType	Long; ADOCE. CursorTypeEnum	For Windows CE Object Store or Pocket Access, only adOpenForwardOnly and adOpenKeyset are implemented.
EditMode	Long; ADOCE. EditModeEnum Read-Only	Specifies the current state of the current record. See ADOCE.EditModeEnum.
EOF	Boolean; Read-Only	Returns True if the AbsolutePosition has been placed past the last record in the recordset.
Fields	Collection; ADOCE.Fields	Collection of all fields in the record. See ADOCE.Fields.
Filter	Variant	Returns or sets the current filtering. Only supports bookmarks and adFilterNone. Not implemented in Windows CE Object Store or Pocket Access.
Index	String|Long	Sets or returns the currently set index of the recordset. Can only be used with base table recordset (adCmdTableDirect). Can be the name of the index or the number of the index (as created). Not implemented in Windows CE Object Store or Pocket Access.

TABLE A.21 Continued

Property	*Type*	*Description*
`LockType`	`Long;`	`ADOCE.LockTypeEnum`
`PageCount`	`Long;` Read-Only	Number of data pages in the recordset.
`PageSize`	`Long;` Read/Write	Number of records to a page.
`Properties`	`Collection; ADOCE.Properties`	Not implemented in Windows CE Object Store or Pocket Access.
`RecordCount`	`Long`	Number of records in recordset. Can return `adUnknown`.
`Source`	`String;` Read-only after the recordset is opened. Write before the recordset is open.	The SQL string that creates the recordset or created the recordset. Set the source before `Open` is called. Or, can be read after therecordset is opened.
`State`	`Long; ADOCE.ObjectStateEnum` Read-Only	Returns the open or closed state of the recordset.

TABLE A.22 ADOCE.Recordset Methods

Property	*Parameters*	*Description*
`AddNew`	`[Fields]`;Array of field to set values for. `[Values]`; Array of the values corresponding to Fields array.	Appends a new record to the recordset. Sets values of fields if arrays provided as parameters.
`CancelUpdate`	None	Discards any changes made to the current record.
`Clone`	[`LockType`]; `ADOCE.LockType`	Returns a copy of the recordset.
`Close`	None	Closes the recordset.
`Delete`	[`AffectRecords`]—only accepts adAffectCurrent, a value of 1.	Deletes the current record.

TABLE A.22 Continued

Property	*Parameters*	*Description*
`Find`	*`Criteria`*; String—String containing the field to search upon, the comparison operator and the value. (*object.*`Find( "LastName = 'Smith'"` [*`SkipRows`*]; Long—offset to start searching from current record. [*`searchDirection`*]; ADOCE. SearchDirectionEnum — direction to search, forward, or backward. *[`start`]*; Variant—Bookmark to begin searching from.	Locates the first record match. ing the criteria provided.
`GetRows`	*[`Rows`]*; Long—Number of rows to return. [*`Start`*]; Long|Variant—Record number of Bookmark of where to start returning rows. [*`Fields`*]; Array—Fields to return values for.	Returns an array of the values from the recordset.
`Move`	*`NumRecords`*; Long—Number of records to offset to. *[`Start`]*; Long|Variant—Record number of Bookmark of where to start returning rows.	Move a specified offset from the current record.
`MoveFirst`	None	Moves to the first record of the recordset.
`MoveLast`	None	Moves to the last record of the record-set.

TABLE A.22 Continued

Property	*Parameters*	*Description*
`MoveNext`	None	Moves to the next record of the recordset.
`MovePrevious`	None	Moves to the previous record of the recordset.
`Open`	*`Source`*; String—Table name or SQL Statement. [*`ActiveConnection`*]; `ADOCE.Connection`—Connection to use. [*`CursorType`*]; ADOCE.CursorType—Cursor type for the recordset. [*`LockType`*]; `ADOCE.LockType`—Lock type for the recordset [*`Options`*]; Long—See provider documentation. AdCmdTableDirect is used with SQL Server CE to provide and updateable recordset.	Opens a new recordset.
`Requery`	None	Refreshes the recordset.
`Supports`	*`CursorOptions`*; `ADOCE.CursorOptionEnum`	Returns Boolean as to whether the recordset supports the requested cursor option. e.g. *object.*`Supports` (adAddNew).
`Update`	[*`Fields`*];Array of field to set values for. [*`Values`*]; Array of the values corresponding to Fields array.	Commits changes to record back to data store.

TABLE A.23 `ADOCE.Error` Properties

Property	*Type*	*Description*
`Description`	`String`; Read-Only	Friendly description of error that occurred.
`ErrorParameters`	`Collection`; `String`	Collection of errors from last execution attempt. Not implemented in Windows CE Object Store or Pocket Access.
`HelpContext`	`Long`	Not implemented in Windows CE at all.
`HelpFile`	`String`; Read-Only	File path to the help file for the error.
`NativeError`	`Long`; Read-Only	Native error returned from the data provider. Limited functionality with Windows CE Object Store or Pocket Access.
`Number`	`Long`; Read-Only	Error number as implemented in OLE.
`Source`	`String`	Name of the object that generated the error. Very limited implementation for Windows CE Object Store or Pocket Access.

The File Control Object Model

The following tables outline the Object Model for the File Control. This control is included in MSCEFile.dll.

TABLE A.24 File Control Methods

Method	*Return*	*Description*
`Close`	Nothing	Closes an open file.
`Get`	Nothing	Reads binary data into a Variant variable. Usually used for data written with the `Put` method.
`Input`	String	Reads a specified number of characters from an open text file.
`InputB`	Byte array	Reads a specified number of bytes from an open binary file.
`InputFields`	Variant array	Reads a specified number of fields from an open sequential, comma-delimited file.

TABLE A.24 File Control Methods

Method	*Return*	*Description*
`LineInputString`	String	Reads the next single line (delimited by vbCr or vbCrLf) from an open sequential text file.
`LinePrint`	Nothing	Appends a line of text to an open sequential text file. `Lineprint` also terminates the line with vbCrLf.
`Open`	Nothing	Opens a file in Input, Output, Append, Random or Binary mode.
`Put`	Nothing	Writes a variant variable to disk as binary data.
`WriteFields`	Nothing	Writes numeric or text data to an open sequential file.

TABLE A.25 File Control Properties

Property	*Return*	*Description*
`Attr`	FileModeEnum	Gets the mode in which a file was opened. Can be confusing, as it does *not* return the FileAttrEnum for the open file.
`EOF`	Boolean	Returns `True` when the end of a file is reached.
`Loc`	Long	Gets the current read/write position of an open file.
`LOF`	Long	Gets the length of a file in bytes.
`Name`	String	Gets the logical name of the File control as set in the Properties window.
`Parent`	Object	Gets a reference to the File control's parent object, such as its containing form.
`Seek`	Long	Sets and returns the current read/write position in an open file. `Seek always` returns Loc + 1, except for when a file is first opened.
`Tag`	String	Sets or gets a string that can be used to hold any additional information the programmer wants to store.

The FileSystem Control Object Model

The following tables outline the Object Model for the FileSystem Control. This control is included in MSCEFile.dll.

TABLE A.26 FileSystem Control Methods

Method	*Return*	*Description*
`Dir`	String	Returns the next file matching the criteria last passed into the `Dir` method. The first call to `Dir` *must* include a criterion.
`FileCopy`	Nothing	Copies an existing file to a new file.
`FileDateTime`	Date	Returns the date and time a file was last modified.
`FileLen`	Long	Returns the length of a file in bytes.
`GetAttr`	FileAttrEnum	Returns a number representing the attributes of a file or directory. A file may have multiple attributes.
`Kill`	Nothing	Deletes the specified file.
`MkDir`	Nothing	Creates a new directory.
`MoveFile`	Nothing	Moves a file or directory. If a directory is moved, all subdirectories and their contents are also moved.
`RmDir`	Nothing	Deletes the specified directory.
`SetAttr`	Nothing	Sets the attributes of the specified file.

TABLE A.27 FileSystem Control Properties

Property	*Return*	*Description*
`Name`	String	Gets the logical name of the FileSystem control as set in the Properties window.
`Parent`	Object	Gets a reference to the `FileSystem` control's parent object, such as its containing form.
`Tag`	String	Sets or gets a string that can be used to hold any additional information the programmer wants to store.

MSCEFileCtl Constants

The following tables list the constants used by the File and FileSystem controls and their underlying values.

TABLE A.28 FileAccessEnum Constants

Constant	*Value*	*Description*
`FsAccessRead`	1	Indicates that a file was opened in read-only mode (input).
`FsAccesWrite`	2	Indicates that a file was opened in write-only mode (output).
`FsAccessReadWrite`	3	Indicates that a file was opened in read/write mode (input-output).

TABLE A.29 FileAttrEnum Constants

Constant	*Value*	*Description*
`FsAttrNormal`	0	Indicates a normal file.
`FsAttrReadOnly`	1	Indicates a file or directory marked as read-only.
`FsAttrHidden`	2	Indicates a file or directory marked as hidden.
`FsAttrSystem`	4	Indicates a system file.
`FsAttrVolume`	8	Indicates a volume set.
`FsAttrDirectory`	16	Indicates a directory.
`FsAttrArchive`	32	Indicates a file has changed since last backup.

TABLE A.30 FileLockEnum Constants

Constant	*Value*	*Description*
`FsLockReadWrite`	0	Indicates other processes may read or write to the file when it is open.
`FsLockWrite`	1	Indicates other processes may write to a file while it is open.
`FsLockRead`	2	Indicates other processes may read from a file while it is open.
`FsLockShared`	3	Indicates that a file is opened by multiple processes.

TABLE A.31 FileModeEnum Constants

Constant	*Value*	*Description*
`FsModeInput`	1	Used to open a file for sequential text input.
`FsModeOutput`	2	Used to open a file for sequential text output. The read/write position is set to the beginning of the file.
`FsModeRandom`	4	Used to open a file for random binary access.
`FsModeAppend`	8	Used to open a file for sequential text output. The read/write position is set to the end of the file.
`FsModeBinary`	32	Used to open a file for binary access.

The CE Treeview Object Model

The following tables outline the Object Model for the CE TreeView Control. This control is included in MSCETreeview.dll.

TABLE A.32 TreeViewCtl Methods

Method	*Return*	*Description*
`GetVisibleCount`	Long	The number of Node objects that fit vertically in the internal area of the TreeView Control. *Note:* This may be greater than the actual number of Nodes in the control.
`Move`	Nothing	Moves the control to the specified location. Can be used to set the Left, Top, Height, and Width simultaneously.
`Refresh`	Nothing	Forces a repaint of the entire control.
`SetFocus`	Nothing	Moves the current focus to the control.
`StartLabelEdit`	Nothing	Allows the user to edit the Text of a node.
`Zorder`	Nothing	Places the control at the front or back of the z-order.

TABLE A.33 TreeViewCtl Properties

Property	*Return*	*Description*
`Container`	Object	Returns a reference to the TreeView control's container object, such as its containing form.
`Enabled`	Boolean	Sets or Gets whether the control responds to user-generated events.

TABLE A.33 Continued

Property	*Return*	*Description*
`Event_Cancel`	Boolean	Determines whether the control processes events.
`FontBold`	Boolean	Sets or Gets the Bold font style for the control.
`FontItalic`	Boolean	Sets or Gets the Italic font style for the control.
`FontName`	String	Sets or Gets the font used to display text in the object.
`FontSize`	Long	Sets or Gets the font size for text displayed in the control.
`FontStrikethrough`	Boolean	Sets or Gets the Strikethrough font style for the control.
`FontUnderline`	Boolean	Sets or Gets the Underline font style for the control.
`Height`	Long	Sets or Gets the current height of the control
`HideSelection`	Boolean	Determines whether selected text remains highlighted when the control loses focus.
`ImageList`	Long	Sets or Gets the handle to the ImageList associated with the control.
`Indentation`	Single	Sets or Gets the distance a child Node is indented below its parent.
`LabelEdit`	LabelEditEnum	Determines whether Labels within the control are user-editable.
`Left`	Long	Sets or Gets the current Left position of the control.
`LineStyle`	LineStyleEnum	Sets or Gets the style of lines displayed between Node objects.
`Name`	String	Gets the logical name of the TreeView control as set in the Properties window.
`Nodes`	Nodes Collection	Gets a reference to the Nodes Collection of the control.
`Parent`	Object	Returns a reference to the `TreeView` control's parent object, such as its containing form.
`PathSeparator`	String	Sets or Gets the delimiting character used for the return of the `FullPath` property.

TABLE A.33 Continued

Property	*Return*	*Description*
`SelectedItem`	Node Object	Gets a reference to the currently selected Node object.
`Sorted`	Boolean	Determines whether Root Nodes within the control are sorted alphabetically by Text.
`Style`	TreeStyleEnum	Sets or Gets the types of graphics, such as lines, pluses and minuses, which appear for each Node.
`TabIndex`	Long	Sets or Gets order in which the Tab key sends focus to the control relative to all other controls on the form.
`TabStop`	Boolean	Determines whether the Tab key can set focus to the control.
`Tag`	String	Sets or Gets a string that can be used to hold any additional information the programmer wants to store.
`Top`	Long	Sets or Gets the current Top position of the control.
`Visible`	Boolean	Determines whether the control is displayed to the user.
`Width`	Long	Sets or Gets the current Width of the control.

TABLE A.34 TreeView Control Events

Event	*Description*
`AfterLabelEdit`	Fires after a user changes the `Text` of a `Node`.
`BeforeLabelEdit`	Fires when a user begins editing the `Text` of a Node.
`Collapse`	Fires when a `Node` is collapsed by the user.
`Expand`	Fires when a `Node` is expanded by the user.
`GotFocus`	Fires when current application focus is set to the control.
`LostFocus`	Fires when current application focus leaves the control.
`NodeClick`	Fires whenever the user clicks on a `Node`.

TABLE A.35 Node Object Methods

Method	*Return*	*Description*
`EnsureVisible`	Nothing	Ensures the specified `Node` is visible by scrolling and expanding nodes if necessary.

TABLE A.36 Node Object Properties

Property	*Return*	*Description*
`Child`	Node Object	Gets a reference to a Node's first child Node.
`Children`	Long	Gets the number of child Nodes a parent Node has.
`Expanded`	Boolean	Sets or Gets whether the specified node is expanded.
`ExpandedImage`	Long	Sets or Gets the index of the ImageList image displayed when a Node is expanded.
`FirstSibling`	Node Object	Gets a reference to a Node's first sibling Node.
`FullPath`	String	Returns the full path to the specified Node.
`Image`	Long	Sets or Gets the index of the ImageList image displayed normally for a Nodes in the control.
`Index`	Long	Gets a number that uniquely identifies the specified Node within the Nodes Collection.
`Key`	String	Sets or Gets a string that uniquely identifies the specified Node within the Nodes Collection.
`LastSibling`	Node Object	Gets a reference to a Node's first sibling Node.
`Next`	Node Object	Gets a reference to a Node's next sibling Node.
`Parent`	Node Object	Gets a reference to a Node's Parent Node.
`Previous`	Node Object	Gets a reference to a Node's previous sibling Node.
`Root`	Node Object	Gets a Reference to the Root Node of the `TreeView` control.
`Selected`	Boolean	Sets or Gets the selection status of a Node.
`SelectedImage`	Long	Sets or Gets the index of the ImageList image displayed when a Node is Selected.
`Sorted`	Boolean	Determines whether a Node's child Nodes are sorted alphabetically by Text.
`Text`	String	Sets or Gets the text displayed for a Node.

TABLE A.37 Nodes Collection Methods

Method	*Return*	*Description*
`Add`	Node Object	Adds a new Node object to the Nodes collection.
`Clear`	Nothing	Removes all Nodes from the Nodes collection.
`Remove`	Nothing	Removes a specific Node from the Nodes collection.

TABLE A.38 Nodes Collection Properties

Property	*Return*	*Description*
`Count`	Long	Gets the total number of Nodes in the Nodes collection.
`Item`	Node Object	Gets a reference to a Node in the Nodes collection based on its Index property.

TABLE A.39 TreeStyleEnum Constants

Constant	*Value*	*Description*
`TvwTextOnly`	0	Indicates the control will not display lines, pictures, or plus/minus.
`TvwPictureText`	1	Indicates the control will display pictures for each Node.
`TvwPlusMinusText`	2	Indicates the control will display a plus/minus box left of each Node.
`TvwPlusPictureText`	3	Indicates the control will display both a picture and a plus/minus box for each Node.
`TvwTreelinesText`	4	Indicates the control will display lines between Nodes.
`TvwTreelinesPictureText`	5	Indicates the control will display lines between each Node as well as pictures for each Node.
`TvwTreelinesPlusMinusText`	6	Indicates the control will display lines between each Node as well as a plus/minus box left of each Node.
`TvwTreelinesPlusMinusPictureText`	7	Indicates the control will display lines between each Node, picture for each Node and a plus/minus box left of each Node.

The CE WinSock Object Model

The following tables outline the Object Model for the CE WinSock Control. This control is included in MSCEWinsock.dll.

TABLE A.40 WinSock Methods

Method	*Return*	*Description*
`Accept`	Nothing	Used to accept a connection after a ConnectionRequest event fires.
`Close`	Nothing	Closes a transmitting or listening socket.
`Connect`	Nothing	Requests a connection with the host named in the `RemoteHost` property of the control through the port named in the `RemotePort` property.
`GetData`	Nothing	Retrieves the current block of data from a `WinSock` control's buffer. Only Strings and Integer arrays are supported. *Note:* The `maxLen` parameter is not implemented and any value provided is ignored.
`Listen`	Nothing	Puts a `WinSock` control into listen mode for the protocol specified in the `Protocol` property.
`SendData`	Nothing	Sends data through the current `WinSock` to the remote host. Only `Strings` and `Integer` arrays are supported.

TABLE A.41 WinSock Properties

Property	*Return*	*Description*
`BytesReceived`	Integer	*Read-Only*. Gets the amount of data, in bytes, received by the `WinSock` control.
`LocalHostName`	String	*Read-Only*. Gets the name of the local machine (device name).
`LocalIP`	String	*Read-Only*. Gets the local IP address in dotted-string format (xxx.xxx.xxx.xxx).
`LocalPort`	Integer	Sets or Gets the local port for use by the `WinSock` control.
`Name`	String	Gets the logical name of the `WinSock` control as set in the Properties window.
`Parent`	Object	Returns a reference to the `WinSock` control's parent object, such as its containing form.

TABLE A.41 Continued

Property	*Return*	*Description*
`Protocol`	SockCtrlProtocol	Sets or gets the protocol used for transfer by the `WinSock` control. Only TCP/IP and IrDA are supported.
`RemoteHost`	String	Sets or Gets the IP or host name of the remote machine the socket is connected or will connect to.
`RemoteHostIP`	String	*Read-Only*. Gets the IP address or the remote host in dotted-string format (xxx.xxx.xxx.xxx) after a successful connection.
`RemotePort`	Integer	Sets or Gets the remote host port the `WinSock` control is connected or will connect to.
`SocketHandle`	Long	*Read-Only*. Gets the window handle for the currently open socket used by the `WinSock` control. This is useful for making calls to the `WinSock` API.
`State`	SockCtrlState	*Read-Only*. Gets the current state of the `WinSock` control.
`ServiceName`	String	Sets or Gets the service name for an IrDA socket connection.
`Tag`	String	Sets or Gets a string that can be used to hold any additional information the programmer wants to store.

TABLE A.42 WinSock Control Events

Event	*Description*
`Close`	Fires when the remote host closes the socket connection.
`ConnectionRequest`	Fires when a request is received on a Listening socket.
`Connect`	Fires when the Connect method succeeds.
`DataArrival`	Fires when the socket's buffer receives new data into an empty buffer.
`Error`	Fires when an error occurs while processing for a socket.
`SendComplete`	Fires when the `SendData` method has completed sending all of its data.
`SendProgress`	Fires after each packet of data has been sent. Data larger than 8k is automatically packetized by the control.

TABLE A.43 SockCtrlError Constants

Constant	*Value*	*Description*
`SckOutOfMemory`	7	The system is out of memory.
`SckInvalidPropertyValue`	380	The property value is invalid.
`SckGetNotSupported`	394	The property cannot be read.
`SckSetNotSupported`	383	The property is read-only.
`SckBadState`	40006	Wrong protocol or connection state for the requested transaction or request.
`SckInvalidArg`	40014	The parameter passed to a function is not in the correct format or in the specified range.
`SckSuccess`	40017	Successful.
`SckUnsupported`	40018	Unsupported variant type.
`SckInvalidOp`	40020	Invalid operation at current state.
`SckOutOfRange`	40021	Parameter is out of range.
`SckWrongProtocol`	40026	Wrong protocol for the requested transaction or request.
`SckOpCanceled`	10004	The operation is canceled.
`SckInvalidArgument`	10014	The requested address is a broadcast address, but flag is not set.
`SckWouldBlock`	10035	Socket is nonblocking and the specified operation will block.
`SckInProgress`	10036	A blocking `WinSock` operation is in progress.
`SckAlreadyComplete`	10037	The operation is completed. No blocking operation in progress.
`SckNotSocket`	10038	The descriptor is not a socket.
`SckMsgTooBig`	10040	The datagram is too large to fit into the buffer and therefore is truncated.
`SckPortNotSupported`	10043	The specified port is not supported.
`SckAddressInUse`	10048	Address in use.
`SckAddressNotAvailable`	10049	Address unavailable from the local computer.
`SckNetworkSubsystemFailed`	10050	Network subsystem failed.
`SckNetworkUnreachable`	10051	The network cannot be reached from this host at this time.
`SckNetReset`	10052	Connection has timed out.
`SckConnectAborted`	10053	Connection aborts due to timeout or other failure.

TABLE A.43 Continued

Constant	*Value*	*Description*
`SckConnectionReset`	10054	The connection is reset by the remote device.
`SckNoBufferSpace`	10055	Buffer space is unavailable.
`SckAlreadyConnected`	10056	Socket is already connected.
`SckNotConnected`	10057	Socket is not connected.
`SckSocketShutdown`	10058	Socket has been shut down.
`SckTimedout`	10060	Socket did not connect with timeout period
`SckConnectionRefused`	10061	Connection is forcefully rejected.
`SckNotInitialized`	10093	WinSockInit should be called first.
`SckHostNotFound`	11001	Authoritative answer: Host not found.
`SckHostNotFoundTryAgain`	11002	Non-Authoritative answer: Host not found.
`SckNonRecoverableError`	11003	Non-recoverable errors.
`SckNoData`	11004	Valid name; no data record of requested type.

TABLE A.44 SockCtrlProtocol Constants

Constant	*Value*	*Description*
`SckIRDAProtocol`	2	Socket will use the TCP/IP protocol.
`SckTCPProtocol`	0	Socket will use the device's infrared port.

TABLE A.45 SockCtrlState Constants

Constant	*Value*	*Description*
`SckClosed`	0	Closed (default)
`SckOpen`	1	Open
`SckListening`	2	Listening
`SckConnectionPending`	3	Connection Pending
`SckResolvingHost`	4	Resolving host
`SckHostResolved`	5	Host resolved
`SckConnecting`	6	Connecting
`SckConnected`	7	Connected
`SckClosing`	8	Peer is closing the connection
`SckError`	9	Error

INDEX

SYMBOLS

A

B

C

D

E

F

G

M

N

O

R

S

T

U

V

W-Z